OXFORD WORLD'S CLASSIC

AN AUTOBIOGRAPI

AND OTHER WRITINGS

ANTHONY TROLLOPE (1815-82) was born in London and grew up in Harrow, where his father, a barrister, ruined himself in an unsuccessful attempt to be a gentleman-farmer. After miserable schooldays at Winchester and Harrow, Anthony became an unsatisfactory clerk in the Post Office. Though his mother, Frances Trollope, restored the family fortunes with a late-flowering career as a novelist and travel-writer, it was not until 1841, when he went to work for the Post Office in Ireland, that Anthony found his feet. Thereafter he combined success as a public official with a remarkable career as a writer, publishing 47 novels and numerous books of other kinds between 1847 and 1884, some of them posthumously. In the words of Gordon N. Ray, Trollope produced, 'more novels of lasting value than any other writer in English', including the perennially popular *Chronicles of Barsetshire* (1855-67) and his 'Palliser' series of political novels (1864-80). His *Autobiography* (1883) is an exceptionally candid account of an author's working life and is accompanied here by some key examples of Trollope's critical writing about other novelists.

NICHOLAS SHRIMPTON is an Emeritus Fellow of Lady Margaret Hall, Oxford. He is the editor of Trollope's *The Prime Minister* and *The Warden* for Oxford World's Classics. His other publications include *The Whole Music of Passion: New Essays on Swinburne* (1993), *Matthew Arnold: Selected Poems* (1998), and *Ruskin and 'War'* (2014).

OXFORD WORLD'S CLASSICS

*For over 100 years Oxford World's Classics have brought
readers closer to the world's great literature. Now with over 700
titles—from the 4,000-year-old myths of Mesopotamia to the
twentieth century's greatest novels—the series makes available
lesser-known as well as celebrated writing.*

*The pocket-sized hardbacks of the early years contained
introductions by Virginia Woolf, T. S. Eliot, Graham Greene,
and other literary figures which enriched the experience of reading.
Today the series is recognized for its fine scholarship and
reliability in texts that span world literature, drama and poetry,
religion, philosophy, and politics. Each edition includes perceptive
commentary and essential background information to meet the
changing needs of readers.*

OXFORD WORLD'S CLASSICS

ANTHONY TROLLOPE

An Autobiography
and Other Writings

Edited with an Introduction and Notes by
NICHOLAS SHRIMPTON

OXFORD
UNIVERSITY PRESS

OXFORD

UNIVERSITY PRESS

Great Clarendon Street, Oxford, OX2 6DP
United Kingdom

Oxford University Press is a department of the University of Oxford.
It furthers the University's objective of excellence in research, scholarship,
and education by publishing worldwide. Oxford is a registered trade mark of
Oxford University Press in the UK and in certain other countries

First published 2014

First published as an Oxford World's Classics paperback 2016

Impression: 6

Published in the United States of America by Oxford University Press
198 Madison Avenue, New York, NY 10016, United States of America

British Library Cataloguing in Publication Data
Data available

Library of Congress Control Number: 2015956650

ISBN 978-0-19-967529-6

Printed in Great Britain by
Clays Ltd, Elcograf S.p.A.

CONTENTS

INTRODUCTION

CROSSING the Atlantic on the SS *Bothnia* in October 1875, Henry James watched his fellow passenger Anthony Trollope at work:

The season was unpropitious, the vessel overcrowded, the voyage detestable; but Trollope shut himself up in his cabin every morning for a purpose which, on the part of a distinguished writer who was also an invulnerable sailor, could only be communion with the muse. He drove his pen as steadily on the tumbling ocean as in Montague Square[.][1]

Though James was right about Trollope's disciplined working methods, he did not realize what was being written on this particular occasion. For once, Trollope was not busy with a novel. Instead, he was writing *An Autobiography*.

The result was the only autobiography by a major Victorian novelist.[2] It was also a book that has sharply divided opinion ever since. For some it is one of the truest, most honest autobiographies ever written: an engrossing account of a young man who unexpectedly rescues himself from drift, doubt, and professional failure in his late twenties, and goes on to achieve a happy marriage and successful career. For others it is a dismayingly philistine picture of the life of a professional writer. Preoccupied with contracts, deadlines, and earnings, unblushingly explicit about the methods used to achieve success, emotionally reticent, and factually unreliable, it can be seen as a mere memoir, or self-help manual, rather than as a genuine exploration of the self.

When the book was published, posthumously, in 1883, it certainly encouraged the view of Trollope as an incessantly productive literary journeyman. As early as 1858, the *Saturday Review* had attacked

---

[1] Henry James, 'Anthony Trollope', *Century Magazine* (New York, July 1883); repr. in *Partial Portraits* (London: Macmillan, 1888); here quoted from Donald Smalley (ed.), *Trollope: The Critical Heritage* (London: Routledge & Kegan Paul, 1969), 526.

[2] George Moore's *Confessions of a Young Man* (1888) and Margaret Oliphant's *Autobiography* (1899) are good books by second-rank novelists; Henry James's so-called *Autobiography* was first published in 1956, having previously appeared between 1913 and 1917 as three separate accounts of parts of his early life, the last of them unfinished. Florence Hardy's *Life of Thomas Hardy* (1928–33) may be a disguised autobiography but is not presented as such.

his 'fecundity', or the rapidity with which he wrote and published fiction: Trollope's gift was a 'mechanical skill' and the 'rapid multi-plication' of his output led to 'carelessness'.[3] Now, in his own account of himself, he seemed to endorse the judgements of his least sympathetic contemporary critics. His purpose, he claimed, was less to depict a personality than to provide an object lesson for would-be writers: 'to speak . . . of what I, and perhaps others round me, have done in literature; of my failures and successes such as they have been, and their causes; and of the opening which a liter-ary career offers to men and women for the earning of their bread' (Chapter 1). The lesson is, for the most part, startlingly literal: 'the surest aid to the writing of a book' is 'a piece of cobbler's wax on my chair', and 'I have always prepared a diary . . . and carried it on for the period which I have allowed myself for the completion of the work. In this I have entered, day by day, the number of pages I have written' (Chapter 7). In Chapter 17 he records the uninterrupted process by which he wrote six novels between the spring of 1867 and the autumn of 1868: '*He Knew He Was Right* . . . was finished while I was at Washington in the spring of 1868, and on the day after I finished it, I commenced *The Vicar of Bullhampton*.' Chapter 15 contains the celebrated account of how he managed to write three thousand words before breakfast every day, by having a servant wake him with a cup of coffee at 5.30 a.m. And the book ends with the proud (or shameless) tabulation of the money he had made from each of his publications between 1847 and 1879. The reviewer of *An Autobiography* in the *Cornhill Magazine* in July 1884 felt that 'He has done his literary reputation as much harm by the revelation of his method of work as by his material views of its result', and suggested that Trollope had taken 'almost a savage pleasure in demolishing the theory of "inspiration" '.[4]

In the early twentieth century this view that the publication of *An Autobiography* had been a form of reputational suicide took firm hold. Frederic Harrison loved Trollope's fiction but argued, in an introduc-tion to a collected edition of The Chronicles of Barsetshire, that, 'in his honest *Autobiography* he artlessly exposed the meagre equipment

---

    [3] *Saturday Review*, 5 (12 June 1858), 618–19; here quoted from Smalley (ed.), *Critical Heritage*, 75–6.
    [4] Review by James Payn, here quoted from David Skilton, *Anthony Trollope and His Contemporaries* (London: Longman, 1972), 35.

of his literary workshop'.[5] Michael Sadleir, in his influential study *Trollope: A Commentary* (1927), linked the decline in Trollope's reputation to the appearance of the book:

A few months after his death his *Autobiography* appeared, and from beyond the grave he flung in the face of fashionable criticism the aggressive horse-sense of his views on life and book-making. Then it was that affectionate depreciation became malevolent hostility; then did the tempest of reaction against his work and against all the principles and opinions that it represented break angrily and overwhelm him.[6]

It is true that *An Autobiography* 'fell', in Sadleir's phrase, 'with a splash into the elegant waters of aestheticism', or, more literally, appeared at a time when the new assumptions of the Jamesian 'art novel' were beginning to make Trollope's mode of High Victorian realism look old-fashioned. But several of the original reviewers praised the book, and it is not the case that it had a decisive effect on his reputation. Those who had previously disliked his novels (such as the critics in the *Saturday Review*) continued to do so, while other people went on reading and enjoying them. His novels stayed in print throughout the first half of the twentieth century, the period when Victorian art and literature were routinely dismissed, retaining a popular readership despite the academic disapproval or neglect to which they were subjected. Although *An Autobiography* may not have helped Trollope's reputation, it cannot be said to have destroyed it.

One reason for this is the fact that the account it gives of the creative process is actually more complex than the references to 'cobbler's wax' and early morning cups of coffee might suggest. In Chapter 12 Trollope gives a remarkable description of the imaginative process by which the writer of realist fiction comes to know and understand his characters:

the novelist has other aims than the elucidation of his plot. He desires to make his readers so intimately acquainted with his characters that the creations of his brain should be to them speaking, moving, living, human creatures. This he can never do unless he know those fictitious personages himself, and he can never know them well unless he can live with them in the full reality of established intimacy. They must be with him as he lies

[5] *The Barsetshire Novels*, with an introduction by Frederic Harrison, 12 vols. (London: G. Bell & Sons, 1906–11), i., p. viii.
[6] Michael Sadleir, *Trollope: A Commentary* (London: Constable, 1927), 362.

down to sleep, and as he wakes from his dreams. He must learn to hate them and to love them. He must argue with them, quarrel with them, forgive them, and even submit to them.

Thus far, this is an impersonal, third-person account of the matter. But in the next paragraph Trollope acknowledges that he is talking here about his own creative method:

It is so that I have lived with my characters, and thence has come whatever success I have obtained. There is a gallery of them, and of all in that gallery I may say that I know the tone of the voice, and the colour of the hair, every flame of the eye, and the very clothes they wear. Of each man I could assert whether he would have said these or the other words; of every woman, whether she would then have smiled or so have frowned.

This process of 'living-with' could sometimes take on an almost frightening intensity, as Trollope reveals in Chapter 10:

When my work has been quicker done . . . the rapidity has been achieved by hot pressure, not in the conception, but in the telling of the story . . . in circumstances which have enabled me to give up all my thoughts for the time to the book I have been writing. This has generally been done at some quiet spot among the mountains . . . At such times I have been able to imbue myself thoroughly with the characters I have had in hand. I have wandered alone among the rocks and woods, crying at their grief, laughing at their absurdities, and thoroughly enjoying their joy. I have been impregnated with my own creations till it has been my only excitement to sit with the pen in my hand, and drive my team before me at as quick a pace as I could make them travel.

Despite Trollope's insistence, elsewhere, that steady application is more important to literary success than 'inspiration', this account of artistic invention, alone and at a 'quiet spot among the mountains', has a distinctly Romantic flavour. When the same suggestion is made in 'A Walk in a Wood', an essay that Trollope published in *Good Words* in September 1879, the description of solitary creation is given an Edenic quality which Romantic writers like Blake and Wordsworth would have recognized:

I have found that I can best command my thoughts on foot, and can do so with the most perfect mastery when wandering through a wood. To be alone is of course essential . . . My eyes . . . should become moist with the troubles of the embryo heroine . . . And it should be a wood,—perhaps a forest,—rather than a skirting of timber. You should feel that, if not lost, you are lose-able. To have trees around you is not enough unless you have many. You must have a feeling as of Adam in the garden.

In *An Autobiography* the narrative format enables Trollope to root such imaginative activity in his own formative experiences. As an unhappy schoolboy, cold-shouldered by his contemporaries, young Anthony was obliged, we are told in Chapter 3, to provide his own, solitary amusement:

I was always going about with some castle in the air firmly built within my mind . . . For weeks, for months, if I remember rightly, from year to year, I would carry on the same tale, binding myself down to certain laws, to certain proportions, and proprieties, and unities . . . I myself was of course my own hero. Such is a necessity of castle-building . . . I was a very clever person, and beautiful young women used to be fond of me. And I strove to be kind of heart, and open of hand, and noble in thought, despising mean things; and altogether I was a very much better fellow than I have ever succeeded in being since . . . There can, I imagine, hardly be a more dangerous mental practice; but . . . I learned in this way to maintain an interest in a fictitious story, to dwell on a work created by my own imagination, and to live in a world altogether outside the world of my own material life. In after years I have done the same,—with this difference, that I have discarded the hero of my early dreams, and have been able to lay my own identity aside.

The two phrases 'castle-building' and 'living-with' have become key terms in modern Trollope criticism. It was, it seems, a psychological compulsion, acquired in early youth, rather than greed or ambition, which drove Trollope to write his forty-seven novels. And the mechanical regularity with which he produced two hundred and fifty words every quarter of an hour for three hours before breakfast was merely part of an extensive process of imaginative contemplation. The American critic Walter M. Kendrick, in 1980, produced a particularly striking version of these new assumptions by reading the 'castle-building' and 'living-with' passages of *An Autobiography* as a brilliant anticipation of the post-structuralist, death-of-the-author theories of Roland Barthes and Michel Foucault. Trollope's shift from private fantasies, in which he was himself the hero, to published fictions with invented protagonists was a literal 'death', or removal, 'of the author'. Still more fundamentally, the 'living-with' process could be seen as a pre-linguistic, imaginative phase in which Trollope achieved 'the full reality of established intimacy' with his characters by a process of 'transmission without signs'.[7] This wordless preliminary experience would be followed by a merely routine act of writing, or rapid transcription, in which the unsatisfactory nature (in a post-structuralist understanding) of language, with its reliance on 'différance' and endless deferral of meaning, was implicitly acknowledged. Trollope wrote by the clock, and in a deliberately commonplace style 'that exists only to efface itself'.[8] The result, in Kendrick's view, is 'the clearest, most comprehensive statement of the theory of realism that realism itself has ever produced'.[9]

Celebrators of 'living-with', whether theoretical or traditional, tend to suggest that this was a phase which significantly preceded the act of putting words on paper. For Kendrick there are three successive stages in Trollope's creative process: 'conception', 'living-with', and, only then, writing. This may possibly have been true in the early years of Trollope's career. But a chronological sequence of this kind is hard to reconcile with what *An Autobiography* tells us about his starting *The Vicar of Bullhampton* 'the day after' he finished *He Knew He Was Right*, and only once having had 'two different novels in my mind at the same time' (in 1859–60, when a clash of contracts obliged him to produce both *Framley Parsonage* and *Castle Richmond*; Chapter 9). What seems more likely is that 'living-with' and writing were distinct but almost simultaneous activities: Trollope would write for three hours in the morning, then 'live with' his characters for the rest of the day, in the intervals of other business. On occasions when there was no other business, he was free to wander 'alone among the rocks and woods', crying at his characters' grief, 'laughing at their absurdities, and thoroughly enjoying their joy'. Trollope's autobiographical short story 'The Panjandrum' (1870) includes a passage which describes his discovery of the 'living-with' experience in the 1830s, and it confirms this simultaneity. The hero is struggling to find a topic to write about. Walking in Regent's Park on a wet November morning, he sees a little girl being dragged along by a servant and hears her say, 'Oh, Anne, I do so wonder what he's like!' Intrigued by this momentary encounter, he builds a 'castle in the air' about it and starts to write his

---

[7] Walter M. Kendrick, *The Novel-Machine: The Theory and Fiction of Anthony Trollope* (Baltimore: Johns Hopkins University Press, 1980), 23.

[8] Kendrick, *The Novel-Machine*, 51.   [9] Kendrick, *The Novel-Machine*, 3.

first short story that same afternoon. He finishes it after five days of intense absorption in the lives of his characters: 'While I was walking, eating, or reading, I was still thinking of my story.'

Like the description of Trollope's creative process in *An Autobiography*, this suggests that the making of his novels had four, rather than three, stages. The first was observation: a constant process, often unconscious, which gathered the experiential data for realistic description. The second was conception: the invention of particular characters and the contrivance of a plot within which they could act. The third and fourth were the separate but overlapping acts of living-with and writing. 'Conception' could be very brief—in Chapter 9 Trollope tells us: 'I have never found myself thinking much about the work that I had to do till I was doing it . . . have indeed for many years now almost abandoned the effort to think, trusting myself with the narrowest thread of a plot, to work the matter out when the pen is in my hand.' 'Living-with', however, was very different: an engrossing state, experienced in the intervals of writing, and one which persisted even after the book was finished. Having 'killed' Mrs Proudie in *The Last Chronicle of Barset*, Trollope tells us in Chapter 15 of *An Autobiography* that, 'I . . . still live much in company with her ghost'. Sadleir and Harrison saw Trollope's account of the way in which he wrote his novels as a regrettably prosaic revelation of 'book-making' in a 'literary workshop'. It seems to me a deliberately simple but wonderfully clear and illuminating account of the way in which prose fiction is created.

Trollope's interest in these issues of literary practice was so strong that he interrupts his life story for three chapters to discuss them: 'On Novels and the Art of Writing Them' (Chapter 12), 'On English Novelists of the Present Day' (Chapter 13), and 'On Criticism' (Chapter 14). But this is, none the less, an autobiography and it was written at an interesting moment in the history of that distinctive literary mode. Self-life-writing is a procedure which can be traced back to the 4th century AD, when St Augustine wrote his *Confessions*. Until the late eighteenth century, however, such texts tended either to be religious, offering spiritual self-scrutiny and doctrinal instruction, or to be 'memoirs'—records of the outward events of a successful professional or political career. The word 'autobiography' entered the English language in the 1790s, and its arrival reflects the fact that *Les Confessions* of Jean-Jacques Rousseau, written in the 1760s and published posthumously in 1781 and 1788, had effectively reinvented the form. Instead of reporting 'What I did', or 'What I believed', the new version of autobiography asked a question: 'Who am I?', and this sense of the self as something complex, mysterious, fascinating, and unstable was to become a characteristic feature of Romantic culture. The obvious masterpieces of Romantic autobiography, apart from Rousseau's, are Wordsworth's poem *The Prelude* (substantially completed by 1805 though not published until 1850), Goethe's *Dichtung und Wahrheit* (published in four parts in 1811–33), and Thomas De Quincey's *Confessions of an English Opium Eater* (1821, enlarged in 1856), which presents a perverse, or self-harming, personality, at odds with the rational self-interest or responsible altruism attributed to the psyche by political economists and Utopian social reformers.

By 1856, however, when the extended version of De Quincey's *Confessions* appeared, the original impetus of Romantic autobiography had faded; its generalized fascination with the mysteries of the self would be taken up, later in the century, by the more technical procedures of psychoanalysis. Instead, in the 1870s and '80s, when Trollope's *An Autobiography* was written and published, the form became more specialized, still asking 'Who am I?' but confining the enquiry to a particular area of the author's life. The outstanding English examples in this period are John Stuart Mill's *Autobiography* (1873), Trollope's *An Autobiography* (written 1875–6, published 1883), and John Ruskin's *Praeterita* (published intermittently between 1871 and 1889). Ruskin explicitly declares, in the preface to his book, that he will pass over 'in total silence things which I have no pleasure in reviewing', and all three of these texts are conspicuously selective. Mill, notoriously, describes his childhood without ever mentioning his mother. Trollope insists that his marriage was, though happy, 'of no special interest to anyone except my wife and me' (Chapter 4). What this narrowed focus permits is a concentration on the particular aspect of the self which the author finds most interesting. Mill, the philosopher, writes the autobiography of an intellect. Ruskin, the art critic, traces the development of a sensibility. Trollope, the novelist, records the formation and exercise of the creative capacity that produced more major novels than any other writer in English.

Trollope insists on his difference from Rousseau at both the beginning and the end of his book. But the similarity to Mill and Ruskin is a coincidental effect of the spirit of the age. There is no evidence to suggest that he had read either Mill's *Autobiography* or the early episodes of *Praeterita*, and the comparable texts which he had in mind when he sat down to write his own life story were probably biographies rather than autobiographies. John Forster's *Life of Charles Dickens* had been published in 1872–4. Trollope strongly disliked it ('distasteful to me', *Letters*, ii. 557), and his account of his own unhappy childhood was probably shaped by a wish to handle such matters more skilfully than Forster (and Dickens, in his autobiographical fragment about the blacking warehouse) had managed to do. A biography of Thackeray was, in 1875–6, a troubling absence. Trollope was conscious of this, and would himself begin to fill it in the biographical first chapter of his life-and-works study, *Thackeray*, published in 1879. If Trollope unconsciously resembles Mill and Ruskin in his decision to write a selective version of autobiography, he consciously differentiates himself from Dickens and Thackeray in the account which he gives of his own personality.

Dickens, Thackeray, and Trollope all experienced early difficulty and disappointment before establishing themselves as major novelists. But, despite this similarity of circumstance, they were, in Trollope's view, very different men. Dickens was the bumptious, irrepressible popularizer, the vulgar genius who swept obstacles aside with humour and panache. Thackeray, a more sensitive and highly cultured man, was the great artist who worked by fits and starts, waiting for inspiration and constantly delaying the moment at which pen must be put to paper. Trollope, by contrast, is, in his own account, the steady, methodical worker, the writer who laboriously achieves success by an infinite capacity for taking pains. Although *An Autobiography* is sometimes seen as brash, it is, in this context, a very modest self-portrait and Trollope enacts this modesty in the narrative he constructs for the story of his life. Born into a prosperous professional family with links to the landed gentry, he is plunged into poverty by his father's failure as lawyer and farmer. Briefly rescued by his mother's literary success, the family is once again devastated, this time by a series of fatal illnesses, and the young Trollope becomes an idle and incompetent Post Office clerk. Only at the age of 26, in 1841, does he begin to glimpse the possibility of happiness and significant achievement. Thereafter the record is one of incessant, arduous labour, and of the rewards which such labour tends to bring. He rises very high in the management of the Post Office, while simultaneously becoming a best-selling novelist. He resigns from the Post Office but continues to combine novel-writing with another career, this time as a journalist and editor. He makes a lot of money. He lives in large and comfortable houses and moves in intellectual high society. Above all, he passes from being despised or neglected to being famous and admired: 'I had created for myself a position among literary men' (Chapter 9). Yet, at the end of the book, there is only one thing for which he is willing to claim 'merit': a 'persevering diligence in my profession'.

Autobiographies are not naive, spontaneous records. They are, necessarily, deliberate interpretations of experience, with an imposed narrative shape. As a novelist, Trollope was thoroughly familiar with the management of narrative and he made sure that the story told in his autobiography had a particular pungency and force. The plot adopted here is the one with which we are familiar from the fable of the ugly duckling, or the folk tale of Cinderella: an exceptionally unhappy and unpromising young creature turns, unexpectedly, into an exceptionally fortunate adult. To achieve this effect, Trollope was not deliberately dishonest. But he did use the events of his life selectively, and in ways which intensified their significance. Although his childhood may not have been ideally happy, it was not in fact as miserable as he here suggests. His brother Thomas Adolphus Trollope, in his own, less interesting but probably more accurate, autobiography, gives a rather different picture, especially of their schooldays, and both brothers misrepresented, or misunderstood, the reasons for their father's financial failure. It was the economic depression of the mid- and late 1820s (the same financial crisis that ruined Sir Walter Scott) which undermined the profitability of the Trollope farms in Harrow, not any individual incompetence on the part of the man who had rented them. Anthony Trollope's life, in the 1830s, as a clerk in the London Post Office, was, similarly, much less feckless than *An Autobiography* suggests. In his spare time, he was hard at work on a demanding process of self-education which had actually begun during his, supposedly wasted, years at school. The surviving evidence of this endeavour includes his marginalia in a copy of Burke's *Philosophical Enquiry into the Origin of Our Ideas of the Sublime and Beautiful* (probably made in 1833), his common-place book for the years 1835–40 (which contains substantial entries on Bulwer-Lytton, George Sand, Shakespeare, Johnson's *Lives of the*

Poets, and Pope's *Essay on Man*), the outline for a proposed 'History of World Literature' (probably written in 1840), and the account, in the autobiographical short story 'The Panjandrum' (1870), of an attempt to found a literary magazine in the late 1830s. In Chapter 3 of *An Autobiography*, Trollope says that at the age of 19 (that is, in 1834) he 'could have given a . . . list of the names of the poets of all countries, with their subjects and periods,—and probably of historians,— . . . knew the names of all the Bishops, all the Judges, all the Heads of Colleges, and all the Cabinet Ministers', and had read Shakespeare, Byron, Scott, Milton, and Austen, but does so in a way which suggests that this was random and impractical knowledge. In fact, it was the product of a remarkable, auto-didactic programme, by means of which he sought to equip himself for a career as an author.

Trollope's intensification of the fecklessness of his youth has had an unfortunate effect on our willingness to take him seriously as a major writer. But it is, at least, easily recognized and understood. Exaggerating the misery of one's teenage years is a familiar practice, and critical judgements on unsatisfactory parents are a common-place. What has been less readily acknowledged is the extent to which the positive account, in *An Autobiography*, of the years after 1841 is the necessary counterpart of this early gloom and idleness. Before the move to Ireland, Trollope is (it seems) exceptionally inefficient. After it, he is a correspondingly perfect model of productive efficiency. One picture is all 'hobbledehoy', without the wide cultural interests and energetic self-education. The other is all successful practicality, with only hints of the creative dreaming and emotional disturbance which made the novels possible. Neither picture is entirely accurate. But the narrative pattern of the book requires, and benefits from, this neat equivalence. The tale is one of transformation, and the techniques of selection and intensification, which Trollope adopts to tell it, serve to make the story vivid.

There were, of course, other examples of autobiography by writers whose careers had included the writing of novels: John Galt's *Autobiography* in 1833, Mary Russell Mitford's *Recollections of a Literary Life* in 1852, and, a little later, Harriet Martineau's *Autobiography*, published posthumously in 1877. All of these are interesting and informative texts. None of them, however, has the strong narrative shape of Trollope's *Autobiography*, and all of them lack the serious enquiry into the practical and theoretical nature of prose fiction with which Trollope accompanies his life story. This edition, for the first time, prints *An Autobiography* side by side with some of the other writings which confirm the seriousness of Trollope's thinking about the novel as a form. Trollope was the Victorian novelist who worked most consciously and effectively in the tradition of Jane Austen. Two examples of his writing about her, both unpublished in his lifetime, are given here; a third can be found in his 1870 lecture 'On English Prose Fiction as a Rational Amusement', his most sustained discussion of the theory and practice of the novel. To modern eyes, one aspect of this lecture, Trollope's anxious insistence on the moral value of prose fiction, can seem quaint or naive. This anxiety arose not from prudishness (the *Cornhill* rejected Trollope's short story 'Mrs General Talboys' on grounds of 'indelicacy') but as a reaction to persistent attacks on the novel as a corrupting form, which it was necessary to contest. His other points are more sophisticated (or more congruent with modern concerns), as is his impressive ability to place his own work in a long perspective of relevant literary history. The subtlety of his understanding of the medium in which he works becomes still more pronounced in *Thackeray*, the monograph published in 1879, which contains his most interesting observations on the difficult concept of 'realism' (and from which extracts are included in this selection). Also reprinted here are passages from his essay 'A Walk in a Wood' (on inspiration), and his review 'The Genius of Nathaniel Hawthorne' (on a novelist of a very different kind from himself, who, none the less, both admired and was admired by Trollope). Sometimes dismissed as 'middle-brow', Trollope was actually an intellectually ambitious and self-conscious literary artist who reflected searchingly on the medium which he was using.

The strong dramatic structure of *An Autobiography* does not, of course, alter the fact that the later chapters are, intrinsically, rather dry and external in their focus. Roy Pascal, in his classic study, *Design and Truth in Autobiography* (1960), admired Trollope's 'moving account of his boyhood' but found the later sections, 'mostly trivial, the career-story of a man of letters'.[10] Another way of putting this would be to say that Trollope wrote a book of two different kinds, the first half genuinely autobiographical, the second merely 'memoir'.

---

[10] Roy Pascal, *Design and Truth in Autobiography* (London: Routledge & Kegan Paul, 1960), 19.

Some critics are untroubled by this shift. Robert D. Aguirre, writing from a Marxian and Foucaultian perspective, argues that the second half of the book 'does not signal the failure of autobiography, but [provides] a recognition of its inseparability from the material conditions of authorship itself', serving 'to demystify the economic milieu in which authors lived and moved as professionals' in 'Victorian commodity culture'.[11] A. L. Rowse, himself once a Marxist, defended the unity of the book more subtly when he argued that, 'To a writer Trollope's *Autobiography* is the most revealing ever written.' Rowse explains this claim by declaring that 'I learned from him myself the essential thing for the real writer—that he must be prepared *to make his work the condition of his life.*' The view (encouraged by Trollope) that the second half of the book omits the inner life is mistaken, 'for his inner life was devoted to story-telling', and 'his real life was the inner life of the imagination'.[12] In this understanding of the book, the question 'Who am I?' is still being put in the later chapters. The unexpected answer to it is, however, 'I am the stories which I tell to myself and the novels which I turn them into', rather than any other, more conventional aspects of human consciousness.

These arguments may not entirely assuage our sense that the second half of *An Autobiography* lacks the candid self-scrutiny of its early chapters. Trollope touches very lightly on his prolonged fascination with a much younger woman, Kate Field (there is a potential parallel with an important Romantic autobiography here, Hazlitt's humiliating *Liber Amoris* (1823), but it is carefully avoided). He acknowledges, though very briefly, his disappointment at the declining public appetite for his recent novels: not for him a golden 'late period' of critical acknowledgement and public esteem. He skirts his disappointment with his unsuccessful sons—both given the early advantages which he himself had lacked, both unwilling or unable to make use of them. Instead we are given the portrait of a smiling public man whose chief regrets are his failure to get into parliament and his inability to continue hunting.

The perfect placidity of this outer self can, however, be understood rather differently—as the index of a successful struggle to control

[11] Robert D. Aguirre, 'Cold Print: Professing Authorship in Anthony Trollope's *An Autobiography*', *Biography*, 25 (2002), 569–70, 585.

[12] A. L. Rowse, 'Trollope's *Autobiography*', in John Halperin (ed.), *Trollope Centenary Essays* (London: Macmillan, 1982), 134, 137, 142.

disturbance and self-doubt. There were so many reasons why the adult Anthony Trollope might have been a deeply troubled man: the child-hood poverty, the humiliating schooldays, the neglectful mother, the failed, irascible, and obsessive father, the deaths of his brothers and sisters, the denial of a university education, the shabbily dissolute years as an incompetent clerk and the crushing debt which they cre-ated. Instead, this big, ugly, awkward man has arrived in middle life as a self-confident and sociable figure whose serenity is both the formal counterpart of the book's unhappy early chapters and a demonstration of how effectively he has (as they say) confronted his demons. The disturbed side of the self has been conquered or, at least, kept under control; its absence is implicitly significant. Rowse, very perceptively, adds a further dimension to this when he suggests that the refusal to reveal, and thus dispel, the troubles of the inner life in the later chapters of *An Autobiography* had a practical and creative purpose. Trollope, he says, 'had been deeply wounded', and 'out of the wound came the genius; the *Autobiography* kept the wound green, as genius does for its own occult purposes'.[13]

When Henry James did finally read the book which he had seen being written in mid-Atlantic, he was dismayed by it: 'Yes, I have read Trollope's autobiography and regard it as one of the most curious and amazing books in all literature, for its density, blockishness and gen-eral thickness and soddenness.'[14] This is an endorsement of the view that *An Autobiography* is a mere memoir, an incongruously philistine portrait of the artist. Yet the details of James's language suggest that he too, with his customary sensitivity, had glimpsed the distinctive-ness of the work. It is, indeed, 'curious' and 'amazing'. No picture of the possibilities of autobiography as a form is complete without it.

[13] Rowse, 'Trollope's *Autobiography*', 138.

[14] Letter to Thomas Perry, 25 November [1883], in *Henry James Letters*, ed. Leon Edel, 4 vols. (London: Macmillan, 1974–84), iii. 14.

NOTE ON THE TEXT

TROLLOPE wrote the first two chapters of *An Autobiography* between 20 and 30 October 1875. He was 60, and was travelling from New York to Liverpool on the SS *Bothnia* after a visit to his younger son, Frederic, in Australia. He started writing again on 1 January 1876 and finished on 11 April;[1] his wife prepared a chronology of events since their marriage in 1844, which helped with the factual detail in Chapters 4 to 20.[2] The manuscript, now in the British Library,[3] is in Trollope's own hand, except for Chapter 1 (a fair copy by his niece Florence Bland, lightly corrected by Trollope) and three inserted quotations in the hand of his wife, Rose (the passage from a letter by Thackeray, the comment on Trollope's work by Nathaniel Hawthorne, and a section from the preface to *The Vicar of Bullhampton*). On 30 April 1876 he wrote a letter to his elder son, Henry, telling him what to do with the material after his death:

My dear Harry,

I wish you to accept as a gift from me, given you now, the accompanying pages which contain a memoir of my life. My intention is that they shall be published after my death, and be edited by you. But I leave it altogether to your discretion whether to publish or to suppress the work;—and also to your discretion whether any part or what part shall be omitted. But I would not wish that anything be added to the memoir. If you wish to say any word as from yourself, let it be done in the shape of a preface or introductory chapter.

I trust you to be careful in editing the work, as much has, I fear, been written hurriedly. Where quotations have been made references have been given in pencil, for your guidance as to correct printing,—but not for publication.

I should wish the book to be published by Fred Chapman if he is in business at the time of my death;—but of course you will do the best you can as to terms, if not with him, then with some other publisher. The volume

---

[1] See Henry Trollope's account in his Preface (p. 3) and the memorandum in his father's hand preserved with the manuscript of *An Autobiography* in the British Library (Add. MS 42856).

[2] Anthony Trollope Papers, 1830–1912, Urbana-Champaign, University of Illinois Library, Post-1650 MS 0442.

[3] London, British Library, Add. MS 42856.

ought to be worth some hundreds of pounds to you. You will understand
that whatever are the proceeds, they are to be yours, and not to go to my
estate.

Now I say how dearly I have loved you.

Your most affectionate father,
Anthony Trollope

The publication, if made at all, should be effected as soon as possible after
my death.[4]

Both the manuscript and the letter were then locked away until the
summer of 1878, when he told Henry about them, explaining that the
letter was not to be opened in his lifetime. In 1878–9 Trollope added
some footnotes to the manuscript and extended the list of his publications to include the books which had appeared since 1876 (but not
Cousin Henry, which would begin its serialization on 8 March 1879);
he may also have cancelled some passages at this time. A slightly
different version of the passage on the foundation of the *Cornhill
Magazine*, in Chapter 8, was published in Chapter 1 of Trollope's
Thackeray (1879).

After Anthony Trollope's death, on 6 December 1882, Henry
made his own copy (now lost) of the manuscript, incorporating
some editorial revisions and further deletions (as the letter author-
ized him to do). An advertisement appeared in *The Athenaeum* on 18
January 1883, which, in effect, invited publishers to bid for the work.
It was published in October 1883 by William Blackwood & Sons, in
two volumes, in an edition of 4,000 copies, with a brief preface by
Henry Trollope (dated September 1883) providing factual information about his father's life between 1878 and 1882.[5] The first reviews
appeared on 13 October 1883 and a second edition in the same format
was published later the same year. Although there was a Tauchnitz
edition (Leipzig, 1884) and several American editions, the book was
not republished in Britain until 1923.

---

[4] *The Letters of Anthony Trollope*, ed. N. John Hall with the assistance of Nina Burgis,
2 vols. (Stanford, Cal.: Stanford University Press, 1983), ii. 685–6.

[5] Henry Trollope's correspondence with Blackwood about the preparation of the
edition is in the Blackwood Papers in the National Library of Scotland, and is discussed by N. John Hall in 'Seeing Trollope's *An Autobiography* through the Press:
The Correspondence of William Blackwood and Henry Merivale Trollope', *Princeton
University Library Chronicle*, 47 (1986), 189–223.

In 1950 Frederick Page published an edition of *An Autobiography* (as part of the Oxford Trollope series, edited by Page and Michael Sadleir), in which 'the text was for the first time made to agree with Trollope's own manuscript'. Page noted that the first edition of 1883, 'needed to be altered in 544 places' and listed the 'Variations between manuscript and first edition' in an appendix. The most celebrated consequences of Page's work were the restoration of the word 'American' to the description of Kate Field in Chapter 17, and the revelation that the mysterious reference to Lily Dale, the heroine of *The Small House at Allington*, as 'a French prig' was a misreading by Henry Trollope of his father's words 'a female prig' (Chapter 10).

Page's text was reprinted in World's Classics paperback editions from 1980, with fresh editorial matter by P. D. Edwards. In 1999 Edwards supplied a new 'Note on the Text', in which he drew attention to some unsatisfactory features of Page's version. The policy of 'giving preference to the manuscript whenever it differed substantively from the first edition' had meant that it retained Trollope's multiple misspellings of the names 'George Eliot' and 'Becky Sharp' (though, inconsistently, it had not reproduced the misspelling of the name James Hannay in Chapter 11 or the inaccurate version of the title of *The Small House at Allington* in Chapter 10). Elsewhere Page had to add footnotes to correct errors of fact, reintroduced in 1950 from manuscript, which had been silently corrected in the 1883 first edition, and on one occasion misread Trollope's handwriting in such a way as to introduce a factual error absent from both manuscript and first edition (the date on which Trollope began writing *The Warden*, Chapter 5). Edwards continued to use the Page text, welcoming the fact that, 'Very sensibly, it retains nearly all the changes that the first edition made to Trollope's sometimes haphazard spelling and slapdash punctuation', but printed a list of thirty-five 'Significant Variations' between it and Trollope's manuscript.

The Page text was, in other words, a composite, and in 1996 David Skilton produced a version more rigorously based on Anthony Trollope's manuscript.[6] This, in Skilton's words, was 'an acceptable reading version . . . which varies from the manuscript as little as

---

[6] Anthony Trollope, *An Autobiography*, ed. with an introduction by David Skilton, Penguin Classics (London: Penguin Books, 1996); reissued, with minor emendations and an introduction by John Sutherland, for the Trollope Society edition, 1999.

would be found tolerable by the reader who reads for pleasure and by a commercial publisher'. Skilton's new transcription produced some corrections to Page's manuscript readings and some further instances of passages cancelled by Trollope while writing or revising his text. Most significantly, however, Skilton retained the spelling and punctuation of the manuscript, in preference to that of the first edition (where, in Skilton's view, 'the copyist and compositor did as they pleased, and were at least as erratic as the manuscript itself'). For the reader who wishes to encounter Trollope's autobiography in the form in which he first wrote it, this is the best available text and it is unnecessary to duplicate it.

A strong case can, however, be made for the merits of encountering *An Autobiography* in a different form—that is, in a version based on the text as it was first published in 1883. One argument for this approach is derived from reception history: this was the book known and discussed between the early 1880s and 1950, when Trollope's reputation was so controversially in question. But it is also supported by what we are told in Trollope's letter to his son in April 1876. Trollope does not recommend a strict adherence to the manuscript as he has left it. On the contrary, he insists that it has 'been written hurriedly' and specifically instructs his son to edit it. As P. D. Edwards put it in 1999, 'anyone who has compared the manuscripts of other Trollope books with the printed texts will be aware that his printers or proofreaders frequently took such liberties: in all probability he would have expected and even, in some measure, relied upon them to do so'.

The school of editorial practice founded by Jerome McGann rejects the conventional stress on authorial intention and sees the text as a social product. In this understanding, correct readings are collectively determined by author, editor, publisher, printer, and proofreader. Whatever one thinks of that as a general principle, in the particular case of *An Autobiography* we are clearly dealing with a text which its writer wished to be produced collaboratively. If Anthony Trollope had wanted to publish the unrevised manuscript text of his autobiography, he could easily have done so. He did not. Instead, he gave instructions for the preparation of a text determined by other hands as well as his own, and that is what was published in 1883.

Unlike Skilton, and to a much greater extent than Page, this edition therefore takes the 1883 first edition as its copy text, making corrections from the manuscript only where they seem absolutely necessary. The substantial passages cancelled in manuscript by Anthony Trollope, or omitted by Henry during the editorial process, are printed as an appendix. Oxford University Press house style has been adopted in the treatment of some accidentals, and misspellings of proper names that persisted into the first edition ('Becky Sharpe', 'Colonel Newcombe') have been silently emended. In the few cases where Henry Trollope's misreadings or alterations of the original manuscript appear to have distorted or obscured his father's meaning, corrections from the manuscript have been made: all such changes are reported in the Explanatory Notes. Repagination has made it impractical to retain the page headings inserted by Henry Trollope. In terms of phrasing, most spelling, and almost all punctuation, however, this edition follows the text as it was published in 1883, and as it was known to readers between then and 1950.

SELECT BIBLIOGRAPHY

An Autobiography

LIFE AND LETTERS

The Letters of Anthony Trollope, ed. N. John Hall with the assistance of Nina Burgis, 2 vols. (Stanford, Cal.: Stanford University Press, 1983).

Escott, T. H. S., *Anthony Trollope: His Work, Associates and Literary Originals* (London: John Lane, Bodley Head, 1913).

Glendinning, Victoria, *Trollope* (London: Hutchinson, 1992).

Hall, N. John, *Trollope: A Biography* (Oxford: Clarendon Press, 1991).

Heineman, Helen, *Mrs. Trollope: The Triumphant Feminine in the Nineteenth Century* (Athens: Ohio University Press, 1979).

Mullen, Richard, *Anthony Trollope: A Victorian in His World* (London: Duckworth, 1990).

Sadleir, Michael, *Trollope: A Commentary* (London: Constable, 1927; new edn., 1928).

Super, R. H., *The Chronicler of Barsetshire: A Life of Anthony Trollope* (Ann Arbor: University of Michigan Press, 1988).

Trollope, Thomas Adolphus, *What I Remember*, 3 vols. (London: Richard Bentley and Son, 1887–9).

TEXT, PUBLICATION AND RECEPTION HISTORY

Chapman, R. W., 'The Text of Trollope's *Autobiography*', *Review of English Studies*, 17 (1941), 90–4.

—— 'The Text of Trollope's *Autobiography*', *Notes and Queries*, 181 (1941), 245.

Hall, N. John, 'Seeing Trollope's *An Autobiography* through the Press: The Correspondence of William Blackwood and Henry Merivale Trollope', *Princeton University Library Chronicle*, 47 (1986), 189–223.

Sadleir, Michael, *Trollope: A Bibliography* (London: Constable, 1928; repr. with addenda and corrigenda, 1934).

Smalley, Donald (ed.), *Trollope: The Critical Heritage* (London: Routledge & Kegan Paul, 1969).

[Tingay, Lance, David Skilton, Claire Connolly, and Christopher Edwards (eds.)], *Anthony Trollope: A Collector's Catalogue, 1847–1990* (London: The Trollope Society, 1992).

CRITICISM AND DISCUSSION

Aguirre, Robert D., 'Cold Print: Professing Authorship in Anthony Trollope's *An Autobiography*', *Biography*, 25 (2002), 569–92.

Anderson, Linda, *Autobiography* (London: Routledge, 2001).

Brown, Sally, '"This so-called autobiography": Anthony Trollope, 1815–1882', *British Library Journal*, 8 (1982), 168–73.

—— 'A Vulnerable Man: Trollope's *An Autobiography*', *Trollopiana*, 23 (November 1993).

Flint, Kate, 'Queer Trollope', in Carolyn Dever and Lisa Niles (eds.), *The Cambridge Companion to Anthony Trollope* (Cambridge: Cambridge University Press, 2011), 99–112.

Gilead, Sarah, 'Trollope's Autobiography: The Strategies of Self-Production', *Modern Language Quarterly*, 47 (1986), 272–90.

Humphreys, Susan L., 'Order—Method: Trollope Learns to Write', *Dickens Studies Annual*, 8 (1980), 251–71.

Kendrick, Walter M., *The Novel-Machine: The Theory and Fiction of Anthony Trollope* (Baltimore: Johns Hopkins University Press, 1980).

Kincaid, James R., 'Trollope's Fictional Autobiography', *Nineteenth-Century Fiction*, 37 (1982), 340–9.

Marcus, Laura, *Autobiographical Discourses: Criticism, Theory, Practice* (Manchester: Manchester University Press, 1994).

Pascal, Roy, *Design and Truth in Autobiography* (London: Routledge & Kegan Paul, 1960).

Roellinger, F. X., 'E. S. Dallas in Trollope's *Autobiography*', *Modern Language Notes*, 55 (1940), 422–4.

Rowse, A. L., 'Trollope's *Autobiography*', in John Halperin (ed.), *Trollope Centenary Essays* (London: Macmillan, 1982).

Shumaker, Wayne, *English Autobiography: Its Emergence, Materials, and Form* (Berkeley: University of California Press, 1954).

Skilton, David, *Anthony Trollope and His Contemporaries: A Study in the Theory and Conventions of Mid-Victorian Fiction* (Harlow: Longman, 1972; repr. with alterations, 1996).

Stone, Donald, *The Romantic Impulse in Victorian Fiction* (Cambridge, Mass.: Harvard University Press, 1980).

Super, R. H., 'Truth and Fiction in Trollope's *Autobiography*', *Nineteenth-Century Literature*, 48 (1993), 74–88.

Swingle, L. J., *Romanticism and Anthony Trollope* (Ann Arbor: University of Michigan Press, 1990).

Other Writings

Booth, Bradford A., 'Trollope and the *Pall Mall Gazette*', *Nineteenth-Century Fiction*, 4 (1949), 51–69, 137–58.

Booth, Bradford A., 'Trollope on "Emma": An Unpublished Note', *Nineteenth-Century Fiction*, 4 (1949), 245–7.

—— 'Trollope on Scott: Some Unpublished Notes', *Nineteenth-Century Fiction*, 5 (1950), 223–30.

—— 'Trollope on the Novel', in *Essays Critical and Historical Dedicated to Lily B. Campbell* (Berkeley: University of California Press, 1950).

Hall, N. John, 'An Unpublished Trollope Manuscript on a Proposed History of World Literature', *Nineteenth-Century Fiction*, 29 (1974), 206–10.

—— 'Trollope's Commonplace Book, 1835–40', *Nineteenth-Century Fiction*, 31 (1976), 15–25.

Humphreys, Susan L., 'Trollope on the Sublime and Beautiful', *Nineteenth-Century Fiction*, 33 (1978), 194–214.

Knelman, Judith, 'Trollope's Journalism', *Library*, 2 (1983), 140–55.

Mason, Michael Y., Introduction to Anthony Trollope, *Miscellaneous Essays and Reviews* (New York: Arno Press, 1981).

Miller, J. Hillis, 'Trollope's Thackeray', *Nineteenth-Century Fiction*, 37 (1982), 350–7.

Sutherland, John, Introduction to Anthony Trollope, *Writings for Saint Paul's Magazine* (New York: Arno Press, 1981).

AN AUTOBIOGRAPHY

PREFACE

IT may be well that I should put a short preface to this book. In the summer of 1878 my father told me that he had written a memoir of his own life. He did not speak about it at length, but said that he had written me a letter, not to be opened until after his death, containing instructions for publication.

This letter was dated 30th April 1876. I will give here as much of it as concerns the public: 'I wish you to accept as a gift from me, given you now, the accompanying pages which contain a memoir of my life. My intention is that they shall be published after my death, and be edited by you. But I leave it altogether to your discretion whether to publish or to suppress the work;—and also to your discretion whether any part or what part shall be omitted. But I would not wish that anything should be added to the memoir. If you wish to say any word as from yourself, let it be done in the shape of a preface or introductory chapter.' At the end there is a postscript: 'The publication, if made at all, should be effected as soon as possible after my death.' My father died on the 6th of December 1882.

It will be seen, therefore, that my duty has been merely to pass the book through the press conformably to the above instructions. I have placed headings to the right-hand pages throughout the book, and I do not conceive that I was precluded from so doing. Additions of any other sort there have been none; the few footnotes are my father's own additions or corrections. And I have made no alterations. I have suppressed some few passages, but not more than would amount to two printed pages has been omitted. My father has not given any of his own letters, nor was it his wish that any should be published.

I see from my father's manuscript, and from his papers, that the first two chapters of this memoir were written in the latter part of 1875, that he began the third chapter early in January 1876, and that he finished the record before the middle of April in that year. I state this, though there are indications in the book by which it might be seen at what time the memoir was being written.

So much I would say by way of preface. And I think I may also give in a few words the main incidents in my father's life after he completed his autobiography.

He has said that he had given up hunting; but he still kept two horses for such riding as may be had in or about the immediate neighbourhood of London. He continued to ride to the end of his life: he liked the exercise, and I think it would have distressed him not to have had a horse in his stable. But he never spoke willingly on hunting matters. He had at last resolved to give up his favourite amusement, and that as far as he was concerned there should be an end of it. In the spring of 1877 he went to South Africa, and returned early in the following year with a book on the colony already written. In the summer of 1878, he was one of a party of ladies and gentlemen who made an expedition to Iceland in the 'Mastiff,' one of Mr John Burns' steam-ships. The journey lasted altogether sixteen days, and during that time Mr and Mrs Burns were the hospitable entertainers. When my father returned, he wrote a short account of *How the 'Mastiff's' went to Iceland*. The book was printed, but was intended only for private circulation.

Every day, until his last illness, my father continued his work. He would not otherwise have been happy. He demanded from himself less than he had done ten years previously, but his daily task was always done. I will mention now the titles of his books that were published after the last included in the list which he himself has given at the end of the second volume:—

An Eye for an Eye	1879
Cousin Henry	1879
Thackeray	1879
The Duke's Children	1880
Life of Cicero	1880
Ayala's Angel	1881
Doctor Wortle's School	1881
Frau Frohmann and other Stories	1882
Lord Palmerston	1882
The Fixed Period	1882
Kept in the Dark	1882
Marion Fay	1882
Mr Scarborough's Family	1883

At the time of his death he had written four-fifths of an Irish story, called *The Landleaguers*, shortly about to be published; and he left in manuscript a completed novel, called *An Old Man's Love*, which will be published by Messrs Blackwood & Sons in 1884.

In the summer of 1880 my father left London, and went to live at Harting, a village in Sussex, but on the confines of Hampshire. I think he chose that spot because he found there a house that suited him, and because of the prettiness of the neighbourhood. His last long journey was a trip to Italy in the late winter and spring of 1881; but he went to Ireland twice in 1882. He went there in May of that year, and was then absent nearly a month. This journey did him much good, for he found that the softer atmosphere relieved his asthma, from which he had been suffering for nearly eighteen months. In August following he made another trip to Ireland, but from this journey he derived less benefit. He was much interested in, and was very much distressed by, the unhappy condition of the country. Few men knew Ireland better than he did. He had lived there for sixteen years, and his Post Office work had taken him into every part of the island. In the summer of 1882 he began his last novel, *The Landleaguers*, which, as stated above, was unfinished when he died. This book was a cause of anxiety to him. He could not rid his mind of the fact that he had a story already in the course of publication, but which he had not yet completed. In no other case, except *Framley Parsonage*, did my father publish even the first number of any novel before he had fully completed the whole tale.

On the evening of the 3rd of November 1882 he was seized with paralysis on the right side, accompanied by loss of speech. His mind also had failed, though at intervals his thoughts would return to him. After the first three weeks these lucid intervals became rarer, but it was always very difficult to tell how far his mind was sound or how far astray. He died on the evening of the 6th of December following, nearly five weeks from the night of his attack.

I have been led to say these few words, not at all from a desire to supplement my father's biography of himself, but to mention the main incidents in his life after he had finished his own record. In what I have here said I do not think I have exceeded his instructions.

HENRY M. TROLLOPE.

September 1883.

CONTENTS

CHAPTER 1

My Education
1815–1834

I N writing these pages, which, for the want of a better name, I shall be fain to call the autobiography of so insignificant a person as myself, it will not be so much my intention to speak of the little details of my private life, as of what I, and perhaps others round me, have done in literature; of my failures and successes such as they have been, and their causes; and of the opening which a literary career offers to men and women for the earning of their bread. And yet the garrulity of old age, and the aptitude of a man's mind to recur to the passages of his own life, will, I know, tempt me to say something of myself,— nor, without doing so, should I know how to throw my matter into any recognised and intelligible form. That I, or any man, should tell everything of himself,* I hold to be impossible. Who could endure to own the doing of a mean thing? Who is there that has done none? But this I protest;—that nothing that I say shall be untrue. I will set down naught in malice;* nor will I give to myself, or others, honour which I do not believe to have been fairly won.

My boyhood was, I think, as unhappy as that of a young gentleman could well be, my misfortunes arising from a mixture of poverty and gentle standing on the part of my father, and from an utter want on my own part of that juvenile manhood which enables some boys to hold up their heads even among the distresses which such a position is sure to produce.

I was born in 1815, in Keppel Street,* Russell Square; and while a baby, was carried down to Harrow, where my father had built a house on a large farm which, in an evil hour he took on a long lease from Lord Northwick.* That farm was the grave of all my father's hopes, ambition, and prosperity, the cause of my mother's sufferings, and of those of her children, and perhaps the director of her destiny and of ours. My father had been a Wykamist and a fellow of New College,* and Winchester was the destination of my brothers and myself; but as he had friends among the masters at Harrow,* and as the school offered an education almost gratuitous to children living in the parish, he, with a certain aptitude to do things differently from others, which accompanied him throughout his life, determined to use that august seminary as a 't'other school' for Winchester, and sent three of us there, one after the other, at the age of seven. My father at this time was a Chancery barrister* practising in London, occupying dingy, almost suicidal chambers, at No. 23 Old Square, Lincoln's Inn,—chambers which on one melancholy occasion did become absolutely suicidal.[1] He was, as I have been informed by those quite competent to know, an excellent and most conscientious lawyer, but plagued with so bad a temper, that he drove the attorneys from him. In his early days he was a man of some small fortune and of higher hopes. These stood so high at the time of my birth, that he was felt to be entitled to a country house, as well as to that in Keppel Street; and in order that he might build such a residence, he took the farm. This place he called Julians,* and the land runs up to the foot of the hill on which the school and church stand,—on the side towards London. Things there went much against him; the farm was ruinous, and I remember that we all regarded the Lord Northwick of those days as a cormorant who was eating us up. My father's clients deserted him. He purchased various dark gloomy chambers in and about Chancery Lane, and his purchases always went wrong. Then, as a final crushing blow, an old uncle,* whose heir he was to have been, married and had a family! The house in London was let; and also the house he built at Harrow, from which he descended to a farmhouse on the land, which I have endeavoured to make known to some readers under the name of Orley Farm. This place, just as it was when we lived there, is to be seen in the frontispiece to the first edition of that novel, having had the good fortune to be delineated by no less a pencil than that of John Millais.*

My two elder brothers had been sent as day-boarders to Harrow School from the bigger house, and may probably have been received among the aristocratic crowd,—not on equal terms, because a day-boarder at Harrow in those days was never so received,—but at any rate as other day-boarders. I do not suppose that they were well treated, but I doubt whether they were subjected to the ignominy which I endured. I was only seven, and I think that boys at seven are now spared among their more considerate seniors. I was never

---

[1] A pupil of his destroyed himself in the rooms.

spared; and was not even allowed to run to and fro between our house and the school without a daily purgatory. No doubt my appearance was against me. I remember well, when I was still the junior boy in the school, Dr Butler,* the head-master, stopping me in the street, and asking me, with all the clouds of Jove upon his brow and all the thunder in his voice, whether it was possible that Harrow School was disgraced by so disreputably dirty a little boy as I! Oh, what I felt at that moment! But I could not look my feelings. I do not doubt that I was dirty;—but I think that he was cruel. He must have known me had he seen me as he was wont to see me, for he was in the habit of flogging me constantly. Perhaps he did not recognise me by my face.

At this time I was three years at Harrow; and, as far as I can remember, I was the junior boy in the school when I left it.

Then I was sent to a private school at Sunbury,* kept by Arthur Drury. This, I think, must have been done in accordance with the advice of Henry Drury,* who was my tutor at Harrow School, and my father's friend, and who may probably have expressed an opinion that my juvenile career was not proceeding in a satisfactory manner at Harrow. To Sunbury I went, and during the two years I was there, though I never had any pocket-money, and seldom had much in the way of clothes, I lived more nearly on terms of equality with other boys than at any other period during my very prolonged school-days. Even here, I was always in disgrace. I remember well how, on one occasion, four boys were selected as having been the perpetrators of some nameless horror. What it was, to this day I cannot even guess; but I was one of the four, innocent as a babe, but adjudged to have been the guiltiest of the guilty. We each had to write out a sermon, and my sermon was the longest of the four. During the whole of one term-time we were helped last at every meal. We were not allowed to visit the playground till the sermon was finished. Mine was only done a day or two before the holidays. Mrs Drury, when she saw us, shook her head with pitying horror. There were ever so many other punishments accumulated on our heads. It broke my heart, knowing myself to be innocent, and suffering also under the almost equally painful feeling that the other three—no doubt wicked boys—were the curled darlings of the school,* who would never have selected me to share their wickedness with them. I contrived to learn, from words that fell from Mr Drury, that he condemned me because I, having come from a public school, might be supposed to be the leader of wickedness!

On the first day of the next term he whispered to me half a word that perhaps he had been wrong. With all a stupid boy's slowness, I said nothing; and he had not the courage to carry reparation further. All that was fifty years ago, and it burns me now as though it were yesterday. What lily-livered curs* those boys must have been not to have told the truth!—at any rate as far as I was concerned. I remember their names well, and almost wish to write them here.

When I was twelve there came the vacancy at Winchester College which I was destined to fill. My two elder brothers had gone there, and the younger had been taken away, being already supposed to have lost his chance of New College. It had been one of the great ambitions of my father's life that his three sons, who lived to go to Winchester, should all become fellows of New College. But that suffering man was never destined to have an ambition gratified. We all lost the prize which he struggled with infinite labour to put within our reach. My eldest brother all but achieved it, and afterwards went to Oxford, taking three exhibitions from the school, though he lost the great glory of a Wykamist. He has since made himself well known to the public as a writer in connection with all Italian subjects. He is still living as I now write. But my other brother died early.

While I was at Winchester my father's affairs went from bad to worse. He gave up his practice at the bar, and, unfortunate that he was, took another farm. It is odd that a man should conceive,—and in this case a highly educated and a very clever man,—that farming should be a business in which he might make money without any special education or apprenticeship. Perhaps of all trades it is the one in which an accurate knowledge of what things should be done, and the best manner of doing them, is most necessary. And it is one also for success in which a sufficient capital is indispensable. He had no knowledge, and, when he took this second farm, no capital. This was the last step preparatory to his final ruin.

Soon after I had been sent to Winchester, my mother went to America, taking with her my brother Henry and my two sisters, who were then no more than children. This was, I think, in 1827. I have no clear knowledge of her object, or of my father's; but I believe that he had an idea that money might be made by sending goods,—little goods, such as pin-cushions, pepper-boxes, and pocket-knives,—out to the still unfurnished States; and that she conceived that an opening might be made for my brother Henry by erecting some bazaar or extended shop in one of the Western cities. Whence the money came I do not know, but the pocket-knives and the pepper-boxes were bought, and the bazaar built. I have seen it since in the town of Cincinnati,*—a sorry building! But I have been told that in those days it was an imposing edifice. My mother went first, with my sisters and second brother. Then my father followed them, taking my elder brother before he went to Oxford. But there was an interval of some year and a half during which he and I were at Winchester together.

Over a period of forty years, since I began my manhood at a desk in the Post Office, I and my brother, Thomas Adolphus, have been fast friends. There have been hot words between us, for perfect friendship bears and allows hot words. Few brothers have had more of brotherhood. But in those schooldays he was, of all my foes, the worst. In accordance with the practice of the college, which submits, or did then submit, much of the tuition of the younger boys to the elder, he was my tutor; and in his capacity of teacher and ruler, he had studied the theories of Draco.* I remember well how he used to exact obedience after the manner of that lawgiver. Hang a little boy for stealing apples, he used to say, and other little boys will not steal apples. The doctrine was already exploded elsewhere, but he stuck to it with con-servative energy. The result was that, as a part of his daily exercise, he thrashed me with a big stick. That such thrashings should have been possible at a school as a continual part of one's daily life, seems to me to argue a very ill condition of school discipline.

At this period I remember to have passed one set of holidays—the midsummer holidays—in my father's chambers in Lincoln's Inn. There was often a difficulty about the holidays,—as to what should be done with me. On this occasion my amusement consisted in wan-dering about among those old deserted buildings, and in reading Shakespeare out of a bi-columned edition, which is still among my books. It was not that I had chosen Shakespeare, but that there was nothing else to read.

After a while my brother left Winchester and accompanied my father to America. Then another and a different horror fell to my fate. My college bills had not been paid, and the school tradesmen who administered to the wants of the boys were told not to extend their credit to me. Boots, waistcoats, and pocket-handkerchiefs, which, with some slight superveillance, were at the command of other schol-ars, were closed luxuries to me. My schoolfellows of course knew that it was so, and I became a Pariah.* It is the nature of boys to be cruel. I have sometimes doubted whether among each other they do usually suffer much, one from the other's cruelty; but I suffered horribly! I could make no stand against it. I had no friend to whom I could pour out my sorrows. I was big, and awkward, and ugly, and, I have no doubt, skulked about in a most unattractive manner. Of course I was ill-dressed and dirty. But, ah! how well I remember all the agonies of my young heart; how I considered whether I should always be alone; whether I could not find my way up to the top of that college tower, and from thence put an end to everything? And a worse thing came than the stoppage of the supplies from the shopkeepers. Every boy had a shilling a week pocket-money, which we called battels, and which was advanced to us out of the pocket of the second master. On one awful day the second master announced to me that my battels would be stopped. He told me the reason,—the battels for the last half-year had not been repaid; and he urged his own unwillingness to advance the money. The loss of a shilling a week would not have been much,—even though pocket-money from other sources never reached me,—but that the other boys all knew it! Every now and again, perhaps three or four times in a half-year, these weekly shillings were given to certain servants of the college, in payment, it may be presumed, for some extra services. And now, when it came to the turn of any servant, he received sixty-nine shillings instead of seventy, and the cause of the defalcation was explained to him. I never saw one of those servants without feeling that I had picked his pocket.

When I had been at Winchester something over three years, my father returned to England and took me away. Whether this was done because of the expense, or because my chance of New College was supposed to have passed away, I do not know. As a fact, I should, I believe, have gained the prize, as there occurred in my year an exceptional number of vacancies. But it would have secured* me nothing, as there would have been no funds for my maintenance at the University till I should have entered in upon the fruition of the founder's endowment, and my career at Oxford must have been unfortunate.

When I left Winchester, I had three more years of school before me, having as yet endured nine. My father at this time having left my mother and sisters with my younger brother in America, took himself to live at a wretched tumble-down farmhouse on the second farm he had hired! And I was taken there with him. It was nearly three miles from Harrow, at Harrow Weald, but in the parish; and from this house I was again sent to that school as a day-boarder. Let those who know what is the usual appearance and what the usual appurtenances of a boy at such a school, consider what must have been my condition among them, with a daily walk of twelve miles* through the lanes, added to the other little troubles and labours of a school life!

Perhaps the eighteen months which I passed in this condition, walking to and fro on those miserably dirty lanes, was the worst period of my life. I was now over fifteen, and had come to an age at which I could appreciate at its full the misery of expulsion from all social intercourse. I had not only no friends, but was despised by all my companions. The farmhouse was not only no more than a farmhouse, but was one of those farmhouses which seem always to be in danger of falling into the neighbouring horse-pond. As it crept downwards from house to stables, from stables to barns, from barns to cowsheds, and from cowsheds to dung-heaps, one could hardly tell where one began and the other ended! There was a parlour in which my father lived, shut up among big books; but I passed my most jocund hours in the kitchen, making innocent love to the bailiff's daughter. The farm kitchen might be very well through the evening, when the horrors of the school were over; but it all added to the cruelty of the days. A sizar at a Cambridge college, or a Bible-clerk* at Oxford, has not pleasant days, or used not to have them half a century ago; but his position was recognised, and the misery was measured. I was a sizar at a fashionable school, a condition never premeditated. What right had a wretched farmer's boy, reeking from a dunghill, to sit next to the sons of peers,—or much worse still, next to the sons of big tradesmen who had made their ten thousand a-year? The indignities I endured are not to be described. As I look back it seems to me that all hands were turned against me,—those of masters as well as boys. I was allowed to join in no plays. Nor did I learn anything,—for I was taught nothing. The only expense, except that of books, to which a home-boarder* was then subject, was the fee to a tutor, amounting, I think, to ten guineas. My tutor took me without the fee; but when I heard him declare the fact in the pupil-room before the boys, I hardly felt grateful for the charity. I was never a coward, and cared for a thrashing as little as any boy, but one cannot make a stand against the acerbities of three hundred tyrants without a moral courage of which at that time I possessed none. I know that I skulked, and was

odious to the eyes of those I admired and envied. At last I was driven
to rebellion, and there came a great fight,*—at the end of which my
opponent had to be taken home for a while. If these words be ever
printed, I trust that some schoolfellow of those days may still be left
alive who will be able to say that, in claiming this solitary glory of my
schooldays, I am not making a false boast.

I wish I could give some adequate picture of the gloom of that
farmhouse. My elder brother—Tom as I must call him in my narrative, though the world, I think, knows him best as Adolphus—was at
Oxford. My father and I lived together, he having no means of living
except what came from the farm. My memory tells me that he was
always in debt to his landlord and to the tradesmen he employed.
Of self-indulgence no one could accuse him. Our table was poorer,
I think, than that of the bailiff who still hung on to our shattered
fortunes. The furniture was mean and scanty. There was a large ram-
bling kitchen-garden, but no gardener; and many times verbal incen-
tives were made to me,—generally, I fear, in vain,—to get me to lend
a hand at digging and planting. Into the hayfield on holidays I was
often compelled to go,—not, I fear, with much profit. My father's
health was very bad. During the last ten years of his life, he spent
nearly the half of his time in bed, suffering agony from sick headaches.
But he was never idle unless when suffering. He had at this time commenced a work,—an Encyclopædia Ecclesiastica,* as he called it,—
on which he laboured to the moment of his death. It was his ambition
to describe all ecclesiastical terms, including the denominations of
every fraternity of monks and every convent of nuns, with all their
orders and subdivisions. Under crushing disadvantages, with few or
no books of reference, with immediate access to no library, he worked
at his most ungrateful task with unflagging industry. When he died,
three numbers out of eight had been published by subscription; and
are now, I fear, unknown, and buried in the midst of that huge pile of
futile literature, the building up of which has broken so many hearts.

And my father, though he would try, as it were by a side wind, to
get a useful spurt of work out of me, either in the garden or in the
hay-field, had constantly an eye to my scholastic improvement. From
my very babyhood, before those first days at Harrow, I had to take
my place alongside of him as he shaved at six o'clock in the morning, and say my early rules from the Latin Grammar, or repeat the
Greek alphabet; and was obliged at these early lessons to hold my

head inclined towards him, so that in the event of guilty fault, he might be able to pull my hair without stopping his razor or dropping his shaving-brush. No father was ever more anxious for the education of his children, though I think none ever knew less how to go about the work. Of amusement, as far as I can remember, he never recognised the need. He allowed himself no distraction, and did not seem to think it was necessary to a child. I cannot bethink me of aught that he ever did for my gratification; but for my welfare,—for the welfare of us all,—he was willing to make any sacrifice. At this time, in the farmhouse at Harrow Weald, he could not give his time to teach me, for every hour that he was not in the fields was devoted to his monks and nuns; but he would require me to sit at a table with Lexicon and Gradus* before me. As I look back on my resolute idleness and fixed determination to make no use whatever of the books thus thrust upon me, or of the hours, and as I bear in mind the consciousness of great energy in after-life, I am in doubt whether my nature is wholly altered, or whether his plan was wholly bad. In those days he never punished me, though I think I grieved him much by my idleness; but in passion he knew not what he did, and he has knocked me down with the great folio Bible which he always used. In the old house were the two first volumes of Cooper's novel, called *The Prairie*, a relic—probably a dishonest relic—of some subscription to Hookham's library.* Other books of the kind there was none. I wonder how many dozen times I read those two first volumes.

It was the horror of those dreadful walks backwards and forwards which made my life so bad. What so pleasant, what so sweet, as a walk along an English lane, when the air is sweet and the weather fine, and when there is a charm in walking? But here were the same lanes four times a-day, in wet and dry, in heat and summer, with all the accompanying mud and dust, and with disordered clothes. I might have been known among all the boys at a hundred yards' distance by my boots and trousers,—and was conscious at all times that I was so known. I remembered constantly that address from Dr Butler when I was a little boy. Dr Longley* might with equal justice have said the same thing any day,—only that Dr Longley never in his life was able to say an ill-natured word. Dr Butler only became Dean of Peterborough, but his successor lived to be Archbishop of Canterbury.

I think it was in the autumn of 1831 that my mother, with the rest of the family, returned from America. She lived at first at the farmhouse, but it was only for a short time. She came back with a book written about the United States,* and the immediate pecuniary success which that work obtained enabled her to take us all back to the house at Harrow,—not to the first house, which would still have been beyond her means, but to that which has since been called Orley Farm, and which was an Eden as compared to our abode at Harrow Weald. Here my schooling went on under somewhat improved circumstances. The three miles became half a mile, and probably some salutary changes were made in my wardrobe. My mother and my sisters, too, were there. And a great element of happiness was added to us all in the affectionate and life-enduring friendship of the family of our close neighbour, Colonel Grant.* But I was never able to overcome—or even to attempt to overcome—the absolute isolation of my school position. Of the cricket-ground or racket-court I was allowed to know nothing. And yet I longed for these things with an exceeding longing. I coveted popularity with a covetousness that was almost mean. It seemed to me that there would be an Elysium* in the intimacy of those very boys whom I was bound to hate because they hated me. Something of the disgrace of my school-days has clung to me all through life. Not that I have ever shunned to speak of them as openly as I am writing now, but that when I have been claimed as schoolfellow by some of those many hundreds who were with me either at Harrow or at Winchester, I have felt that I had no right to talk of things from most of which I was kept in estrangement.

Through all my father's troubles he still desired to send me either to Oxford or Cambridge. My elder brother went to Oxford, and Henry to Cambridge. It all depended on my ability to get some scholarship that would help me to live at the University. I had many chances. There were exhibitions from Harrow—which I never got. Twice I tried for a sizarship at Clare Hall,—but in vain. Once I made a futile attempt for a scholarship at Trinity, Oxford,—but failed again. Then the idea of a university career was abandoned. And very fortunate it was that I did not succeed, for my career with such assistance only as a scholarship would have given me, would have ended in debt and ignominy.

When I left Harrow I was all but nineteen, and I had at first gone there at seven. During the whole of those twelve years no attempt had been made to teach me anything but Latin and Greek, and very little attempt to teach me those languages. I do not remember any lessons either in writing or arithmetic. French and German I certainly was not taught. The assertion will scarcely be credited, but I do assert that I have no recollection of other tuition except that in the dead languages. At the school at Sunbury there was certainly a writing master and a French master. The latter was an extra, and I never had extras. I suppose I must have been in the writing master's class, but though I can call to mind the man, I cannot call to mind his ferule.* It was by their ferules that I always knew them, and they me. I feel convinced in my mind that I have been flogged oftener than any human being alive. It was just possible to obtain five scourgings in one day at Winchester, and I have often boasted that I obtained them all. Looking back over half a century, I am not quite sure whether the boast is true; but if I did not, nobody ever did.

And yet when I think how little I knew of Latin or Greek* on leaving Harrow at nineteen, I am astonished at the possibility of such waste of time. I am now a fair Latin scholar,—that is to say, I read and enjoy the Latin classics, and could probably make myself understood in Latin prose. But the knowledge which I have, I have acquired since I left school,—no doubt aided much by that groundwork of the language which will in the process of years make its way slowly, even through the skin. There were twelve years of tuition in which I do not remember that I ever knew a lesson! When I left Harrow I was nearly at the top of the school, being a monitor, and, I think, the seventh boy. This position I achieved by gravitation upwards. I bear in mind well with how prodigal a hand prizes used to be showered about; but I never got a prize.* From the first to the last there was nothing satisfactory in my school career,—except the way in which I licked the boy who had to be taken home to be cured.

CHAPTER 2

My Mother

THOUGH I do not wish in these pages to go back to the origin of all the Trollopes, I must say a few words of my mother,—partly because filial duty will not allow me to be silent as to a parent who made for herself a considerable name in the literature of her day, and partly because there were circumstances in her career well worthy of notice. She was the daughter of the Rev. William Milton,* vicar of Heckfield, who, as well as my father, had been a fellow of New College. She was nearly thirty when, in 1809, she married my father. Six or seven years ago a bundle of love-letters from her to him fell into my hand in a very singular way, having been found in the house of a stranger, who, with much courtesy, sent them to me. They were then about sixty years old, and had been written some before and some after her marriage, over the space of perhaps a year. In no novel of Richardson's or Miss Burney's* have I seen a correspondence at the same time so sweet, so graceful, and so well expressed. But the marvel of these letters was in the strange difference they bore to the love-letters of the present day. They are, all of them, on square paper, folded and sealed, and addressed to my father on circuit;* but the language in each, though it almost borders on the romantic, is beautifully chosen, and fit, without change of a syllable, for the most critical eye. What girl now studies the words with which she shall address her lover, or seeks to charm him with grace of diction? She dearly likes a little slang, and revels in the luxury of entire familiarity with a new and strange being. There is something in that, too, pleasant to our thoughts, but I fear that this phase of life does not conduce to a taste for poetry among our girls. Though my mother was a writer of prose, and revelled in satire, the poetic feeling clung to her to the last.

In the first ten years of her married life she became the mother of six children, four of whom died of consumption at different ages. My elder sister married, and had children, of whom one still lives; but she was one of the four who followed each other at intervals during my mother's lifetime. Then my brother Tom and I were left to her,—with the destiny before us three of writing more books than were probably ever before produced by a single family.[1] My married sister added to the number by one little anonymous high church story, called *Chollerton.**

From the date of their marriage up to 1827, when my mother went to America, my father's affairs had always been going down in the world. She had loved society, affecting a somewhat liberal *rôle*, and professing an emotional dislike to tyrants, which sprung from the wrongs of would-be regicides and the poverty of patriot exiles. An Italian marquis who had escaped with only a second shirt from the clutches of some archduke whom he had wished to exterminate, or a French *prolétaire* with distant ideas of sacrificing himself to the cause of liberty, were always welcome to the modest hospitality of her house. In after years, when marquises of another caste had been gracious to her, she became a strong Tory, and thought that archduchesses were sweet. But with her politics were always an affair of the heart,—as, indeed, were all her convictions. Of reasoning from causes, I think that she knew nothing. Her heart was in every way so perfect, her desire to do good to all around her so thorough, and her power of self-sacrifice so complete, that she generally got herself right in spite of her want of logic; but it must be acknowledged that she was emotional. I can remember now her books, and can see her at her pursuits. The poets she loved best were Dante and Spenser. But she raved also of him of whom all such ladies were raving then, and rejoiced in the popularity and wept over the persecution of Lord Byron.* She was among those who seized with avidity on the novels, as they came out, of the then unknown Scott, and who could still talk of the triumphs of Miss Edgeworth.* With the literature of the day she was familiar, and with the poets of the past. Of other reading I do not think she had mastered much. Her life, I take it, though latterly clouded by money troubles,* was easy, luxurious, and idle, till my father's affairs and her own aspirations sent her to America. She had dear friends among literary people, of whom I remember Mathias,* Henry Milman,* and Miss Landon;* but till long after middle life she never herself wrote a line for publication.

---

[1] The family of Estienne, the great French printers of the fifteenth and sixteenth centuries, of whom there were at least nine or ten, did more perhaps for the production of literature than any other family. But they, though they edited, and not unfrequently translated the works which they published, were not authors in the ordinary sense.

In 1827 she went to America, having been partly instigated by the social and communistic ideas of a lady whom I well remember,—a certain Miss Wright,*—who was, I think, the first of the American female lecturers. Her chief desire, however, was to establish my brother Henry; and perhaps joined with that was the additional object of breaking up her English home without pleading broken fortunes to all the world. At Cincinnati, in the State of Ohio, she built a bazaar, and I fancy lost all the money which may have been embarked in that speculation. It could not have been much, and I think that others also must have suffered. But she looked about her, at her American cousins, and resolved to write a book about them. This book she brought back with her in 1831, and published it early in 1832. When she did this she was already fifty. When doing this she was aware that unless she could so succeed in making money, there was no money for any of the family. She had never before earned a shilling. She almost immediately received a considerable sum from the publishers,—if I remember rightly, amounting to two sums of £400 each within a few months; and from that moment till nearly the time of her death, at any rate for more than twenty years, she was in the receipt of a considerable income from her writings. It was a late age at which to begin such a career.

The Domestic Manners of the Americans was the first of a series of books of travels, of which it was probably the best, and was certainly the best known. It will not be too much to say of it that it had a material effect upon the manners of the Americans of the day, and that that effect has been fully appreciated by them. No observer was certainly ever less qualified to judge of the prospects or even of the happiness of a young people. No one could have been worse adapted by nature for the task of learning whether a nation was in a way to thrive. Whatever she saw she judged, as most women do, from her own standing-point. If a thing were ugly to her eyes, it ought to be ugly to all eyes,—and if ugly, it must be bad. What though people had plenty to eat and clothes to wear, if they put their feet upon the tables and did not reverence their betters? The Americans were to her rough, uncouth, and vulgar,—and she told them so. Those communistic and social ideas, which had been so pretty in a drawing-room, were scattered to the winds. Her volumes were very bitter; but they were very clever, and they saved the family from ruin.

Book followed book immediately,—first two novels, and then a book on Belgium and Western Germany.* She refurnished the house which I have called Orley Farm, and surrounded us again with moderate comforts. Of the mixture of joviality and industry which formed her character, it is almost impossible to speak with exaggeration. The industry was a thing apart, kept to herself. It was not necessary that any one who lived with her should see it. She was at her table at four in the morning, and had finished her work before the world had begun to be aroused. But the joviality was all for others. She could dance with other people's legs, eat and drink with other people's palates, be proud with the lustre of other people's finery. Every mother can do that for her own daughters; but she could do it for any girl whose look, and voice, and manners pleased her. Even when she was at work, the laughter of those she loved was a pleasure to her. She had much, very much, to suffer. Work sometimes came hard to her, so much being required,—for she was extravagant, and liked to have money to spend; but of all people I have known she was the most joyous, or, at any rate, the most capable of joy.

We continued this renewed life at Harrow for nearly two years, during which I was still at the school, and at the end of which I was nearly nineteen. Then there came a great catastrophe. My father, who, when he was well, lived a sad life among his monks and nuns, still kept a horse and gig. One day in March 1834, just as it had been decided that I should leave the school then, instead of remaining, as had been intended, till midsummer, I was summoned very early in the morning, to drive him up to London. He had been ill, and must still have been very ill indeed when he submitted to be driven by any one. It was not till we had started that he told me that I was to put him on board the Ostend boat. This I did, driving him through the city down to the docks. It was not within his nature to be communicative, and to the last he never told me why he was going to Ostend. Something of a general flitting abroad I had heard before, but why he should have flown the first, and flown so suddenly, I did not in the least know till I returned. When I got back with the gig, the house and furniture were all in the charge of the sheriff's officers.

The gardener who had been with us in former days stopped me as I drove up the road, and with gestures, signs, and whispered words, gave me to understand that the whole affair—horse, gig, and harness—would be made prize of if I went but a few yards farther. Why they should not have been made prize of I do not know. The little piece of dishonest business which I at once took in hand and carried through successfully was of no special service to any of us. I drove the gig into the village, and sold the entire equipage to the ironmonger for £17, the exact sum which he claimed as being due to himself. I was much complimented by the gardener, who seemed to think that so much had been rescued out of the fire. I fancy that the ironmonger was the only gainer by my smartness.

When I got back to the house a scene of devastation was in progress, which still was not without its amusement. My mother, through her various troubles, had contrived to keep a certain number of pretty-pretties which were dear to her heart. They were not much, for in those days the ornamentation of houses was not lavish as it is now; but there was some china, and a little glass, a few books, and a very moderate supply of household silver. These things, and things like them, were being carried down surreptitiously, through a gap between the two gardens, on to the premises of our friend Colonel Grant. My two sisters, then sixteen and seventeen, and the Grant girls, who were just younger, were the chief marauders. To such forces I was happy to add myself for any enterprise, and between us we cheated the creditors to the extent of our powers, amidst the anathemas, but good-humoured abstinence from personal violence, of the men in charge of the property. I still own a few books that were thus purloined.

For a few days the whole family bivouacked under the Colonel's hospitable roof, cared for and comforted by that dearest of all women, his wife. Then we followed my father to Belgium, and established ourselves in a large house just outside the walls of Bruges.* At this time, and till my father's death, everything was done with money earned by my mother. She now again furnished the house,—this being the third that she had put in order since she came back from America two years and a half ago.

There were six of us went into this new banishment. My brother Henry had left Cambridge and was ill. My younger sister was ill. And though as yet we hardly told each other that it was so, we began to feel that that desolating fiend, consumption, was among us. My father was broken-hearted as well as ill, but whenever he could sit at his table he still worked at his ecclesiastical records. My elder sister and I were in good health, but I was an idle, desolate hanger-on, that most hopeless of human beings, a hobbledehoy of nineteen, without any idea of a career, or a profession, or a trade. As well as I can remember I was fairly happy, for there were pretty girls at Bruges with whom

I could fancy that I was in love; and I had been removed from the real misery of school. But as to my future life I had not even an aspiration. Now and again there would arise a feeling that it was hard upon my mother that she should have to do so much for us, that we should be idle while she was forced to work so constantly; but we should probably have thought more of that had she not taken to work as though it were the recognised condition of life for an old lady of fifty-five.

Then, by degrees, an established sorrow was at home among us. My brother was an invalid, and the horrid word, which of all words were for some years after the most dreadful to us, had been pronounced. It was no longer a delicate chest, and some temporary necessity for peculiar care,—but consumption! The Bruges doctor had said so, and we knew that he was right. From that time forth my mother's most visible occupation was that of nursing. There were two sick men in the house, and hers were the hands that tended them. The novels went on, of course. We had already learned to know that they would be forthcoming at stated intervals,—and they always were forthcoming. The doctor's vials and the ink-bottle held equal places in my mother's rooms. I have written many novels under many circumstances; but I doubt much whether I could write one when my whole heart was by the bedside of a dying son. Her power of dividing herself into two parts, and keeping her intellect by itself clear from the troubles of the world, and fit for the duty it had to do, I never saw equalled. I do not think that the writing of a novel is the most difficult task which a man may be called upon to do; but it is a task that may be supposed to demand a spirit fairly at ease. The work of doing it with a troubled spirit killed Sir Walter Scott. My mother went through it unscathed in strength, though she performed all the work of day-nurse and night-nurse to a sick household;—for there were soon three of them dying.

At this time there came from some quarter an offer to me of a commission in an Austrian cavalry regiment; and so it was apparently my destiny to be a soldier. But I must first learn German and French, of which languages I knew almost nothing. For this a year was allowed me, and in order that it might be accomplished without expense, I undertook the duties of a classical usher* to a school then kept by William Drury at Brussels. Mr Drury had been one of the masters at Harrow when I went there at seven years old, and is now, after an interval of fifty-three years, even yet officiating as clergyman at that place.[1] To Brussels I went, and my heart still sinks within me as I reflect that any one should have intrusted to me the tuition of thirty boys. I can only hope that those boys went there to learn French, and that their parents were not particular as to their classical acquirements. I remember that on two occasions I was sent to take the school out for a walk; but that after the second attempt Mrs Drury declared that the boys' clothes would not stand any further experiments of that kind. I cannot call to mind any learning by me of other languages; but as I only remained in that position for six weeks, perhaps the return lessons had not been as yet commenced. At the end of the six weeks a letter reached me, offering me a clerkship in the General Post Office, and I accepted it. Among my mother's dearest friends she reckoned Mrs Freeling, the wife of Clayton Freeling, whose father, Sir Francis Freeling,* then ruled the Post Office. She had heard of my desolate position, and had begged from her father-in-law the offer of a berth in his own office.

I hurried back from Brussels to Bruges on my way to London, and found that the number of invalids had been increased. My younger sister, Emily, who, when I had left the house, was trembling on the balance,—who had been pronounced to be delicate, but with that false-tongued hope which knows the truth, but will lie lest the heart should faint, had been called delicate, but only delicate,—was now ill. Of course she was doomed. I knew it of both of them, though I had never heard the word spoken, or had spoken it to any one. And my father was very ill,—ill to dying, though I did not know it. And my mother had decreed to send my elder sister away to England, thinking that the vicinity of so much sickness might be injurious to her. All this happened late in the autumn of 1834, in the spring of which year we had come to Bruges; and then my mother was left alone in a big house outside the town, with two Belgian women-servants, to nurse three* dying patients—the patients being her husband and children—and to write novels for the sustenance of the family! It was about this period of her career that her best novels were written.*

To my own initiation at the Post Office I will return in the next chapter. Just before Christmas my brother died, and was buried at Bruges. In the following February my father died, and was buried alongside of him,—and with him died that tedious task of his, which I can only

---

[1] He died two years after these words were written.

hope may have solaced many of his latter hours. I sometimes look back, meditating for hours together, on his adverse fate. He was a man, finely educated, of great parts, with immense capacity for work, physically strong very much beyond the average of men, addicted to no vices, carried off by no pleasures, affectionate by nature, most anxious for the welfare of his children, born to fair fortunes,—who, when he started in the world, may be said to have had everything at his feet. But everything went wrong with him. The touch of his hand seemed to create failure. He embarked in one hopeless enterprise after another, spending on each all the money he could at the time command. But the worse curse to him of all was a temper so irritable that even those whom he loved the best could not endure it. We were all estranged from him, and yet I believe that he would have given his heart's blood for any of us. His life as I knew it was one long tragedy.

After his death my mother moved to England, and took and furnished a small house at Hadley,* near Barnet. I was then a clerk in the London Post Office, and I remember well how gay she made the place with little dinners, little dances, and little picnics, while she herself was at work every morning long before others had left their beds. But she did not stay at Hadley much above a year. She went up to London, where she again took and furnished a house, from which my remaining sister was married and carried away into Cumberland. My mother soon followed her, and on this occasion did more than take a house. She bought a bit of land,—a field of three acres near the town,—and built a residence for herself. This, I think, was in 1841, and she had thus established and reestablished herself six times in ten years. But in Cumberland she found the climate too severe, and in 1844 she moved herself to Florence, where she remained till her death in 1863. She continued writing up to 1856, when she was seventy-six years old,—and had at that time produced 114 volumes, of which the first was not written till she was fifty. Her career offers great encouragement to those who have not begun early in life, but are still ambitious to do something before they depart hence.

She was an unselfish, affectionate, and most industrious woman, with great capacity for enjoyment and high physical gifts. She was endowed too, with much creative power, with considerable humour, and a genuine feeling for romance. But she was neither clear-sighted nor accurate; and in her attempts to describe morals, manners, and even facts, was unable to avoid the pitfalls of exaggeration.

CHAPTER 3

The General Post Office
1834–1841

WHILE I was still learning my duty as an usher at Mr Drury's
school at Brussels, I was summoned to my clerkship in the
London Post Office, and on my way passed through Bruges. I then
saw my father and my brother Henry for the last time. A sadder
household never was held together. They were all dying; except my
mother, who would sit up night after night nursing the dying ones
and writing novels the while,—so that there might be a decent roof for
them to die under. Had she failed to write the novels, I do not know
where the roof would have been found. It is now more than forty
years ago, and looking back over so long a lapse of time I can tell the
story, though it be the story of my own father and mother, of my own
brother and sister, almost as coldly as I have often done some scene
of intended pathos in fiction; but that scene was indeed full of pathos.
I was then becoming alive to the blighted ambition of my father's
life, and becoming alive also to the violence of the strain which my
mother was enduring. But I could do nothing but go and leave them.
There was something that comforted me in the idea that I need no
longer be a burden,—a fallacious idea, as it soon proved. My salary
was to be £90 a year, and on that I was to live in London, keep up my
character as a gentleman, and be happy. That I should have thought
this possible at the age of nineteen, and should have been delighted
at being able to make the attempt, does not surprise me now; but that
others should have thought it possible, friends who knew something
of the world, does astonish me. A lad might have done so, no doubt,
or might do so even in these days, who was properly looked after and
kept under control,—on whose behalf some law of life had been laid
down. Let him pay so much a week for his board and lodging, so much
for his clothes, so much for his washing, and then let him understand
that he has—shall we say?—sixpence a day left for pocket-money and
omnibuses. Any one making the calculation will find the sixpence far
too much. No such calculation was made for me or by me. It was

supposed that a sufficient income had been secured to me, and that I should live upon it as other clerks lived.

But as yet the £90 a year was not secured to me. On reaching London I went to my friend Clayton Freeling, who was then secretary at the Stamp Office, and was taken by him to the scene of my future labours in St Martin's le Grand.* Sir Francis Freeling was the secretary, but he was greatly too high an official to be seen at first by a new junior clerk. I was taken, therefore, to his eldest son Henry Freeling,* who was the assistant secretary, and by him I was examined as to my fitness. The story of that examination is given accurately in one of the opening chapters of a novel written by me, called *The Three Clerks.* If any reader of this memoir would refer to that chapter and see how Charley Tudor was supposed to have been admitted into the Internal Navigation Office, that reader will learn how Anthony Trollope was actually admitted into the Secretary's office of the General Post Office in 1834. I was asked to copy some lines from the *Times* newspaper with an old quill pen, and at once made a series of blots and false spellings. 'That won't do, you know,' said Henry Freeling to his brother Clayton. Clayton, who was my friend, urged that I was nervous, and asked that I might be allowed to do a bit of writing at home and bring it as a sample on the next day. I was then asked whether I was a proficient in arithmetic. What could I say ? I had never learned the multiplication table, and had no more idea of the rule of three than of conic sections.* 'I know a little of it,' I said humbly, whereupon I was sternly assured that on the morrow, should I succeed in showing that my handwriting was all that it ought to be, I should be examined as to that little of arithmetic. If that little should not be found to comprise a thorough knowledge of all the ordinary rules, together with practised and quick skill, my career in life could not be made at the Post Office. Going down the main stairs of the building,—stairs which have I believe been now pulled down to make room for sorters and stampers,—Clayton Freeling told me not to be too downhearted. I was myself inclined to think that I had better go back to the school in Brussels. But nevertheless I went to work, and under the surveillance of my elder brother made a beautiful transcript of four or five pages of Gibbon.* With a faltering heart I took these on the next day to the office. With my caligraphy I was contented, but was certain that I should come to the ground among the figures. But when I got to 'The Grand,' as we used to call our office in those days, from its site in St Martin's le Grand, I was seated at a desk without any further reference to my competency. No one condescended even to look at my beautiful penmanship.

That was the way in which candidates for the Civil Service were examined in my young days. It was at any rate the way in which I was examined. Since that time there has been a very great change indeed;*—and in some respects a great improvement. But in regard to the absolute fitness of the young men selected for the public service, I doubt whether more harm has not been done than good. And I think that good might have been done without the harm. The rule of the present day is, that every place shall be open to public competition, and that it shall be given to the best among the comers. I object to this, that at present there exists no known mode of learning who is best, and that the method employed has no tendency to elicit the best. That method pretends only to decide who among a certain number of lads will best answer a string of questions, for the answering of which they are prepared by tutors, who have sprung up for the purpose since this fashion of election has been adopted. When it is decided in a family that a boy shall 'try the Civil Service,' he is made to undergo a certain amount of cramming. But such treatment has, I maintain, no connection whatever with education. The lad is no better fitted after it than he was before for the future work of his life. But his very success fills him with false ideas of his own educational standing, and so far unfits him. And, by the plan now in vogue, it has come to pass that no one is in truth responsible either for the conduct, the manners, or even for the character of the youth. The responsibility was perhaps slight before; but existed, and was on the increase.

There might have been,—in some future time of still increased wisdom, there yet may be,—a department established to test the fitness of acolytes without recourse to the dangerous optimism of competitive choice. I will not say but that there should have been some one to reject me,—though I will have the hardihood to say that, had I been so rejected, the Civil Service would have lost a valuable public servant. This is a statement that will not, I think, be denied by those who, after I am gone, may remember anything of my work. Lads, no doubt, should not be admitted who have none of the small acquirements that are wanted. Our offices should not be schools in which writing and early lessons in geography, arithmetic, or French should be learned. But all that could be ascertained without the perils of competitive examination.

The desire to insure the efficiency of the young men selected, has not been the only object—perhaps not the chief object—of those who have yielded in this matter to the arguments of the reformers. There had arisen in England a system of patronage, under which it had become gradually necessary for politicians to use their influence for the purchase of political support. A member of the House of Commons, holding office, who might chance to have five clerkships to give away in a year, found himself compelled to distribute them among those who sent him to the House. In this there was nothing pleasant to the distributer of patronage. Do away with the system altogether, and he would have as much chance of support as another. He bartered his patronage only because another did so also. The beggings, the refusings, the jealousies, the correspondence, were simply troublesome. Gentlemen in office were not therefore indisposed to rid themselves of the care of patronage. I have no doubt their hands are the cleaner and their hearts are the lighter; but I do doubt whether the offices are on the whole better manned.

As what I now write will certainly never be read till I am dead, I may dare to say what no one now does dare to say in print,—though some of us whisper it occasionally into our friends' ears. There are places in life which can hardly be well filled except by 'Gentlemen.' The word is one the use of which almost subjects one to ignominy. If I say that a judge should be a gentleman, or a bishop, I am met with a scornful allusion to 'Nature's Gentlemen.' Were I to make such an assertion with reference to the House of Commons, nothing that I ever said again would receive the slightest attention. A man in public life could not do himself a greater injury than by saying in public that the commissions in the army or navy, or berths in the Civil Service, should be given exclusively to gentlemen. He would be defied to define the term,—and would fail should he attempt to do so. But he would know what he meant, and so very probably would they who defied him. It may be that the son of the butcher of the village shall become as well fitted for employments requiring gentle culture as the son of the parson. Such is often the case. When such is the case, no one has been more prone to give the butcher's son all the welcome he has merited than I myself; but the chances are greatly in favour of the parson's son. The gates of the one class should be open to the other; but neither to the one class nor to the other can good be done by declaring that there are no gates, no barrier, no difference. The system of competitive examination is, I think, based on a supposition that there is no difference.

I got into my place without any examining. Looking back now, I think I can see with accuracy what was then the condition of my own mind and intelligence. Of things to be learned by lessons I knew almost less than could be supposed possible after the amount of schooling I had received. I could read neither French, Latin, nor Greek. I could speak no foreign language,—and I may as well say here as elsewhere that I never acquired the power of really talking French. I have been able to order my dinner and take a railway ticket, but never got much beyond that. Of the merest rudiments of the sciences I was completely ignorant. My handwriting was in truth wretched. My spelling was imperfect. There was no subject as to which examination would have been possible on which I could have gone through an examination otherwise than disgracefully. And yet I think I knew more than the average of young men of the same rank who began life at nineteen. I could have given a fuller list of the names of the poets of all countries, with their subjects and periods,—and probably of historians,—than many others; and had, perhaps, a more accurate idea of the manner in which my own country was governed. I knew the names of all the Bishops, all the Judges, all the Heads of Colleges, and all the Cabinet Ministers,— not a very useful knowledge indeed, but one that had not been acquired without other matter which was more useful. I had read Shakespeare and Byron and Scott, and could talk about them. The music of the Miltonic line* was familiar to me. I had already made up my mind that *Pride and Prejudice* was the best novel in the English language,—a palm which I only partially withdrew after a second reading of *Ivanhoe*, and did not completely bestow elsewhere till *Esmond** was written. And though I would occasionally break down in my spelling, I could write a letter. If I had a thing to say, I could so say it in written words that the readers should know what I meant,—a power which is by no means at the command of all those who come out from these competitive examinations with triumph. Early in life, at the age of fifteen, I had commenced the dangerous habit of keeping a journal, and this I maintained for ten years. The volumes remained in my possession unregarded—never looked at—till 1870, when I examined them, and, with many blushes, destroyed them. They convicted me of folly, ignorance, indiscretion, idleness, extravagance, and conceit. But they had habituated me to the rapid use of pen and ink, and taught me how to express myself with facility.

I will mention here another habit which had grown upon me from still earlier years,—which I myself often regarded with dismay when I thought of the hours devoted to it, but which, I suppose, must have tended to make me what I have been. As a boy, even as a child, I was thrown much upon myself. I have explained, when speaking of my school-days, how it came to pass that other boys would not play with me. I was therefore alone, and had to form my plays within myself. Play of some kind was necessary to me then, as it has always been. Study was not my bent, and I could not please myself by being all idle. Thus it came to pass that I was always going about with some castle in the air firmly built within my mind. Nor were these efforts in architecture spasmodic, or subject to constant change from day to day. For weeks, for months, if I remember rightly, from year to year, I would carry on the same tale, binding myself down to certain laws, to certain proportions, and proprieties, and unities. Nothing impossible was ever introduced,—nor even anything which, from outward circumstances, would seem to be violently improbable. I myself was of course my own hero. Such is a necessity of castle-building. But I never became a king, or a duke,—much less when my height and personal appearance were fixed could I be an Antinous,* or six feet high. I never was a learned man, nor even a philosopher. But I was a very clever person, and beautiful young women used to be fond of me. And I strove to be kind of heart, and open of hand, and noble in thought, despising mean things; and altogether I was a very much better fellow than I have ever succeeded in being since. This had been the occupation of my life for six or seven years before I went to the Post Office, and was by no means abandoned when I commenced my work. There can, I imagine, hardly be a more dangerous mental practice; but I have often doubted whether, had it not been my practice, I should ever have written a novel. I learned in this way to maintain an interest in a fictitious story, to dwell on a work created by my own imagination, and to live in a world altogether outside the world of my own material life. In after years I have done the same,—with this difference, that I have discarded the hero of my early dreams, and have been able to lay my own identity aside.

I must certainly acknowledge that the first seven years of my official life were neither creditable to myself nor useful to the public service.

These seven years were passed in London, and during this period of my life it was my duty to be present every morning at the office punctually at 10 a.m. I think I commenced my quarrels with the authorities there by having in my possession a watch which was always ten minutes late. I know that I very soon achieved a character for irregularity, and came to be regarded as a black sheep by men around me who were not themselves, I think, very good public servants. From time to time rumours reached me that if I did not take care I should be dismissed; especially one rumour in my early days, through my dearly beloved friend Mrs Clayton Freeling,—who, as I write this, is still living, and who, with tears in her eyes, besought me to think of my mother. That was during the life of Sir Francis Freeling, who died,—still in harness,—a little more than twelve months after I joined the office. And yet the old man showed me signs of almost affectionate kindness, writing to me with his own hand more than once from his death-bed.

Sir Francis Freeling was followed at the Post Office by Colonel Maberly,* who certainly was not my friend. I do not know that I deserved to find a friend in my new master, but I think that a man with better judgment would not have formed so low an opinion of me as he did. Years have gone by, and I can write now, and almost feel, without anger; but I can remember well the keenness of my anguish when I was treated as though I were unfit for any useful work. I did struggle—not to do the work, for there was nothing which was not easy without any struggling—but to show that I was willing to do it. My bad character nevertheless stuck to me, and was not to be got rid of by any efforts within my power. I do admit that I was irregular. It was not considered to be much in my favour that I could write letters—which was mainly the work of our office—rapidly, correctly, and to the purpose. The man who came at ten, and who was always still at his desk at half-past four, was preferred before me, though when at his desk he might be less efficient. Such preference was no doubt proper; but, with a little encouragement, I also would have been punctual. I got credit for nothing, and was reckless.

As it was, the conduct of some of us was very bad. There was a comfortable sitting-room up-stairs, devoted to the use of some one of our number who in turn was required to remain in the place all night. Hither one or two of us would adjourn after lunch, and play *écarté** for an hour or two. I do not know whether such ways are possible now in our public offices. And here we used to have suppers and card-parties at night—great symposiums,* with much smoking of tobacco; for in our part of the building there lived a whole bevy of clerks. These were gentlemen whose duty it then was to make up and receive the foreign mails. I do not remember that they worked later or earlier than the other sorting-clerks; but there was supposed to be something special in foreign letters, which required that the men who handled them should have minds undistracted by the outer world. Their salaries, too, were higher than those of their more homely brethren; and they paid nothing for their lodgings. Consequently there was a somewhat fast set in those apartments, given to cards and to tobacco, who drank spirits and water in preference to tea. I was not one of them, but was a good deal with them.

I do not know that I should interest my readers by saying much of my Post Office experiences in those days. I was always on the eve of being dismissed, and yet was always striving to show how good a public servant I could become, if only a chance were given me. But the chance went the wrong way. On one occasion, in the performance of my duty, I had to put a private letter containing bank-notes on the secretary's table,—which letter I had duly opened, as it was not marked private. The letter was seen by the Colonel, but had not been moved by him when he left the room. On his return it was gone. In the meantime I had returned to the room, again in the performance of some duty. When the letter was missed I was sent for, and there I found the Colonel much moved about his letter, and a certain chief clerk, who, with a long face, was making suggestions as to the probable fate of the money. 'The letter has been taken,' said the Colonel, turning to me angrily, 'and, by G——! there has been nobody in the room but you and I.' As he spoke, he thundered his fist down upon the table. 'Then,' said I, 'by G——! you have taken it.' And I also thundered my fist down;—but, accidentally, not upon the table. There was there a standing movable desk, at which, I presume, it was the Colonel's habit to write, and on this movable desk was a large bottle full of ink. My fist unfortunately came on the desk, and the ink at once flew up, covering the Colonel's face and shirt-front. Then it was a sight to see that senior clerk, as he seized a quire of blotting-paper, and rushed to the aid of his superior officer, striving to mop up the ink; and a sight also to see the Colonel, in his agony, hit right out through the blotting-paper at that senior clerk's unoffending stomach. At that moment there came in the Colonel's private secretary, with the letter and the money, and I was desired to go back to my own room. This was an incident not much in my favour, though I do not know that it did me special harm.

I was always in trouble. A young woman down in the country had taken it into her head that she would like to marry me,—and a very foolish young woman she must have been to entertain such a wish. I need not tell that part of the story more at length, otherwise than by protesting that no young man in such a position was ever much less to blame than I had been in this. The invitation had come from her, and I had lacked the pluck to give it a decided negative; but I had left the house within half an hour, going away without my dinner, and had never returned to it. Then there was a correspondence,—if that can be called a correspondence in which all the letters came from one side. At last the mother appeared at the Post Office. My hair almost stands on my head now as I remember the figure of the woman walking into the big room in which I sat with six or seven other clerks, having a large basket on her arm and an immense bonnet on her head. The messenger had vainly endeavoured to persuade her to remain in the ante-room. She followed the man in, and walking up the centre of the room, addressed me in a loud voice: 'Anthony Trollope, when are you going to marry my daughter?' We have all had our worst moments, and that was one of my worst. I lived through it, however, and did not marry the young lady. These little incidents were all against me in the office.

And then a certain other phase of my private life crept into official view, and did me a damage. As I shall explain just now, I rarely at this time had any money wherewith to pay my bills. In this state of things a certain tailor had taken from me an acceptance for, I think £12, which found its way into the hands of a money-lender. With that man, who lived in a little street near Mecklenburgh Square,* I formed a most heart-rending but a most intimate acquaintance. In cash I once received from him £4. For that and for the original amount of the tailor's bill, which grew monstrously under repeated renewals, I paid ultimately something over £200. That is so common a story as to be hardly worth the telling; but the peculiarity of this man was that he became so attached to me as to visit me every day at my office. For a long period he found it to be worth his while to walk up those stone steps daily, and come and stand behind my chair, whispering to me always the same words: 'Now I wish you would be punctual. If you only would be punctual, I should like you to have anything you want.' He was a little, clean, old man, who always wore a high starched white cravat, inside which he had a habit of twisting his chin as he uttered his caution. When I remember the constant persistency of his visits, I cannot but feel that he was paid very badly for time and trouble. Those visits were very terrible, and can have hardly been of service to me in the office.

Of one other misfortune which happened to me in those days I must tell the tale. A junior clerk in the secretary's office was always told off to sleep upon the premises, and he was supposed to be the presiding genius of the establishment when the other members of the Secretary's department had left the building. On an occasion when I was still little more than a lad,—perhaps one-and-twenty years old,—I was filling this responsible position. At about seven in the evening word was brought to me that the Queen of,—I think Saxony,* but I am sure it was a Queen,—wanted to see the night mails sent out. At this time, when there were many mail-coaches, this was a show, and august visitors would sometimes come to see it. But preparation was generally made beforehand, and some pundit of the office would be at hand to do the honours. On this occasion we were taken by surprise, and there was no pundit. I therefore gave the orders, and accompanied her Majesty around the building, walking backwards, as I conceived to be proper, and often in great peril as I did so, up and down the stairs. I was, however, quite satisfied with my own manner of performing an unaccustomed and most important duty. There were two old gentlemen with her Majesty, who, no doubt, were German barons, and an ancient baroness also. They had come and, when they had seen the sights, took their departure in two glass coaches. As they were preparing to go, I saw the two barons consulting together in deep whispers, and then as the result of that conversation one of them handed me half-a-crown! That also was a bad moment.

I came up to town, as I said before, purporting to live a jolly life upon £90 per annum. I remained seven years in the General Post Office, and when I left it my income was £140. During the whole of this time I was hopelessly in debt. There were two intervals,* amounting together to nearly two years, in which I lived with my mother, and therefore lived in comfort,—but even then I was overwhelmed with debt. She paid much for me,—paid all that I asked her to pay, and all that she could find out that I owed. But who in such a condition ever

tells all and makes a clean breast of it? The debts, of course, were not
large, but I cannot think now how I could have lived, and sometimes
have enjoyed life, with such a burden of duns as I endured. Sheriff's
officers with uncanny documents, of which I never understood anything, were common attendants on me. And yet I do not remember
that I was ever locked up, though I think I was twice a prisoner.* In
such emergencies some one paid for me. And now, looking back at
it, I have to ask myself whether my youth was very wicked. I did no
good in it; but was there fair ground for expecting good from me?
When I reached London no mode of life was prepared for me,—no
advice ever* given to me. I went into lodgings, and then had to dispose of my time. I belonged to no club, and knew very few friends
who would receive me into their houses. In such a condition of life
a young man should no doubt go home after his work, and spend
the long hours of the evening in reading good books and drinking
tea. A lad brought up by strict parents, and without having had even
a view of gayer things, might perhaps do so. I had passed all my life
at public schools, where I had seen gay things, but had never enjoyed
them. Towards the good books and tea no training had been given me.
There was no house in which I could habitually see a lady's face and
hear a lady's voice. No allurement to decent respectability came in
my way. It seems to me that in such circumstances the temptations of
loose life will almost certainly prevail with a young man. Of course if
the mind be strong enough, and the general stuff knitted together of
sufficiently stern material, the temptations will not prevail. But such
minds and such material are, I think, uncommon. The temptation at
any rate prevailed with me.

I wonder how many young men fall utterly to pieces from being
turned loose into London after the same fashion. Mine was, I think,
of all phases of such life the most dangerous. The lad who is sent
to mechanical work has longer hours, during which he is kept from
danger, and has not generally been taught in his boyhood to antici-
pate pleasure. He looks for hard work and grinding circumstances.
I certainly had enjoyed but little pleasure, but I had been among
those who did enjoy it and were taught to expect it. And I had filled
my mind with the ideas of such joys. And now, except during official
hours, I was entirely without control,—without the influences of any
decent household around me. I have said something of the comedy
of such life, but it certainly had its tragic aspect. Turning it all over

in my own mind, as I have constantly done in after years, the tragedy has always been uppermost. And so it was as the time was passing. Could there be any escape from such dirt? I would ask myself; and I always answered that there was no escape. The mode of life was itself wretched. I hated the office. I hated my work. More than all I hated my idleness. I had often told myself since I left school that the only career in life within my reach was that of an author, and the only mode of authorship open to me that of a writer of novels. In the journal which I read and destroyed a few years since, I found the matter argued out before I had been in the Post Office two years. Parliament was out of the question. I had not means to go to the Bar. In official life, such as that to which I had been introduced, there did not seem to be any opening for real success. Pens and paper I could command. Poetry I did not believe to be within my grasp. The drama, too, which I would fain have chosen, I believed to be above me. For history, biography, or essay writing I had not sufficient erudition. But I thought it possible that I might write a novel. I had resolved very early that in that shape must the attempt be made. But the months and years ran on, and no attempt was made. And yet no day was passed without thoughts of attempting, and a mental acknowledgment of the disgrace of postponing it. What reader will not understand the agony of remorse produced by such a condition of mind? The gentleman from Mecklenburgh Square was always with me in the morning,—always angering me by his hateful presence,—but when the evening came I could make no struggle towards getting rid of him.

In those days I read a little, and did learn to read French and Latin. I made myself familiar with Horace,* and became acquainted with the works of our own greatest poets. I had my strong enthusiasms, and remember throwing out of the window in Northumberland Street, where I lived, a volume of Johnson's *Lives of the Poets*, because he spoke sneeringly of *Lycidas*.* That was Northumberland Street by the Marylebone Workhouse,* on to the back-door of which establishment my room looked out—a most dreary abode, at which I fancy I must have almost ruined the good-natured lodging-house keeper by my constant inability to pay her what I owed.

How I got my daily bread I can hardly remember. But I do remember that I was often unable to get myself a dinner. Young men generally now have their meals provided for them. I kept house, as it were. Every day I had to find myself with the day's food. For my breakfast

I could get some credit at the lodgings, though that credit would frequently come to an end. But for all that I had after breakfast I had to pay day by day;* and at your eating-house credit is not given. I had no friends on whom I could sponge regularly. Out on the Fulham Road I had an uncle,* but his house was four miles from the Post Office, and almost as far from my own lodgings. Then came borrowings of money, sometimes absolute want, and almost constant misery.

Before I tell how it came about that I left this wretched life, I must say a word or two of the friendships which lessened its misfortunes. My earliest friend in life was John Merivale, with whom I had been at school at Sunbury and Harrow, and who was a nephew of my tutor, Harry Drury. Herman Merivale, who afterwards became my friend, was his brother, as is also Charles Merivale,* the historian and Dean of Ely. I knew John when I was ten years old, and am happy to be able to say that he is going to dine with me one day this week. I hope I may not injure his character by stating that in those days I lived very much with him. He, too, was impecunious, but he had a home in London, and knew but little of the sort of penury which I endured. For more than fifty years he and I have been close friends. And then there was one W—— A——,* whose misfortunes in life will not permit me to give his full name, but whom I dearly loved. He had been at Winchester and at Oxford, and at both places had fallen into trouble. He then became a schoolmaster,—or perhaps I had better say usher,—and finally he took orders. But he was unfortunate in all things, and died some years ago in poverty. He was most perverse; bashful to very fear of the rustle of a lady's dress;* unable to restrain himself in anything, but yet with a conscience that was always stinging him; a loving friend, though very quarrelsome; and, perhaps, of all men I have known, the most humorous. And he was entirely unconscious of his own humour. He did not know that he could so handle all matters as to create infinite amusement out of them. Poor W—— A——! To him there came no happy turning-point at which life first loomed* seriously on him, and then became prosperous.

W—— A——, Merivale, and I formed a little club, which we called the Tramp Society, and subjected to certain rules, in obedience to which we wandered on foot about the counties adjacent to London. Southampton was the furthest point we ever reached; but Buckinghamshire and Hertfordshire were more dear to us. These were the happiest hours of my then life—and perhaps not the least innocent, although we were frequently in peril from the village authorities whom we outraged. Not to pay for any conveyance, never to spend above five shillings a day, to obey all orders from the elected ruler of the hour (this enforced under heavy fines), were among our statutes. I would fain tell here some of our adventures:—how A—— enacted an escaped madman and we his pursuing keepers, and so got ourselves a lift in a cart, from which we ran away as we approached the lunatic asylum; how we were turned out of a little town at night, the townsfolk frightened by the loudness of our mirth; and how we once crept into a hayloft and were wakened in the dark morning by a pitchfork,—and how the juvenile owner of that pitchfork fled through the window when he heard the complaints of the wounded man! But the fun was the fun of W—— A——, and would cease to be fun as told by me.

It was during these years that John Tilley,* who has now been for many years the permanent senior officer of the Post Office, married my sister, whom he took with him into Cumberland, where he was stationed as one of our surveyors. He has been my friend for more than forty years; as has also Peregrine Birch, a clerk in the House of Lords, who married one of those daughters of Colonel Grant* who assisted us in the raid we made on the goods which had been seized by the Sheriff's officer at Harrow. These have been the oldest and dearest friends of my life; and I can thank God that three of them are still alive.

When I had been nearly seven years in the Secretary's office of the Post Office, always hating my position there, and yet always fearing that I should be dismissed from it, there came a way of escape. There had latterly been created in the service a new body of officers called surveyors' clerks. There were at that time seven surveyors in England, two in Scotland, and three in Ireland. To each of these officers a clerk had been lately attached, whose duty it was to travel about the country under the surveyor's orders. There had been much doubt among the young men in the office whether they should or should not apply for these places. The emoluments were good and the work alluring; but there was at first supposed to be something derogatory in the position. There was a rumour that the first surveyor who got a clerk sent the clerk out to fetch his beer; and that another had called upon his clerk to send the linen to the wash. There was, however, a conviction that nothing could be worse than the berth of a surveyor's clerk

in Ireland. The clerks were all appointed, however. To me it had not
occurred to ask for anything, nor would anything have been given me.
But after a while there came a report from the far west of Ireland that
the man sent there was absurdly incapable. It was probably thought
then that none but a man absurdly incapable would go on such a mission to the west of Ireland. When the report reached the London
office I was the first to read it. I was at that time in dire trouble, having
debts on my head and quarrels with our Secretary-Colonel, and a full
conviction that my life was taking me downwards to the lowest pits.
So I went to the Colonel boldly, and volunteered for Ireland if he
would send me. He was glad to be so rid of me, and I went. This happened in August 1841, when I was twenty-six years old. My salary in
Ireland was to be but £100 a year; but I was to receive fifteen shillings
a day for every day that I was away from home, and sixpence for every
mile that I travelled. The same allowances were made in England;
but at that time travelling in Ireland was done at half the English
prices. My income in Ireland, after paying my expenses, became at
once £400.* This was the first good fortune of my life.

CHAPTER 4

Ireland—My First Two Novels
1841–1848

I N the preceding pages I have given a short record of the first twenty-six years of my life,—years of suffering, disgrace, and inward remorse. I fear that my mode of telling will have left an idea simply of their absurdities; but in truth I was wretched,—sometimes almost unto death, and have often cursed the hour in which I was born.* There had clung to me a feeling that I had been looked upon always as an evil, an encumbrance, a useless thing,—as a creature of whom those connected with him had to be ashamed. And I feel certain now that in my young days I was so regarded. Even my few friends who had found with me a certain capacity for enjoyment were half afraid of me. I acknowledge the weakness of a great desire to be loved,—of a strong wish to be popular with my associates. No child, no boy, no lad, no young man, had ever been less so. And I had been so poor; and so little able to bear poverty. But from the day on which I set my foot in Ireland all these evils went away from me. Since that time who has had a happier life than mine? Looking round upon all those I know, I cannot put my hand upon one. But all is not over yet. And, mindful of that, remembering how great is the agony of adversity, how crushing the despondency of degradation, how susceptible I am myself to the misery coming from contempt,—remembering also how quickly good things may go and evil things come,—I am often again tempted to hope, almost to pray, that the end may be near. Things may be going well now—

'Sin aliquem infandum casum, Fortuna, minaris;
Nunc, o nunc liceat crudelem abrumpere vitam.'*

There is unhappiness so great that the very fear of it is an alloy to happiness. I had then lost my father, and sister, and brother,—have since lost another sister and my mother;—but I have never as yet lost a wife or a child.

When I told my friends that I was going on this mission to Ireland they shook their heads, but said nothing to dissuade me. I think it must have been evident to all who were my friends that my life in London was not a success. My mother and elder brother were at this time abroad, and were not consulted;—did not even know my intention in time to protest against it. Indeed, I consulted no one, except a dear old cousin,* our family lawyer, from whom I borrowed £200 to help me out of England. He lent me the money, and looked upon me with pitying eyes,—shaking his head. 'After all you were right to go,' he said to me when I paid him the money a few years afterwards.

But nobody then thought I was right to go. To become clerk to an Irish surveyor, in Connaught,* with a salary of £100 a year, at twenty-six years of age! I did not think it right even myself,—except that anything was right which would take me away from the General Post Office and from London.

My ideas of the duties I was to perform were very vague, as were also my ideas of Ireland generally. Hitherto I had passed my time, seated at a desk, either writing letters myself, or copying into books those which others had written. I had never been called upon to do anything I was unable or unfitted to do. I now understood that in Ireland I was to be a deputy-inspector of country post offices, and that among other things to be inspected would be the postmasters' accounts! But as no other person asked a question as to my fitness for this work, it seemed unnecessary for me to do so.

On the 15th of September 1841, I landed in Dublin, without an acquaintance in the country, and with only two or three letters of introduction from a brother clerk in the Post Office. I had learned to think that Ireland was a land flowing with fun and whisky, in which irregularity was the rule of life, and where broken heads were looked upon as honourable badges. I was to live at a place called Banagher,* on the Shannon, which I had heard of because of its having once been conquered, though it had heretofore conquered everything, including the devil. And from Banagher my inspecting tours were to be made, chiefly into Connaught, but also over a strip of country eastwards, which would enable me occasionally to run up to Dublin. I went to a hotel which was very dirty, and after dinner I ordered some whisky punch. There was an excitement in this, but when the punch was gone I was very dull. It seemed so strange to be in a country in which there was not a single individual whom I had ever spoken to or ever seen. And it was to be my destiny to go down into Connaught and adjust accounts,—the destiny of me who had never learned the multiplication table, or done a sum in long division!

On the next morning I called on the Secretary of the Irish Post Office,* and learned from him that Colonel Maberly had sent a very bad character with me. He could not have sent a very good one; but I felt a little hurt when I was informed by this new master that he had been informed that I was worthless, and must in all probability be dismissed. 'But,' said the new master, 'I shall judge you by your own merits.' From that time to the day on which I left the service, I never heard a word of censure, nor had many months passed before I found that my services were valued. Before a year was over, I had acquired the character of a thoroughly good public servant.

The time went very pleasantly. Some adventures I had;—two of which I told in the *Tales of All Countries*,* under the names of *The O'Conors of Castle Conor*, and *Father Giles of Ballymoy*. I will not swear to every detail in these stories, but the main purport of each is true. I could tell many others of the same nature, were this the place for them. I found that the surveyor to whom I had been sent kept a pack of hounds, and therefore I bought a hunter. I do not think he liked it, but he could not well complain. He never rode to hounds himself, but I did; and then and thus began one of the great joys of my life. I have ever since been constant to the sport, having learned to love it with an affection which I cannot myself fathom or understand. Surely no man has laboured at it as I have done, or hunted under such drawbacks as to distances, money, and natural disadvantages. I am very heavy, very blind, have been—in reference to hunting—a poor man, and am now an old man. I have often had to travel all night outside a mail-coach, in order that I might hunt the next day. Nor have I ever been in truth a good horseman. And I have passed the greater part of my hunting life under the discipline of the Civil Service. But it has been for more than thirty years a duty to me to ride to hounds; and I have performed that duty with a persistent energy. Nothing has ever been allowed to stand in the way of hunting,—neither the writing of books, nor the work of the Post Office, nor other pleasures. As regarded the Post Office, it soon seemed to be understood that I was to hunt; and when my services were re-transferred to England, no word of difficulty ever reached me about it. I have written on very many subjects, and on most of them with pleasure; but on no subject with such delight as that on hunting. I have dragged it into many novels,—into too many no doubt,—but I have always felt myself deprived of a legitimate joy when the nature of the tale has not allowed me a hunting chapter. Perhaps that which gave me the greatest delight was the description of a run on a horse accidentally taken from another sportsman,—a circumstance which occurred to my dear friend Charles Buxton,* who will be remembered as one of the members for Surrey.

It was altogether a very jolly life that I led in Ireland. I was always moving about, and soon found myself to be in pecuniary circumstances which were opulent in comparison with those of my past life. The Irish people did not murder me, nor did they even break my head. I soon found them to be good-humoured, clever—the working classes very much more intelligent than those of England—economical, and hospitable. We hear much of their spendthrift nature; but extravagance is not the nature of an Irishman. He will count the shillings in a pound much more accurately than an Englishman, and will with much more certainty get twelve pennyworth from each. But they are perverse, irrational, and but little bound by the love of truth. I lived for many years among them—not finally leaving the country until 1859, and I had the means of studying their character.

I had not been a fortnight in Ireland before I was sent down to a little town in the far west of county Galway, to balance a defaulting postmaster's accounts, find out how much he owed, and report upon his capacity to pay. In these days such accounts are very simple. They adjust themselves from day to day, and a Post Office surveyor has nothing to do with them. At that time, though the sums dealt with were small, the forms of dealing with them were very intricate. I went to work, however, and made that defaulting postmaster teach me the use of those forms. I then succeeded in balancing the account, and had no difficulty whatever in reporting that he was altogether unable to pay his debt. Of course he was dismissed;—but he had been a very useful man to me. I never had any further difficulty in the matter.

But my chief work was the investigating of complaints made by the public as to postal matters. The practice of the office was and is to send one of its servants to the spot to see the complainant and to inquire into the facts, when the complainant is sufficiently energetic or sufficiently big to make himself well heard. A great expense is often incurred for a very small object; but the system works well on the whole as confidence is engendered, and a feeling is produced in the country that the department has eyes of its own and does keep them open. This employment was very pleasant, and to me always easy, as it required at its close no more than the writing of a report. There were no accounts in this business, no keeping of books, no necessary manipulation of multitudinous forms. I must tell of one such complaint and inquiry, because in its result I think it was emblematic of many.

A gentleman in county Cavan* had complained most bitterly of the injury done to him by some arrangement of the Post Office. The nature of his grievance has no present significance; but it was so unendurable that he had written many letters, couched in the strongest language. He was most irate, and indulged himself in that scorn which is so easy to an angry mind. The place was not in my district, but I was borrowed, being young and strong, that I might encounter* the edge of his personal wrath. It was mid-winter, and I drove up to his house, a squire's country seat, in the middle of a snow-storm, just as it was becoming dark. I was on an open jaunting-car, and was on my way from one little town to another, the cause of his complaint having reference to some mail conveyance between the two. I was certainly very cold, and very wet, and very uncomfortable when I entered his house. I was admitted by a butler, but the gentleman himself hurried into the hall. I at once began to explain my business. 'God bless me!' he said, 'you are wet through. John, get Mr Trollope some brandy and water,—very hot.' I was beginning my story about the post again when he himself took off my greatcoat, and suggested that I should go up to my bedroom before I troubled myself with business. 'Bedroom!' I exclaimed. Then he assured me that he would not turn a dog out on such a night as that, and into a bedroom I was shown, having first drank the brandy and water standing at the drawing-room fire. When I came down I was introduced to his daughter, and the three of us went into dinner. I shall never forget his righteous indignation when I again brought up the postal question on the departure of the young lady. Was I such a Goth as to contaminate wine with business? So I drank my wine, and then heard the young lady sing while her father slept in his arm-chair. I spent a very pleasant evening, but my host was too sleepy to hear anything about the Post Office that night. It was absolutely necessary that I should go away the next morning after breakfast, and I explained that the matter must be discussed then. He shook his head and wrung his hands in unmistakable disgust,—almost in despair. 'But what am I to say in my report?' I asked. 'Anything you please,' he said. 'Don't spare me, if you want an excuse for yourself. Here I sit all the day,—with nothing to do; and I like writing letters.' I did report that Mr —— was now quite satisfied with the postal arrangement of his district; and I felt a soft regret that I should have robbed my friend of his occupation. Perhaps he was able to take up the Poor Law Board, or to attack the Excise. At the Post Office nothing more was heard from him.

I went on with the hunting surveyor at Banagher for three years, during which, at Kingstown, the watering-place near Dublin, I met Rose Heseltine,* the lady who has since become my wife. The engagement took place when I had been just one year in Ireland; but there was still a delay of two years before we could be married. She had no fortune, nor had I any income beyond that which came from the Post Office; and there were still a few debts, which would have been paid off no doubt sooner, but for that purchase of the horse. When I had been nearly three years in Ireland we were married on the 11th of June 1844;—and perhaps I ought to name that happy day as the commencement of my better life, rather than the day on which I first landed in Ireland.

For though during these three years I had been jolly enough, I had not been altogether happy. The hunting, the whisky punch, the rattling Irish life,—of which I could write a volume of stories were this the place to tell them,—were continually driving from my mind the still cherished determination to become a writer of novels. When I reached Ireland I had never put pen to paper; nor had I done so when I became engaged. And when I was married, being then twenty-nine, I had only written the first volume of my first work. This constant putting off of the day of work was a great sorrow to me. I certainly had not been idle in my new berth. I had learned my work, so that every one concerned knew that it was safe in my hands; and I held a position altogether the reverse of that in which I was always trembling while I remained in London. But that did not suffice,—did not nearly suffice. I still felt that there might be a career before me, if I could only bring myself to begin the work. I do not think I much doubted my own intellectual sufficiency for the writing of a readable novel. What I did doubt was my own industry, and the chances of the market.

The vigour necessary to prosecute two professions at the same time is not given to every one, and it was only lately that I had found the vigour necessary for one. There must be early hours, and I had not as yet learned to love early hours. I was still, indeed, a young man; but hardly young enough to trust myself to find the power to alter the habits of my life. And I had heard of the difficulties of publishing,—a subject of which I shall have to say much should I ever bring this memoir to a close. I had dealt already with publishers on my mother's behalf, and knew that many a tyro who could fill a manuscript lacked the power to put his matter before the public;—and I knew, too, that when the matter was printed, how little had then been done towards the winning of the battle! I had already learned that many a book—many a good book—

> 'is born to blush unseen
> And waste its sweetness on the desert air.'*

But still the purpose was strong within me, and the first effort was made after the following fashion. I was located at a little town called Drumsna,* or rather village, in the county Leitrim, where the postmaster had come to some sorrow about his money; and my friend John Merivale was staying with me for a day or two. As we were taking a walk in that most uninteresting country, we turned up through a deserted gateway, along a weedy, grass-grown avenue, till we came to the modern ruins of a country house. It was one of the most melancholy spots I ever visited. I will not describe it here, because I have done so in the first chapter of my first novel. We wandered about the place, suggesting to each other causes for the misery we saw there, and while I was still among the ruined walls and decayed beams I fabricated the plot of *The Macdermots of Ballycloran*. As to the plot itself, I do not know that I ever made one so good,—or, at any rate, one so susceptible of pathos. I am aware that I broke down in the telling, not having yet studied the art. Nevertheless, *The Macdermots* is a good novel, and worth reading by any one who wishes to understand what Irish life was before the potato disease, the famine, and the Encumbered Estates Bill.*

When my friend left me, I set to work and wrote the first chapter or two. Up to this time I had continued that practice of castle-building of which I have spoken; but now the castle I built was among the ruins of that old house. The book, however, hung with me. It was only now and then that I found either time or energy for a few pages. I commenced the book in September 1843, and had only written a volume when I was married in June 1844.

My marriage was like the marriage of other people, and of no special interest to any one except my wife and me. It took place at Rotherham in Yorkshire, where her father was the manager of a bank. We were not very rich, having about £400 a year on which to live. Many people would say that we were two fools to encounter such poverty together. I can only reply that since that day I have never been without money in my pocket, and that I soon acquired the means of paying what I owed. Nevertheless, more than twelve years had to pass over our heads before I received any payment for any literary work which afforded an appreciable increase to our income.

Immediately after our marriage, I left the west of Ireland and the hunting surveyor, and joined another in the south. It was a better district, and I was enabled to live at Clonmel,* a town of some importance, instead of at Banagher, which is little more than a village. I had not felt myself to be comfortable in my old residence as a married man. On my arrival there as a bachelor I had been received most kindly, but when I brought my English wife I fancied that there was a feeling that I had behaved badly to Ireland generally. When a young man has been received hospitably in an Irish circle, I will not say that it is expected of him that he should marry some young lady in that society;—but it certainly is expected of him that he shall not marry any young lady out of it. I had given offence, and I was made to feel it.

There has taken place a great change in Ireland since the days in which I lived at Banagher, and a change so much for the better, that I have sometimes wondered at the obduracy with which people have spoken of the permanent ill condition of the country. Wages are now nearly double what they were then. The Post Office at any rate is paying almost double for its rural labour,—9s. a week when it used to pay 5s., and 12s. a week when it used to pay 7s. Banks have sprung up in almost every village. Rents are paid with more than English punctuality. And the religious enmity between the classes, though it is not yet dead, is dying out. Soon after I reached Banagher in 1841, I dined one evening with a Roman Catholic. I was informed next day by a Protestant gentleman who had been very hospitable to me that I must choose my party. I could not sit both at Protestant and Catholic tables. Such a caution would now be impossible in any part of Ireland. Home-rule no doubt is a nuisance,—and especially a nuisance because the professors of the doctrine do not at all believe it themselves. There are probably no other twenty men in England or Ireland who would be so utterly dumfounded and prostrated were Home-rule to have its way as the twenty Irish members who profess to support it in the House of Commons. But it is not to be expected that nuisances such as these should be abolished at a blow. Home-rule is at any rate better and more easily managed than the rebellion at the close of the last century; it is better than the treachery of the Union; less troublesome than O'Connell's monster meetings; less dangerous than Smith O'Brien and the battle of the cabbage-garden at Ballingary; and very much less bloody than Fenianism. The descent from O'Connell to Mr Butt* has been the natural declension of a political disease, which we had no right to hope would be cured by any one remedy.

When I had been married a year my first novel was finished. In July 1845 I took it with me to the north of England, and intrusted the MS. to my mother to do with it the best she could among the publishers in London. No one had read it but my wife; nor, as far as I am aware, has any other friend of mine ever read a word of my writing before it was printed. She, I think, has so read almost everything, to my very great advantage in matters of taste. I am sure I have never asked a friend to read a line; nor have I ever read a word of my own writing aloud,—even to her. With one exception,— which shall be mentioned as I come to it,—I have never consulted a friend as to a plot, or spoken to any one of the work I have been doing. My first manuscript I gave up to my mother, agreeing with her that it would be as well that she should not look at it before she gave it to a publisher. I knew that she did not give me credit for the sort of cleverness necessary for such work. I could see in the faces and hear in the voices of those of my friends who were around me at the house in Cumberland—my mother, my sister, my brother-in-law, and, I think, my brother—that they had not expected me to come out as one of the family authors. There were three or four in the field before me, and it seemed to be almost absurd that another should wish to add himself to the number. My father had written much—those long ecclesiastical descriptions—quite unsuccessfully. My mother had become one of the popular authors of the day. My brother had commenced,* and had been fairly well paid for his work. My sister, Mrs Tilley, had also written a novel, which was at the time in manuscript—which was published afterwards without her name, and was called *Chollerton*. I could perceive that this attempt of mine was felt to be an unfortunate aggravation of the disease.

My mother however did the best she could for me, and soon reported that Mr Newby* of Mortimer Street was to publish the book. It was to be printed at his expense, and he was to give me half the profits. Half the profits! Many a young author expects much from such an undertaking. I can with truth declare that I expected nothing. And I got nothing. Nor did I expect fame, or even acknowledgment. I was sure that the book would fail, and it did fail most absolutely. I never heard of a person reading it in those days. If there was any notice taken of it* by any critic of the day, I did not see it. I never asked any questions about it, or wrote a single letter on the subject to the publisher. I have Mr Newby's agreement with me, in duplicate, and one or two preliminary notes; but beyond that I did not have a word from Mr Newby. I am sure that he did not wrong me in that he paid me nothing. It is probable that he did not sell fifty copies of the work;—but of what he did sell he gave me no account.

I do not remember that I felt in any way disappointed or hurt. I am quite sure that no word of complaint passed my lips. I think I may say that after the publication I never said a word about the book, even to my wife. The fact that I had written and published it, and that I was writing another, did not in the least interfere with my life or with my determination to make the best I could of the Post Office. In Ireland, I think that no one knew that I had written a novel. But I went on writing. *The Macdermots* was published in 1847, and *The Kellys and the O'Kellys* followed in 1848. I changed my publisher, but did not change my fortune. This second Irish story was sent into the world by Mr Colburn,* who had long been my mother's publisher, who reigned in Great Marlborough Street, and I believe created the business which is now carried on by Messrs Hurst & Blackett. He had previously been in partnership with Mr Bentley in New Burlington Street. I made the same agreement as before as to half profits, and with precisely the same results. The book was not only not read, but was never heard of,—at any rate in Ireland. And yet it is a good Irish story, much inferior to *The Macdermots* as to plot, but superior in the mode of telling. Again I held my tongue, and not only said nothing but felt nothing. Any success would, I think, have carried me off my legs, but I was altogether prepared for failure. Though I thoroughly enjoyed the writing of these books, I did not imagine, when the time came for publishing them, that any one would condescend to read them.

But in reference to *The O'Kellys* there arose a circumstance which set my mind to work on a subject which has exercised it much ever since. I made my first acquaintance with criticism. A dear friend of mine to whom the book had been sent—as have all my books—wrote me word to Ireland that he had been dining at some club with a man high in authority among the gods of the *Times* newspaper, and that this special god had almost promised that *The O'Kellys* should be noticed in that most influential of 'organs.' The information moved me very much; but it set me thinking whether the notice, should it ever appear, would not have been more valuable, at any rate more honest, if it had been produced by other means;—if for instance the writer of the notice had been instigated by the merits or demerits of the book instead of by the friendship of a friend. And I made up my mind then that, should I continue this trade of authorship, I would have no dealings with any critic on my own behalf. I would neither ask for nor deplore criticism, nor would I ever thank a critic for praise, or quarrel with him, even in my own heart, for censure. To this rule I have adhered with absolute strictness, and this rule I would recommend to all young authors. What can be got by touting among the critics is never worth the ignominy. The same may of course be said of all things acquired by ignominious means. But in this matter it is so easy to fall into the dirt. *Facilis descensus Averni.** There seems to be but little fault in suggesting to a friend that a few words in this or that journal would be of service. But any praise so obtained must be an injustice to the public, for whose instruction, and not for the sustentation of the author, such notices are intended. And from such mild suggestion the descent to crawling at the critic's feet, to the sending of presents, and at last to a mutual understanding between critics and criticised, is only too easy. Other evils follow, for the denouncing of which this is hardly the place;—though I trust I may find such place before my work is finished. I took no notice of my friend's letter, but I was not the less careful in watching *The Times*. At last the review came,—a real review in *The Times*.* I learned it by heart, and can now give, if not the words, the exact purport. 'Of *The Kellys and the O'Kellys* we may say what the master said to his footman, when the man complained of the constant supply of legs of mutton on the kitchen table. "Well, John, legs of mutton are good substantial food;" and we may say also what John replied: "Substantial, sir;—yes, they are substantial, but a little coarse." ' That was the review, and even that did not sell the book!

From Mr Colburn I did receive an account, showing that 375 copies of the book had been printed, that 140 had been sold,—to those, I presume, who liked substantial food though it was coarse,—and that he had incurred a loss of £63, 10s. 1½d. The truth of the account I never for a moment doubted; nor did I doubt the wisdom of the advice given to me in the following letter, though I never thought of obeying it—

'GREAT MARLBOROUGH STREET,
'*November* 11, 1848.

'MY DEAR SIR,—I am sorry to say that absence from town and other circumstances have prevented me from earlier inquiring into the results of the sale of *The Kellys and the O'Kellys*, with which the greatest efforts have been used, but in vain. The sale has been, I regret to say, so small that the loss upon the publication is very considerable; and it appears clear to me that, although in consequence of the great number of novels that are published, the sale of each, with some few exceptions, must be small, yet it is evident that readers do not like novels on Irish subjects as well as on others. Thus you will perceive it is impossible for me to give any encouragement to you to proceed in novel-writing.

'As, however, I understand you have nearly finished the novel *La Vendée*, perhaps you will favour me with a sight of it when convenient.—I remain, &c. &c.

'H. COLBURN.'

This, though not strictly logical, was a rational letter, telling a plain truth plainly. I did not like the assurance that 'the greatest efforts had been used,' thinking that any efforts which might be made for the popularity of a book ought to have come from the author;—but I took in good part Mr Colburn's assurance that he could not encourage me in the career I had commenced. I would have bet twenty to one against my own success. But by continuing I could lose only pen and paper; and if the one chance in twenty did turn up in my favour, then how much might I win!

CHAPTER 5

My First Success
1849–1855

I HAD at once gone to work on a third novel, and had nearly completed it, when I was informed of the absolute failure of the former.
I find however that the agreement for its publication was not made till
1850, by which time I imagine that Mr Colburn must have forgotten
the disastrous result of *The O'Kellys*, as he thereby agrees to give me
£20 down for my 'new historical novel, to be called *La Vendée*.' He
agreed also to pay me £30 more when he had sold 350 copies, and £50
more should he sell 450 within six months. I got my £20, and then
heard no more of *La Vendée*, not even receiving any account. Perhaps
the historical title had appeared more alluring to him than an Irish
subject; though it was not long afterwards that I received a warning
from the very same house of business against historical novels,—as
I will tell at length when the proper time comes.

I have no doubt that the result of the sale of this story was no better than that of the two that had gone before. I asked no questions,
however, and to this day have received no information. The story is
certainly inferior to those which had gone before;—chiefly because
I knew accurately the life of the people in Ireland, and knew, in truth,
nothing of life in the La Vendée country, and also because the facts of
the present time came more within the limits of my powers of story-
telling than those of past years. But I read the book the other day, and
am not ashamed of it. The conception as to the feeling of the people
is, I think, true; the characters are distinct; and the tale is not dull. As
far as I can remember, this morsel of criticism* is the only one that
was ever written on the book.

I had, however, received £20. Alas! alas! years were to roll by before
I should earn by my pen another shilling. And, indeed, I was well
aware that I had not earned that; but that the money had been 'talked
out of' the worthy publisher by the earnestness of my brother, who
made the bargain for me. I have known very much of publishers and
have been surprised by much in their mode of business,—by the

apparent lavishness and by the apparent hardness to authors in the same men;—but by nothing so much as by the ease with which they can occasionally be persuaded to throw away small sums of money. If you will only make the payment future instead of present, you may generally twist a few pounds in your own or your client's favour. 'You might as well promise her £20. This day six months will do very well.' The publisher, though he knows that the money will never come back to him, thinks it worth his while to rid himself of your importunity at so cheap a price.

But while I was writing *La Vendée* I made a literary attempt in another direction. In 1847 and 1848 there had come upon Ireland the desolation and destruction, first of the famine, and then of the pestilence which succeeded the famine. It was my duty at that time to be travelling constantly in those parts of Ireland in which the misery and troubles thence arising were, perhaps, at their worst. The western parts of Cork, Kerry, and Clare were pre-eminently unfortunate. The efforts—I may say the successful efforts—made by the Government to stay the hands of death will still be in the remembrance of many:— how Sir Robert Peel was instigated to repeal the Corn Laws; and how, subsequently, Lord John Russell* took measures for employing the people, and supplying the country with Indian corn. The expediency of these latter measures was questioned by many. The people themselves wished of course to be fed without working; and the gentry, who were mainly responsible for the rates, were disposed to think that the management of affairs was taken too much out of their own hands. My mind at the time was busy with the matter, and, thinking that the Government was right, I was inclined to defend them as far as my small powers went. S. G. O.* (Lord Sydney Godolphin Osborne) was at that time denouncing the Irish scheme of the Administration in the *Times*, using very strong language,—as those who remember his style will know. I fancied then—as I still think—that I understood the country much better than he did; and I was anxious to show that the steps taken for mitigating the terrible evil of the times were the best which the Minister of the day could have adopted. In 1848 I was in London, and, full of my purpose, I presented myself to Mr John Forster*—who has since been an intimate and valued friend—but who was at that time the editor of the *Examiner*. I think that that portion of the literary world which understands the fabrication of newspapers will admit that neither before his time, nor since, has there been a more capable editor of a weekly newspaper. As a literary man, he was not without his faults. That which the cabman is reported to have said of him before the magistrate is quite true. He was always 'an arbitrary cove.' As a critic, he belonged to the school of Bentley and Gifford,*—who would always bray in a literary mortar all critics who disagreed from them, as though such disagreement were a personal offence requiring personal castigation. But that very eagerness made him a good editor. Into whatever he did he put his very heart and soul. During his time the *Examiner* was almost all that a Liberal weekly paper should be. So to John Forster I went, and was shown into that room in Lincoln's Inn Fields in which, some three or four years earlier, Dickens had given that reading* of which there is an illustration with portraits in the second volume of his life.

At this time I knew no literary men. A few I had met when living with my mother, but that had been now so long ago that all such acquaintance had died out. I knew who they were as far as a man could get such knowledge from the papers of the day, and felt myself as in part belonging to the guild, through my mother, and in some degree by my own unsuccessful efforts. But it was not probable that any one would admit my claim;—nor on this occasion did I make any claim. I stated my name and official position, and the fact that opportunities had been given me of seeing the poor-houses in Ireland, and of making myself acquainted with the circumstances of the time. Would a series of letters on the subject be accepted by the *Examiner*? The great man, who loomed very large to me, was pleased to say that if the letters should recommend themselves by their style and matter, if they were not too long, and if—every reader will know how on such occasions an editor will guard himself—if this and if that, they should be favourably entertained. They were favourably entertained,—if printing and publication be favourable entertainment. But I heard no more of them. The world in Ireland did not declare that the Government had at last been adequately defended, nor did the treasurer of the *Examiner* send me a cheque in return.

Whether there ought to have been a cheque I do not even yet know. A man who writes a single letter to a newspaper of course is not paid for it,—nor for any number of letters on some point personal to himself. I have since written sets of letters to newspapers, and have been paid for them; but then I have bargained for a price. On this occasion I had hopes; but they never ran high, and I was not much disappointed. I have no copy now of those letters, and could not refer to them without much trouble; nor do I remember what I said. But I know that I did my best in writing them.

When my historical novel failed, as completely as had its predecessors, the two Irish novels, I began to ask myself whether, after all, that was my proper line. I had never thought of questioning the justice of the verdict expressed against me. The idea that I was the unfortunate owner of unappreciated genius never troubled me. I did not look at the books after they were published, feeling sure that they had been, as it were, damned with good reason. But still I was clear in my mind that I would not lay down my pen. Then and therefore I determined to change my hand, and to attempt a play. I did attempt the play, and in 1850 I wrote a comedy, partly in blank verse, and partly in prose, called *The Noble Jilt*.* The plot I afterwards used in a novel called *Can You Forgive Her?* I believe that I did give the best of my intellect to the play, and I must own that when it was completed it pleased me much, I copied it, and re-copied it, touching it here and touching it there, and then sent it to my very old friend, George Bartley* the actor, who had when I was in London been stage-manager of one of the great theatres, and who would I thought, for my own sake and for my mother's, give me the full benefit of his professional experience.

I have now before me the letter which he wrote to me,—a letter which I have read a score of times. It was altogether condemnatory. 'When I commenced,' he said, 'I had great hopes of your production. I did not think it opened dramatically, but that might have been remedied.' I knew then that it was all over. But, as my old friend warmed to the subject, the criticism became stronger and stronger, till my ears tingled. At last came the fatal blow. 'As to the character of your heroine, I felt at a loss how to describe it, but you have done it for me in the last speech of Madame Brudo.' Madame Brudo was the heroine's aunt. ' "Margaret, my child, never play the jilt again; 'tis a most unbecoming character. Play it with what skill you will, it meets but little sympathy." And this, be assured would be its effect upon an audience. So that I must reluctantly add that, had I been still a manager, *The Noble Jilt* is not a play I could have recommended for production.' This was a blow that I did feel. The neglect of a book is a disagreeable fact which grows upon an author by degrees. There is no special moment of agony,—no stunning violence of condemnation. But a piece of criticism such as this, from a friend, and from a man undoubtedly capable of forming an opinion, was a blow in the face! But I accepted the judgment loyally, and said not a word on the subject to any one. I merely showed the letter to my wife, declaring my conviction, that it must be taken as gospel. And as critical gospel it has since been accepted. In later days I have more than once read the play, and I know that he was right. The dialogue, however, I think to be good, and I doubt whether some of the scenes be not the brightest and best work I ever did.

Just at this time another literary project loomed before my eyes, and for six or eight months had considerable size. I was introduced to Mr John Murray,* and proposed to him to write a handbook for Ireland. I explained to him that I knew the country better than most other people, perhaps better than any other person, and could do it well. He asked me to make a trial of my skill, and to send him a certain number of pages, undertaking to give me an answer within a fortnight after he should have received my work. I came back to Ireland, and for some weeks I laboured very hard. I 'did' the city of Dublin, and the county of Kerry, in which lies the lake scenery of Killarney; and I 'did' the route from Dublin to Killarney, altogether completing nearly a quarter of the proposed volume. The roll of MS. was sent to Albemarle Street,—but was never opened. At the expiration of nine months from the date on which it reached that time-honoured spot it was returned without a word, in answer to a very angry letter from myself. I insisted on having back my property,—and got it. I need hardly say that my property has never been of the slightest use to me. In all honesty I think that had he been less dilatory, John Murray would have got a very good Irish Guide at a cheap rate.

Early in 1851 I was sent upon a job of special official work, which for two years so completely absorbed my time that I was able to write nothing. A plan was formed for extending the rural delivery of letters, and for adjusting the work, which up to that time had been done in a very irregular manner. A country letter-carrier would be sent in one direction in which there were but few letters to be delivered, the arrangement having originated probably at the request of some influential person, while in another direction there was no letter-carrier because no influential person had exerted himself. It was intended to set this right throughout England, Ireland, and Scotland; and I quickly did the work in the Irish district to which I was attached. I was then invited to do the same in a portion of England, and I spent two of the happiest years of my life at the task. I began in Devonshire; and visited, I think I may say, every nook in that county, in Cornwall, Somersetshire, the greater part of Dorsetshire, the Channel Islands, part of Oxfordshire, Wiltshire, Gloucestershire, Worcestershire, Herefordshire, Monmouthshire, and the six southern Welsh counties. In this way I had an opportunity of seeing a considerable portion of Great Britain, with a minuteness which few have enjoyed. And I did my business after a fashion in which no other official man has worked, at least for many years. I went almost everywhere on horseback. I had two hunters of my own, and here and there, where I could, I hired a third horse. I had an Irish groom* with me,—an old man, who has now been in my service for thirty-five years; and in this manner I saw almost every house—I think I may say every house of importance— in this large district. The object was to create a postal network which should catch all recipients of letters. In France it was, and I suppose still is, the practice to deliver every letter. Wherever the man may live to whom a letter is addressed, it is the duty of some letter-carrier to take that letter to his house, sooner or later. But this, of course, must be done slowly. With us a delivery much delayed was thought to be worse than none at all. In some places we did establish posts three times a week, and perhaps occasionally twice a week; but such halting arrangements were considered to be objectionable, and we were bound down by a salutary law as to expense, which came from our masters at the Treasury. We were not allowed to establish any messenger's walk on which a sufficient number of letters would not be delivered to pay the man's wages, counted at a halfpenny a letter. But then the counting was in our own hands, and an enterprising official might be sanguine in his figures. I think I was sanguine. I did not prepare false accounts; but I fear that the postmasters and clerks who absolutely had the country to do became aware that I was anxious for good results. It is amusing to watch how a passion will grow upon a man. During those two years it was the ambition of my life to cover the country with rural letter-carriers. I do not remember that in any case a rural post proposed by me was negatived by the authorities; but I fear that some of them broke down afterwards as being too poor, or because, in my anxiety to include this house and that, I had sent the men too far afield. Our law was that a man should not be required to walk more than sixteen miles a day. Had the work to be done been all on a measured road, there would have been no need for doubt as to the distances. But my letter-carriers went here and there across the fields. It was my special delight to take them by all short cuts; and as I measured on horseback the short cuts which they would have to make on foot, perhaps I was sometimes a little unjust to them.

All this I did on horseback, riding on an average forty miles a day. I was paid sixpence a mile for the distance travelled, and it was necessary that I should at any rate travel enough to pay for my equipage. This I did, and got my hunting out of it also. I have often surprised some small country postmaster, who had never seen or heard of me before, by coming down upon him at nine in the morning, with a red coat and boots and breeches, and interrogating him as to the disposal of every letter which came into his office. And in the same guise I would ride up to farmhouses, or parsonages, or other lone residences about the country, and ask the people how they got their letters, at what hour, and especially whether they were delivered free or at a certain charge. For a damnable habit* had crept into use, which came to be, in my eyes, at that time, the one sin for which there was no pardon, in accordance with which these rural letter-carriers used to charge a penny a letter, alleging that the house was out of their beat, and that they must be paid for their extra work. I think that I did stamp out that evil. In all these visits I was, in truth, a beneficent angel to the public, bringing everywhere with me an earlier, cheaper, and much more regular delivery of letters. But not unfrequently the angelic nature of my mission was imperfectly understood. I was perhaps a little in a hurry to get on, and did not allow as much time as was necessary to explain to the wondering mistress of the house, or to an open-mouthed farmer, why it was that a man arrayed for hunting asked so many questions which might be considered impertinent, as applying to his or her private affairs. 'Good morning, sir. I have just called to ask a few questions. I am a surveyor of the Post Office. How do you get your letters? As I am a little in a hurry, perhaps you can explain at once.' Then I would take out my pencil and notebook, and wait for information. And in fact there was no other way in which the truth could be ascertained. Unless I came down suddenly as a summer's storm upon them, the very people who were robbed by our messengers would not confess the robbery, fearing the ill-will of the men. It was necessary to startle them into the revelations which I required them to make for their own good. And I did startle them. I became thoroughly used to it, and soon lost my native bashfulness;—but sometimes my visits astonished the retiring inhabitants of country houses. I did, however, do my work, and can look back upon what I did with thorough satisfaction. I was altogether in earnest; and I believe that many a farmer now has his letters brought daily to his house free of charge, who but for me would still have had to send to the post-town for them twice a week, or to have paid a man for bringing them irregularly to his door.

This work took up my time so completely, and entailed upon me so great an amount of writing, that I was in fact unable to do any literary work. From day to day I thought of it, still purporting to make another effort, and often turning over in my head some fragment of a plot which had occurred to me. But the day did not come in which I could sit down with pen and paper and begin another novel. For, after all, what could it be but a novel? The play had failed more absolutely than the novels, for the novels had attained the honour of print. The cause of this pressure of official work lay, not in the demands of the General Post Office, which more than once expressed itself as astonished by my celerity, but in the necessity which was incumbent on me to travel miles enough to pay for my horses, and upon the amount of correspondence, returns, figures, and reports which such an amount of daily travelling brought with it. I may boast that the work was done very quickly and very thoroughly,—with no fault but an over-eagerness to extend postal arrangements far and wide.

In the course of the job I visited Salisbury, and whilst wandering there one mid-summer evening round the purlieus of the cathedral I conceived the story of *The Warden*,—from whence came that series of novels of which Barchester, with its bishops, deans, and archdeacon, was the central site. I may as well declare at once that no one at their commencement could have had less reason than myself to presume himself to be able to write about clergymen. I have been often asked in what period of my early life I had lived so long in a cathedral city as to have become intimate with the ways of a Close. I never lived in any cathedral city,—except London, never knew anything of any Close, and at that time had enjoyed no peculiar intimacy with any clergyman.* My archdeacon, who has been said to be life-like, and for whom I confess that I have all a parent's fond affection, was, I think, the simple result of an effort of my moral consciousness. It was such as that, in my opinion, that an archdeacon should be,—or, at any rate, would be with such advantages as an archdeacon might have; and lo!

an archdeacon was produced, who has been declared by competent authorities to be a real archdeacon down to the very ground. And yet, as far as I can remember, I had not then even spoken to an archdeacon. I have felt the compliment to be very great. The archdeacon came whole from my brain after this fashion;—but in writing about clergymen generally, I had to pick up as I went whatever I might know or pretend to know about them. But my first idea had no reference to clergymen in general. I had been struck by two opposite evils,—or what seemed to me to be evils,—and with an absence of all art-judgment in such matters, I thought that I might be able to expose them, or rather to describe them, both in one and the same tale. The first evil was the possession by the Church of certain funds and endowments which had been intended for charitable purposes, but which had been allowed to become incomes for idle Church dignitaries. There had been more than one such case brought to public notice at the time, in which there seemed to have been an egregious malversation of charitable purposes. The second evil was its very opposite. Though I had been much struck by the injustice above described, I had also often been angered by the undeserved severity of the newspapers towards the recipients of such incomes, who could hardly be considered to be the chief sinners in the matter. When a man is appointed to a place, it is natural that he should accept the income allotted to that place without much inquiry. It is seldom that he will be the first to find out that his services are overpaid. Though he be called upon only to look beautiful and to be dignified upon State occasions, he will think £2000 a year little enough for such beauty and dignity as he brings to the task. I felt that there had been some tearing to pieces which might have been spared. But I was altogether wrong in supposing that the two things could be combined. Any writer in advocating a cause must do so after the fashion of an advocate,—or his writing will be ineffective. He should take up one side and cling to that, and then he may be powerful. There should be no scruples of conscience. Such scruples make a man impotent for such work. It was open to me to have described a bloated parson, with a red nose and all other iniquities, openly neglecting every duty required from him, and living riotously on funds purloined from the poor,—defying as he did do so the moderate remonstrances of a virtuous press. Or I might have painted a man as good, as sweet, and as mild as my warden, who should also have been a hard-working, ill-paid minister of

God's word, and might have subjected him to the rancorous venom of some daily *Jupiter*,* who, without a leg to stand on, without any true case, might have been induced, by personal spite, to tear to rags the poor clergyman with poisonous, anonymous, and ferocious leading articles. But neither of these programmes recommended itself to my honesty. Satire, though it may exaggerate the vice it lashes, is not justified in creating it in order that it may be lashed. Caricature may too easily become a slander, and satire a libel. I believed in the existence neither of the red-nosed clerical cormorant, nor in that of the venomous assassin of the journals. I did believe that through want of care and the natural tendency of every class to take care of itself, money had slipped into the pockets of certain clergymen which should have gone elsewhere; and I believed also that through the equally natural propensity of men to be as strong as they know how to be, certain writers of the press had allowed themselves to use language which was cruel, though it was in a good cause. But the two objects should not have been combined—and I now know myself well enough to be aware that I was not the man to have carried out either of them.

Nevertheless I thought much about it, and on the 29th of July 1853,—having been then two years without having made any literary effort,—I began *The Warden*, at Tenbury in Worcestershire.* It was then more than twelve months since I had stood for an hour on the little bridge in Salisbury, and had made out to my own satisfaction the spot on which Hiram's hospital should stand. Certainly no work that I ever did took up so much of my thoughts. On this occasion I did no more than write the first chapter, even if so much. I had determined that my official work should be moderated, so as to allow me some time for writing; but then, just at this time,* I was sent to take the postal charge of the northern counties in Ireland,—of Ulster, and the counties Meath and Louth. Hitherto in official language I had been a surveyor's clerk,— now I was to be a surveyor. The difference consisted mainly in an increase of income from about £450 to about £800;—for at that time the sum netted still depended on the number of miles travelled. Of course that English work to which I had become so warmly wedded had to be abandoned. Other parts of England were being done by other men, and I had nearly finished the area which had been entrusted to me. I should have liked to ride over the whole country, and to have sent a rural post letter-carrier to every parish, every village, every hamlet, and every grange in England.

We were at this time very much unsettled as regards any residence. While we were living at Clonmel two sons* had been born, who certainly were important enough to have been mentioned sooner. At Clonmel we had lived in lodgings, and from there had moved to Mallow,* a town in the county Cork, where we had taken a house. Mallow was in the centre of a hunting country, and had been very pleasant to me. But our house there had been given up when it was known that I should be detained in England; and then we had wandered about in the western counties, moving our headquarters from one town to another. During this time we had lived at Exeter, at Bristol, at Caermarthen, at Cheltenham, and at Worcester. Now we again moved, and settled ourselves for eighteen months at Belfast. After that we took a house at Donnybrook,* the well-known suburb of Dublin.

The work of taking up a new district, which requires not only that the man doing it should know the nature of the postal arrangements, but also the characters and the peculiarities of the postmasters and their clerks, was too heavy to allow of my going on with my book at once. It was not till the end of 1853 that I recommenced it, and it was in the autumn of 1854* that I finished the work. It was only one small volume, and in later days would have been completed in six weeks,—or in two months at the longest, if other work had pressed. On looking at the title-page, I find it was not published till 1855. I had made acquaintance, through my friend John Merivale, with William Longman* the publisher, and had received from him an assurance that the manuscript should be 'looked at.' It was 'looked at,' and Messrs Longman made me an offer to publish it at half profits. I had no reason to love 'half profits,' but I was very anxious to have my book published, and I acceded. It was now more than ten years since I had commenced writing *The Macdermots*, and I thought that if any success was to be achieved, the time surely had come. I had not been impatient; but, if there was to be a time, surely it had come.

The novel-reading world did not go mad about *The Warden*; but I soon felt that it had not failed as the others had failed. There were notices* of it in the press, and I could discover that people around me knew that I had written a book. Mr Longman was complimentary, and after a while informed me that there would be profits to divide. At the end of 1855 I received a cheque for £9, 8s. 8d., which was the first money I had ever earned by literary work;—that £20 which poor Mr Colburn had been made to pay certainly never having been earned at all. At the end of 1856 I received another sum of £10, 15s. 1d. The pecuniary success was not great. Indeed, as regarded remuneration for the time, stone-breaking* would have done better. A thousand copies were printed, of which, after a lapse of five or six years, about 300 had to be converted into another form, and sold as belonging to a cheap edition. In its original form *The Warden* never reached the essential honour of a second edition.

I have already said of the work that it failed altogether in the purport for which it was intended. But it has a merit of its own,—a merit by my own perception of which I was enabled to see wherein lay whatever strength I did possess. The characters of the bishop, of the archdeacon, of the archdeacon's wife, and especially of the warden, are all well and clearly drawn. I had realised to myself a series of portraits, and had been able so to put them on the canvas that my readers should see that which I meant them to see. There is no gift which an author can have more useful to him than this. And the style of the English was good, though from most unpardonable carelessness the grammar was not unfrequently faulty. With such results I had no doubt but that I would at once begin another novel.

I will here say one word as a long-deferred answer to an item of criticism which appeared in the *Times* newspaper as to *The Warden*. In an article*—if I remember rightly, on *The Warden* and *Barchester Towers* combined—which I would call good-natured, but that I take it for granted that the critics of the *Times* are actuated by higher motives than good-nature, that little book and its sequel are spoken of in terms which were very pleasant to the author. But there was added to this a gentle word of rebuke at the morbid condition of the author's mind which had prompted him to indulge in personalities,—the personalities in question having reference to some editor or manager of the *Times* newspaper. For I had introduced one Tom Towers as being potent among the contributors to the *Jupiter*, under which name I certainly did allude to the *Times*. But at that time, living away in Ireland, I had not even heard the name of any gentleman connected with the *Times* newspaper, and could not have intended to represent any individual by Tom Towers. As I had created an archdeacon, so had I created a journalist, and the one creation was no more personal or indicative of morbid tendencies than the other. If Tom Towers was at all like any gentleman then connected with the *Times*, my moral consciousness must again have been very powerful.

CHAPTER 6

'Barchester Towers' and the 'Three Clerks'
1855–1858

IT was, I think, before I started on my English tours among the
rural posts that I made my first attempt at writing for a magazine.
I had read, soon after they came out, the two first volumes of Charles
Merivale's *History of the Romans under the Empire*, and had got into
some correspondence with the author's brother as to the author's
views about Cæsar. Hence arose in my mind a tendency to investi-
gate the character of probably the greatest man who ever lived, which
tendency in after years produced a little book* of which I shall have
to speak when its time comes,—and also a taste generally for Latin literature, which has been one of the chief delights of my later life. And
I may say that I became at this time as anxious about Cæsar, and as
desirous of reaching the truth as to his character, as we have all been in
regard to Bismarck* in these latter days. I lived in Cæsar, and debated
with myself constantly whether he crossed the Rubicon as a tyrant or
as a patriot. In order that I might review Mr Merivale's book without
feeling that I was dealing unwarrantably with a subject beyond me,
I studied the Commentaries thoroughly, and went through a mass
of other reading which the object of a magazine article hardly justified,—but which has thoroughly justified itself in the subsequent
pursuits of my life. I did write two articles, the first mainly on Julius
Cæsar, and the second on Augustus, which appeared in the *Dublin
University Magazine.* They were the result of very much labour, but
there came from them no pecuniary product. I had been very modest
when I sent them to the editor, as I had been when I called on John
Forster, not venturing to suggest the subject of money. After a while
I did call upon the proprietor of the magazine in Dublin, and was told
by him that such articles were generally written to oblige friends, and
that articles written to oblige friends were not usually paid for. The
Dean of Ely, as the author of the work in question now is, was my
friend; but I think I was wronged, as I certainly had no intention of
obliging him by my criticism. Afterwards, when I returned to Ireland,

I wrote other articles* for the same magazine, one of which, intended to be very savage in its denunciation, was on an official blue-book just then brought out, preparatory to the introduction of competitive examinations for the Civil Service. For that and some other article, I now forget what, I was paid. Up to the end of 1857 I had received £55 for the hard work of ten years.

It was while I was engaged on *Barchester Towers* that I adopted a system of writing which, for some years afterwards, I found to be very serviceable to me. My time was greatly occupied in travelling, and the nature of my travelling was now changed. I could not any longer do it on horseback. Railroads afforded me my means of conveyance, and I found that I passed in railway-carriages very many hours of my existence. Like others, I used to read,—though Carlyle* has since told me that a man when travelling should not read, but 'sit still and label his thoughts.' But if I intended to make a profitable business out of my writing, and, at the same time, to do my best for the Post Office, I must turn these hours to more account than I could do even by reading. I made for myself therefore a little tablet, and found after a few days' exercise that I could write as quickly in a railway-carriage as I could at my desk. I worked with a pencil, and what I wrote my wife copied afterwards. In this way was composed the greater part of *Barchester Towers* and of the novel which succeeded it, and much also of others subsequent to them. My only objection to the practice came from the appearance of literary ostentation, to which I felt myself to be subject when going to work before four or five fellow-passengers. But I got used to it, as I had done to the amazement of the west country farmers' wives when asking them after their letters.

In the writing of *Barchester Towers* I took great delight. The bishop and Mrs Proudie were very real to me, as were also the troubles of the archdeacon and the loves of Mr Slope. When it was done, Mr W. Longman required that it should be subjected to his reader; and he returned the MS. to me, with a most laborious and voluminous criticism,*—coming from whom I never knew. This was accompanied by an offer to print the novel on the half-profit system, with a payment of £100 in advance out of my half-profits,—on condition that I would comply with the suggestions made by his critic. One of these suggestions required that I should cut the novel down to two volumes. In my reply, I went through the criticisms, rejecting one and accepting another, almost alternately, but declaring at last that no

consideration should induce me to put out a third of my work. I am
at a loss to know how such a task could be performed. I could burn
the MS., no doubt, and write another book on the same story; but
how two words out of six are to be withdrawn from a written novel,
I cannot conceive. I believe such tasks have been attempted—perhaps
performed; but I refused to make even the attempt. Mr Longman
was too gracious to insist on his critic's terms; and the book was published, certainly none the worse, and I do not think much the better,
for the care that had been taken with it.

The work succeeded just as *The Warden* had succeeded. It achieved
no great reputation, but it was one of the novels which novel readers
were called upon to read. Perhaps I may be assuming upon myself
more than I have a right to do in saying now that *Barchester Towers*
has become one of those novels which do not die quite at once, which
live and are read for perhaps a quarter of a century; but if that be
so, its life has been so far prolonged by the vitality of some of its
younger brothers. *Barchester Towers* would hardly be so well known
as it is had there been no *Framley Parsonage* and no *Last Chronicle
of Barset*.

I received my £100, in advance, with profound delight. It was
a positive and most welcome increase to my income, and might probably be regarded as a first real step on the road to substantial success.
I am well aware that there are many who think that an author in his
authorship should not regard money,—nor a painter, or sculptor, or
composer in his art. I do not know that this unnatural self-sacrifice is
supposed to extend itself further. A barrister, a clergyman, a doctor,
an engineer, and even actors and architects, may without disgrace
follow the bent of human nature, and endeavour to fill their bellies
and clothe their backs, and also those of their wives and children,
as comfortably as they can by the exercise of their abilities and their
crafts. They may be as rationally realistic, as may the butchers and
the bakers; but the artist and the author forget the high glories of
their calling if they condescend to make a money return a first object.
They who preach this doctrine will be much offended by my theory,
and by this book of mine, if my theory and my book come beneath
their notice. They require the practice of a so-called virtue which
is contrary to nature, and which, in my eyes, would be no virtue
if it were practised. They are like clergymen who preach sermons
against the love of money, but who know that the love of money is so

distinctive a characteristic of humanity that such sermons are mere platitudes called for by customary but unintelligent piety. All material progress has come from man's desire to do the best he can for himself and those about him, and civilisation and Christianity itself have been made possible by such progress. Though we do not all of us argue this matter out within our breasts, we do all feel it; and we know that the more a man earns the more useful he is to his fellow-men. The most useful lawyers, as a rule, have been those who have made the greatest incomes,—and it is the same with the doctors. It would be the same in the Church if they who have the choosing of bishops always chose the best man. And it has in truth been so too in art and authorship. Did Titian or Rubens disregard their pecuniary rewards? As far as we know, Shakespeare worked always for money, giving the best of his intellect to support his trade as an actor. In our own century what literary names stand higher than those of Byron, Tennyson, Scott, Dickens, Macaulay, and Carlyle? And I think I may say that none of those great men neglected the pecuniary result of their labours. Now and then a man may arise among us who in any calling, whether it be in law, in physic, in religious teaching, in art, or literature, may in his professional enthusiasm utterly disregard money. All will honour his enthusiasm, and if he be wifeless and childless, his disregard of the great object of men's work will be blameless. But it is a mistake to suppose that a man is a better man because he despises money. Few do so, and those few in doing so suffer a defeat. Who does not desire to be hospitable to his friends, generous to the poor, liberal to all, munificent to his children, and to be himself free from the carking fear which poverty creates? The subject will not stand an argument;—and yet authors are told that they should disregard payment for their work, and be content to devote their unbought brains to the welfare of the public. Brains that are unbought will never serve the public much. Take away from English authors their copyrights, and you would very soon take away from England her authors.

I say this here, because it is my purpose as I go on to state what to me has been the result of my profession in the ordinary way in which professions are regarded, so that by my example may be seen what prospect there is that a man devoting himself to literature with industry, perseverance, certain necessary aptitudes, and fair average talents, may succeed in gaining a livelihood, as another man does in another profession. The result with me has been comfortable but not splendid, as I think was to have been expected from the combination of such gifts.

I have certainly always had also before my eyes the charms of reputation. Over and above the money view of the question, I wished from the beginning to be something more than a clerk in the Post Office. To be known as somebody,—to be Anthony Trollope if it be no more,—is to me much. The feeling is a very general one, and I think beneficent. It is that which has been called the 'last infirmity of noble mind.'* The infirmity is so human that the man who lacks it is either above or below humanity. I own to the infirmity. But I confess that my first object in taking to literature as a profession was that which is common to the barrister when he goes to the Bar, and to the baker when he sets up his oven. I wished to make an income on which I and those belonging to me might live in comfort.

If indeed a man writes his books badly, or paints his pictures badly, because he can make his money faster in that fashion than by doing them well, and at the same time proclaims them to be the best he can do,—if in fact he sells shoddy for broadcloth,—he is dishonest, as is any other fraudulent dealer. So may be the barrister who takes money that he does not earn, or the clergyman who is content to live on a sinecure. No doubt the artist or the author may have a difficulty which will not occur to the seller of cloth, in settling within himself what is good work and what is bad,—when labour enough has been given, and when the task has been scamped. It is a danger as to which he is bound to be severe with himself—in which he should feel that his conscience should be set fairly in the balance against the natural bias of his interest. If he do not do so, sooner or later his dishonesty will be discovered, and will be estimated accordingly. But in this he is to be governed only by the plain rules of honesty which should govern us all. Having said so much, I shall not scruple as I go on to attribute to the pecuniary result of my labours all the importance which I felt them to have at the time.

Barchester Towers, for which I had received £100 in advance, sold well enough to bring me further payments—moderate payments— from the publishers. From that day up to this very time in which I am writing, that book and *The Warden* together have given me almost every year some small income. I get the accounts very regularly, and I find that I have received £727, 11s. 3d. for the two. It is more than

I got for the three or four works that came afterwards, but the payments have been spread over twenty years.

When I went to Mr Longman with my next novel, *The Three Clerks*, in my hand, I could not induce him to understand that a lump sum down was more pleasant than a deferred annuity. I wished him to buy it from me at a price which he might think to be a fair value, and I argued with him that as soon as an author has put himself into a position which insures a sufficient sale of his works to give a profit, the publisher is not entitled to expect the half of such proceeds. While there is a pecuniary risk, the whole of which must be borne by the publisher, such division is fair enough; but such a demand on the part of the publisher is monstrous as soon as the article produced is known to be a marketable commodity. I thought that I had now reached that point, but Mr Longman did not agree with me. And he endeavoured to convince me that I might lose more than I gained, even though I should get more money by going elsewhere. 'It is for you,' said he, 'to think whether our names on your title-page are not worth more to you than the increased payment.' This seemed to me to savour of that high-flown doctrine of the contempt of money which I have never admired. I did think much of Messrs Longman's name, but I liked it best at the bottom of a cheque.

I was also scared from the august columns of Paternoster Row* by a remark made to myself by one of the firm, which seemed to imply that they did not much care for works of fiction. Speaking of a fertile writer of tales who was not then dead, he declared that —— (naming the author in question) had spawned upon them (the publishers) three novels a year! Such language is perhaps justifiable in regard to a man who shows so much of the fecundity of the herring; but I did not know how fruitful might be my own muse, and I thought that I had better go elsewhere.

I had then written *The Three Clerks*, which, when I could not sell it to Messrs Longman, I took in the first instance to Messrs Hurst & Blackett,* who had become successors to Mr Colburn. I had made an appointment with one of the firm, which, however, that gentleman was unable to keep. I was on my way from Ireland to Italy, and had but one day in London in which to dispose of my manuscript. I sat for an hour in Great Marlborough Street, expecting the return of the peccant publisher who had broken his tryst, and I was about to depart with my bundle under my arm when the foreman of the house came to me. He seemed to think it a pity that I should go, and wished me to leave my work with him. This, however, I would not do, unless he would undertake to buy it then and there. Perhaps he lacked authority. Perhaps his judgment was against such purchase. But while we debated the matter, he gave me some advice. 'I hope it's not historical, Mr Trollope?' he said. 'Whatever you do, don't be historical; your historical novel is not worth a damn.' Thence I took *The Three Clerks* to Mr Bentley;* and on the same afternoon succeeded in selling it to him for £250. His son still possesses it, and the firm has, I believe, done very well with the purchase. It was certainly the best novel I had as yet written. The plot is not so good as that of the *Macdermots*; nor are there any characters in the book equal to those of Mrs Proudie and the Warden; but the work has a more continued interest, and contains the first well-described love-scene that I ever wrote. The passage in which Kate Woodward, thinking that she will die, tries to take leave of the lad she loves, still brings tears to my eyes when I read it. I had not the heart to kill her. I never could do that. And I do not doubt but that they are living happily together to this day.

The lawyer Chaffanbrass* made his first appearance in this novel, and I do not think that I have cause to be ashamed of him. But this novel now is chiefly noticeable to me from the fact that in it I introduced a character under the name of Sir Gregory Hardlines, by which I intended to lean very heavily on that much loathed scheme of competitive examination, of which at that time Sir Charles Trevelyan was the great apostle. Sir Gregory Hardlines was intended for Sir Charles Trevelyan,—as any one at the time would know who had taken an interest in the Civil Service. 'We always call him Sir Gregory,' Lady Trevelyan said to me afterwards, when I came to know her and her husband. I never learned to love competitive examination; but I became, and am, very fond of Sir Charles Trevelyan. Sir Stafford Northcote,* who is now Chancellor of the Exchequer, was then leagued with his friend Sir Charles, and he too appears in *The Three Clerks* under the feebly facetious name of Sir Warwick West End.

But for all that *The Three Clerks* was a good novel.

When that sale was made I was on my way to Italy with my wife, paying a third visit there to my mother and brother. This was in 1857, and she had then given up her pen. It was the first year in which she had not written, and she expressed to me her delight that her labours should be at an end, and that mine should be beginning in the same field. In truth they had already been continued for a dozen years, but a man's career will generally be held to date itself from the commencement of his success. On those foreign tours I always encountered adventures, which, as I look back upon them now, tempt me almost to write a little book of my long past Continental travels. On this occasion, as we made our way slowly through Switzerland and over the Alps, we encountered again and again a poor forlorn Englishman, who had no friend and no aptitude for travelling. He was always losing his way, and finding himself with no seat in the coaches and no bed at the inns. On one occasion I found him at Coire seated at 5 a.m. in the *coupé* of a diligence which was intended to start at noon for the Engadine, while it was his purpose to go over the Alps in another which was to leave at 5.30, and which was already crowded with passengers. 'Ah!' he said, 'I am in time now, and nobody shall turn me out of this seat,' alluding to former little misfortunes of which I had been a witness. When I explained to him his position, he was as one to whom life was too bitter to be borne. But he made his way into Italy, and encountered me again at the Pitti Palace in Florence. 'Can you tell me something?' he said to me in a whisper, having touched my shoulder. 'The people are so ill-natured I don't like to ask them. Where is it they keep the Medical Venus?'* I sent him to the Uffizzi, but I fear he was disappointed.

We ourselves, however, on entering Milan had been in quite as much distress as any that he suffered. We had not written for beds, and on driving up to a hotel at ten in the evening found it full. Thence we went from one hotel to another, finding them all full. The misery is one well known to travellers, but I never heard of another case in which a man and his wife were told at midnight to get out of the conveyance into the middle of the street because the horse could not be made to go any further. Such was our condition. I induced the driver, however, to go again to the hotel which was nearest to him, and which was kept by a German. Then I bribed the porter to get the master to come down to me; and, though my French is ordinarily very defective, I spoke with such eloquence to that German innkeeper that he, throwing his arms round my neck in a transport of compassion, swore that he would never leave me nor my wife till he had put us to bed. And he did so; but, ah! there were so many in those beds! It is such an experience as this which teaches a travelling foreigner how different on the Continent is the accommodation provided for him, from that which is supplied for the inhabitants of the country.

It was on a previous visit to Milan, when the telegraph-wires were only just opened to the public by the Austrian authorities,* that we had decided one day at dinner that we would go to Verona that night. There was a train at six, reaching Verona at midnight, and we asked some servant of the hotel to telegraph for us, ordering supper and beds. The demand seemed to create some surprise; but we persisted, and were only mildly grieved when we found ourselves charged twenty zwanzigers* for the message. Telegraphy was new at Milan, and the prices were intended to be almost prohibitory. We paid our twenty zwanzigers and went on, consoling ourselves with the thought of our ready supper and our assured beds. When we reached Verona, there arose a great cry along the platform for Signor Trollopè. I put out my head and declared my identity, when I was waited upon by a glorious personage dressed like a beau for a ball, with half-a-dozen others almost as glorious behind him, who informed me, with his hat in his hand, that he was the landlord of the 'Due Torre.' It was a heating moment, but it became more hot when he asked me after my people,—'mes gens.' I could only turn round, and point to my wife and brother-in-law. I had no other 'people.' There were three carriages provided for us, each with a pair of grey horses. When we reached the house it was all lit up. We were not allowed to move without an attendant with a lighted candle. It was only gradually that the mistake came to be understood. On us there was still the horror of the bill, the extent of which could not be known till the hour of departure had come. The landlord, however, had acknowledged to himself that his inductions had been ill-founded, and he treated us with clemency. He had never before received a telegram.

I apologise for these tales, which are certainly outside my purpose, and will endeavour to tell no more that shall not have a closer relation to my story. I had finished *The Three Clerks* just before I left England, and when in Florence was cudgelling my brain for a new plot. Being then with my brother, I asked him to sketch me a plot, and he drew out that of my next novel, called *Doctor Thorne*. I mention this particularly, because it was the only occasion in which I have had recourse to some other source than my own brains for the thread of a story. How far I may unconsciously have adopted incidents from what I have read,— either from history or from works of imagination,—I do not know. It is beyond question that a man employed as I have been must do so. But when doing it I have not been aware that I have done it. I have never taken another man's work, and deliberately framed my work upon it. I am far from censuring this practice in others. Our greatest masters in works of imagination have obtained such aid for themselves. Shakespeare dug out of such quarries wherever he could find them. Ben Jonson, with heavier hand, built up his structures on his studies of the classics, not thinking it beneath him to give, without direct acknowledgment, whole pieces translated both from poets and historians. But in those days no such acknowledgment was usual. Plagiary existed, and was very common, but was not known as a sin. It is different now; and I think that an author, when he uses either the words or the plot of another, should own as much, demanding to be credited with no more of the work than he has himself produced. I may say also that I have never printed as my own a word that has been written by others.[1] It might probably have been better for my readers had I done so, as I am informed that *Doctor Thorne*, the novel of which I am now speaking, has a larger sale than any other book of mine.

Early in 1858, while I was writing *Doctor Thorne*, I was asked by the great men at the General Post Office to go to Egypt to make a treaty with the Pasha* for the conveyance of our mails through that country by railway. There was a treaty in existence, but that had reference to the carriage of bags and boxes by camels from Alexandria to Suez. Since its date the railway had grown, and was now nearly completed, and a new treaty was wanted. So I came over from Dublin to London, on my road, and again went to work among the publishers. The other novel was not finished; but I thought I had now progressed far enough to arrange a sale while the work was still on the stocks. I went to Mr Bentley and demanded £400,—for the copyright. He acceded, but came to me the next morning* at the General Post Office to say that it could not be. He had gone to work at his figures after I had left him, and had found that £300 would be the outside value of the novel. I was intent upon the larger sum; and in furious haste,—for I had but an hour at my disposal,—I rushed to Chapman & Hall* in Piccadilly, and said what I had to say to Mr Edward Chapman in a quick torrent of words. They were the first of a great many words which have since

---

[1] I must make one exception to this declaration. The legal opinion as to heirlooms in *The Eustace Diamonds* was written for me by Charles Merewether,* the present Member for Northampton. I am told that it has become the ruling authority on the subject.

been spoken by me in that back-shop. Looking at me as he might have done at a highway robber who had stopped him on Hounslow Heath,* he said that he supposed he might as well do as I desired. I considered this to be a sale, and it was a sale. I remember that he held the poker in his hand all the time that I was with him;—but in truth, even though he had declined to buy the book, there would have been no danger.

CHAPTER 7

'Doctor Thorne'—'The Bertrams'—'The West Indies and the Spanish Main'

As I journeyed across France to Marseilles, and made thence a terribly rough voyage to Alexandria, I wrote my allotted number of pages every day. On this occasion more than once I left my paper on the cabin table, rushing away to be sick in the privacy of my state room. It was February, and the weather was miserable; but still I did my work. *Labor omnia vincit improbus.** I do not say that to all men has been given physical strength sufficient for such exertion as this, but I do believe that real exertion will enable most men to work at almost any season. I had previously to this arranged a system of taskwork for myself, which I would strongly recommend to those who feel as I have felt, that labour, when not made absolutely obligatory by the circumstances of the hour, should never be allowed to become spasmodic. There was no day on which it was my positive duty to write for the publishers, as it was my duty to write reports for the Post Office. I was free to be idle if I pleased. But as I had made up my mind to undertake this second profession, I found it to be expedient to bind myself by certain self-imposed laws. When I have commenced a new book, I have always prepared a diary,* divided into weeks, and carried it on for the period which I have allowed myself for the completion of the work. In this I have entered, day by day, the number of pages I have written, so that if at any time I have slipped into idleness for a day or two, the record of that idleness has been there, staring me in the face, and demanding of me increased labour, so that the deficiency might be supplied. According to the circumstances of the time,—whether my other business might be then heavy or light, or whether the book which I was writing was or was not wanted with speed,—I have allotted myself so many pages a week. The average number has been about 40. It has been placed as low as 20, and has risen to 112. And as a page is an ambiguous term, my page has been made to contain 250 words; and as words, if not watched, will have a tendency to straggle, I have had every word counted as I went. In the bargains I have made with publishers I have,—not, of course, with their knowledge, but in my own mind,—undertaken always to supply them with so many words, and I have never put a book out of hand short of the number by a single word. I may also say that the excess has been very small. I have prided myself on completing my work exactly within the proposed dimensions. But I have prided myself especially in completing it within the proposed time,—and I have always done so. There has ever been the record before me, and a week passed with an insufficient number of pages has been a blister to my eye, and a month so disgraced would have been a sorrow to my heart.

I have been told that such appliances are beneath the notice of a man of genius. I have never fancied myself to be a man of genius, but had I been so I think I might well have subjected myself to these trammels. Nothing surely is so potent as a law that may not be disobeyed. It has the force of the water-drop that hollows the stone. A small daily task, if it be really daily, will beat the labours of a spasmodic Hercules. It is the tortoise* which always catches the hare. The hare has no chance. He loses more time in glorifying himself for a quick spurt than suffices for the tortoise to make half his journey.

I have known authors whose lives have always been troublesome and painful because their tasks have never been done in time. They have ever been as boys struggling to learn their lesson as they entered the school gates. Publishers have distrusted them, and they have failed to write their best because they have seldom written at ease. I have done double their work,—though burdened with another profession,—and have done it almost without an effort. I have not once, through all my literary career, felt myself even in danger of being late with my task. I have known no anxiety as to 'copy.' The needed pages far ahead—very far ahead—have almost always been in the drawer beside me. And that little diary, with its dates and ruled spaces, its record that must be seen, its daily, weekly demand upon my industry, has done all that for me.

There are those who would be ashamed to subject themselves to such a taskmaster, and who think that the man who works with his imagination should allow himself to wait till—inspiration moves him. When I have heard such doctrine preached, I have hardly been able to repress my scorn. To me it would not be more absurd if the shoemaker were to wait for inspiration, or the tallow-chandler for the divine moment of melting. If the man whose business it is to write has eaten too many good things, or has drunk too much, or smoked too many cigars,—as men who write sometimes will do,—then his condition may be unfavourable for work; but so will be the condition of a shoemaker who has been similarly imprudent. I have sometimes thought that the inspiration wanted has been the remedy which time will give to the evil results of such imprudence.—*Mens sana in corpore sano.** The author wants that as does every other workman,—that and a habit of industry. I was once told that the surest aid to the writing of a book was a piece of cobbler's wax* on my chair. I certainly believe in the cobbler's wax much more than the inspiration.

It will be said, perhaps, that a man whose work has risen to no higher pitch than mine has attained, has no right to speak of the strains and impulses to which real genius is exposed. I am ready to admit the great variations in brain power which are exhibited by the products of different men, and am not disposed to rank my own very high; but my own experience tells me that a man can always do the work for which his brain is fitted if he will give himself the habit of regarding his work as a normal condition of his life. I therefore venture to advise young men who look forward to authorship as the business of their lives, even when they propose that that authorship be of the highest class known, to avoid enthusiastic rushes with their pens, and to seat themselves at their desks day by day as though they were lawyers' clerks;—and so let them sit until the allotted task shall be accomplished.

While I was in Egypt, I finished *Doctor Thorne*, and on the following day began *The Bertrams*. I was moved now by a determination to excel, if not in quality, at any rate in quantity. An ignoble ambition for an author, my readers will no doubt say. But not, I think, altogether ignoble, if an author can bring himself to look at his work as does any other workman. This had become my task, this was the furrow in which my plough was set, this was the thing the doing of which had fallen into my hands, and I was minded to work at it with a will. It is not on my conscience that I have ever scamped my work. My novels, whether good or bad, have been as good as I could make them. Had I taken three months of idleness between each they would have been no better. Feeling convinced of that, I finished *Doctor Thorne* on one day, and began *The Bertrams* on the next.

I had then been nearly two months in Egypt, and had at last succeeded in settling the terms of a postal treaty. Nearly twenty years have passed since that time, and other years may yet run on before these pages are printed. I trust I may commit no official sin by describing here the nature of the difficulty which met me. I found, on my arrival, that I was to communicate with an officer of the Pasha, who was then called Nubar Bey.* I presume him to have been the gentleman who has lately dealt with our Government as to the Suez Canal shares, and who is now well known to the political world as Nubar Pasha. I found him a most courteous gentleman, an Armenian. I never went to his office, nor do I know that he had an office. Every other day he would come to me at my hotel, and bring with him servants, and pipes, and coffee. I enjoyed his coming greatly; but there was one point on which we could not agree. As to money and other details, it seemed as though he could hardly accede fast enough to the wishes of the Postmaster-General; but on one point he was firmly opposed to me. I was desirous that the mails should be carried through Egypt in twenty-four hours, and he thought that forty eight hours should be allowed. I was obstinate, and he was obstinate; and for a long time we could come to no agreement. At last his oriental tranquillity seemed to desert him, and he took upon himself to assure me, with almost more than British energy, that, if I insisted on the quick transit, a terrible responsibility would rest on my head. I made this mistake, he said,— that I supposed that a rate of travelling which would be easy and secure in England could be attained with safety in Egypt. 'The Pasha, his master, would,' he said, 'no doubt accede to any terms demanded by the British Post Office, so great was his reverence for everything British. In that case he, Nubar, would at once resign his position, and retire into obscurity. He would be ruined; but the loss of life and bloodshed which would certainly follow so rash an attempt should not be on his head.' I smoked my pipe, or rather his, and drank his coffee, with oriental quiescence but British firmness. Every now and again, through three or four visits, I renewed the expression of my opinion that the transit could easily be made in twenty-four hours. At last he gave way,—and astonished me by the cordiality of his greeting. There was no longer any question of bloodshed or of resignation of office, and he assured me, with energetic complaisance, that it should be his care to see that the time was punctually kept. It was punctually kept, and, I believe, is so still. I must confess, however, that my persistency was not the result of any courage specially personal to myself. While the matter was being debated, it had been whispered to me that the Peninsular and Oriental Steamship Company had conceived that forty-eight hours would suit the purposes of their traffic better than twenty-four, and that, as they were the great paymasters on the railway, the Minister of the Egyptian State, who managed the railway, might probably wish to accommodate them. I often wondered who originated that frightful picture of blood and desolation. That it came from an English heart and an English hand I was always sure.

From Egypt I visited the Holy Land, and on my way inspected the Post Offices at Malta and Gibraltar. I could fill a volume with true tales of my adventures. The *Tales of All Countries* have, most of them, some foundation in such occurrences. There is one called 'John Bull on the Guadalquivir',* the chief incident in which occurred to me and a friend of mine on our way up that river to Seville. We both of us handled the gold ornaments of a man whom we believed to be a bull-fighter, but who turned out to be a duke,—and a duke, too, who could speak English! How gracious he was to us, and yet how thoroughly he covered us with ridicule!

On my return home I received £400 from Messrs Chapman & Hall for *Doctor Thorne*, and agreed to sell them *The Bertrams* for the same sum. This latter novel was written under very vagrant circumstances,—at Alexandria, Malta, Gibraltar, Glasgow, then at sea, and at last finished in Jamaica. Of my journey to the West Indies I will say a few words presently, but I may as well speak of these two novels here. *Doctor Thorne* has, I believe, been the most popular book that I have written,—if I may take the sale as a proof of comparative popularity. *The Bertrams* has had quite an opposite fortune.* I do not know that I have ever heard it well spoken of even by my friends, and I cannot remember that there is any character in it that has dwelt in the minds of novel-readers. I myself think that they are of about equal merit, but that neither of them is good. They fall away very much from *The Three Clerks*, both in pathos and humour. There is no personage in either of them comparable to Chaffanbrass the lawyer. The plot of *Doctor Thorne* is good, and I am led therefore to suppose that a good plot,—which, to my own feeling, is the most insignificant part of a tale,—is that which will most raise it or most condemn it in the public judgment. The plots of *Tom Jones* and of *Ivanhoe* are almost perfect, and they are probably the most popular novels of the schools of the last and of this century; but to me the delicacy of Amelia, and the rugged strength of Burley and Meg Merrilies,* say more for the

power of those great novelists than the gift of construction shown in
the two works I have named. A novel should give a picture of common life enlivened by humour and sweetened by pathos. To make
that picture worthy of attention, the canvas should be crowded with
real portraits, not of individuals known to the world or to the author,
but of created personages impregnated with traits of character which
are known. To my thinking, the plot is but the vehicle for all this; and
when you have the vehicle without the passengers, a story of mystery
in which the agents never spring to life, you have but a wooden show.
There must, however, be a story. You must provide a vehicle of some
sort. That of *The Bertrams* was more than ordinarily bad; and as the
book was relieved by no special character, it failed. Its failure never
surprised me; but I have been surprised by the success of *Doctor
Thorne.*

At this time there was nothing in the success of the one or the failure of the other to affect me very greatly. The immediate sale, and the
notices elicited from the critics, and the feeling which had now come
to me of a confident standing with the publishers, all made me know
that I had achieved my object. If I wrote a novel, I could certainly
sell it. And if I could publish three in two years,——confining myself
to half the fecundity of that terrible author of whom the publisher in
Paternoster Row had complained to me,——I might add £600 a-year
to my official income. I was still living in Ireland, and could keep
a good house over my head, insure my life, educate my two boys, and
hunt perhaps twice a-week, on £1400 a-year. If more should come, it
would be well;——but £600 a-year I was prepared to reckon as success.
It had been slow in coming, but was very pleasant when it came.

On my return from Egypt I was sent down to Scotland to revise
the Glasgow Post Office. I almost forget now what it was that I had
to do there, but I know that I walked all over the city with the letter-
carriers, going up to the top flats of the houses, as the men would have
declared me incompetent to judge the extent of their labours had
I not trudged every step with them. It was midsummer, and wearier
work I never performed. The men would grumble, and then I would
think how it would be with them if they had to go home afterwards
and write a love-scene. But the love-scenes written in Glasgow, all
belonging to *The Bertrams*, are not good.

Then in the autumn of that year, 1858, I was asked to go to the West
Indies, and cleanse the Augean stables* of our Post Office system

there. Up to that time, and at that time, our Colonial Post Offices generally were managed from home, and were subject to the British Postmaster-General. Gentlemen were sent out from England to be postmasters, surveyors, and what not; and as our West Indian islands have never been regarded as being of themselves happily situated for residence, the gentlemen so sent were sometimes more conspicuous for want of income than for official zeal and ability. Hence the stables had become Augean. I was also instructed to carry out in some of the islands a plan for giving up this postal authority to the island Governor, and in others to propose some such plan. I was then to go on to Cuba, to make a postal treaty with the Spanish authorities, and to Panama for the same purpose with the Government of New Grenada. All this work I performed to my satisfaction, and I hope to that of my masters in St Martin's le Grand.

But the trip is at the present moment of importance to my subject, as having enabled me to write that which, on the whole, I regard as the best book* that has come from my pen. It is short, and, I think I may venture to say, amusing, useful, and true. As soon as I had learned from the secretary at the General Post Office that this journey would be required, I proposed the book to Messrs Chapman & Hall, demanding £250 for a single volume. The contract was made without any difficulty, and when I returned home the work was complete in my desk. I began it on board the ship in which I left Kingston, Jamaica, for Cuba,—and from week to week I carried it on as I went. From Cuba I made my way to St Thomas, and through the island down to Demerara, then back to St Thomas,—which is the starting-point for all places in that part of the globe,—to Santa Martha, Carthagena, Aspinwall, over the Isthmus to Panama, up the Pacific to a little harbour on the coast of Costa Rica, thence across Central America, through Costa Rica, and down the Nicaragua river to the Mosquito coast, and after that home by Bermuda and New York. Should any one want further details of the voyage, are they not written in my book? The fact memorable to me now is that I never made a single note while writing or preparing it. Preparation, indeed, there was none. The descriptions and opinions came hot on to the paper from their causes. I will not say that this is the best way of writing a book intended to give accurate information. But it is the best way of producing to the eye of the reader, and to his ear, that which the eye of the writer has seen and his ear heard. There are two kinds of confidence which a reader may have in his author,—which two kinds the reader who wishes to use his reading well should carefully discriminate. There is a confidence in facts and a confidence in vision. The one man tells you accurately what has been. The other suggests to you what may, or perhaps what must have been, or what ought to have been. The former requires simple faith. The latter calls upon you to judge for yourself, and form your own conclusions. The former does not intend to be prescient, nor the latter accurate. Research is the weapon used by the former; observation by the latter. Either may be false,—wilfully false; as also may either be steadfastly true. As to that, the reader must judge for himself. But the man who writes *currente calamo*,* who works with a rapidity which will not admit of accuracy, may be as true, and in one sense as trustworthy, as he who bases every word upon a rock of facts. I have written very much as I have travelled about; and though I have been very inaccurate, I have always written the exact truth as I saw it;—and I have, I think, drawn my pictures correctly.

The view I took of the relative position in the West Indies of black men and white men was the view of the *Times* newspaper at that period; and there appeared three articles* in that journal, one closely after another, which made the fortune of the book. Had it been very bad, I suppose its fortune could not have been made for it even by the *Times* newspaper. I afterwards became acquainted with the writer of those articles, the contributor himself informing me that he had written them. I told him that he had done me a greater service than can often be done by one man to another, but that I was under no obligation to him. I do not think that he saw the matter quite in the same light.

I am aware that by that criticism I was much raised in my position as an author. Whether such lifting up by such means is good or bad for literature is a question which I hope to discuss in a future chapter. But the result was immediate to me, for I at once went to Chapman & Hall and successfully demanded £600 for my next novel.

CHAPTER 8

---∞∞∞---

The 'Cornhill Magazine' and 'Framley Parsonage'

SOON after my return from the West Indies I was enabled to change my district in Ireland for one in England. For some time past my official work had been of a special nature, taking me out of my own district; but through all that, Dublin had been my home, and there my wife and children had lived. I had often sighed to return to England,—with a silly longing. My life in England for twenty-six years from the time of my birth to the day on which I left it, had been wretched. I had been poor, friendless, and joyless. In Ireland it had constantly been happy. I had achieved the respect of all with whom I was concerned, I had made for myself a comfortable home, and I had enjoyed many pleasures. Hunting itself was a great delight to me; and now, as I contemplated a move to England, and a house in the neighbourhood of London, I felt that hunting must be abandoned.[1] Nevertheless I thought that a man who could write books ought not to live in Ireland,—ought to live within the reach of the publishers, the clubs, and the dinner-parties of the metropolis. So I made my request at headquarters, and with some little difficulty got myself appointed to the Eastern District of England,—which comprised Essex, Suffolk, Norfolk, Cambridgeshire, Huntingdonshire, and the greater part of Hertfordshire.

At this time I did not stand very well with the dominant interest at the General Post Office. My old friend Colonel Maberly had been, some time since, squeezed out,* and his place was filled by Mr Rowland Hill,* the originator of the penny post. With him I never had any sympathy, nor he with me. In figures and facts he was most accurate, but I never came across any one who so little understood the ways of men,—unless it was his brother Frederic. To the two brothers the servants of the Post Office,—men numerous enough to have formed a large army in old days,—were so many machines who

---

[1] It was not abandoned till sixteen more years had passed away.

could be counted on for their exact work without deviation, as wheels may be counted on, which are kept going always at the same pace and always by the same power. Rowland Hill was an industrious public servant, anxious for the good of his country; but he was a hard task-master, and one who would, I think, have put the great department with which he was concerned altogether out of gear by his hardness, had he not been at last controlled. He was the Chief Secretary, my brother-in-law—who afterwards succeeded him—came next to him, and Mr Hill's brother was the Junior Secretary. In the natural course of things, I had not, from my position, anything to do with the man-agement of affairs;—but from time to time I found myself more or less mixed up in it. I was known to be a thoroughly efficient public servant; I am sure I may say so much of myself without fear of con-tradiction from any one who has known the Post Office;—I was very fond of the department, and when matters came to be considered, I generally had an opinion of my own. I have no doubt that I often made myself very disagreeable. I know that I sometimes tried to do so. But I could hold my own because I knew my business and was useful. I had given official offence by the publication of *The Three Clerks*. I afterwards gave greater offence by a lecture on The Civil Service* which I delivered in one of the large rooms at the General Post Office to the clerks there. On this occasion, the Postmaster-General, with whom personally I enjoyed friendly terms, sent for me and told me that Mr Hill had told him that I ought to be dismissed. When I asked his lordship whether he was prepared to dismiss me, he only laughed. The threat was no threat to me, as I knew myself to be too good to be treated in that fashion. The lecture had been permitted, and I had disobeyed no order. In the lecture which I delivered, there was nothing to bring me to shame,—but it advocated the doctrine that a civil servant is only a servant as far as his contract goes, and that he is beyond that entitled to be as free a man in politics, as free in his general pursuits, and as free in opinion, as those who are in open professions and open trades. All this is very nearly admitted now, but it certainly was not admitted then. At that time no one in the Post Office could even vote* for a Member of Parliament.

Through my whole official life I did my best to improve the style of official writing. I have written, I should think, some thousands of reports,—many of them necessarily very long; some of them dealing with subjects so absurd as to allow a touch of burlesque; some few in which a spark of indignation or a slight glow of pathos might find an entrance. I have taken infinite pains with these reports, habituating myself always to write them in the form in which they should be sent,—without a copy. It is by writing thus that a man can throw on to his paper the exact feeling with which his mind is impressed at the moment. A rough copy, or that which is called a draft, is written in order that it may be touched and altered and put upon stilts. The waste of time, moreover, in such an operation, is terrible. If a man knows his craft with his pen, he will have learned to write without the necessity of changing his words or the form of his sentences. I had learned so to write my reports that they who read them should know what it was that I meant them to understand. But I do not think that they were regarded with favour. I have heard horror expressed because the old forms were disregarded and language used which had no savour of red-tape. During the whole of this work in the Post Office it was my principle always to obey authority in everything instantly, but never to allow my mouth to be closed as to the expression of my opinion. They who had the ordering of me very often did not know the work as I knew it,—could not tell as I could what would be the effect of this or that change. When carrying out instructions which I knew should not have been given, I never scrupled to point out the fatuity of the improper order in the strongest language that I could decently employ. I have revelled in these official correspondences, and look back to some of them as among the great* delights of my life. But I am not sure that they were so delightful to others.

I succeeded, however, in getting the English district,—which could hardly have been refused to me,—and prepared to change our residence towards the end of 1859. At the time I was writing *Castle Richmond*, the novel which I had sold to Messrs Chapman & Hall for £600. But there arose at this time a certain literary project which probably had a great effect upon my career. Whilst travelling on postal service abroad, or riding over the rural districts in England, or arranging the mails in Ireland,—and such for the last eighteen years had now been my life,—I had no opportunity of becoming acquainted with literary life in London. It was probably some feeling of this which had made me anxious to move my penates* back to England. But even in Ireland, where I was still living in October 1859, I had heard of the *Cornhill Magazine*,* which was to come out on the 1st of January 1860, under the editorship of Thackeray.*

I had at this time written from time to time certain short stories, which had been published in different periodicals, and which in due time were republished under the name of *Tales of All Countries*. On the 23d of October 1859 I wrote to Thackeray, whom I had, I think, never then seen, offering to send him for the magazine certain of these stories. In reply to this I received two letters,—one from Messrs Smith & Elder, the proprietors of the *Cornhill*, dated 26th of October, and the other from the editor, written two days later. That from Mr Thackeray was as follows:—

'36 ONSLOW SQUARE, S.W.,
'*October 28th.*

'MY DEAR MR TROLLOPE,—Smith & Elder have sent you their proposals; and the business part done, let me come to the pleasure, and say how very glad indeed I shall be to have you as a co-operator in our new magazine. And looking over the annexed programme, you will see whether you can't help us in many other ways besides tale-telling. Whatever a man knows about life and its doings, that let us hear about. You must have tossed a good deal about the world, and have countless sketches in your memory and your portfolio. Please to think if you can furbish up any of these besides a novel. When events occur, and you have a good lively tale, bear us in mind. One of our chief objects in this magazine is the getting out of novel spinning, and back into the world. Don't understand me to disparage our craft, especially *your* wares. I often say I am like the pastrycook, and don't care for tarts, but prefer bread and cheese; but the public love the tarts (luckily for us), and we must bake and sell them. There was quite an excitement in my family one evening when Paterfamilias* (who goes to sleep on a novel almost always when he tries it after dinner) came up-stairs into the drawing-room wide awake and calling for the second volume* of *The Three Clerks*. I hope the *Cornhill Magazine* will have as pleasant a story. And the Chapmans, if they are the honest men I take them to be, I've no doubt have told you with what sincere liking your works have been read by yours very faithfully,

'W. M. THACKERAY.'

This was very pleasant, and so was the letter from Smith & Elder offering me £1000 for the copyright of a three-volume novel, to come out in the new magazine,—on condition that the first portion of it should be in their hands by December 12th. There was much in all this that astonished me;—in the first place the price, which was more than double what I had yet received, and nearly double that which I was about to receive from Messrs Chapman & Hall. Then there was the suddenness of the call. It was already the end of October, and a portion of the work was required to be in the printer's hands within six weeks. *Castle Richmond* was indeed half written, but that was sold to Chapman. And it had already been a principle with me in my art, that no part of a novel should be published till the entire story was completed.* I knew, from what I read from month to month, that this hurried publication of incompleted work was frequently, I might perhaps say always, adopted by the leading novelists of the day. That such has been the case, is proved by the fact that Dickens, Thackeray, and Mrs Gaskell died with unfinished novels, of which portions had been already published. I had not yet entered upon the system of publishing novels in parts, and therefore had never been tempted. But I was aware that an artist should keep in his hand the power of fitting the beginning of his work to the end. No doubt it is his first duty to fit the end to the beginning, and he will endeavour to do so. But he should still keep in his hands the power of remedying any defect in this respect.

'Servetur ad imum
Qualis ab incepto processerit,'*

should be kept in view as to every character and every string of action. Your Achilles* should all through, from beginning to end, be 'impatient, fiery, ruthless, keen.' Your Achilles, such as he is, will probably keep up his character. But your Davus* also should be always Davus, and that is more difficult. The rustic driving his pigs to market cannot always make them travel by the exact path which he has intended for them. When some young lady at the end of a story cannot be made quite perfect in her conduct, that vivid description of angelic purity with which you laid the first lines of her portrait should be slightly toned down. I had felt that the rushing mode of publication to which the system of serial stories had given rise, and by which small parts as they were written were sent hot to the press, was injurious to the work done. If I now complied with the proposition made to me, I must act against my own principle. But such a principle becomes a tyrant if it cannot be superseded on a just occasion. If the reason be 'tanti,'* the principle should for the occasion be put in abeyance. I sat as judge, and decreed that the present reason was 'tanti.' On this my first attempt at a serial story, I thought it fit to break my own rule. I can say, however, that I have never broken it since.*

But what astonished me most was the fact that at so late a day this new *Cornhill Magazine* should be in want of a novel! Perhaps some of my future readers will be able to remember the great expectations which were raised as to this periodical. Thackeray's was a good name with which to conjure. The proprietors, Messrs Smith & Elder, were most liberal in their manner of initiating the work, and were able to make an expectant world of readers believe that something was to be given them for a shilling very much in excess of anything they had ever received for that or double the money. Whether these hopes were or were not fulfilled it is not for me to say, as, for the first few years of the magazine's existence, I wrote for it more than any other one person. But such was certainly the prospect;—and how had it come to pass that, with such promises made, the editor and the proprietors were, at the end of October, without anything fixed as to what must be regarded as the chief dish in the banquet to be provided?

I fear that the answer to this question must be found in the habits of procrastination which had at that time grown upon the editor. He had, I imagine, undertaken the work himself, and had postponed its commencement till there was left to him no time for commencing. There was still, it may be said, as much time for him as for me. I think there was,—for though he had his magazine to look after, I had the Post Office. But he thought, when unable to trust his own energy, that he might rely upon that of a new recruit. He was but four years my senior in life, but he was at the top of the tree, while I was still at the bottom.

Having made up my mind to break my principle, I started at once from Dublin to London. I arrived there on the morning of Thursday, 3d of November, and left it on the evening of Friday. In the meantime* I had made my agreement with Messrs Smith & Elder, and had arranged my plot. But when in London, I first went to Edward Chapman, at 193 Piccadilly. If the novel I was then writing for him would suit the *Cornhill*, might I consider my arrangement with him to be at an end? Yes; I might. But if that story would not suit the *Cornhill*, was I to consider my arrangement with him as still standing,—that agreement requiring that my MS. should be in his hands in the following March? As to that, I might do as I pleased. In our dealings together Mr Edward Chapman always acceded to every suggestion made to him. He never refused a book, and never haggled at a price. Then I hurried into the City, and had my first interview with Mr George Smith. When he heard that *Castle Richmond* was an Irish story, he begged that I would endeavour to frame some other for his magazine. He was sure that an Irish story would not do for a commencement;—and he suggested the Church, as though it were my peculiar subject. I told him that *Castle Richmond* would have to 'come out' while any other novel that I might write for him would be running through the magazine;—but to that he expressed himself altogether indifferent. He wanted an English tale, on English life, with a clerical flavour. On these orders I went to work, and framed what I suppose I must call the plot of *Framley Parsonage*.

On my journey back to Ireland, in the railway carriage, I wrote the first few pages of that story. I had got into my head an idea of what I meant to write,—a morsel of the biography of an English clergyman who should not be a bad man, but one led into temptation by his own youth and by the unclerical accidents of the life of those around him. The love of his sister for the young lord was an adjunct necessary, because there must be love in a novel. And then by placing Framley Parsonage near Barchester, I was able to fall back upon my old friends Mrs Proudie and the archdeacon. Out of these slight elements I fabricated a hodge-podge in which the real plot consisted at last simply of a girl refusing to marry the man she loved till the man's friends agreed to accept her lovingly. Nothing could be less efficient or artistic. But the characters were so well handled, that the work from the first to the last was popular,—and was received as it went on with still increasing favour by both editor and proprietor of the magazine. The story was thoroughly English. There was a little fox-hunting and a little tuft-hunting,* some Christian virtue and some Christian cant. There was no heroism and no villainy. There was much Church, but more love-making. And it was downright honest love,—in which there was no pretence on the part of the lady that she was too ethereal to be fond of a man, no half-and-half inclination on the part of the man to pay a certain price and no more for a pretty toy. Each of them longed for the other, and they were not ashamed to say so. Consequently they in England who were living, or had lived, the same sort of life, liked *Framley Parsonage*. I think myself that Lucy Robarts is perhaps the most natural English girl that I ever drew,—the most natural, at any rate, of those who have been good girls. She was not as dear to me as Kate Woodward in *The Three Clerks*, but I think she is more like real human life. Indeed I doubt whether such a character could be made more lifelike than Lucy Robarts.

And I will say also that in this novel there is no very weak part,—no long succession of dull pages. The production of novels in serial form forces upon the author the conviction that he should not allow himself to be tedious in any single part. I hope no reader will misunderstand me. In spite of that conviction, the writer of stories in parts will often be tedious. That I have been so myself is a fault that will lie heavy on my tombstone. But the writer when he embarks in such a business should feel that he cannot afford to have many pages skipped out of the few which are to meet the reader's eye at the same time. Who can imagine the first half of the first volume of *Waverley* coming out in shilling numbers? I had realised this when I was writing *Framley Parsonage*; and working on the conviction which had thus come home to me, I fell into no bathos of dulness.

I subsequently came across a piece of criticism which was written on me as a novelist by a brother novelist very much greater than myself, and whose brilliant intellect and warm imagination led him to a kind of work the very opposite of mine. This was Nathaniel Hawthorne,* the American, whom I did not then know, but whose works I knew. Though it praises myself highly, I will insert it here, because it certainly is true in its nature: 'It is odd enough,' he says, 'that my own individual taste is for quite another class of works than those which I myself am able to write. If I were to meet with such books as mine by another writer, I don't believe I should be able to get through them. Have you ever read the novels of Anthony Trollope? They precisely suit my taste,—solid and substantial, written on the strength of beef and through the inspiration of ale, and just as real as if some giant had hewn a great lump out of the earth and put it under a glass case, with all its inhabitants going about their daily business, and not suspecting that they were being made a show of. And these books are just as English as a beef-steak. Have they ever been tried in America? It needs an English residence to make them thoroughly comprehensible; but still I should think that human nature would give them success anywhere.'

This was dated early in 1860, and could have had no reference to *Framley Parsonage*; but it was as true of that work as of any that I have written. And the criticism, whether just or unjust, describes with wonderful accuracy the purport that I have ever had in view in my writing. I have always desired to 'hew out some lump of the earth,' and to make men and women walk upon it just as they do walk here among us,—with not more of excellence, nor with exaggerated baseness,—so that my readers might recognise human beings like to themselves, and not feel themselves to be carried away among gods or demons. If I could do this, then I thought I might succeed in impregnating the mind of the novel-reader with a feeling that honesty is the best policy; that truth prevails while falsehood fails; that a girl will be loved as she is pure, and sweet, and unselfish; that a man will be honoured as he is true, and honest, and brave of heart; that things meanly done are ugly and odious, and things nobly done beautiful and gracious. I do not say that lessons such as these may not be more grandly taught by higher flights than mine. Such lessons come to us from our greatest poets. But there are so many who will read novels and understand them, who either do not read the works of our great poets, or reading them miss the lesson! And even in prose fiction the character whom the fervid imagination of the writer has lifted somewhat into the clouds, will hardly give so plain an example to the hasty normal reader as the humbler personage whom that reader unconsciously feels to resemble himself or herself. I do think that a girl would more probably dress her own mind after Lucy Robarts than after Flora Macdonald.*

There are many who would laugh at the idea of a novelist teaching either virtue or nobility,—those, for instance, who regard the reading of novels as a sin, and those also who think it to be simply an idle pastime. They look upon the tellers of stories as among the tribe of those who pander to the wicked pleasures of a wicked world. I have regarded my art from so different a point of view that I have ever thought of myself as a preacher of sermons, and my pulpit as one which I could make both salutary and agreeable to my audience. I do believe that no girl has risen from the reading of my pages less modest than she was before, and that some may have learned from them that modesty is a charm well worth preserving. I think that no youth has been taught that in falseness and flashness is to be found the road to manliness; but some may perhaps have learned from me that it is to be found in truth and a high but gentle spirit. Such are the lessons I have striven to teach; and I have thought it might best be done by representing to my readers characters like themselves,—or to which they might liken themselves.

Framley Parsonage—or, rather, my connection with the *Cornhill*—was the means of introducing me very quickly to that literary world from which I had hitherto been severed by the fact of my residence in Ireland. In December 1859, while I was still very hard at work on my novel, I came over to take charge of the Eastern District, and settled myself at a residence about twelve miles from London, in Hertfordshire, but on the borders both of Essex and Middlesex,—which was somewhat too grandly called Waltham House. This I took on lease, and subsequently bought after I had spent about £1000 on improvements. From hence I was able to make myself frequent both in Cornhill and Piccadilly, and to live, when the opportunity came, among men of my own pursuit.

It was in January 1860 that Mr George Smith*—to whose enterprise we owe not only the *Cornhill Magazine* but the *Pall Mall Gazette*—gave a sumptuous dinner to his contributors. It was a memorable banquet in many ways, but chiefly so to me because on that occasion I first met many men who afterwards became my most intimate associates. It can rarely happen that one such occasion can be the first starting-point of so many friendships. It was at that table, and on that day, that I first saw Thackeray, Charles Taylor* (Sir)—than whom in latter life I have loved no man better,—Robert Bell,* G. H. Lewes,* Russell of the *Times*,* and John Everett Millais. With all these men I afterwards lived on affectionate terms;—but I will here speak specially of the last, because from that time he was joined with me in so much of the work that I did.

Mr Millais was engaged to illustrate *Framley Parsonage*, but this was not the first work he did for the magazine. In the second number there is a picture of his accompanying Monckton Milne's* 'Unspoken Dialogue'. The first drawing he did for *Framley Parsonage* did not appear till after the dinner of which I have spoken, and I do not think that I knew at the time that he was engaged on my novel. When I did know it, it made me very proud. He afterwards illustrated *Orley Farm*, *The Small House at Allington*, *Rachel Ray*, and *Phineas Finn*. Altogether he drew from my tales eighty-seven drawings, and I do not think that more conscientious work was ever done by man. Writers of novels know well—and so ought readers of novels to have learned—that there are two modes of illustrating, either of which may be adopted equally by a bad and by a good artist. To which class Mr Millais belongs I need not say; but, as a good artist, it was open to him simply to make a pretty picture, or to study the work of the author from whose writing he was bound to take his subject. I have too often found that the former alternative has been thought to be the better, as it certainly is the easier method. An artist will frequently dislike to subordinate his ideas to those of an author, and will sometimes be too idle to find out what those ideas are. But this artist was neither proud nor idle. In every figure that he drew it was his object to promote the views of the writer whose work he had undertaken to illustrate, and he never spared himself any pains in studying that work, so as to enable him to do so. I have carried on some of those characters from book to book, and have had my own early ideas impressed indelibly on my memory by the excellence of his delineations. Those illustrations were commenced fifteen years ago, and from that time up to this day my affection for the man of whom I am speaking has increased. To see him has always been a pleasure. His voice has been a sweet sound in my ears. Behind his back I have never heard him praised without joining the eulogist; I have never heard a word spoken against him without opposing the censurer. These words, should he ever see them, will come to him from the grave, and will tell him of my regard,—as one living man never tells another.

Sir Charles Taylor, who carried me home in his brougham that evening, and thus commenced an intimacy which has since been very close, was born to wealth, and was therefore not compelled by the necessities of a profession to enter the lists as an author. But he lived much with those who did so,—and could have done it himself had want or ambition stirred him. He was our king at the Garrick Club,* to which, however, I did not yet belong. He gave the best dinners of my time, and was,—happily I may say is,[1]—the best giver of dinners. A man rough of tongue, brusque in his manners, odious to those who dislike him, somewhat inclined to tyranny, he is the prince of friends, honest as the sun, and as openhanded as Charity itself.

Robert Bell has now been dead nearly ten years. As I look back over the interval and remember how intimate we were, it seems odd to me that we should have known each other for no more than six years.

---

[1] Alas! within a year of the writing of this he went from us.

He was a man who had lived by his pen from his very youth; and was so far successful that I do not think that want ever came near him. But he never made that mark which his industry and talents would have seemed to ensure. He was a man well known to literary men, but not known to readers. As a journalist he was useful and conscientious, but his plays and novels never made themselves popular. He wrote a life of Canning,* and he brought out an annotated edition of the British poets; but he achieved no great success. I have known no man better read in English literature. Hence his conversation had a peculiar charm, but he was not equally happy with his pen. He will long be remembered at the Literary Fund Committees,* of which he was a staunch and most trusted supporter. I think it was he who first introduced me to that board. It has often been said that literary men are peculiarly apt to think that they are slighted and unappreciated. Robert Bell certainly never achieved the position in literature which he once aspired to fill, and which he was justified in thinking that he could earn for himself. I have frequently discussed these subjects with him, but I never heard from his mouth a word of complaint as to his own literary fate. He liked to hear the chimes go at midnight, and he loved to have ginger hot in his mouth.* On such occasions no sound ever came out of a man's lips sweeter than his wit and gentle revelry.

George Lewes,—with his wife, whom all the world knows as George Eliot,*—has also been and still is one of my dearest friends. He is, I think, the acutest critic I know,—and the severest. His severity, however, is a fault. His intention to be honest, even when honesty may give pain, has caused him to give pain when honesty has not required it. He is essentially a doubter, and has encouraged himself to doubt till the faculty of trusting has almost left him. I am not speaking of the personal trust which one man feels in another, but of that confidence in literary excellence, which is, I think, necessary for the full enjoyment of literature. In one modern writer he did believe thoroughly. Nothing can be more charming than the unstinted admiration which he has accorded to everything that comes from the pen of the wonderful woman to whom his lot has been united. To her name I shall recur again when speaking of the novelists of the present day.

Of 'Billy Russell,' as we always used to call him, I may say that I never knew but one man equal to him in the quickness and continuance of witty speech. That one man was Charles Lever*—also an Irishman—whom

I had known from an earlier date, and also with close intimacy. Of the two, I think that Lever was perhaps the more astounding producer of good things. His manner was perhaps a little the happier, and his turns more sharp and unexpected. But 'Billy' also was marvellous. Whether abroad as special correspondent, or at home amidst the flurry of his newspaper work, he was a charming companion;* his ready wit always gave him the last word.*

Of Thackeray I will speak again when I record his death.

There were many others whom I met for the first time at George Smith's table. Albert Smith,* for the first, and indeed for the last time, as he died soon after; Higgins, whom all the world knew as Jacob Omnium,* a man I greatly regarded; Dallas,* who for a time was literary critic to the *Times*, and who certainly in that capacity did better work than has appeared since in the same department; George Augustus Sala,* who, had he given himself fair play, would have risen to higher eminence than that of being the best writer in his day of sensational leading articles; and Fitz-James Stephen,* a man of very different calibre, who has not yet culminated, but who, no doubt, will culminate among our judges. There were many others;—but I cannot now recall their various names as identified with those banquets.*

Of *Framley Parsonage* I need only further say, that as I wrote it I became more closely than ever acquainted with the new shire which I had added to the English counties. I had it all in my mind,—its roads and railroads, its towns and parishes, its members of Parliament, and the different hunts which rode over it. I knew all the great lords and their castles, the squires and their parks, the rectors and their churches. This was the fourth novel of which I had placed the scene in Barsetshire, and as I wrote it I made a map of the dear county.* Throughout these stories there has been no name given to a fictitious site which does not represent to me a spot of which I know all the accessories, as though I had lived and wandered there.

CHAPTER 9

———— ∞∞∞ ————

'Castle Richmond', 'Brown, Jones, and Robinson', 'North America', 'Orley Farm'

WHEN I had half-finished *Framley Parsonage*, I went back to my other story, *Castle Richmond*, which I was writing for Messrs Chapman & Hall, and completed that. I think that this was the only occasion on which I have had two different novels in my mind at the same time. This, however, did not create either difficulty or confusion. Many of us live in different circles; and when we go from our friends in the town to our friends in the country, we do not usually fail to remember the little details of the one life or the other. The parson at Rusticum,* with his wife and his wife's mother, and all his belongings; and our old friend, the Squire, with his family history; and Farmer Mudge, who has been cross with us, because we rode so unnecessarily over his barley; and that rascally poacher, once a gamekeeper, who now traps all the foxes; and pretty Mary Cann, whose marriage with the wheelwright we did something to expedite;—though we are alive to them all, do not drive out of our brain the club gossip, or the memories of last season's dinners, or any incident of our London intimacies. In our lives we are always weaving novels, and we manage to keep the different tales distinct. A man does, in truth, remember that which it interests him to remember; and when we hear that memory has gone as age has come on, we should understand that the capacity for interest in the matter concerned has perished. A man will be generally very old and feeble before he forgets how much money he has in the funds. There is a good deal to be learned by any one who wishes to write a novel well; but when the art has been acquired, I do not see why two or three should not be well written at the same time. I have never found myself thinking much about the work that I had to do till I was doing it. I have indeed for many years almost abandoned the effort to think, trusting myself, with the narrowest thread of a plot, to work the matter out when the pen is in my hand. But my mind is constantly employing itself on the work I have done. Had I left either *Framley Parsonage* or *Castle Richmond* half-finished fifteen years ago, I think I could complete the tales now with very little trouble. I have not looked at *Castle Richmond* since it was published; and poor as the work is, I remember all the incidents.

Castle Richmond certainly was not a success,—though the plot is a fairly good plot, and is much more of a plot than I have generally been able to find. The scene is laid in Ireland, during the famine; and I am well aware now that English readers no longer like Irish stories. I cannot understand why it should be so, as the Irish character is peculiarly well fitted for romance. But Irish subjects generally have become distasteful. This novel, however, is of itself a weak production. The characters do not excite sympathy. The heroine has two lovers, one of whom is a scamp and the other a prig. As regards the scamp, the girl's mother is her own rival. Rivalry of the same nature has been admirably depicted by Thackeray in his *Esmond*; but there the mother's love seems to be justified by the girl's indifference. In *Castle Richmond* the mother strives to rob her daughter of the man's love. The girl herself has no character; and the mother, who is strong enough, is almost revolting. The dialogue is often lively, and some of the incidents are well told; but the story as a whole was a failure. I cannot remember, however, that it was roughly handled by the critics when it came out; and I much doubt whether anything so hard was said of it then as that which I have said here.

I was now settled at Waltham Cross,* in a house in which I could entertain a few friends modestly, where we grew our cabbages and strawberries, made our own butter, and killed our own pigs. I occupied it for twelve years, and they were years to me of great prosperity. In 1861* I became a member of the Garrick Club, with which institution I have since been much identified. I had belonged to it about two years, when, on Thackeray's death, I was invited to fill his place on the Committee, and I have been one of that august body ever since. Having up to that time lived very little among men, having known hitherto nothing of clubs, having even as a boy been banished from social gatherings, I enjoyed infinitely at first the gaiety of the Garrick. It was a festival to me to dine there—which I did indeed but seldom; and a great delight to play a rubber in the little room up-stairs of an afternoon. I am speaking now of the old club in King Street.* This playing of whist before dinner has since that become a habit with me, so that unless there be something else special to do—unless there be hunting, or I am wanted to ride in the park by the young tyrant of my

household*—it is 'my custom always in the afternoon.'* I have sometimes felt sore with myself for this persistency, feeling that I was making myself a slave to an amusement which has not after all very much
to recommend it. I have often thought that I would break myself away
from it, and 'swear off,' as Rip Van Winkle* says. But my swearing off
has been like that of Rip Van Winkle. And now, as I think of it coolly,
I do not know but that I have been right to cling to it. As a man grows
old he wants amusement, more even than when he is young; and then
it becomes so difficult to find amusement. Reading should, no doubt,
be the delight of one's* leisure hours. Had I to choose between books
and cards, I should no doubt take the books. But I find that I can
seldom read with pleasure for above an hour and a half at a time, or
more than three hours a day. As I write this I am aware that hunting
must soon be abandoned. After sixty it is given but to few men to ride
straight across country, and I cannot bring myself to adopt any other
mode of riding. I think that without cards I should now be much at
a loss. When I began to play at the Garrick, I did so chiefly* because
I liked the society of the men who played.

I think that I became popular among those with whom I associated.
I have long been aware of a certain weakness in my own character,
which I may call a craving for love. I have ever had a wish to be liked
by those around me,—a wish that during the first half of my life was
never gratified. In my school-days no small part of my misery came
from the envy with which I regarded the popularity of popular boys.
They seemed to me to live in a social paradise, while the desolation
of my pandemonium* was complete. And afterwards, when I was in
London as a young man, I had but few friends. Among the clerks in
the Post Office I held my own fairly after* the first two or three years;
but even then I regarded myself as something of a pariah. My Irish
life had been much better. I had had my wife and children, and had
been sustained by a feeling of general respect. But even in Ireland
I had in truth lived but little in society. Our means had been sufficient
for our wants, but insufficient for entertaining others. It was not till
we had settled ourselves at Waltham that I really began to live much
with others. The Garrick Club was the first assemblage of men at
which I felt myself to be popular.

I soon became a member of other clubs. There was the Arts Club
in Hanover Square, of which I saw the opening, but from which,
after three or four years, I withdrew my name, having found that

during these three or four years I had not once entered the building. Then I was one of the originators of the Civil Service Club—not from judgment, but instigated to do so by others. That also I left for the same reason. In 1864 I received the honour of being elected by the Committee at the Athenaeum.* For this I was indebted to the kindness of Lord Stanhope;* and I never was more surprised than when I was informed of the fact. About the same time I became a member of the Cosmopolitan,* a little club that meets twice a week in Charles Street, Berkeley Square, and supplies to all its members, and its members' friends, tea and brandy and water without charge! The gatherings there I used to think very delightful. One met Jacob Omnium, Monckton Milnes, Tom Hughes, William Stirling, Henry Reeve, Arthur Russell, Tom Taylor,* and such like; and generally a strong political element, thoroughly well mixed, gave a certain spirit to the place. Lord Ripon, Lord Stanley, William Forster, Lord Enfield, Lord Kimberley, George Bentinck, Vernon Harcourt, Bromley Davenport, Knatchbull Huguessen,* with many others, used to whisper the secrets of Parliament with free tongues. Afterwards I became a member of the Turf,* which I found to be serviceable—or the reverse—only for the playing of whist at high points.

In August 1861 I wrote another novel for the *Cornhill Magazine*. It was a short story, about one volume in length, and was called *The Struggles of Brown, Jones, and Robinson*. In this I attempted a style for which I certainly was not qualified, and to which I never had again recourse. It was meant to be funny, was full of slang, and was intended as a satire on the ways of trade. Still I think that there is some good fun in it, but I have heard no one else express such an opinion. I do not know that I ever heard any opinion expressed on it, except by the publisher, who kindly remarked that he did not think it was equal to my usual work. Though he had purchased the copyright, he did not republish the story in a book form till 1870, and then it passed into the world of letters *sub silentio*.* I do not know that it was ever criticised or ever read. I received £600 for it. From that time to this I have been paid at about that rate for my work—£600 for the quantity contained in an ordinary novel volume, or £3000 for a long tale published in twenty parts, which is equal in length to five such volumes. I have occasionally, I think, received something more than this, never I think less for any tale, except when I have published my work anonymously.[1]* Having said so much, I need not further specify the prices as I mention the books as they were written. I will, however, when I am completing this memoir, give a list of all the sums I have received for my literary labours. I think that *Brown, Jones, and Robinson* was the hardest bargain I ever sold to a publisher.

In 1861 the War of Secession* had broken out in America, and from the first I interested myself much in the question. My mother had thirty years previously written a very popular, but, as I had thought, a somewhat unjust book about our cousins over the water. She had seen what was distasteful in the manners of a young people, but had hardly recognised their energy. I had entertained for many years an ambition to follow her footsteps there, and to write another book. I had already paid a short visit to New York City and State on my way home from the West Indies, but had not seen enough then to justify me in the expression of any opinion. The breaking out of the war did not make me think that the time was peculiarly fit for such inquiry as I wished to make, but it did represent itself as an occasion on which a book might be popular. I consequently consulted the two great powers with whom I was concerned. Messrs Chapman & Hall, the publishers, were one power, and I had no difficulty in arranging my affairs with them. They agreed to publish the book on my terms, and bade me God-speed on my journey. The other power was the Postmaster-General and Mr Rowland Hill, the Secretary of the Post Office. I wanted leave of absence for the unusual period of nine months, and fearing that I should not get it by the ordinary process of asking the Secretary, I went direct to his lordship. 'Is it on the plea of ill-health?' he asked, looking into my face, which was then that of a very robust man. His lordship knew the Civil Service as well as any one living, and must have seen much of falseness and fraudulent pretence, or he could not have asked that question. I told him that I was very well, but that I wanted to write a book. 'Had I any special ground to go upon in asking for such indulgence?' I had, I said, done my duty well by the service. There was a good deal of demurring, but I got my leave for nine months,—and I knew that I had earned it. Mr Hill attached to the minute granting me the leave an intimation that it was to be considered as a full equivalent for the special services rendered by me to the department. I declined, however, to accept the

[1] Since the date at which this was written I have encountered a diminution in price.

grace with such a stipulation, and it was withdrawn by the directions of the Postmaster-General.[1]*

I started for the States in August* and returned in the following May. The war was raging during the time that I was there, and the country was full of soldiers. A part of the time I spent in Virginia, Kentucky, and Missouri, among the troops, along the line of attack. I visited all the States (excepting California) which had not then seceded,—failing to make my way into the seceding States unless I was prepared to visit them with an amount of discomfort I did not choose to endure. I worked very hard at the task I had assigned to myself, and did, I think, see much of the manners and institutions of the people. Nothing struck me more than their persistence in the ordinary pursuits of life in spite of the war which was around them. Neither industry nor amusement seemed to meet with any check. Schools, hospitals, and institutes were by no means neglected because new regiments were daily required. The truth, I take it, is that we, all of us, soon adapt ourselves to the circumstances around us. Though three parts of London were in flames I should no doubt expect to have my dinner served to me if I lived in the quarter which was free from fire.

The book I wrote was very much longer than that on the West Indies, but was also written almost without a note. It contained much information, and, with many inaccuracies, was a true book. But it was not well done. It is tedious and confused, and will hardly, I think, be of future value to those who wish to make themselves acquainted with the United States. It was published about the middle of the war,—just at the time in which the hopes of those who loved the South were most buoyant, and the fears of those who stood by the North were the strongest. But it expressed an assured confidence—which never quavered in a page or in a line—that the North would win. This assurance was based on the merits of the Northern cause, on the superior strength of the Northern party, and on a conviction that England would never recognise the South, and that France would be guided in her policy by England. I was right in my prophecies, and right, I think, on the

[1] During the period of my service in the Post Office I did very much special work for which I never asked any remuneration,—and never received any, though payments for special services were common in the department at that time. But if there was to be a question of such remuneration, I did not choose that my work should be valued at the price put upon it by Mr Hill.

grounds on which they were made. The Southern cause was bad. The South had provoked the quarrel because its political supremacy was checked by the election of Mr Lincoln to the Presidency. It had to fight as a little man against a big man, and fought gallantly. That gallantry,— and a feeling based on a misconception as to American character that the Southerners are better gentlemen than their Northern brethren,— did create great sympathy here; but I believe that the country was too just to be led into political action by a spirit of romance, and I was warranted in that belief. There was a moment in which the Northern cause was in danger, and the danger lay certainly in the prospect of British interference. Messrs Slidell and Mason,*—two men insignificant in themselves,—had been sent to Europe by the Southern party, and had managed to get on board the British mail steamer called 'The Trent,' at the Havannah. A most undue importance was attached to this mission by Mr Lincoln's government, and efforts were made to stop them. A certain Commodore Wilkes, doing duty as policeman on the seas, did stop the Trent, and took the men out. They were carried, one to Boston and one to New York, and were incarcerated, amidst the triumph of the nation. Commodore Wilkes, who had done nothing in which a brave man could take glory, was made a hero and received a prize sword. England of course demanded her passengers back, and the States for a while refused to surrender them. But Mr Seward was at that time the Secretary of State, and Mr Seward, with many political faults, was a wise man. I was at Washington at the time, and it was known there that the contest among the leading Northerners was very sharp on the matter. Mr Sumner and Mr Seward were, under Mr Lincoln, the two chiefs of the party. It was understood that Mr Sumner was opposed to the rendition of the men, and Mr Seward in favour of it. Mr Seward's counsels at last prevailed with the President, and England's declaration of war was prevented. I dined with Mr Seward on the day of the decision, meeting Mr Sumner at his house, and was told as I left the dining-room what the decision had been. During the afternoon I and others had received intimation through the embassy that we might probably have to leave Washington at an hour's notice. This, I think, was the severest danger that the Northern cause encountered during the war.

But my book, though it was right in its views on this subject,—and wrong in none other as far as I know,—was not a good book. I can recommend no one to read it now in order that he may be either instructed or amused,—as I can do that on the West Indies. It served its purpose at the time, and was well received by the public and by the critics.

Before starting to America I had completed *Orley Farm*, a novel which appeared in shilling numbers,—after the manner in which *Pickwick*, *Nicholas Nickleby*, and many others had been published. Most of those among my friends who talk to me now about my novels, and are competent to form an opinion on the subject, say that this is the best I have written. In this opinion I do not coincide. I think that the highest merit which a novel can have consists in perfect delineation of character, rather than in plot, or humour, or pathos, and I shall before long mention a subsequent work in which I think the main character of the story is so well developed as to justify me in asserting its claim above the others. The plot of *Orley Farm* is probably the best I have ever made; but it has the fault of declaring itself, and thus coming to an end too early in the book. When Lady Mason tells her ancient lover that she did forge the will, the plot of *Orley Farm* has unravelled itself;—and this she does in the middle of the tale. Independently, however, of this the novel is good. Sir Peregrine Orme, his grandson, Madeline Stavely, Mr Furnival, Mr Chaffanbrass, and the commercial gentlemen, are all good. The hunting is good. The lawyer's talk is good. Mr Moulder carves his turkey admirably, and Mr Kantwise sells his tables and chairs with spirit. I do not know that there is a dull page in the book. I am proud of *Orley Farm*;—and am especially proud* of its illustrations by Millais, which are the best I have seen in any novel in any language.

I now felt that I had gained my object. In 1862 I had achieved that which I contemplated when I went to London in 1834, and towards which I made my first attempt when I began the *Macdermots* in 1843. I had created for myself a position among literary men, and had secured to myself an income on which I might live in ease and comfort,—which ease and comfort have been made to include many luxuries. From this time for a period of twelve years my income averaged £4500 a year. Of this I spent about two-thirds, and put by one. I ought perhaps to have done better,—to have spent one-third, and put by two; but I have ever been too well inclined to spend freely that which has come easily.

This, however, has been so exactly the life which my thoughts and aspirations had marked out,—thoughts and aspirations which used to cause me to blush with shame because I was so slow in forcing myself to the work which they demanded,—that I have felt some pride in having attained it. I have before said how entirely I fail to reach the altitude of those who think that a man devoted to letters should be indifferent to the pecuniary results for which work is generally done. An easy income has always been regarded by me as a great bless-ing. Not to have to think of sixpences, or very much of shillings; not to be unhappy because the coals have been burned too quickly, and the house linen wants renewing; not to be debarred by the rigour of necessity from opening one's hands, perhaps foolishly, to one's friends;—all this to me has been essential to the comfort of life. I have enjoyed the comfort for I may almost say the last twenty years, though no man in his youth had less prospect of doing so, or would have been less likely at twenty-five to have had such luxuries foretold to him by his friends.

But though the money has been sweet, the respect, the friend-ships, and the mode of life which has been achieved, have been much sweeter. In my boyhood, when I would be crawling up to school with dirty boots and trousers through the muddy lanes, I was always tell-ing myself that the misery of the hour was not the worst of it, but that the mud and solitude and poverty of the time would insure me mud and solitude and poverty through my life. Those lads about me would go into Parliament, or become rectors and deans, or squires of parishes, or advocates thundering at the Bar. They would not live with me now,—but neither should I be able to live with them in after years. Nevertheless I have lived with them. When, at the age in which others go to the universities, I became a clerk in the Post Office, I felt that my old visions were being realised. I did not think it a high call-ing. I did not know then how very much good work may be done by a member of the Civil Service who will show himself capable of doing it. The Post Office at last grew upon me and forced itself into my affections. I became intensely anxious that people should have their letters delivered to them punctually. But my hope to rise had always been built on the writing of novels, and at last by the writing of novels I had risen.

I do not think that I ever toadied any one, or that I have acquired the character of a tuft-hunter. But here I do not scruple to say that I prefer the society of distinguished people, and that even the dis-tinction of wealth confers many advantages. The best education is to be had at a price as well as the best broadcloth. The son of a peer is more likely to rub his shoulders against well-informed men than the son of a tradesman. The graces come easier to the wife of him who has had great-grandfathers than they do to her whose husband has been less,—or more fortunate, as he may think it. The discerning man will recognise the information and the graces when they are achieved without such assistance, and will honour the owners of them the more because of the difficulties they have overcome;—but the fact remains that the society of the well-born and of the wealthy will as a rule be worth seeking. I say this now, because these are the rules by which I have lived, and these are the causes which have instigated me to work.

I have heard the question argued—On what terms should a man of inferior rank live with those who are manifestly superior to him? If a marquis or an earl honour me, who have no rank, with his intimacy, am I in my intercourse with him to remember our close acquaintance or his high rank? I have always said that where the difference in position is quite marked, the overtures to intimacy should always come from the higher rank; but if the intimacy be ever fixed, then that rank should be held of no account. It seems to me that intimate friendship admits of no standing but that of equality. I cannot be the Sovereign's friend, nor probably the friend of many very much beneath the Sovereign, because such equality is impossible.

When I first came to Waltham Cross in the winter of 1859-1860, I had almost made up my mind that my hunting was over. I could not then count upon an income which would enable me to carry on an amusement which I should doubtless find much more expensive in England than in Ireland. I brought with me out of Ireland one mare, but she was too light for me to ride in the hunting-field. As, however, the money came in, I very quickly fell back into my old habits. First one horse was bought, then another, and then a third, till it became established as a fixed rule that I should not have less than four hunters in the stable. Sometimes when my boys have been at home I have had as many as six. Essex was the chief scene of my sport, and gradually I became known there almost as well as though I had been an Essex squire, to the manner born. Few have investigated more closely than I have done the depth, and breadth, and water-holding capacities of an Essex ditch. It will, I think, be accorded to me by Essex men generally that I have ridden hard. The cause of my delight in the amusement I have never been able to analyse to my own satisfaction. In the first place, even now, I know very little about hunting,—though I know very much of the accessories of the field. I am too blind to see hounds turning, and cannot therefore tell whether the fox has gone this way or that. Indeed all the notice I take of hounds is not to ride over them. My eyes are so constituted that I can never see the nature of a fence. I either follow some one, or ride at it with the full conviction that I may be going into a horse-pond or a gravel-pit. I have jumped into both one and the other. I am very heavy, and have never ridden expensive horses. I am also now old for such work, being so stiff that I cannot get on to my horse without the aid of a block or a bank. But I ride still after the same fashion, with a boy's energy, determined to get ahead if it may possibly be done, hating the roads, despising young men who ride them, and with a feeling that life can not, with all her riches, have given me anything better than when I have gone through a long run to the finish, keeping a place, not of glory, but of credit, among my juniors.*

CHAPTER 10

'The Small House at Allington', 'Can You Forgive Her?', 'Rachel Ray', and The 'Fortnightly Review'

D URING the early months of 1862 *Orley Farm* was still being brought out in numbers, and at the same time *Brown, Jones, and Robinson* was appearing in the *Cornhill Magazine*. In September 1862 *The Small House at Allington* began its career in the same periodical. The work on North America had also come out in 1862. In August 1863 the first number of *Can You Forgive Her?* was published as a separate serial, and was continued through 1864. In 1863 a short novel was produced in the ordinary volume form, called *Rachel Ray*. In addition to these I published during the time two volumes of stories called *The Tales of all Countries*. In the early spring of 1865 *Miss Mackenzie* was issued in the same form as *Rachel Ray*; and in May of the same year *The Belton Estate* was commenced with the commencement of the *Fortnightly Review*,* of which periodical I will say a few words in this chapter.

I quite admit that I crowded my wares into the market too quickly,—because the reading world could not want such a quantity of matter from the hands of one author in so short a space of time. I had not been quite so fertile as the unfortunate gentleman who disgusted the publisher in Paternoster Row,—in the story of whose productiveness I have always thought there was a touch of romance,—but I had probably done enough to make both publishers and readers think that I was coming too often beneath their notice. Of publishers, however, I must speak collectively, as my sins were, I think, chiefly due to the encouragement which I received from them individually. What I wrote for the *Cornhill Magazine*, I always wrote at the instigation of Mr Smith. My other works were published by Messrs Chapman & Hall, in compliance with contracts made by me with them, and always made with their good-will. Could I have been two separate persons at one and the same time, of whom one might have been devoted to Cornhill and the other to the interests of the firm in Piccadilly, it might have been very well;—but as I preserved my identity in both places, I myself became aware that my name was too frequent on title-pages.

Critics, if they ever trouble themselves with these pages, will, of course, say that in what I have now said I have ignored altogether the one great evil of rapid production,—namely, that of inferior work. And of course if the work was inferior because of the too great rapidity of production, the critics would be right. Giving to the subject the best of my critical abilities, and judging of my own work as nearly as possible as I would that of another, I believe that the work which has been done quickest has been done the best. I have composed better stories—that is, have created better plots—than those of *The Small House at Allington* and *Can You Forgive Her?* and I have portrayed two or three better characters than are to be found in the pages of either of them; but taking these books all through, I do not think that I have ever done better work. Nor would these have been improved by any effort in the art of story telling, had each of these been the isolated labour of a couple of years. How short is the time devoted to the manipulation of a plot can be known only to those who have written plays and novels;—I may say also, how very little time the brain is able to devote to such wearing work. There are usually some hours of agonising doubt, almost of despair,—so at least it has been with me,—or perhaps some days. And then, with nothing settled in my brain as to the final development of events, with no capability of settling anything, but with a most distinct conception of some character or characters, I have rushed at the work as a rider rushes at a fence which he does not see. Sometimes I have encountered what, in hunting language, we call a cropper. I had such a fall in two novels of mine, of which I have already spoken—*The Bertrams* and *Castle Richmond.* I shall have to speak of other such troubles. But these failures have not arisen from over-hurried work. When my work has been quicker done,—and it has sometimes been done very quickly—the rapidity has been achieved by hot pressure, not in the conception, but in the telling of the story. Instead of writing eight pages a day, I have written sixteen; instead of working five days a week, I have worked seven. I have trebled my usual average, and have done so in circumstances which have enabled me to give up all my thoughts for the time to the book I have been writing. This has generally been done at some quiet spot among the mountains,—where there has been no society, no hunting, no whist, no ordinary household duties. And I am sure that the work so done has had in it the best truth and the highest spirit that I have been able to produce. At such times I have been able to imbue myself thoroughly with the characters I have had in hand. I have wandered alone among the rocks and woods, crying at their grief, laughing at their absurdities, and thoroughly enjoying their joy. I have been impregnated with my own creations till it has been my only excitement to sit with the pen in my hand, and drive my team before me at as quick a pace as I could make them travel.

The critics will again say that all this may be very well as to the rough work of the author's own brain, but it will be very far from well in reference to the style in which that work has been given to the public. After all, the vehicle which a writer uses for conveying his thoughts to the public should not be less important to him than the thoughts themselves. An author can hardly hope to be popular unless he can use popular language. That is quite true; but then comes the question of achieving a popular—in other words, I may say, a good and lucid style. How may an author best acquire a mode of writing which shall be agreeable and easily intelligible to the reader? He must be correct, because without correctness he can be neither agreeable nor intelligible. Readers will expect him to obey those rules which they, consciously or unconsciously, have been taught to regard as binding on language; and unless he does obey them, he will disgust. Without much labour, no writer will achieve such a style. He has very much to learn; and, when he has learned that much, he has to acquire the habit of using what he has learned with ease. But all this must be learned and acquired,—not while he is writing that which shall please, but long before. His language must come from him as music comes from the rapid touch of the great performer's fingers; as words come from the mouth of the indignant orator; as letters fly from the fingers of the trained compositor; as the syllables tinkled out by little bells form themselves to the ear of the telegraphist. A man who thinks much of his words as he writes them will generally leave behind him work that smells of oil. I speak here, of course, of prose; for in poetry we know what care is necessary, and we form our taste accordingly.

Rapid writing will no doubt give rise to inaccuracy,—chiefly because the ear, quick and true as may be its operation, will occasion-ally break down under pressure, and, before a sentence be closed, will forget the nature of the composition with which it was commenced. A singular nominative will be disgraced by a plural verb, because other pluralities have intervened and have tempted the ear into plural tendencies. Tautologies will occur, because the ear, in demanding fresh emphasis, has forgotten that the desired force has been already expressed. I need not multiply these causes of error, which must have been stumbling-blocks indeed when men wrote in the long sentences of Gibbon, but which Macaulay,* with his multiplicity of divisions, has done so much to enable us to avoid. A rapid writer will hardly avoid these errors altogether. Speaking of myself, I am ready to declare that, with much training, I have been unable to avoid them. But the writer for the press is rarely called upon—a writer of books should never be called upon—to send his manuscript hot from his hand to the printer. It has been my practice to read everything four times at least—thrice in manuscript and once in print. Very much of my work I have read twice in print. In spite of this I know that inaccuracies have crept through,—not single spies, but in battalions.* From this I gather that the supervision has been insufficient, not that the work itself has been done too fast. I am quite sure that those passages which have been written with the greatest stress of labour, and consequently with the greatest haste, have been the most effective and by no means the most inaccurate.

The Small House at Allington redeemed my reputation with the spirited proprietor of the Cornhill, which must, I should think, have been damaged by Brown, Jones, and Robinson. In it appeared Lily Dale, one of the characters which readers of my novels have liked the best. In the love with which she has been greeted I have hardly joined with much enthusiasm, feeling that she is somewhat of a female prig.* She became first engaged to a snob, who jilted her; and then, though in truth she loved another man who was hardly good enough, she could not extricate herself sufficiently from the collapse of her first great misfortune to be able to make up her mind to be the wife of one whom, though she loved him, she did not altogether reverence. Prig as she was, she made her way into the hearts of many readers, both young and old; so that, from that time to this, I have been continually honoured with letters, the purport of which has always been to beg me to marry Lily Dale to Johnny Eames. Had I done so, however, Lily would never have so endeared herself to these people as to induce them to write letters to the author concerning her fate. It was because she could not get over her troubles that they loved her. Outside Lily Dale and the chief interest of the novel, The Small House at Allington is, I think, good. The De Courcy family are alive, as is also Sir Raffle Buffle, who is a hero of the Civil Service. Sir Raffle was intended to represent a type, not a man; but the man for the picture was soon chosen, and I was often assured that the portrait was very like. I have never seen the gentleman with whom I am supposed to have taken the liberty. There is also an old squire down at Allington, whose life as a country gentleman with rather straitened means is, I think, well described.

Of *Can You Forgive Her?* I cannot speak with too great affection, though I do not know that of itself it did very much to increase my reputation. As regards the story, it was formed chiefly on that of the play which my friend Mr Bartley had rejected long since, the circumstances of which the reader may perhaps remember. The play had been called *The Noble Jilt*; but I was afraid of the name for a novel, lest the critics might throw a doubt on the nobility. There was more of tentative humility in that which I at last adopted. The character of the girl is carried through with considerable strength, but is not attractive. The humorous characters, which are also taken from the play,— a buxom widow who with her eyes open chooses the most scampish of two selfish suitors because he is the better looking,—are well done. Mrs Greenow, between Captain Bellfield and Mr Cheeseacre, is very good fun—as far as the fun of novels is. But that which endears the book to me is the first presentation which I made in it of Plantagenet Palliser, with his wife, Lady Glencora.

By no amount of description or asseveration could I succeed in making any reader understand how much these characters with their belongings have been to me in my latter life; or how frequently I have used them for the expression of my political or social convictions. They have been as real to me as free trade was to Mr Cobden, or the dominion of a party to Mr Disraeli;* and as I have not been able to speak from the benches of the House of Commons, or to thunder from platforms, or to be efficacious as a lecturer, they have served me as safety-valves by which to deliver my soul. Mr Plantagenet Palliser had appeared in *The Small House at Allington*, but his birth had not been accompanied by many hopes. In the last pages of that novel he is made to seek a remedy for a foolish false step in life by marrying the grand heiress of the day;—but the personage of the great heiress does not appear till she comes on the scene as a married woman in *Can You Forgive Her?* He is the nephew and heir to a duke—the

Duke of Omnium—who was first introduced in *Doctor Thorne*, and afterwards in *Framley Parsonage*, and who is one of the belongings of whom I have spoken. In these personages and their friends, political and social, I have endeavoured to depict the faults and frailties and vices,—as also the virtues, the graces, and the strength of our highest classes; and if I have not made the strength and virtues predominant over the faults and vices, I have not painted the picture as I intended. Plantagenet Palliser I think to be a very noble gentleman,—such a one as justifies to the nation the seeming anomaly of an hereditary peerage and of primogeniture.* His wife is in all respects very* inferior to him; but she, too, has, or has been intended to have, beneath the thin stratum of her follies a basis of good principle, which enabled her to live down the conviction of the original wrong which was done to her, and taught her to endeavour to do her duty* in the position to which she was called. She had received a great wrong,—having been made, when little more than a child, to marry a man for whom she cared nothing;—when, however, though she was little more than a child, her love had been given elsewhere. She had very heavy troubles, but they did not overcome her.

As to the heaviest of these troubles, I will say a word in vindication of myself and of the way I handled it in my work. In the pages of *Can You Forgive Her?* the girl's first love is introduced,—beautiful, well-born, and utterly worthless. To save a girl from wasting herself, and an heiress from wasting her property on such a scamp, was certainly the duty of the girl's friends. But it must ever be wrong to force a girl into a marriage with a man she does not love,—and certainly the more so when there is another whom she does love. In my endeavour to teach this lesson I subjected the young wife to the terrible danger of overtures from the man to whom her heart had been given. I was walking no doubt on ticklish ground, leaving for a while a doubt on the question whether the lover might or might not succeed. Then there came to me a letter from a distinguished dignitary of our Church,* a man whom all men honoured, treating me with severity for what I was doing. It had been one of the innocent joys of his life, said the clergyman, to have my novels read to him by his daughters. But now I was writing a book which caused him to bid them close it! Must I also turn away to vicious sensation such as this? Did I think that a wife contemplating adultery was a character fit for my pages? I asked him in return, whether from his pulpit, or at any rate from his communion-table, he did not denounce adultery to his audience; and if so, why should it not be open to me to preach the same doctrine to mine. I made known nothing which the purest girl could not but have learned, and ought not to have learned, elsewhere, and I certainly lent no attraction to the sin which I indicated. His rejoinder was full of grace, and enabled him to avoid the annoyance of argumentation without abandoning his cause. He said that the subject was so much too long for letters; that he hoped I would go and stay a week with him in the country,—so that we might have it out. That opportunity, however, has never yet arrived.

Lady Glencora overcomes that trouble, and is brought, partly by her own sense of right and wrong, and partly by the genuine nobility of her husband's conduct, to attach herself to him after a certain fashion. The romance of her life is gone, but there remains a rich reality of which she is fully able to taste the flavour. She loves her rank and becomes ambitious, first of social, and then of political ascendancy. He is thoroughly true to her, after his thorough nature, and she, after her less perfect nature, is imperfectly true to him.

In conducting these characters from one story to another I realised the necessity, not only of consistency,—which, had it been maintained by a hard exactitude, would have been untrue to nature,—but also of those changes which time always produces. There are, perhaps, but few of us who, after the lapse of ten years, will be found to have changed our chief characteristics. The selfish man will still be selfish, and the false man false. But our manner of showing or of hiding these characteristics will be changed,—as also our power of adding to or diminishing their intensity. It was my study that these people, as they grew in years, should encounter the changes which come upon us all; and I think that I have succeeded. The Duchess of Omnium, when she is playing the part of Prime Minister's wife, is the same woman as that Lady Glencora who almost longs to go off with Burgo Fitzgerald, but yet knows that she will never do so; and the Prime Minister Duke, with his wounded pride and sore spirit, is he who, for his wife's sake, left power and place when they were first offered to him;—but they have undergone the changes which a life so stirring as theirs would naturally produce. To do all this thoroughly was in my heart from first to last; but I do not know that the game has been worth the candle. To carry out my scheme I have had to spread my picture over so wide a canvas that I cannot expect that any lover of such art should trouble himself to look at it as a whole. Who will read *Can You Forgive Her?*, *Phineas Finn*, *Phineas Redux*, and *The Prime Minister* consecutively, in order that they may understand the characters of the Duke of Omnium, of Plantagenet Palliser, and of Lady Glencora? Who will even* know that they should be so read? But in the performance of the work I had much gratification, and was enabled from time to time to have in this way that fling at the political doings of the day which every man likes to take, if not in one fashion then in another. I look upon this string of characters,—carried sometimes into other novels than those just named,—as the best work of my life. Taking him altogether, I think that Plantagenet Palliser stands more firmly on the ground than any other personage I have created.

On Christmas day 1863 we were startled by the news of Thackeray's death. He had then for many months given up the editorship of the *Cornhill Magazine*,—a position for which he was hardly fitted either by his habits or temperament—but was still employed in writing for its pages. I had known him only for four years, but had grown into much intimacy with him and his family. I regard him as one of the most tender-hearted human beings I ever knew, who, with an exaggerated contempt for the foibles of the world at large, would entertain an almost equally exaggerated sympathy with the joys and troubles of individuals around him. He had been unfortunate* in early life— unfortunate in regard to money—unfortunate with an afflicted wife— unfortunate in having his home broken up before his children were fit to be his companions. This threw him too much upon clubs, and taught him to dislike general society. But it never affected his heart, or clouded his imagination. He could still revel in the pangs and joys of fictitious life, and could still feel—as he did to the very last—the duty of showing to his readers the evil consequences of evil conduct. It was perhaps his chief fault as a writer that he could never abstain from that dash of satire which he felt to be demanded by the weaknesses which he saw around him. The satirist who writes nothing but satire should write but little,—or it will seem that his satire springs rather from his own caustic nature than from the sins of the world in which he lives. I myself regard *Esmond* as the greatest novel in the English language, basing that judgment upon the excellence of its language, on the clear individuality of the characters, on the truth of its delineations in regard to the time selected, and on its great pathos. There are also in it a few scenes so told that even Scott has never equalled the telling. Let any one who doubts this read the passage in which Lady Castlewood* induces the Duke of Hamilton to think that his nuptials with Beatrice will be honoured if Colonel Esmond will give away the bride. When he went from us he left behind living novelists with great names; but I think that they who best understood the matter felt that the greatest master of fiction of this age had gone.

Rachel Ray underwent a fate which no other novel of mine has encountered. Some years before this a periodical called *Good Words** had been established under the editorship of my friend Dr Norman Macleod, a well-known Presbyterian pastor in Glasgow. In 1863 he asked me to write a novel for his magazine, explaining to me that his principles did not teach him to confine his matter to religious subjects, and paying me the compliment of saying that he would feel himself quite safe in my hands. In reply I told him I thought he was wrong in his choice; that though he might wish to give a novel to the readers of *Good Words*, a novel from me would hardly be what he wanted, and that I could not undertake to write either with any specially religious tendency, or in any fashion different from that which was usual to me. As worldly and—if any one thought me wicked—as wicked as I had heretofore been, I must still be, should I write for *Good Words*. He persisted in his request, and I came to terms as to a story for the periodical. I wrote it and sent it to him, and shortly afterwards received it back— a considerable portion having been printed—with an intimation that it would not do. A letter more full of wailing and repentance no man ever wrote. It was, he said, all his own fault. He should have taken my advice. He should have known better. But the story, such as it was, he could not give to his readers in the pages of *Good Words*. Would I forgive him? Any pecuniary loss to which his decision might subject me the owner of the publication would willingly make good.* There was some loss—or rather would have been—and that money I exacted, feeling that the fault had in truth been with the editor. There is the tale now to speak for itself. It is not brilliant, nor in any way very excellent; but it certainly is not very wicked. There is some dancing in one of the early chapters, described, no doubt, with that approval of the amusement which I have always entertained; and it was this to which my friend demurred. It is more true of novels than perhaps of anything else, that one man's food is another man's poison.

Miss Mackenzie was written with a desire to prove that a novel may be produced without any love; but even in this attempt it breaks down before the conclusion. In order that I might be strong in my purpose, I took for my heroine a very unattractive old maid, who was overwhelmed with money troubles; but even she was in love before the end of the book, and made a romantic marriage with an old man. There is in this story an attack upon charitable bazaars, made with a violence which will, I think, convince any reader that such attempts at raising money were at the time very odious to me. I beg to say that since that I have had no occasion to alter my opinion. *Miss Mackenzie* was published in the early spring of 1865.

At the same time I was engaged with others in establishing a periodical Review, in which some of us trusted much, and from which we expected great things. There was, however, in truth so little combination of idea among us, that we were not justified in our trust or in our expectations. And yet we were honest in our purpose, and have, I think, done some good by our honesty. The matter on which we were all agreed was freedom of speech, combined with personal responsibility. We would be neither conservative nor liberal, neither religious nor free-thinking, neither popular nor exclusive;—but we would let any man who had a thing to say, and knew how to say it, speak freely. But he should always speak with the responsibility of his name attached.* In the very beginning I militated against this impossible negation of principles,—and did so most irrationally, seeing that I had agreed to the negation of principles,—by declaring that nothing should appear denying or questioning the divinity of Christ. It was a most preposterous claim to make for such a publication as we proposed, and it at once drove from us one or two who had proposed to join us. But we went on, and our company—limited—was formed. We subscribed, I think, £1250 each. I at least subscribed that amount, and—having agreed to bring out our publication every fortnight, after the manner of the well-known French publication,*—we called it *The Fortnightly.* We secured the services of G. H. Lewes as our editor. We agreed to manage our finances by a Board, which was to meet once a fortnight, and of which I was the Chairman. And we determined that the payments for our literature should be made on a liberal and strictly ready-money system. We carried out our principles till our money was all gone, and then we sold the copyright to Messrs Chapman & Hall for a trifle. But before we parted with our property we found that a fortnightly issue was not popular with the trade through whose hands the work must reach the public; and, as our periodical had not become sufficiently popular itself to bear down such opposition, we succumbed, and brought it out once a month. Still it was *The Fortnightly*, and still it is *The Fortnightly*. Of all the serial publications of the day, it probably is the most serious, the most earnest, the least devoted to amusement, the least flippant, the least jocose,—and yet it has the face to show itself month after month to the world, with so absurd a misnomer! It is, as all who know the laws of modern literature are aware, a very serious thing to change the name of a periodical. By doing so you begin an altogether new enterprise. Therefore should the name be well chosen;—whereas this was very ill chosen, a fault for which I alone was responsible.

That theory of eclecticism was altogether impracticable. It was as though a gentleman should go into the House of Commons determined to support no party, but to serve his country by individual utterances. Such gentlemen have gone into the House of Commons, but they have not served their country much. Of course the project broke down. Liberalism, free-thinking, and open inquiry will never object to appear in company with their opposites, because they have the conceit to think that they can quell those opposites; but the opposites will not appear in conjunction with liberalism, free-thinking, and open inquiry. As a natural consequence, our new publication became an organ of liberalism, free-thinking, and open inquiry. The result has been good; and though there is much in the now established principles of *The Fortnightly* with which I do not myself agree, I may safely say that the publication has assured an individuality, and asserted for itself a position in our periodical literature, which is well understood and highly respected.

As to myself and my own hopes in the matter,—I was craving after some increase in literary honesty, which I think is still desirable, but which is hardly to be attained by the means which then recommended themselves to me. In one of the early numbers I wrote a paper advocating the signature of the authors to periodical writing, admitting that the system should not be extended to journalistic articles on political subjects. I think that I made the best of my case; but further consideration has caused me to doubt whether the reasons which induced me to make an exception in favour of political writing do not extend themselves also to writing on other subjects. Much of the literary criticism which we now have is very bad indeed;—so bad as to be open to the charge both of dishonesty and incapacity. Books are criticised without being read,—are criticised by favour,—and are trusted by editors to the criticism of the incompetent. If the names of the critics were demanded, editors would be more careful. But I fear the effect would be that we should get but little criticism, and that the public would put but little trust in that little. An ordinary reader would not care to have his books recommended to him by Jones; but the recommendation of the great unknown comes to him with all the weight of the *Times*, the *Spectator*, or the *Saturday*.

Though I admit so much, I am not a recreant from the doctrine I then preached. I think that the name of the author does tend to honesty, and that the knowledge that it will be inserted adds much to the author's industry and care. It debars him also from illegitimate license and dishonest assertions. A man should never be ashamed to acknowledge that which he is not ashamed to publish. In *The Fortnightly* everything has been signed, and in this way good has, I think, been done. Signatures to articles in other periodicals have become much more common since *The Fortnightly* was commenced.

After a time Mr Lewes retired from the editorship, feeling that the work pressed too severely on his moderate strength. Our loss in him was very great, and there was considerable difficulty in finding a successor. I must say that the present proprietor has been fortunate in the choice he did make. Mr John Morley* has done the work with admirable patience, zeal, and capacity. Of course he has got around him a set of contributors whose modes of thought are what we may call much advanced; he being 'much advanced' himself, would not work with other aids. The periodical has a peculiar tone of its own; but it holds its own with ability, and though there are many who perhaps hate it, there are none who despise it. When the company sold it, having spent about £9000 on it, it was worth little or nothing. Now I believe it to be a good property.

My own last personal concern with it was on a matter of fox-hunting.[1] There came out in it an article from the pen of Mr Freeman* the historian, condemning the amusement, which I love, on the grounds of cruelty and general brutality. Was it possible, asked Mr Freeman, quoting from Cicero, that any educated man should

---

[1] I have written various articles for it since, especially two on Cicero,* to which I devoted great labour.

find delight in so coarse a pursuit? Always bearing in mind my own connection with *The Fortnightly*, I regarded this almost as a rising of a child against the father. I felt at any rate bound to answer Mr Freeman in the same columns, and I obtained Mr Morley's permission to do so. I wrote my defence of fox-hunting, and there it is. In regard to the charge of cruelty, Mr Freeman seems to assert that nothing unpleasant should be done to any of God's creatures except for a useful purpose. The protection of a lady's shoulders from the cold is a useful purpose; and therefore a dozen fur-bearing animals may be snared in the snow and left to starve to death in the wires, in order that the lady may have the tippet,—though a tippet of wool would serve the purpose as well as a tippet of fur. But the congregation and healthful amusement of one or two hundred persons, on whose behalf a single fox may or may not be killed, is not a useful purpose. I think that Mr Freeman has failed to perceive that amusement is as needful and almost as necessary as food and raiment. The absurdity of the further charge as to the general brutality of the pursuit, and its consequent unfitness for an educated man, is to be attributed to Mr Freeman's ignorance of what is really done and said in the hunting-field,—perhaps to his misunderstanding of Cicero's words. There was a rejoinder to my answer, and I asked for space for further remarks. I could have it, the editor said, if I much wished it; but he preferred that the subject should be closed. Of course I was silent. His sympathies were all with Mr Freeman,—and against the foxes, who, but for foxhunting, would cease to exist in England. And I felt that *The Fortnightly* was hardly the place for the defence of the sport. Afterwards Mr Freeman kindly suggested to me that he would be glad to publish my article in a little book to be put out by him condemnatory of fox-hunting generally. He was to have the last word and the first word, and that power of picking to pieces which he is known to use in so masterly a manner, without any reply from me! This I was obliged to decline. If he would give me the last word, as he would have the first, then, I told him, I should be proud to join him in the book. This offer did not however meet his views.

It had been decided by the Board of Management, somewhat in opposition to my own ideas on the subject, that the *Fortnightly Review* should always contain a novel. It was of course natural that I should write the first novel, and I wrote *The Belton Estate*. It is similar in its attributes to *Rachel Ray* and to *Miss Mackenzie*. It is readable, and contains scenes which are true to life; but it has no peculiar merits, and will add nothing to my reputation as a novelist. I have not looked at it since it was published; and now turning back to it in my memory, I seem to remember almost less of it than of any book that I have written.

CHAPTER 11

'The Claverings', the 'Pall Mall Gazette', 'Nina Balatka', and 'Linda Tressel'

*T*HE *Claverings*, which came out in 1866 and 1867, was the last novel which I wrote for the *Cornhill*; and it was for this that I received the highest rate of pay that was ever accorded to me. It was the same length as *Framley Parsonage*, and the price was £2800. Whether much or little, it was offered by the proprietor of the magazine, and was paid in a single cheque.

In *The Claverings* I did not follow the habit* which had now become very common to me, of introducing personages whose names are already known to the readers of novels, and whose characters were familiar to myself. If I remember rightly, no one appears here who had appeared before or who has been allowed to appear since. I consider the story as a whole to be good, though I am not aware that the public has ever corroborated that verdict. The chief character is that of a young woman who has married manifestly for money and rank,—so manifestly that she does not herself pretend, even while she is making the marriage, that she has any other reason. The man is old, disreputable, and a worn-out debauchee. Then comes the punishment natural to the offence. When she is free, the man whom she had loved, and who had loved her, is engaged to another woman. He vacillates and is weak,—in which weakness is the fault of the book, as he plays the part of hero. But she is strong—strong in her purpose, strong in her desires, and strong in her consciousness that the punishment which comes upon her has been deserved.

But the chief merit of *The Claverings* is in the genuine fun of some of the scenes. Humour has not been my forte, but I am inclined to think that the characters of Captain Boodle, Archie Clavering, and Sophie Gordeloup are humorous. Count Pateroff, the brother of Sophie, is also good, and disposes of the young hero's interference in a somewhat masterly manner. In *The Claverings*, too, there is a wife whose husband is a brute to her, who loses an only child—his heir—and who is rebuked by her lord because the boy dies. Her sorrow is,

I think, pathetic. From beginning to end the story is well told, But I doubt now whether any one reads *The Claverings*. When I remember how many novels I have written, I have no right to expect that above a few of them shall endure even to the second year beyond publication. This story closed my connection with the *Cornhill Magazine*;—— but not with its owner, Mr George Smith, who subsequently brought out a further novel of mine* in a separate form, and who about this time established the *Pall Mall Gazette*,* to which paper I was for some years a contributor.

It was in 1865 that the *Pall Mall Gazette* was commenced, the name having been taken from a fictitious periodical, which was the offspring of Thackeray's brain. It was set on foot by the unassisted energy and resources of George Smith, who had succeeded by means of his magazine and his publishing connection in getting around him a society of literary men who sufficed, as far as literary ability went, to float the paper at once under favourable auspices. His two strongest staffs probably were 'Jacob Omnium,' whom I regard as the most forcible newspaper writer of my days, and Fitz-James Stephen, the most conscientious and industrious. To them the *Pall Mall Gazette* owed very much of its early success,—and to the untiring energy and general ability of its proprietor. Among its other contributors were George Lewes, Hannay,—who, I think, came up from Edinburgh for employment on its columns,—Lord Houghton, Lord Strangford, Charles Merivale, Greenwood the present editor, Greg,* myself, and very many others;—so many others, that I have met at a Pall Mall dinner a crowd of guests who would have filled the House of Commons more respectably than I have seen it filled even on important occasions. There are many who now remember—and no doubt when this is published there will be left some to remember—the great stroke of business which was done by the revelations of a visitor* to one of the casual wards in London. A person had to be selected who would undergo the misery of a night among the usual occupants of a casual ward in a London poor-house, and who should at the same time be able to record what he felt and saw. The choice fell upon Mr Greenwood's brother, who certainly possessed the courage and the powers of endurance. The description, which was very well given, was, I think, chiefly written by the brother of the Casual himself. It had a great effect, which was increased by secrecy as to the person who encountered all the horrors of that night. I was more than once assured that Lord Houghton was the man. I heard it asserted also that I myself had been the hero. At last the unknown one could no longer endure that his honours should be hidden, and revealed the truth,— in opposition, I fear, to promises to the contrary, and instigated by a conviction that if known he could turn his honours to account. In the meantime, however, that record of a night passed in a workhouse had done more to establish the sale of the journal than all the legal lore of Stephen, or the polemical power of Higgins, or the critical acumen of Lewes.

My work was very various. I wrote much on the subject of the American War, on which my feelings were at the time very keen,— subscribing, if I remember right, my name to all that I wrote. I contributed also some sets of sketches, of which those concerning hunting found favour with the public. They were republished afterwards, and had a considerable sale, and may, I think, still be recommended to those who are fond of hunting, as being accurate in their description of the different classes of people who are to be met in the hunting-field. There was also a set of clerical sketches, which was considered to be of sufficient importance to bring down upon my head the critical wrath of a great dean* of that period. The most ill-natured review that was ever written upon any work of mine appeared in the *Contemporary Review* with reference to these Clerical Sketches. The critic told me that I did not understand Greek. That charge has been made not unfrequently by those who have felt themselves strong in that pride-producing language. It is much to read Greek with ease, but it is not disgraceful to be unable to do so. To pretend to read it without being able,—that is disgraceful. The critic, however, had been driven to wrath by my saying that Deans of the Church of England loved to revisit the glimpses of the metropolitan moon.

I also did some critical work for the *Pall Mall*,—as I did also for *The Fortnightly*. It was not to my taste, but was done in conformity with strict conscientious scruples. I read what I took in hand, and said what I believed to be true,—always giving to the matter time altogether incommensurate with the pecuniary result to myself. In doing this for the *Pall Mall*, I fell into great sorrow. A gentleman,* whose wife was dear to me as if she were my own sister, was in some trouble as to his conduct in the public service. He had been blamed, as he thought unjustly, and vindicated himself in a pamphlet. This he handed to me one day, asking me to read it, and express my opinion about it if I found that

I had an opinion. I thought the request injudicious, and I did not read the pamphlet. He met me again, and, handing me a second pamphlet, pressed me very hard. I promised him that I would read it, and that if I found myself able I would express myself;—but that I must say not what I wished to think, but what I did think. To this of course he assented. I then went very much out of my way to study the subject,—which was one requiring study. I found, or thought that I found, that the conduct of the gentleman in his office had been indiscreet; but that charges made against himself affecting his honour were baseless. This I said, emphasising much more strongly than was necessary the opinion which I had formed of his indiscretion,—as will so often be the case when a man has a pen in his hand. It is like a club or a sledge-hammer,—in using which, either for defence or attack, a man can hardly measure the strength of the blows he gives. Of course, there was offence,—and a breaking off of intercourse between loving friends,—and a sense of wrong received, and I must own, too, of wrong done. It certainly was not open to me to whitewash with honesty him whom I did not find to be white; but there was no duty incumbent on me to declare what was his colour in my eyes,—no duty even to ascertain. But I had been ruffled by the persistency of the gentleman's request,—which should not have been made,—and I punished him for his wrong-doing by doing a wrong myself. I must add, that before he died his wife succeeded in bringing us together.

In the early days of the paper, the proprietor, who at that time acted also as chief editor, asked me to undertake a duty,—of which the agony would indeed at no one moment have been so sharp as that endured in the casual ward, but might have been prolonged until human nature sank under it. He suggested to me that I should during an entire season attend the May meetings in Exeter Hall,* and give a graphic and, if possible, amusing description of the proceedings. I did attend one,—which lasted three hours,—and wrote a paper which I think was called *A Zulu in Search of a Religion*. But when the meeting was over I went to that spirited proprietor, and begged him to impose upon me some task more equal to my strength. Not even on behalf of the *Pall Mall Gazette*, which was very dear to me, could I go through a second May meeting,—much less endure a season of such martyrdom.

I have to acknowledge that I found myself unfit for work on a newspaper. I had not taken to it early enough in life to learn its ways and bear its trammels. I was fidgety when any word was altered in accordance with the judgment of the editor, who, of course, was responsible for what appeared. I wanted to select my own subjects,—not to have them selected for me; to write when I pleased,—and not when it suited others. As a permanent member of a staff I was no use, and after two or three years I dropped out of the work.

From the commencement of my success as a writer, which I date from the beginning of the *Cornhill Magazine*, I had always felt an injustice in literary affairs which had never afflicted me or even suggested itself to me while I was unsuccessful. It seemed to me that a name once earned carried with it too much favour. I indeed had never reached a height to which praise was awarded as a matter of course; but there were others who sat on higher seats to whom the critics brought unmeasured incense and adulation, even when they wrote, as they sometimes did write, trash which from a beginner would not have been thought worthy of the slightest notice. I hope no one will think that in saying this I am actuated by jealousy of others. Though I never reached that height, still I had so far progressed that that which I wrote was received with too much favour. The injustice which struck me did not consist in that which was withheld from me, but in that which was given to me. I felt that aspirants coming up below me might do work as good as mine, and probably much better work, and yet fail to have it appreciated. In order to test this, I determined to be such an aspirant myself, and to begin a course of novels anonymously, in order that I might see whether I could obtain a second identity,—whether as I had made one mark by such literary ability as I possessed, I might succeed in doing so again. In 1865 I began a short tale called *Nina Balatka*, which in 1866 was published anonymously in *Blackwood's Magazine*. In 1867 this was followed by another of the same length, called *Linda Tressel*. I will speak of them together, as they are of the same nature and of nearly equal merit. Mr Blackwood, who himself read the MS. of *Nina Balatka*, expressed an opinion that it would not from its style be discovered to have been written by me;—but it was discovered by Mr Hutton* of the *Spectator*, who found the repeated use of some special phrase which had rested upon his ear too frequently when reading for the purpose of criticism other works of mine. He declared in his paper that *Nina Balatka* was by me, showing I think more sagacity than good nature. I ought not, however, to complain of him, as of all the critics of my work he has been the most observant, and generally the most eulogistic. *Nina Balatka* never rose sufficiently high in reputation to make its detection a matter of any importance. Once or twice I heard the story mentioned by readers who did not know me to be the author, and always with praise; but it had no real success. The same may be said of *Linda Tressel*. Blackwood, who of course knew the author, was willing to publish them, trusting that works by an experienced writer would make their way, even without the writer's name, and he was willing to pay me for them, perhaps half what they would have fetched with my name. But he did not find the speculation answer, and declined a third attempt, though a third such tale was written for him.

Nevertheless I am sure that the two stories are good. Perhaps the first is somewhat the better, as being the less lachrymose. They were both written very quickly, but with a considerable amount of labour; and both were written immediately after visits to the towns in which the scenes are laid,—Prague, mainly, and Nuremberg.* Of course I had endeavoured to change not only my manner of language, but my manner of story-telling also; and in this, *pace* Mr Hutton, I think that I was successful. English life in them there was none. There was more of romance proper than had been usual with me. And I made an attempt at local colouring, at descriptions of scenes and places, which has not been usual with me. In all this I am confident that I was in a measure successful. In the loves, and fears, and hatreds, both of Nina and of Linda, there is much that is pathetic. Prague is Prague, and Nuremberg is Nuremberg. I know that the stories are good, but they missed the object with which they had been written. Of course there is not in this any evidence that I might not have succeeded a second time as I succeeded before, had I gone on with the same dogged perseverance. Mr Blackwood, had I still further reduced my price, would probably have continued the experiment.* Another ten years of unpaid unflagging labour might have built up a second reputation. But this at any rate did seem clear to me, that with all the increased advantages which practice in my art must have given me, I could not at once induce English readers to read what I gave to them, unless I gave it with my name.

I do not wish to have it supposed from this that I quarrel with public judgment in affairs of literature. It is a matter of course that in all things the public should trust to established reputation. It is as natural that a novel reader wanting novels should send to a library for those by George Eliot or Wilkie Collins, as that a lady when she wants a pie for a picnic should go to Fortnum & Mason.* Fortnum & Mason can only make themselves Fortnum & Mason by dint of time and good pies combined. If Titian were to send us a portrait from the other world, as certain dead poets send their poetry, by means of a medium, it would be some time before the art critic of the *Times* would discover its value. We may sneer at the want of judgment thus displayed, but such slowness of judgment is human and has always existed. I say all this here because my thoughts on the matter have forced upon me the conviction that very much consideration is due to the bitter feelings of disappointed authors.

We who have succeeded are so apt to tell new aspirants not to aspire, because the thing to be done may probably be beyond their reach. 'My dear young lady, had you not better stay at home and darn your stockings?' 'As, sir, you have asked for my candid opinion, I can only counsel you to try some other walk* of life which may be better suited to your abilities.' What old-established successful author has not said such words as these to humble aspirants for critical advice, till they have become almost formulas? No doubt there is cruelty in such answers; but the man who makes them has considered the matter within himself, and has resolved that such cruelty is the best mercy. No doubt the chances against literary aspirants are very great. It is so easy to aspire,—and to begin! A man cannot make a watch or a shoe without a variety of tools and many materials. He must also have learned much. But any young lady can write a book who has a sufficiency of pens and paper. It can be done anywhere; in any clothes—which is a great thing; at any hours—to which happy accident in literature I owe my success. And the success, when achieved, is so pleasant! The aspirants, of course, are very many; and the experienced councillor, when asked for his candid judgment as to this or that effort, knows that among every hundred efforts there will be ninety-nine failures. Then the answer is so ready: 'My dear young lady, do darn your stockings; it will be for the best.' Or perhaps, less tenderly, to the male aspirant: 'You must earn some money, you say. Don't you think that a stool in a counting-house might be better?' The advice will probably be good advice,—probably, no doubt, as may be proved by the terrible majority of failures. But who is to be sure that he is not expelling an angel from the heaven to which, if less roughly treated, he would soar,—that he is not dooming some Milton to be mute and inglorious,* who, but for such cruel ill-judgment, would become vocal to all ages?

The answer to all this seems to be ready enough. The judgment, whether cruel or tender, should not be ill-judgment. He who consents to sit as judge should have capacity for judging. But in this matter no accuracy of judgment is possible. It may be that the matter subjected to the critic is so bad or so good as to make an assured answer possible. 'You, at any rate, cannot make this your vocation;' or 'You, at any rate, can succeed, if you will try.' But cases as to which such certainty can be expressed are rare. The critic who wrote the article on the early verses of Lord Byron,* which produced the *English Bards and Scotch Reviewers*, was justified in his criticism by the merits of the *Hours of Idleness.* The lines had nevertheless been written by that Lord Byron who became our Byron. In a little satire called *The Biliad*,* which, I think, nobody knows, are the following well-expressed lines:—

> 'When Payne Knight's *Taste* was issued to the town,
> A few Greek verses in the text set down
> Were torn to pieces, mangled into hash,
> Doomed to the flames as execrable trash,—
> In short, were butchered rather than dissected,
> And several false quantities detected,—
> Till, when the smoke had vanished from the cinders,
> 'Twas just discovered that—*the lines were Pindar's!*'

There can be no assurance against cases such as these; and yet we are so free with our advice, always bidding the young aspirant to desist.

There is perhaps no career of life so charming as that of a successful man of letters. Those little unthought of advantages which I just now named are in themselves attractive. If you like the town, live in the town, and do your work there; if you like the country, choose the country. It may be done on the top of a mountain or in the bottom of a pit. It is compatible with the rolling of the sea and the motion of a railway. The clergyman, the lawyer, the doctor, the member of Parliament, the clerk in a public office, the tradesman, and even his assistant in the shop, must dress in accordance with certain fixed laws; but the author need sacrifice to no grace, hardly even to Propriety. He is subject to no bonds such as those which bind other men. Who else is free from all shackle as to hours? The judge must sit at ten, and the attorney-general,* who is making his £20,000 a year, must be there with his bag. The Prime Minister must be in his place on that weary front bench shortly after prayers, and must sit there, either asleep or awake, even though —— or —— should be addressing the House. During all that Sunday which he maintains should be a day of rest, the active clergyman toils like a galley-slave. The actor, when eight o'clock comes, is bound to his footlights. The Civil Service clerk must sit there from ten till four,—unless his office be fashionable, when twelve to six is just as heavy on him. The author may do his work at five in the morning when he is fresh from his bed, or at three in the morning before he goes there. And the author wants no capital, and encounters no risks. When once he is afloat, the publisher finds all that;—and indeed, unless he be rash, finds it whether he be afloat or not. But it is in the consideration which he enjoys that the successful author finds his richest reward. He is, if not of equal rank, yet of equal standing with the highest; and if he be open to the amenities of society, may choose his own circles. He without money can enter doors which are closed against almost all but him and the wealthy. I have often heard it said that in this country the man of letters is not recognised. I believe the meaning of this to be that men of letters are not often invited to be knights and baronets. I do not think that they wish it;—and if they had it they would, as a body, lose much more than they would gain. I do not at all desire to have letters put after my name, or to be called Sir Anthony, but if my friends Tom Hughes and Charles Reade* became Sir Thomas and Sir Charles, I do not know how I might feel,—or how my wife might feel, if we were left unbedecked. As it is, the man of letters who would be selected for titular honour, if such bestowal of honours were customary, receives from the general respect of those around him a much more pleasant recognition of his worth.

If this be so,—if it be true that the career of the successful literary man be thus pleasant,—it is not wonderful that many should attempt to win the prize. But how is a man to know whether or not he has within him the qualities necessary for such a career? He makes an attempt, and fails; repeats his attempt, and fails again! So many have succeeded at last who have failed more than once or twice! Who will tell him the truth as to himself? Who has power to find out that truth? The hard man sends him off without a scruple to that office-stool; the soft man assures him that there is much merit in his MS.

Oh, my young aspirant,—if ever such a one should read these pages,—be sure that no one can tell you! To do so it would be necessary not only to know what there is now within you, but also to foresee what time will produce there. This, however, I think may be said to you, without any doubt as to the wisdom of the counsel given, that if it be necessary for you to live by your work, do not begin by trusting to literature. Take the stool in the office as recommended to you by the hard man; and then, in such leisure hours as may belong to you, let the praise which has come from the lips of that soft man induce you to persevere in your literary attempts. Should you fail, then your failure will not be fatal,—and what better could you have done with the leisure hours had you not so failed? Such double toil, you will say, is severe. Yes; but if you want this thing, you must submit to severe toil.

Sometime before this I had become one of the Committee appointed for the distribution of the moneys of the Royal Literary Fund, and in that capacity I heard and saw much of the sufferings of authors. I may in a future chapter speak further of this Institution, which I regard with great affection, and in reference to which I should be glad to record certain convictions of my own; but I allude to it now, because the experience I have acquired in being active in its cause forbids me to advise any young man or woman to enter boldly on a literary career in search of bread. I know how utterly I should have failed myself had my bread not been earned elsewhere while I was making my efforts. During ten years of work, which I commenced with some aid from the fact that others of my family were in the same profession, I did not earn enough to buy me the pens, ink, and paper which I was using; and then when, with all my experience in my art, I began again as from a new springing point, I should have failed again unless again I could have given years to the task. Of course there have been many who have done better than I,—many whose powers have been infinitely greater. But then, too, I have seen the failure of many who were greater.

The career, when success has been achieved, is certainly very pleasant; but the agonies which are endured in the search for that success are often terrible. And the author's poverty is, I think, harder to be borne than any other poverty. The man, whether rightly or wrongly, feels that the world is using him with extreme injustice. The more absolutely he fails, the higher, it is probable, he will reckon his own merits; and the keener will be the sense of injury in that he whose work is of so high a nature cannot get bread, while they whose tasks are mean are lapped in luxury. 'I, with my well-filled mind, with my clear intellect, with all my gifts, cannot earn a poor crown* a day, while that fool, who simpers in a little room behind a shop, makes his thousands every year.' The very charity, to which he too often is driven, is bitterer to him than to others. While he takes it he almost spurns the hand that gives it to him, and every fibre of his heart within him is bleeding with a sense of injury.

The career, when successful, is pleasant enough certainly; but when unsuccessful, it is of all careers the most agonising.

CHAPTER 12

On Novels and the Art of Writing Them

I T is nearly twenty years since I proposed to myself to write a history of English prose fiction.* I shall never do it now, but the subject is so good a one that I recommend it heartily to some man of letters, who shall at the same time be indefatigable and light-handed. I acknowledge that I broke down in the task, because I could not endure the labour in addition to the other labours of my life. Though the book might be charming, the work was very much the reverse. It came to have a terrible aspect to me, as did that proposition that I should sit out all the May meetings* of a season. According to my plan of such a history it would be necessary to read an infinity of novels, and not only to read them, but so to read them as to point out the excellences of those which are most excellent, and to explain the defects of those which, though defective, had still reached sufficient reputation to make them worthy of notice. I did read many after this fashion,—and here and there I have the criticisms which I wrote. In regard to many, they were written on some blank page within the book. I have not, however, even a list of the books so criticised. I think that the *Arcadia* was the first, and *Ivanhoe* the last. My plan, as I settled it at last, had been to begin with *Robinson Crusoe*,* which is the earliest really popular novel which we have in our language, and to continue the review so as to include the works of all English novelists of reputation, except those who might still be living when my task should be completed. But when Dickens and Bulwer died,* my spirit flagged, and that which I had already found to be very difficult had become almost impossible to me at my then period of life.

I began my own studies on the subject with works much earlier than *Robinson Crusoe*, and made my way through a variety of novels which were necessary for my purpose, but which in the reading gave me no pleasure whatever. I never worked harder than at the *Arcadia*, or read more detestable trash than the stories written by Mrs Aphra Behn;* but these two were necessary to my purpose, which was not only to give an estimate of the novels as I found them, but to describe how it had come to pass that the English novels of the present day have become what they are, to point out the effects which they have produced, and to inquire whether their great popularity has on the whole done good or evil to the people who read them. I still think that the book is one well worthy to be written.

I intended to write that book to vindicate my own profession as a novelist, and also to vindicate that public taste in literature which has created and nourished the profession which I follow. And I was stirred up to make such an attempt by a conviction that there still exists among us Englishmen a prejudice in respect to novels which might, perhaps, be lessened by such a work. This prejudice is not against the reading of novels, as is proved by their general acceptance among us. But it exists strongly in reference to the appreciation in which they are professed to be held; and it robs them of much of that high character which they may claim to have earned by their grace, their honesty, and good teaching.

No man can work long at any trade without being brought to consider much whether that which he is daily doing tends to evil or to good. I have written many novels, and have known many writers of novels, and I can assert that such thoughts have been strong with them and with myself. But in acknowledging that these writers have received from the public a full measure of credit for such genius, ingenuity, or perseverance as each may have displayed, I feel that there is still wanting to them a just appreciation of the excellence of their calling, and a general understanding of the high nature of the work which they perform.

By the common consent of all mankind who have read, poetry takes the highest place in literature. That nobility of expression, and all but divine grace of words, which she is bound to attain before she can make her footing good, is not compatible with prose. Indeed it is that which turns prose into poetry. When that has been in truth achieved, the reader knows that the writer has soared above the earth, and can teach his lessons somewhat as a god might teach. He who sits down to write his tale in prose makes no such attempt, nor does he dream that the poet's honour is within his reach;—but his teaching is of the same nature, and his lessons all tend to the same end. By either, false sentiments may be fostered; false notions of humanity may be engendered; false honour, false love, false worship may be created; by either, vice instead of virtue may be taught. But by each, equally, may true honour, true love, true worship, and true humanity be inculcated; and that will be the greatest teacher who will spread such truth the widest. But at present, much as novels, as novels, are bought and read, there exists still an idea, a feeling which is very prevalent, that novels at their best are but innocent. Young men and women,—and old men and women too,—read more of them than of poetry, because such reading is easier than the reading of poetry; but they read them,—as men eat pastry after dinner,—not without some inward conviction that the taste is vain if not vicious. I take upon myself to say that it is neither vicious nor vain.

But all writers of fiction who have desired to think well of their own work, will probably have had doubts on their minds before they have arrived at this conclusion. Thinking much of my own daily labour and of its nature, I felt myself at first to be much afflicted and then to be deeply grieved by the opinion expressed by wise and thinking men as to the work done by novelists.* But when, by degrees, I dared to examine and sift the sayings of such men, I found them to be some-times silly and often arrogant. I began to inquire what had been the nature of English novels since they first became common in our own language, and to be desirous of ascertaining whether they had done harm or good. I could well remember that, in my own young days, they had not taken that undisputed possession of drawing-rooms which they now hold. Fifty years ago, when George IV was king, they were not indeed treated as Lydia had been forced to treat them in the preceding reign, when, on the approach of elders, *Peregrine Pickle* was hidden beneath the bolster, and *Lord Ainsworth* put away under the sofa.* But the families in which an unrestricted permission was given for the reading of novels were very few, and from many they were altogether banished. The high poetic genius and correct morality of Walter Scott had not altogether succeeded in making men and women understand that lessons which were good in poetry could not be bad in prose. I remember that in those days an embargo was laid upon novel-reading as a pursuit, which was to the novelist a much heavier tax than that want of full appreciation of which I now complain.

There is, we all know, no such embargo now. May we not say that people of an age to read have got too much power into their own hands to endure any very complete embargo? Novels are read right and left, above stairs and below, in town houses and in country parsonages, by young countesses and by farmer's daughters, by old lawyers and by young students. It has not only come to pass that a special provision of them has to be made for the godly, but that the provision so made must now include books which a few years since the godly would have thought to be profane. It was this necessity which, a few years since, induced the editor of *Good Words* to apply to me for a novel,—which, indeed, when supplied was rejected, but which now, probably, owing to further change in the same direction, would have been accepted.

If such be the case—if the extension of novel-reading be so wide as I have described it—then very much good or harm must be done by novels. The amusement of the time can hardly be the only result of any book that is read, and certainly not so with a novel, which appeals especially to the imagination, and solicits the sympathy of the young. A vast proportion of the teaching of the day,—greater probably than many of us have acknowledged to ourselves,—comes from these books, which are in the hands of all readers. It is from them that girls learn what is expected from them, and what they are to expect when lovers come; and also from them that young men unconsciously learn what are, or should be, or may be, the charms of love,—though I fancy that few young men will think so little of their natural instincts and powers as to believe that I am right in saying so. Many other lessons also are taught. In these times, when the desire to be honest is pressed so hard, is so violently assaulted by the ambition to be great; in which riches are the easiest road to greatness; when the temptations to which men are subjected dulls their eyes to the perfected iniquities of others; when it is so hard for a man to decide vigorously that the pitch, which so many are handling, will defile him if it be touched;—men's conduct will be actuated much by that which is from day to day depicted to them as leading to glorious or inglorious results. The woman who is described as having obtained all that the world holds to be precious, by lavishing her charms and her caresses unworthily and heartlessly, will induce other women to do the same with theirs,—as will she who is made interesting by exhibitions of bold passion teach others to be spuriously passionate. The young man who in a novel becomes a hero, perhaps a Member of Parliament, and almost a Prime Minister, by trickery, falsehood, and flash cleverness, will have many followers, whose attempts to rise in the world ought to lie heavily on the conscience of the novelists who create fictitious Cagliostros.* There are Jack Sheppards other than those who break into houses and out of prisons,—Macheaths,* who deserve the gallows more than Gay's hero.

Thinking of all this, as a novelist surely must do,—as I certainly have done through my whole career,—it becomes to him a matter of deep conscience how he shall handle those characters by whose words and doings he hopes to interest his readers. It will very frequently be the case that he will be tempted to sacrifice something for effect, to say a word or two here, or to draw a picture there, for which he feels that he has the power, and which when spoken or drawn would be alluring. The regions of absolute vice are foul and odious. The savour of them, till custom has hardened the palate and the nose, is disgusting. In these he will hardly tread. But there are outskirts on these regions, on which sweet-smelling flowers seem to grow, and grass to be green. It is in these border-lands that the danger lies. The novelist may not be dull. If he commit that fault he can do neither harm nor good. He must please, and the flowers and the grass in these neutral territories sometimes seem to give him so easy an opportunity of pleasing!

The writer of stories must please, or he will be nothing. And he must teach whether he wish to teach or no. How shall he teach lessons of virtue and at the same time make himself a delight to his readers? That sermons are not in themselves often thought to be agreeable we all know. Nor are disquisitions on moral philosophy supposed to be pleasant reading for our idle hours. But the novelist, if he have a conscience, must preach his sermons with the same purpose as the clergyman, and must have his own system of ethics. If he can do this efficiently, if he can make virtue alluring and vice ugly, while he charms his readers instead of wearying them, then I think Mr Carlyle need not call him distressed, nor talk of that long ear of fiction, nor question whether he be or not the most foolish of existing mortals.

I think that many have done so; so many that we English novelists may boast as a class that such has been the general result of our own work. Looking back to the past generation, I may say with certainty that such was the operation of the novels of Miss Edgeworth, Miss Austen, and Walter Scott. Coming down to my own times, I find such to have been the teaching of Thackeray, of Dickens, and of George Eliot. Speaking, as I shall speak to any who may read these words, with that absence of self-personality which the dead may claim, I will boast that such has been the result of my own writing.

Can any one by search through the works of the six great English novelists I have named, find a scene, a passage, or a word that would teach a girl to be immodest, or a man to be dishonest? When men in their pages have been described as dishonest and women as immodest, have they not ever been punished? It is not for the novelist to say, baldly and simply: 'Because you lied here, or were heartless there, because you Lydia Bennet forgot the lessons of your honest home, or you Earl Leicester were false through your ambition, or you Beatrix* loved too well the glitter of the world, therefore you shall be scourged with scourges either in this world or in the next;' but it is for him to show, as he carries on his tale, that his Lydia, or his Leicester, or his Beatrix, will be dishonoured in the estimation of all readers by his or her vices. Let a woman be drawn clever, beautiful, attractive,—so as to make men love her, and women almost envy her,—and let her be made also heartless, unfeminine, and ambitious of evil grandeur, as was Beatrix, what a danger is there not in such a character! To the novelist who shall handle it, what peril of doing harm! But if at last it have been so handled that every girl who reads of Beatrix shall say: 'Oh! not like that;—let me not be like that!' and that every youth shall say: 'Let me not have such a one as that to press my bosom, anything rather than that!'—then will not the novelist have preached his sermon as perhaps no clergyman can preach it?

Very much of a novelist's work must appertain to the intercourse between young men and young women. It is admitted that a novel can hardly be made interesting or successful without love. Some few might be named, but even in those the attempt breaks down, and the softness of love is found to be necessary to complete the story. *Pickwick* has been named as an exception to the rule, but even in *Pickwick* there are three or four sets of lovers, whose little amatory longings give a softness to the work. I tried it once with *Miss Mackenzie*, but I had to make her fall in love at last. In this frequent allusion to the passion which most stirs the imagination of the young, there must be danger. Of that the writer of fiction is probably well aware. Then the question has to be asked, whether the danger may not be so averted that good may be the result,—and to be answered.

In one respect the necessity of dealing with love is advantageous,—advantageous from the very circumstance which has made love necessary to all novelists. It is necessary because the passion is one which interests or has interested all. Every one feels it, has felt it, or expects to feel it,—or else rejects it with an eagerness which still perpetuates the interest. If the novelist, therefore, can so handle the subject as to do good by his handling, as to teach wholesome lessons in regard to love, the good which he does will be very wide. If I can teach politicians that they can do their business better by truth than by falsehood, I do a great service; but it is done to a limited number of persons. But if I can make young men and women believe that truth in love will make them happy, then, if my writings be popular, I shall have a very large class of pupils. No doubt the cause for that fear which did exist as to novels arose from an idea that the matter of love would be treated in an inflammatory and generally unwholesome manner. 'Madam,' says Sir Anthony in the play, 'a circulating library in a town is an ever-green tree of diabolical knowledge. It blossoms through the year; and depend on it, Mrs Malaprop,* that they who are so fond of handling the leaves will long for the fruit at last.' Sir Anthony was no doubt right. But he takes it for granted that the longing for the fruit is an evil. The novelist who writes of love thinks differently, and thinks that the honest love of an honest man is a treasure which a good girl may fairly hope to win,— and that if she can be taught to wish only for that, she will have been taught to entertain only wholesome wishes.

I can easily believe that a girl should be taught to wish to love by reading how Laura Bell* loved Pendennis. Pendennis was not in truth a very worthy man, nor did he make a very good husband; but the girl's love was so beautiful, and the wife's love when she became a wife so womanlike, and at the same time so sweet, so unselfish, so wifely, so worshipful,—in the sense in which wives are told that they ought to worship their husbands,— that I cannot believe that any girl can be injured, or even not benefited, by reading of Laura's love.

There once used to be many who thought, and probably there still are some, even here in England, who think that a girl should hear nothing of love till the time come in which she is to be married. That, no doubt, was the opinion of Sir Anthony Absolute and of Mrs Malaprop. But I am hardly disposed to believe that the old system was more favourable than ours to the purity of manners. Lydia Languish, though she was constrained by fear of her aunt to hide the book, yet had *Peregrine Pickle* in her collection. While human nature talks of love so forcibly it can hardly serve our turn to be silent on the subject. 'Naturam expellas furcâ, tamen usque recurret.'* There are countries in which it has been in accordance with the manners of the upper classes that the girl should be brought to marry the man almost out of the nursery—or rather perhaps out of the convent—without having enjoyed that freedom of thought which the reading of novels and of poetry will certainly produce; but I do not know that the marriages so made have been thought to be happier than our own.

Among English novels of the present day, and among English novelists, a great division is made. There are sensational novels* and anti-sensational, sensational novelists and anti-sensational, sensational readers and anti-sensational. The novelists who are considered to be anti-sensational are generally called realistic. I am realistic. My friend Wilkie Collins is generally supposed to be sensational. The readers who prefer the one are supposed to take delight in the elucidation of character. Those who hold by the other are charmed by the continuation and gradual development of a plot. All this is, I think, a mistake,—which mistake arises from the inability of the imperfect artist to be at the same time realistic and sensational. A good novel should be both, and both in the highest degree. If a novel fail in either, there is a failure in art. Let those readers who believe that they do not like sensational scenes in novels think of some of those passages from our great novelists which have charmed them most:—of Rebecca in the castle with Ivanhoe; of Burley in the cave with Morton; of the mad lady tearing the veil of the expectant bride, in *Jane Eyre*; of Lady Castlewood as, in her indignation, she explains to the Duke of Hamilton Henry Esmond's right to be present at the marriage of his Grace with Beatrix;—may I add, of Lady Mason,* as she makes her confession at the feet of Sir Peregrine Orme? Will any one say that the authors of these passages have sinned in being over-sensational? No doubt, a string of horrible incidents, bound together without truth in detail, and told as affecting personages without character,— wooden blocks, who cannot make themselves known to the reader as men and women,—does not instruct or amuse, or even fill the mind with awe. Horrors heaped upon horrors, and which are horrors only in themselves, and not as touching any recognised and known person, are not tragic, and soon cease even to horrify. And such would-be tragic elements of a story may be increased without end, and without difficulty. I may tell you of a woman murdered,—murdered in the same street with you, in the next house,—that she was a wife murdered by her husband,—a bride not yet a week a wife. I may add to it for ever. I may say that the murderer roasted her alive. There is no end to it. I may declare that a former wife was treated with equal barbarity; and may assert that, as the murderer was led away to execution, he declared his only sorrow, his only regret to be, that he could not live to treat a third wife after the same fashion. There is nothing so easy as the creation and the cumulation of fearful incidents after this fashion. If such creation and cumulation be the beginning and the end of the novelist's work,—and novels have been written which seem to be without other attractions,—nothing can be more dull or more useless. But not on that account are we averse to tragedy in prose fiction. As in poetry, so in prose, he who can deal adequately with tragic elements is a greater artist and reaches a higher aim than the writer whose efforts never carry him above the mild walks of everyday life. *The Bride of Lammermoor** is a tragedy throughout, in spite of its comic elements. The life of Lady Castlewood, of whom I have spoken, is a tragedy. Rochester's wretched thraldom to his mad wife, in *Jane Eyre*, is a tragedy. But these stories charm us not simply because they are tragic, but because we feel that men and women with flesh and blood, creatures with whom we can sympathise, are struggling amidst their woes. It all lies in that. No novel is anything, for the purposes either of comedy or tragedy, unless the reader can sympathise with the characters whose names he finds upon the pages. Let an author so tell his tale as to touch his reader's heart and draw his tears, and he has, so far, done his work well. Truth let there be,—truth of description, truth of character, human truth as to men and women. If there be such truth, I do not know that a novel can be too sensational.

I did intend when I meditated that history of English fiction to include within its pages some rules for the writing of novels;—or I might perhaps say, with more modesty, to offer some advice on the art to such tyros in it as might be willing to take advantage of the experience of an old hand. But the matter would, I fear, be too long for this episode, and I am not sure that I have as yet got the rules quite settled in my own mind. I will, however, say a few words on one or two points which my own practice has pointed out to me.

I have from the first felt sure that the writer, when he sits down to commence his novel, should do so, not because he has to tell a story, but because he has a story to tell. The novelist's first novel will generally have sprung from the right cause. Some series of events, or some development of character, will have presented itself to his imagination,—and this he feels so strongly that he thinks he can present his picture in strong and agreeable language to others. He sits down and tells his story because he has a story to tell; as you, my friend, when you have heard something which has at once tickled your fancy or moved your pathos, will hurry to tell it to the first person you meet. But when that first novel has been received graciously by the public and has made for itself a success, then the writer, naturally feeling that the writing of novels is within his grasp, looks about for something to tell in another. He cudgels his brains, not always successfully, and sits down to write, not because he has something which he burns to tell, but because he feels it to be incumbent on him to be telling something. As you, my friend, if you are very successful in the telling of that first story, will become ambitious of further story-telling, and will look out for anecdotes,—in the narration of which you will not improbably sometimes distress your audience.

So it has been with many novelists, who, after some good work, perhaps after very much good work, have distressed their audience because they have gone on with their work till their work has become simply a trade with them. Need I make a list of such, seeing that it would contain the names of those who have been greatest in the art of British novel-writing. They have at last become weary of that portion of a novelist's work which is of all the most essential to success. That a man as he grows old should feel the labour of writing to be a fatigue is natural enough. But a man to whom writing has become a habit may write well though he be fatigued. But the weary novelist refuses any longer to give his mind to that work of observation and reception from which has come his power, without which work his power cannot be continued,—which work should be going on not only when he is at his desk, but in all his walks abroad, in all his movements through the world, in all his intercourse with his fellow-creatures. He has become a novelist, as another has become a poet, because he has in those walks abroad, unconsciously for the most part, been drawing in matter from all that he has seen and heard. But this has not been done without labour, even when the labour has been unconscious. Then there comes a time when he shuts his eyes and shuts his ears. When we talk of memory fading as age comes on, it is such shutting of eyes and ears that we mean. The things around cease to interest us, and we cannot exercise our minds upon them. To the novelist thus wearied there comes the demand for further novels. He does not know his own defect, and even if he did he does not wish to abandon his own profession. He still writes; but he writes because he has to tell a story, not because he has a story to tell. What reader of novels has not felt the 'woodenness' of this mode of telling? The characters do not live and move, but are cut out of blocks and are propped against the wall. The incidents are arranged in certain lines—the arrangement being as palpable to the reader as it has been to the writer—but do not follow each other as results naturally demanded by previous action. The reader can never feel—as he ought to feel—that only for that flame of the eye, only for that angry word, only for that moment of weakness, all might have been different. The course of the tale is one piece of stiff mechanism, in which there is no room for a doubt.

These, it may be said, are reflections which I, being an old novelist, might make useful to myself for discontinuing my work, but can hardly be needed by those tyros of whom I have spoken. That they are applicable to myself I readily admit, but I also find that they apply to many beginners. Some of us who are old fail at last because we are old. It would be well that each of us should say to himself,

> 'Solve senescentem mature sanus equum, ne
> Peccet ad extremum ridendus.'*

But many young fail also, because they endeavour to tell stories when they have none to tell. And this comes from idleness rather than from innate incapacity. The mind has not been sufficiently at work when the tale has been commenced, nor is it kept sufficiently at work as the tale is continued. I have never troubled myself much about the construction of plots, and am not now insisting specially on thoroughness in a branch of work in which I myself have not been very thorough. I am not sure that the construction of a perfected plot has been at any period within my power. But the novelist has other aims than the elucidation of his plot. He desires to make his readers so intimately acquainted with his characters that the creatures of his brain should be to them speaking, moving, living, human creatures. This he can never do unless he know those fictitious personages himself, and he can never know them well unless* he can live with them in the full reality of established intimacy. They must be with him as he lies down to sleep, and as he wakes from his dreams. He must learn to hate them and to love them. He must argue with them, quarrel with them, forgive them, and even submit to them. He must know of them whether they be cold-blooded or passionate, whether true or false, and how far true, and how far false. The depth and the breadth, and the narrowness and the shallowness of each should be clear to him. And, as here, in our outer world, we know that men and women change,—become worse or better as temptation or conscience may guide them,—so should these creations of his change, and every change should be noted by him. On the last day of each month recorded, every person in his novel should be a month older than on the first. If the would-be novelist have aptitudes that way, all this will come to him without much struggling;—but if it do not come, I think he can only make novels of wood.

It is so that I have lived with my characters, and thence has come whatever success I have obtained. There is a gallery of them, and of all in that gallery I may say that I know the tone of the voice, and the colour of the hair, every flame of the eye, and the very clothes they wear. Of each man I could assert whether he would have said these or the other words; of every woman, whether she would then have smiled or so have frowned. When I shall feel that this intimacy ceases, then I shall know that the old horse should be turned out to grass. That I shall feel it when I ought to feel it, I will by no means say. I do not know that I am at all wiser than Gil Blas' canon;* but I do know that the power indicated is one without which the teller of tales cannot tell them to any good effect.

The language in which the novelist is to put forth his story, the colours with which he is to paint his picture, must of course be to him matter of much consideration. Let him have all other possible gifts,—imagination, observation, erudition, and industry,—they will avail him nothing for his purpose, unless he can put forth his work in pleasant words. If he be confused, tedious, harsh, or unharmonious, readers will certainly reject him. The reading of a volume of history or on science may represent itself as a duty; and though the duty may by a bad style be made very disagreeable, the conscientious reader will perhaps perform it. But the novelist will be assisted by no such feeling. Any reader may reject his work without the burden of a sin. It is the first necessity of his position that he make himself pleasant. To do this, much more is necessary than to write correctly. He may indeed be pleasant without being correct,—as I think can be proved by the works of more than one distinguished novelist. But he must be intelligible,—intelligible without trouble; and he must be harmonious.

Any writer who has read even a little will know what is meant by the word intelligible. It is not sufficient that there be a meaning that may be hammered out of the sentence, but that the language should be so pellucid that the meaning should be rendered without an effort of the reader;—and not only some proposition of meaning, but the very sense, no more and no less, which the writer has intended to put into his words. What Macaulay says should be remembered by all writers: 'How little the all-important art of making meaning pellucid is studied now! Hardly any popular author except myself thinks of it.'* The language used should be as ready and as efficient a conductor of the mind of the writer to the mind of the reader as is the electric spark which passes from one battery to another battery. In all written matter the spark should carry everything; but in matters recondite the recipient will search to see that he misses nothing, and that he takes nothing away too much. The novelist cannot expect that any such search will be made. A young writer, who will acknowledge the truth of what I am saying, will often feel himself tempted by the difficulties of language to tell himself that some one little doubtful passage, some single collocation of words which is not quite what it ought to be, will not matter. I know well what a stumbling-block such a passage may be. But he should leave none such behind him as he goes on. The habit of writing clearly soon comes to the writer who is a severe critic to himself.

As to that harmonious expression which I think is required, I shall find it more difficult to express my meaning. It will be granted, I think, by readers that a style may be rough, and yet both forcible and intelligible; but it will seldom come to pass that a novel written in a rough style will be popular,—and less often that a novelist who habitually uses such a style will become so. The harmony which is required must come from the practice of the ear. There are few ears naturally so dull that they cannot, if time be allowed to them, decide whether a sentence, when read, be or be not harmonious. And the sense of such harmony grows on the ear, when the intelligence has once informed itself as to what is, and what is not harmonious. The boy, for instance, who learns with accuracy the prosody of a Sapphic stanza,* and has received through his intelligence a knowledge of its parts, will soon tell by his ear whether a Sapphic stanza be or be not correct. Take a girl, endowed with gifts of music, well instructed in her art, with perfect ear, and read to her such a stanza with two words transposed, as, for instance—

> 'Mercuri, nam te docilis magistro
> Movit Amphion *canendo lapides*,
> Tuque testudo resonare septem
> Callida nervis—'*

and she will find no halt in the rhythm. But a schoolboy with none of her musical acquirements or capacities, who has, however, become familiar with the metres of the poet, will at once discover the fault. And so will the writer become familiar with what is harmonious in prose. But in order that familiarity may serve him in his business, he must so train his ear that he shall be able to weigh the rhythm of every word as it falls from his pen. This, when it has been done for a time, even for a short time, will become so habitual to him that he will have appreciated the metrical duration of every syllable before it shall have dared to show itself upon paper. The art of the orator is the same. He knows beforehand how each sound which he is about to utter will affect the force of his climax. If a writer will do so he will charm his readers, though his readers will probably not know how they have been charmed.

In writing a novel the author soon becomes aware that a burden of many pages is before him. Circumstances require that he should cover a certain and generally not a very confined space. Short novels are not popular with readers generally. Critics often complain of the ordinary length of novels,—of the three volumes to which they are subjected; but few novels which have attained great success in England have been told in fewer pages. The novel-writer who sticks to novel-writing as his profession will certainly find that this burden of length is incumbent on him. How shall he carry his burden to the end? How shall he cover his space? Many great artists have by their practice opposed the doctrine which I now propose to preach;—but they have succeeded I think in spite of their fault and by dint of their greatness. There should be no episodes in a novel. Every sentence, every word, through all those pages, should tend to the telling of the story. Such episodes distract the attention of the reader, and always do so disagreeably. Who has not felt this to be the case even with *The Curious Impertinent* and with the *History of the Man of the Hill*.* And if it be so with Cervantes and Fielding, who can hope to succeed? Though the novel which you have to write must be long, let it be all one. And this exclusion of episodes should be carried down into the smallest details. Every sentence and every word used should tend to the telling of the story. 'But,' the young novelist will say, 'with so many pages before me to be filled, how shall I succeed if I thus confine myself;—how am I to know beforehand what space this story of mine will require? There must be the three volumes, or the certain number of magazine pages which I have contracted to supply. If I may not be discursive should occasion require, how shall I complete my task? The painter suits the size of his canvas to his subject, and must I in my art stretch my subject to my canvas?' This undoubtedly must be done by the novelist; and if he will learn his business, may be done without injury to his effect. He may not paint different pictures on the same canvas, which he will do if he allow himself to wander away to matters outside his own story; but by studying proportion in his work, he may teach himself so to tell his story that it shall naturally fall into the required length. Though his story should be all one, yet it may have many parts. Though the plot itself may require but few characters, it may be so enlarged as to find its full development in many. There may be subsidiary plots, which shall all tend to the elucidation of the main story, and which will take their places as part of one and the same work,—as there may be many figures on a canvas which shall not to the spectator seem to form themselves into separate pictures.

There is no portion of a novelist's work in which this fault of episodes is so common as in the dialogue. It is so easy to make any two persons talk on any casual subject with which the writer presumes himself to be conversant! Literature, philosophy, politics, or sport, may thus be handled in a loosely discursive style; and the writer, while indulging himself and filling his pages, is apt to think that he is pleasing his reader. I think he can make no greater mistake. The dialogue is generally the most agreeable part of a novel; but it is only so as long as it tends in some way to the telling of the main story. It need not seem to be confined to that, but it should always have a tendency in that direction. The unconscious critical acumen of a reader is both just and severe. When a long dialogue on extraneous matter reaches his mind, he at once feels that he is being cheated into taking something which he did not bargain to accept when he took up that novel. He does not at that moment require politics or philosophy, but he wants his story. He will not perhaps be able to say in so many words that at some certain point the dialogue has deviated from the story; but when it does so he will feel it, and the feeling will be unpleasant. Let the intending novel-writer, if he doubt this, read one of Bulwer's novels,—in which there is very much to charm,—and then ask himself whether he has not been offended by devious conversations.

And the dialogue, on which the modern novelist in consulting the taste of his probable readers must depend most, has to be constrained also by other rules. The writer may tell much of his story in conversations, but he may only do so by putting such words into the mouths of his personages as persons so situated would probably use. He is not allowed for the sake of his tale to make his characters give utterance to long speeches, such as are not customarily heard from men and women. The ordinary talk of ordinary people is carried on in short sharp expressive sentences, which very frequently are never completed,—the language of which even among educated people is often incorrect. The novel-writer in constructing his dialogue must so steer between absolute accuracy of language—which would give to his conversation an air of pedantry, and the slovenly inaccuracy of ordinary talkers, which if closely followed would offend by an appearance of grimace—as to produce upon the ear of his readers a sense of reality. If he be quite real he will seem to attempt to be funny. If he be quite correct he will seem to be unreal. And above all, let the speeches be short. No character should utter much above a dozen words at a breath,—unless the writer can justify to himself a longer flood of speech by the speciality of the occasion.

In all this human nature must be the novel-writer's guide. No doubt effective novels have been written in which human nature has been set at defiance. I might name *Caleb Williams* as one and *Adam Blair** as another. But the exceptions are not more than enough to prove the rule. But in following human nature he must remember that he does so with a pen in his hand, and that the reader who will appreciate human nature will also demand artistic ability and literary aptitude.

The young novelist will probably ask, or more probably bethink himself how he is to acquire that knowledge of human nature which will tell him with accuracy what men and women would say in this or that position. He must acquire it as the compositor, who is to print his words, has learned the art of distributing his type—by constant and intelligent practice. Unless it be given to him to listen and to observe,—so to carry away, as it were, the manners of people in his memory, as to be able to say to himself with assurance that these words might have been said in a given position, and that those other words could not have been said,—I do not think that in these days he can succeed as a novelist.

And then let him beware of creating tedium! Who has not felt the charm of a spoken story up to a certain point, and then suddenly become aware that it has become too long and is the reverse of charming. It is not only that the entire book may have this fault, but that this fault may occur in chapters, in passages, in pages, in paragraphs. I know no guard against this so likely to be effective as the feeling of the writer himself. When once the sense that the thing is becoming long has grown upon him, he may be sure that it will grow upon his readers. I see the smile of some who will declare to themselves that the words of a writer will never be tedious to himself. Of the writer of whom this may be truly said, it may be said with equal truth that he will always be tedious to his readers.

CHAPTER 13

On English Novelists of the Present Day

I N this chapter I will venture to name a few successful novelists of my own time, with whose works I am acquainted; and will endeavour to point whence their success has come, and why they have failed when there has been failure.

I do not hesitate to name Thackeray the first. His knowledge of human nature was supreme, and his characters stand out as human beings, with a force and a truth which has not, I think, been within the reach of any other English novelist in any period. I know no character in fiction, unless it be Don Quixote, with whom the reader becomes so intimately acquainted as with Colonel Newcome.* How great a thing it is to be a gentleman at all parts! How we admire the man of whom so much may be said with truth! Is there any one of whom we feel more sure in this respect than of Colonel Newcome? It is not because Colonel Newcome is a perfect gentleman that we think Thackeray's work to have been so excellent, but because he has had the power to describe him as such, and to force us to love him, a weak and silly old man, on account of this grace of character.

It is evident from all Thackeray's best work that he lived with the characters he was creating. He had always a story to tell until quite late in life; and he shows us that this was so, not by the interest which he had in his own plots,—for I doubt whether his plots did occupy much of his mind,—but by convincing us that his characters were alive to himself. With Becky Sharp, with Lady Castlewood and her daughter, and with Esmond, with Warrington, Pendennis, and the Major, with Colonel Newcome, and with Barry Lyndon,* he must have lived in perpetual intercourse. Therefore he has made these personages real to us.

Among all our novelists his style is the purest, as to my ear it is also the most harmonious. Sometimes it is disfigured by a slight touch of affectation, by little conceits which smell of the oil;—but the language is always lucid. The reader, without labour, knows what he means, and knows all that he means. As well as I can remember, he deals with no episodes. I think that any critic, examining his work minutely, would find that every scene, and every part of every scene, adds something to the clearness with which the story is told. Among all his stories there is not one which does not leave on the mind a feeling of distress that women should ever be immodest or men dishonest,—and of joy that women should be so devoted and men so honest. How we hate the idle selfishness of Pendennis, the worldliness of Beatrix, the craft of Becky Sharp!—how we love the honesty of Colonel Newcome, the nobility of Esmond, and the devoted affection of Mrs Pendennis! The hatred of evil and love of good can hardly have come upon so many readers without doing much good.

Late in Thackeray's life,—he never was an old man, but towards the end of his career,—he failed in his power of charming, because he allowed his mind to become idle. In the plots which he conceived, and in the language which he used, I do not know that there is any perceptible change, but in *The Virginians* and in *Philip** the reader is introduced to no character with which he makes a close and undying acquaintance. And this, I have no doubt, is so because Thackeray himself had no such intimacy. His mind had come to be weary of that fictitious life which is always demanding the labour of new creation, and he troubled himself with his two Virginians and his Philip only when he was seated at his desk.

At the present moment George Eliot is the first of English novelists, and I am disposed to place her second of those of my time. She is best known to the literary world as a writer of prose fiction, and not improbably whatever of permanent fame she may acquire will come from her novels. But the nature of her intellect is very far removed indeed from that which is common to the tellers of stories. Her imagination is no doubt strong, but it acts in analysing rather than in creating. Everything that comes before her is pulled to pieces so that the inside of it shall be seen, and be seen if possible by her readers as clearly as by herself. This searching analysis is carried so far that, in studying her latter writings, one feels oneself to be in company with some philosopher rather than with a novelist. I doubt whether any young person can read with pleasure either *Felix Holt*, *Middlemarch*, or *Daniel Deronda*.* I know that they are very difficult to many that are not young.

Her personifications of character have been singularly terse and graphic, and from them has come her great hold on the public,—though by no means the greatest effect which she has produced. The lessons which she teaches remain, though it is not for the sake of the lessons that her pages are read. Seth Bede, Adam Bede, Maggie and Tom Tulliver, old Silas Marner, and, much above all, Tito, in *Romola*, are characters which, when once known, can never be forgotten. I cannot say quite so much for any of those in her later works, because in them the philosopher so greatly overtops the portrait-painter, that, in the dissection of the mind, the outward signs seem to have been forgotten. In her, as yet, there is no symptom whatever of that weariness of mind which, when felt by the reader, induces him to declare that the author has written himself out. It is not from decadence that we do not have another Mrs Poyser,* but because the author soars to things which seem to her to be higher than Mrs Poyser.

It is, I think, the defect of George Eliot that she struggles too hard to do work that shall be excellent. She lacks ease. Latterly the signs of this have been conspicuous in her style, which has always been and is singularly correct, but which has become occasionally obscure from her too great desire to be pungent. It is impossible not to feel the struggle, and that feeling begets a flavour of affectation. In *Daniel Deronda*, of which at this moment only a portion has been published, there are sentences which I have found myself compelled to read three times before I have been able to take home to myself all that the writer has intended. Perhaps I may be permitted here to say, that this gifted woman was among my dearest and most intimate friends. As I am speaking here of novelists, I will not attempt to speak of George Eliot's merit as a poet.

There can be no doubt that the most popular novelist of my time—probably the most popular English novelist of any time—has been Charles Dickens. He has now been dead nearly six years, and the sale of his books goes on as it did during his life. The certainty with which his novels are found in every house—the familiarity of his name in all English-speaking countries—the popularity of such characters as Mrs Gamp, Micawber, and Pecksniff,* and many others whose names have entered into the English language and become well-known words—the grief of the country at his death, and the honours paid to him at his funeral,—all testify to his popularity. Since the last book he wrote himself, I doubt whether any book has been so popular as his biography by John Forster.* There is no withstanding such testimony as this. Such evidence of popular appreciation should go for very much, almost for everything, in criticism on the work of a novelist. The primary object of a novelist is to please; and this man's novels have been found more pleasant than those of any other writer. It might of course be objected to this, that though the books have pleased they have been injurious, that their tendency has been immoral and their teaching vicious; but it is almost needless to say that no such charge has ever been made against Dickens. His teaching has ever been good. From all which, there arises to the critic a question whether, with such evidence against him as to the excellence of this writer, he should not subordinate his own opinion to the collected opinion of the world of readers. To me it almost seems that I must be wrong to place Dickens after Thackeray and George Eliot, knowing as I do that so great a majority put him above those authors.

My own peculiar idiosyncrasy in the matter forbids me to do so. I do acknowledge that Mrs Gamp, Micawber, Pecksniff, and others have become household words in every house, as though they were human beings; but to my judgment they are not human beings, nor are any of the characters human which Dickens has portrayed. It has been the peculiarity and the marvel of this man's power, that he has invested his puppets with a charm that has enabled him to dispense with human nature. There is a drollery about them, in my estimation, very much below the humour of Thackeray, but which has reached the intellect of all; while Thackeray's humour has escaped the intellect of many. Nor is the pathos of Dickens human. It is stagey and melodramatic. But it is so expressed that it touches every heart a little. There is no real life in Smike. His misery, his idiotcy, his devotion for Nicholas, his love for Kate,* are all overdone and incompatible with each other. But still the reader sheds a tear. Every reader can find a tear for Smike. Dickens's novels are like Boucicault's* plays. He has known how to draw his lines broadly, so that all should see the colour.

He, too, in his best days, always lived with his characters;—and he, too, as he gradually ceased to have the power of doing so, ceased to charm. Though they are not human beings, we all remember Mrs Gamp and Pickwick. The Boffins and Veneerings* do not, I think, dwell in the minds of so many.

Of Dickens's style it is impossible to speak in praise. It is jerky, ungrammatical, and created by himself in defiance of rules—almost as completely as that created by Carlyle. To readers who have taught themselves to regard language, it must therefore be unpleasant.

But the critic is driven to feel the weakness of his criticism, when he acknowledges to himself—as he is compelled in all honesty to do—that with the language, such as it is, the writer has satisfied the great mass of the readers of his country. Both these great writers have satisfied the readers of their own pages; but both have done infinite harm by creating a school of imitators. No young novelist should ever dare to imitate the style of Dickens. If such a one wants a model for his language, let him take Thackeray.

Bulwer, or Lord Lytton,—but I think that he is still better known by his earlier name,—was a man of very great parts. Better educated than either of those I have named before him, he was always able to use his erudition, and he thus produced novels from which very much not only may be but must be learned by his readers. He thoroughly understood the political status of his own country, a subject on which, I think, Dickens was marvellously ignorant, and which Thackeray had never studied. He had read extensively, and was always apt to give his readers the benefit of what he knew. The result has been that very much more than amusement may be obtained from Bulwer's novels. There is also a brightness about them—the result rather of thought than of imagination, of study and of care, than of mere intellect—which has made many of them excellent in their way. It is perhaps improper to class all his novels together, as he wrote in varied manners, making in his earlier works, such as *Pelham* and *Ernest Maltravers*, pictures of a fictitious life, and afterwards pictures of life as he believed it to be, as in *My Novel* and *The Caxtons*.* But from all of them there comes the same flavour of an effort to produce effect. The effects are produced, but it would have been better if the flavour had not been there.

I cannot say of Bulwer as I have of the other novelists whom I have named that he lived with his characters. He lived with his work, with the doctrines which at the time he wished to preach, thinking always of the effects which he wished to produce; but I do not think he ever knew his own personages,—and therefore neither do we know them. Even Pelham and Eugene Aram are not human beings to us, as are Pickwick, and Colonel Newcome, and Mrs Poyser.

In his plots Bulwer has generally been simple, facile, and successful. The reader never feels with him, as he does with Wilkie Collins, that it is all plot, or, as with George Eliot, that there is no plot. The story comes naturally without calling for too much attention, and is thus proof of the completeness of the man's intellect. His language is clear, good, intelligible English, but it is defaced by mannerism. In all that he did, affectation was his fault.

How shall I speak of my dear old friend Charles Lever, and his rattling, jolly, joyous, swearing Irishmen. Surely never did a sense of vitality come so constantly from a man's pen, nor from man's voice, as from his! I knew him well for many years, and whether in sickness or in health, I have never come across him without finding him to be running over with wit and fun. Of all the men I have encountered, he was the surest fund of drollery. I have known many witty men, many who could say good things, many who would sometimes be ready to say them when wanted, though they would sometimes fail;—but he never failed. Rouse him in the middle of the night, and wit would come from him before he was half awake. And yet he never monopolised the talk, was never a bore. He would take no more than his own share of the words spoken, and would yet seem to brighten all that was said during the night. His earlier novels the later I have not read—are just like his conversation. The fun never flags, and to me, when I read them, they were never tedious. As to character he can hardly be said to have produced it. Corney Delaney,* the old man-servant, may perhaps be named as an exception.

Lever's novels will not live long,—even if they may be said to be alive now,—because it is so. What was his manner of working I do not know, but I should think it must have been very quick, and that he never troubled himself on the subject, except when he was seated with a pen in his hand.

Charlotte Brontë was surely a marvellous woman. If it could be right to judge the work of a novelist from one small portion of one novel, and to say of an author that he is to be accounted as strong as he shows himself to be in his strongest morsel of work, I should be inclined to put Miss Brontë very high indeed. I know no interest more thrilling than that which she has been able to throw into the characters of Rochester and the governess, in the second volume of *Jane Eyre*. She lived with those characters, and felt with* every fibre of the heart, the longings of the one and the sufferings of the other. And therefore, though the end of the book is weak, and the beginning not very good, I venture to predict that *Jane Eyre* will be read among English novels when many whose names are now better known shall have been forgotten. *Jane Eyre*, and *Esmond*, and *Adam Bede* will be in the hands of our grandchildren, when *Pickwick*, and *Pelham*, and

Harry Lorrequer are forgotten; because the men and women depicted are human in their aspirations, human in their sympathies, and human in their actions.

In *Villette*, too, and in *Shirley*,* there is to be found human life as natural and as real, though in circumstances not so full of interest as those told in *Jane Eyre*. The character of Paul in the former of the two is a wonderful study. She must herself have been in love with some Paul when she wrote the book, and have been determined to prove to herself that she was capable of loving one whose exterior circumstances were mean and in every way unprepossessing.

There is no writer of the present day who has so much puzzled me by his eccentricities, impracticabilities, and capabilities as Charles Reade. I look upon him as endowed almost with genius, but as one who has not been gifted by nature with ordinary powers of reasoning. He can see what is grandly noble and admire it with all his heart. He can see, too, what is foully vicious and hate it with equal ardour. But in the common affairs of life he cannot see what is right or wrong; and as he is altogether unwilling to be guided by the opinion of others, he is constantly making mistakes in his literary career, and subjecting himself to reproach which he hardly deserves. He means to be honest. He means to be especially honest,—more honest than other people. He has written a book called *The Eighth Commandment* on behalf of honesty in literary transactions,—a wonderful work, which has I believe been read by a very few. I never saw a copy except that in my own library, or heard of any one who knew the book. Nevertheless it is a volume that must have taken very great labour, and have been writ-ten,—as indeed he declares that it was written,—without the hope of pecuniary reward. He makes an appeal to the British Parliament and British people on behalf of literary honesty, declaring that should he fail—'I shall have to go on blushing for the people I was born among.' And yet of all the writers of my day he has seemed to me to under-stand literary honesty the least. On one occasion, as he tells us in this book, he bought for a certain sum from a French author the right of using a plot taken from a play,*—which he probably might have used without such purchase, and also without infringing any international copyright act. The French author not unnaturally praises him for the transaction, telling him that he is 'un vrai gentleman.' The plot was used by Reade in a novel; and a critic discovering the adaptation, made known his discovery to the public. Whereupon the novelist became angry, called his critic a pseudonymuncle, and defended himself by stating the fact of his own purchase. In all this he seems to me to ignore what we all mean when we talk of literary plagiarism and literary honesty. The sin of which the author is accused is not that of taking another man's property, but of passing off as his own creation that which he does not himself create. When an author puts his name to a book he claims to have written all that there is therein, unless he makes direct signification to the contrary. Some years subsequently there arose another similar question, in which Mr Reade's opinion was declared even more plainly, and certainly very much more publicly. In a tale which he wrote he inserted a dialogue which he took from Swift,* and took without any acknowledgment. As might have been expected, one of the critics of the day fell foul of him for this barefaced plagiarism. The author, however, defended himself, with much abuse of the critic, by asserting, that whereas Swift had found the jewel he had supplied the setting;—an argument in which there was some little wit, and would have been much excellent truth, had he given the words as belonging to Swift and not to himself.*

The novels of a man possessed of so singular a mind must themselves be very strange,—and they are strange. It has generally been his object to write down some abuse with which he has been particularly struck,—the harshness, for instance, with which paupers or lunatics are treated, or the wickedness of certain classes,—and he always, I think, leaves upon his readers an idea of great earnestness of purpose. But he has always left at the same time on my mind so strong a conviction that he has not really understood his subject, that I have ever found myself taking the part of those whom he has accused. So good a heart, and so wrong a head, surely no novelist ever before had combined! In story-telling he has occasionally been almost great. Among his novels I would especially recommend *The Cloister and the Hearth.** I do not know that in this work, or in any, that he has left a character that will remain; but he has written some of his scenes so brightly that to read them would always be a pleasure.

Of Wilkie Collins it is impossible for a true critic not to speak with admiration, because he has excelled all his contemporaries in a certain most difficult branch of his art; but as it is a branch which I have not myself at all cultivated, it is not unnatural that his work should be very much lost upon me individually. When I sit down to write a novel I do not at all know, and I do not very much care, how it is to end. Wilkie Collins seems so to construct his that he not only, before writing, plans everything on, down to the minutest detail, from the beginning to the end; but then plots it all back again, to see that there is no piece of necessary dove-tailing which does not dove-tail with absolute accuracy. The construction is most minute and most wonderful. But I can never lose the taste of the construction. The author seems always to be warning me to remember that something happened at exactly half-past two o'clock on Tuesday morning; or that a woman disappeared from the road just fifteen yards beyond the fourth milestone. One is constrained by mysteries and hemmed in by difficulties, knowing, however, that the mysteries will be made clear, and the difficulties overcome at the end of the third volume. Such work gives me no pleasure. I am, however, quite prepared to acknowledge that the want of pleasure comes from fault of my intellect.

There are two ladies of whom I would fain say a word, though I feel that I am making my list too long, in order that I may declare how much I have admired their work. They are Annie Thackeray and Rhoda Broughton.* I have known them both, and have loved the former almost as though she belonged to me. No two writers were ever more dissimilar,—except in this that they are both feminine. Miss Thackeray's characters are sweet, charming, and quite true to human nature. In her writings she is always endeavouring to prove that good produces good, and evil evil. There is not a line of which she need be ashamed,—not a sentiment of which she should not be proud. But she writes like a lazy writer who dislikes her work, and who allows her own want of energy to show itself in her pages.

Miss Broughton, on the other hand, is full of energy,—though she too, I think, can become tired over her work. She, however, does take the trouble to make her personages stand upright on the ground. And she has the gift of making them speak as men and women do speak. 'You beast!' said Nancy, sitting on the wall, to the man who was to be her husband,—thinking that she was speaking to her brother. Now Nancy, whether right or wrong, was just the girl who would, as circumstances then were, have called her brother a beast. There is nothing wooden about any of Miss Broughton's novels; and in these days so many novels are wooden! But they are not sweet-savoured as are those by Miss Thackeray, and are, therefore, less true to nature. In Miss Broughton's determination not to be mawkish and missish, she has made her ladies do and say things which ladies would not do and say. They throw themselves at men's heads, and when they are not accepted only think how they may throw themselves again. Miss Broughton is still so young that I hope she may live to overcome her fault in this direction.

There is one other name, without which the list of the best known English novelists of my own time would certainly be incomplete, and that is the name of the present Prime Minister of England. Mr Disraeli* has written so many novels, and has been so popular as a novelist that, whether for good or for ill, I feel myself compelled to speak of him. He began his career as an author early in life, publishing *Vivian Grey* when he was twenty-three years old. He was very young for such work, though hardly young enough to justify the excuse that he makes in his own preface, that it is a book written by a boy. Dickens was, I think, younger when he wrote his *Sketches by Boz*, and as young when he was writing the *Pickwick Papers*. It was hardly longer ago than the other day when Mr Disraeli brought out *Lothair*, and between the two there were eight or ten others. To me they have all had the same flavour of paint and unreality. In whatever he has written he has affected something which has been intended to strike his readers as uncommon and therefore grand. Because he has been bright and a man of genius, he has carried his object as regards the young. He has struck them with astonishment and aroused in their imagination ideas of a world more glorious, more rich, more witty, more enterprising, than their own. But the glory has been the glory of pasteboard, and the wealth has been a wealth of tinsel. The wit has been the wit of hairdressers, and the enterprise has been the enterprise of mountebanks. An audacious conjurer has generally been his hero,—some youth who, by wonderful cleverness, can obtain success by every intrigue that comes to his hand. Through it all there is a feeling of stage properties, a smell of hair-oil, an aspect of buhl,* a remembrance of tailors, and that pricking of the conscience which must be the general accompaniment of paste diamonds. I can understand that Mr Disraeli should by his novels have instigated many a young man and many a young woman on their way in life, but I cannot understand that he should have instigated any one to good. Vivian Grey has had probably as many followers as Jack Sheppard, and has led his followers in the same direction.

Lothair, which is as yet Mr Disraeli's last work, and, I think, undoubtedly his worst, has been defended on a plea somewhat similar to that by which he has defended *Vivian Grey*. As that was written when he was too young, so was the other when he was too old,—too old for work of that nature, though not too old to be Prime Minister. If his mind were so occupied with greater things as to allow him to write such a work, yet his judgment should have sufficed to induce him to destroy it when written. Here that flavour of hair-oil, that flavour of false jewels, that remembrance of tailors, comes out stronger than in all the others. Lothair is falser even than Vivian Grey, and Lady Corisande, the daughter of the Duchess, more inane and unwoman-like than Venetia or Henrietta Temple. It is the very bathos of story-telling. I have often lamented, and have as often excused to myself, that lack of public judgment which enables readers to put up with bad work because it comes from good or from lofty hands. I never felt the feeling so strongly, or was so little able to excuse it, as when a portion of the reading public received *Lothair* with satisfaction.

CHAPTER 14

On Criticism

L ITERARY criticism in the present day has become a profession,—
but it has ceased to be an art. Its object is no longer that of prov-
ing that certain literary work is good and other literary work is bad, in
accordance with rules which the critic is able to define. English criticism at present rarely even pretends to go so far as this. It attempts,
in the first place, to tell the public whether a book be or be not worth
public attention; and, in the second place, so to describe the purport
of the work as to enable those who have not time or inclination for
reading it to feel that by a short cut they can become acquainted with
its contents. Both these objects, if fairly well carried out, are salutary.
Though the critic may not be a profound judge himself; though not
unfrequently he be a young man making his first literary attempts,
with tastes and judgment still unfixed, yet he probably has a conscience in the matter, and would not have been selected for that work
had he not shown some aptitude for it. Though he may be not the best
possible guide to the undiscerning, he will be better than no guide at
all. Real substantial criticism must, from its nature, be costly, and that
which the public wants should at any rate be cheap. Advice is given
to many thousands, which, though it may not be the best advice possible, is better than no advice at all. Then that description of the work
criticised, that compressing of the much into very little,—which is
the work of many modern critics or reviewers,—does enable many
to know something of what is being said, who without it would know
nothing.

I do not think it is incumbent on me at present to name periodicals
in which this work is well done, and to make complaints of others by
which it is scamped. I should give offence, and might probably be
unjust. But I think I may certainly say that as some of these periodicals
are certainly entitled to great praise for the manner in which the work
is done generally, so are others open to very severe censure,—and that
the praise and that the censure are chiefly due on behalf of one virtue

and its opposite vice. It is not critical ability that we have a right to demand, or its absence that we are bound to deplore. Critical ability for the price we pay is not attainable. It is a faculty not peculiar to Englishmen, and when displayed is very frequently not appreciated. But that critics should be honest we have a right to demand, and critical dishonesty we are bound to expose. If the writer will tell us what he thinks, though his thoughts be absolutely vague and useless, we can forgive him; but when he tells us what he does not think, actuated either by friendship or by animosity, then there should be no pardon for him. This is the sin in modern English criticism of which there is most reason to complain.

It is a lamentable fact that men and women lend themselves to this practice who are neither vindictive nor ordinarily dishonest. It has become 'the custom of the trade,' under the veil of which excuse so many tradesmen justify their malpractices! When a struggling author learns that so much has been done for A by the *Barsetshire Gazette*, so much for B by the *Dillsborough Herald*, and, again, so much for C by that powerful metropolitan organ the *Evening Pulpit*,* and is told also that A and B and C have been favoured through personal interest, he also goes to work among the editors, or the editors' wives,—or perhaps, if he cannot reach their wives, with their wives' first or second cousins. When once the feeling has come upon an editor or a critic that he may allow himself to be influenced by other considerations than the duty he owes to the public, all sense of critical or of editorial honesty falls from him at once. *Facilis descensus Averni.** In a very short time that editorial honesty becomes ridiculous to himself. It is for other purpose that he wields the power; and when he is told what is his duty, and what should be his conduct, the preacher of such doctrine seems to him to be quixotic. 'Where have you lived, my friend, for the last twenty years,' he says in spirit, if not in word, 'that you come out now with such stuff as old-fashioned as this?' And thus dishonesty begets dishonesty, till dishonesty seems to be beautiful. How nice to be good-natured! How glorious to assist struggling young authors, especially if the young author be also a pretty woman! How gracious to oblige a friend! Then the motive, though still pleasing, departs further from the border of what is good. In what way can the critic better repay the hospitality of his wealthy literary friend than by good-natured criticism,—or more certainly ensure for himself a continuation of hospitable favours?

Some years since a critic of the day,* a gentleman well known then in literary circles, showed me the manuscript of a book recently published,—the work of a popular author. It was handsomely bound, and was a valuable and desirable possession. It had just been given to him by the author as an acknowledgment for a laudatory review in one of the leading journals of the day. As I was expressly asked whether I did not regard such a token as a sign of grace both in the giver and in the receiver, I said that I thought it should neither have been given nor have been taken. My theory was repudiated with scorn, and I was told that I was strait-laced, visionary, and impracticable! In all that the damage did not lie in the fact of that one present, but in the feeling on the part of the critic that his office was not debased by the acceptance of presents from those whom he criticised. This man was a professional critic, bound by his contract with certain employers to review such books as were sent to him. How could he, when he had received a valuable present for praising one book, censure another by the same author?

While I write this I well know that what I say, if it be ever noticed at all, will be taken as a straining at gnats,* as a pretence of honesty, or at any rate as an exaggeration of scruples. I have said the same thing before, and have been ridiculed for saying it. But none the less am I sure that English literature generally is suffering much under this evil. All those who are struggling for success have forced upon them the idea that their strongest efforts should be made in touting for praise. Those who are not familiar with the lives of authors will hardly believe how low will be the forms which their struggles will take:—how little presents will be sent to men who write little articles; how much flattery may be expended even on the keeper of a circulating library; with what profuse and distant genuflexions approaches are made to the outside railing of the temple which contains within it the great thunderer of some metropolitan periodical publication! The evil here is not only that done to the public when interested counsel is given to them, but extends to the debasement of those who have at any rate considered themselves fit to provide literature for the public.

I am satisfied that the remedy for this evil must lie in the conscience and deportment of authors themselves. If once the feeling could be produced that it is disgraceful for an author to ask for praise,—and demands for praise are, I think, disgraceful in every walk of life,—the practice would gradually fall into the hands only of the lowest, and that which is done only by the lowest soon becomes despicable even to them. The sin, when perpetuated with unflagging labour, brings with it at best very poor reward. That work of running after critics, editors, publishers, the keepers of circulating libraries, and their clerks, is very hard, and must be very disagreeable. He who does it must feel himself to be dishonoured,—or she. It may perhaps help to sell an edition, but can never make an author successful.*

I think it may be laid down as a golden rule in literature that there should be no intercourse at all between an author and his critic. The critic, as critic, should not know his author, nor the author, as author, his critic. As censure should beget no anger, so should praise beget no gratitude. The young author should feel that criticisms fall upon him as dew or hail from heaven,*—which, as coming from heaven, man accepts as fate. Praise let the author try to obtain by wholesome effort; censure let him avoid, if possible, by care and industry. But when they come, let him take them as coming from some source which he cannot influence, and with which he should not meddle.

I know no more disagreeable trouble into which an author may plunge himself than of a quarrel with his critics, or any more useless labour than that of answering them. It is wise to presume, at any rate, that the reviewer has simply done his duty, and has spoken of the book according to the dictates of his conscience. Nothing can be gained by combating the reviewer's opinion. If the book which he has disparaged be good, his judgment will be condemned by the praise of others; if bad, his judgment will be confirmed by others. Or if, unfortunately, the criticism of the day be in so evil a condition generally that such ultimate truth cannot be expected, the author may be sure that his efforts made on behalf of his own book will not set matters right. If injustice be done him, let him bear it. To do so is consonant with the dignity of the position which he ought to assume. To shriek, and scream, and sputter, to threaten actions, and to swear about the town that he has been belied and defamed in that he has been accused of bad grammar or a false metaphor, of a dull chapter, or even of a borrowed heroine, will leave on the minds of the public nothing but a sense of irritated impotence.

If, indeed, there should spring from an author's work any assertion by a critic injurious to the author's honour, if the author be accused of falsehood or of personal motives which are discreditable to him, then, indeed, he may be bound to answer the charge. It is hoped, however, that he may be able to do so with clean hands, or he will so stir the mud in the pool as to come forth dirtier than he went into it.

I have lived much among men by whom the English criticism of the day has been vehemently abused. I have heard it said that to the public it is a false guide, and that to authors it is never a trustworthy Mentor.* I do not concur in this wholesale censure. There is, of course, criticism and criticism. There are at this moment one or two periodicals to which both public and authors may safely look for guidance, though there are many others from which no spark of literary advantage may be obtained. But it is well that both public and authors should know what is the advantage which they have a right to expect. There have been critics,—and there probably will be again, though the circumstances of English literature do not tend to produce them,—with power sufficient to entitle them to speak with authority. These great men have declared, *tanquam ex cathedrâ*,* that such a book has been so far good and so far bad, or that it has been altogether good or altogether bad,—and the world has believed them. When making such assertions they have given their reasons, explained their causes, and have carried conviction. Very great reputations have been achieved by such critics, but not without infinite study and the labour of many years.

Such are not the critics of the day, of whom we are now speaking. In the literary world as it lives at present some writer is selected for the place of critic to a newspaper, generally some young writer, who for so many shillings a column shall review whatever book is sent to him and express an opinion,—reading the book through for the purpose, if the amount of honorarium as measured with the amount of labour will enable him to do so. A labourer must measure his work by his pay or he cannot live. From criticism such as this must for the most part be, the general reader has no right to expect philosophical analysis, or literary judgment on which confidence may be placed. But he probably may believe that the books praised will be better than the books censured, and that those which are praised by periodicals which never censure are better worth his attention than those which are not noticed. And readers will also find that by devoting an hour or two on Saturday to the criticisms of the week, they will enable themselves to have an opinion about the books of the day. The knowledge so acquired will not be great, nor will that little be lasting; but it adds something to the pleasure of life to be able to talk on subjects of which others are speaking; and the man who has sedulously gone through the literary notices in the *Spectator* and the *Saturday* may perhaps be justified in thinking himself as well able to talk about the new book as his friend who has brought that new book on the *tapis*,* and who, not improbably, obtained his information from the same source.

As an author, I have paid careful attention to the reviews which have been written on my own work; and I think that now I well know where I may look for a little instruction, where I may expect only greasy adulation, where I shall be cut up into mince-meat for the delight of those who love sharp invective, and where I shall find an equal mixture of praise and censure so adjusted, without much judgment, as to exhibit the impartiality of the newspaper and its staff. Among it all there is much chaff, which I have learned how to throw to the winds, with equal disregard whether it praises or blames;—but I have also found some corn, on which I have fed and nourished myself, and for which I have been thankful.

CHAPTER 15

---∞∞∞---

'The Last Chronicle of Barset'—Leaving
the Post Office—'St Paul's Magazine'

I WILL now go back to the year 1867, in which I was still living at
Waltham Cross. I had some time since bought the house there which
I had at first hired, and added rooms to it, and made it for our purposes very comfortable. It was, however, a rickety old place, requiring
much repair, and occasionally not as weather-tight as it should be. We
had a domain there sufficient for the cows, and for the making of our
butter and hay. For strawberries, asparagus, green peas, out-of-door
peaches, for roses especially, and such everyday luxuries, no place
was ever more excellent. It was only twelve miles from London, and
admitted therefore of frequent intercourse with the metropolis. It was
also near enough to the Roothing country* for hunting purposes. No
doubt the Shoreditch Station,* by which it had to be reached, had its
drawbacks. My average distance also to the Essex meets was twenty
miles. But the place combined as much or more than I had a right to
expect. It was within my own postal district, and had, upon the whole,
been well chosen.

The work I did during the twelve years that I remained there, from
1859 to 1871, was certainly very great. I feel confident that in amount
no other writer contributed so much during that time to English literature. Over and above my novels, I wrote political articles, critical,
social, and sporting articles, for periodicals, without number. I did
the work of a surveyor of the General Post Office, and so did it as to
give the authorities of the department no slightest pretext for fault-
finding. I hunted always at least twice a week. I was frequent in the
whist-room at the Garrick. I lived much in society in London, and
was made happy by the presence of many friends at Waltham Cross.
In addition to this we always spent six weeks at least out of England.
Few men, I think, ever lived a fuller life. And I attribute the power of
doing this altogether to the virtue of early hours. It was my practice to
be at my table every morning at 5.30 a.m.;* and it was also my practice to allow myself no mercy. An old groom, whose business it was

to call me, and to whom I paid £5 a year extra for the duty, allowed himself no mercy. During all those years at Waltham Cross he was never once late with the coffee which it was his duty to bring me. I do not know that I ought not to feel that I owe more to him than to any one else for the success I have had. By beginning at that hour I could complete my literary work before I dressed for breakfast.

All those I think who have lived as literary men,—working daily as literary labourers,—will agree with me that three hours a day will produce as much as a man ought to write. But then he should so have trained himself that he shall be able to work continuously during those three hours,—so have tutored his mind that it shall not be necessary for him to sit nibbling his pen, and gazing at the wall before him, till he shall have found the words with which he wants to express his ideas. It had at this time become my custom,—and it still is my custom, though of late I have become a little lenient to myself,—to write with my watch before me, and to require from myself 250 words every quarter of an hour. I have found that the 250 words have been forthcoming as regularly as my watch went. But my three hours were not devoted entirely to writing. I always began my task by reading the work of the day before, an operation which would take me half an hour, and which consisted chiefly in weighing with my ear the sound of the words and phrases. I would strongly recommend this practice to all tyros in writing. That their work should be read after it has been written is a matter of course,—that it should be read twice at least before it goes to the printers, I take to be a matter of course. But by reading what he has last written, just before he recommences his task, the writer will catch the tone and spirit of what he is then saying, and will avoid the fault of seeming to be unlike himself. This division of time allowed me to produce over ten pages of an ordinary novel volume a day, and if kept up through ten months, would have given as its results three novels of three volumes each in the year;—the precise amount which so greatly acerbated the publisher in Paternoster Row, and which must at any rate be felt to be quite as much as the novel-readers of the world can want from the hands of one man.

I have never written three novels in a year, but by following the plan above described I have written more than as much as three volumes; and by adhering to it over a course of years, I have been enabled to have always on hand,—for some time back now,—one or two or even three unpublished novels in my desk beside me. Were I to die now there are three such* besides *The Prime Minister*, half of which has only yet been issued. One of these has been six years finished, and has never seen the light since it was first tied up in the wrapper which now contains it. I look forward with some grim pleasantry to its publication after another period of six years, and to the declaration of the critics that it has been the work of a period of life at which the power of writing novels had passed from me. Not improbably, however, these pages may be printed first.

In 1866 and 1867 *The Last Chronicle of Barset* was brought out by George Smith in sixpenny monthly numbers. I do not know that this mode of publication had been tried before, or that it answered very well on this occasion. Indeed the shilling magazines had interfered greatly with the success of novels published in numbers without other accompanying matter. The public finding that so much might be had for a shilling, in which a portion of one or more novels was always included, were unwilling to spend their money on the novel alone. Feeling that this certainly had become the case in reference to novels published in shilling numbers, Mr Smith and I determined to make the experiment with sixpenny parts. As he paid me £3000 for the use of my MS., the loss, if any, did not fall upon me. If I remember right, the enterprise was not altogether successful.

Taking it as a whole, I regard this as the best novel I have written. I was never quite satisfied with the development of the plot, which consisted in the loss of a cheque, of a charge made against a clergyman for stealing it, and of absolute uncertainty on the part of the clergyman himself as to the manner in which the cheque had found its way into his hands. I cannot quite make myself believe that even such a man as Mr Crawley could have forgotten how he got it; nor would the generous friend who was anxious to supply his wants have supplied them by tendering the cheque of a third person. Such fault I acknowledge,—acknowledging at the same time that I have never been capable of constructing with complete success the intricacies of a plot that required to be unravelled. But while confessing so much, I claim to have portrayed the mind of the unfortunate man with great accuracy and great delicacy. The pride, the humility, the manliness, the weakness, the conscientious rectitude and bitter prejudices of Mr Crawley were, I feel, true to nature and well described. The surroundings too are good. Mrs Proudie at the palace is a real woman; and the poor old dean dying at the deanery* is also real. The archdeacon in his rectory* is very real. There is a true savour of

English country life all through the book. It was with many misgivings that I killed my old friend Mrs Proudie. I could not, I think, have done it, but for a resolution taken and declared under circumstances of great momentary pressure.

It was thus that it came about.* I was sitting one morning at work upon the novel at the end of the long drawing-room of the Athenæum Club,—as was then my wont when I had slept the previous night in London. As I was there, two clergymen, each with a magazine in his hand, seated themselves, one on one side of the fire and one on the other, close to me. They soon began to abuse what they were reading, and each was reading some part of some novel of mine. The gravamen of their complaint lay in the fact that I reintroduced the same characters so often! 'Here,' said one, 'is that archdeacon whom we have had in every novel he has ever written.' 'And here,' said the other, 'is the old duke whom he has talked about till everybody is tired of him. If I could not invent new characters, I would not write novels at all.' Then one of them fell foul of Mrs Proudie. It was impossible for me not to hear their words, and almost impossible to hear them and be quiet. I got up, and standing between them, I acknowledged myself to be the culprit. 'As to Mrs Proudie,' I said, 'I will go home and kill her before the week is over.' And so I did. The two gentlemen were utterly confounded, and one of them begged me to forget his frivolous observations.

I have sometimes regretted the deed, so great was my delight in writing about Mrs Proudie, so thorough was my knowledge of all the little shades of her character. It was not only that she was a tyrant, a bully, a would-be priestess, a very vulgar woman, and one who would send headlong to the nethermost pit all who disagreed with her; but that at the same time she was conscientious, by no means a hypocrite, really believing in the brimstone which she threatened, and anxious to save the souls around her from its horrors. And as her tyranny increased so did the bitterness of the moments of her repentance increase, in that she knew herself to be a tyrant,—till that bitterness killed her. Since her time others have grown up equally dear to me,—Lady Glencora and her husband, for instance; but I have never dissevered myself from Mrs Proudie, and still live much in company with her ghost.

I have in a previous chapter said how I wrote *Can You Forgive Her?* after the plot of a play which had been rejected,—which play had been called *The Noble Jilt*. Some year or two after the completion of

The Last Chronicle, I was asked by the manager of a theatre to prepare a piece for his stage, and I did so, taking the plot of this novel. I called the comedy *Did He Steal It?** But my friend the manager did not approve of my attempt. My mind at this time was less attentive to such a matter than when dear old George Bartley nearly crushed me by his criticism,—so that I forget the reason given. I have little doubt but that the manager was right. That he intended to express a true opinion, and would have been glad to have taken the piece had he thought it suitable, I am quite sure.*

I have sometimes wished to see during my lifetime a combined republication* of those tales which are occupied with the fictitious county of Barsetshire. These would be *The Warden, Barchester Towers, Doctor Thorne, Framley Parsonage*, and *The Last Chronicle of Barset*. But I have hitherto failed. The copyrights are in the hands of four different persons, including myself, and with one of the four I have not been able to prevail to act in concert with the others.[1]

In 1867 I made up my mind to take a step in life which was not unattended with peril, which many would call rash, and which, when taken, I should be sure at some period to regret. This step was the resignation of my place in the Post Office. I have described how it was that I contrived to combine the performance of its duties with my other avocations in life. I got up always very early; but even this did not suffice. I worked always on Sundays,—as to which no scruple of religion made me unhappy,—and not unfrequently I was driven to work at night. In the winter when hunting was going on, I had to keep myself very much on the alert. And during the London season, when I was generally two or three days of the week in town, I found the official work to be a burden. I had determined some years previously, after due consideration with my wife, to abandon the Post Office when I had put by an income equal to the pension to which I should be entitled if I remained in the department till I was sixty. That I had now done, and I sighed for liberty.

The exact time chosen, the autumn of 1867, was selected because I was then about to undertake other literary work in editing a new magazine,—of which I shall speak very shortly. But in addition to these reasons there was another, which was, I think, at last the actuating

---

[1] Since this was written I have made arrangements for doing as I have wished, and the first volume of the series will now very shortly be published.

cause. When Sir Rowland Hill left the Post Office, and my brother-in-law, Mr Tilley, became Secretary in his place, I applied for the vacant office of Under-Secretary. Had I obtained this I should have given up my hunting, have given up much of my literary work,—at any rate would have edited no magazine,—and would have returned to the habit of my youth in going daily to the General Post Office. There was very much against such a change in life. The increase of salary would not have amounted to above £400 a year, and I should have lost much more than that in literary remuneration. I should have felt bitterly the slavery of attendance at an office, from which I had then been exempt for five-and-twenty years. I should, too, have greatly missed the sport which I loved. But I was attached to the department, had imbued myself with a thorough love of letters,—I mean the letters which are carried by the post,—and was anxious for their welfare as though they were all my own. In short, I wished to continue the connection. I did not wish, moreover, that any younger officer should again pass over my head. I believed that I had been a valuable public servant, and I will own to a feeling existing at that time that I had not altogether been well treated. I was probably wrong in this. I had been allowed to hunt,—and to do as I pleased, and to say what I liked, and had in that way received my reward. I applied for the office, but Mr Scudamore* was appointed to it. He no doubt was possessed of gifts which I did not possess. He understood the manipulation of money and the use of figures, and was a great accountant. I think that I might have been more useful in regard to the labours and wages of the immense body of men employed by the Post Office. However, Mr Scudamore was appointed; and I made up my mind that I would fall back upon my old intention, and leave the department. I think I allowed two years to pass before I took the step; and the day on which I sent the letter was to me most melancholy.

The rule of the service in regard to pensions is very just. A man shall serve till he is sixty before he is entitled to a pension,— unless his health fail him. At that age he is entitled to one-sixtieth of his salary for every year he has served up to forty years. If his health do fail him so that he is unfit for further work before the age named, then he may go with a pension amounting to one-sixtieth for every year he has served. I could not say that my health had failed me, and therefore I went without any pension. I have since felt occasionally that it has been supposed that I left the Post Office under pressure,—because

I attended to hunting and to my literary work rather than to postal matters. As it had for many years been my ambition to be a thoroughly good servant to the public, and to give to the public much more than I took in the shape of salary, this feeling has sometimes annoyed me. And as I am still a little sore on the subject, and as I would not have it imagined after my death that I had slighted the public service to which I belonged, I will venture here to give the reply which was sent to the letter containing my resignation.

'GENERAL POST OFFICE,
'*October 9th,* 1867.

'SIR,— I have received your letter of the 3d inst., in which you tender your resignation as Surveyor in the Post Office service, and state as your reason for this step that you have adopted another profession, the exigencies of which are so great as to make you feel you cannot give to the duties of the Post Office that amount of attention which you consider the Postmaster-General has a right to expect.

'You have for many years ranked among the most conspicuous members of the Post Office, which, on several occasions when you have been employed on large and difficult matters, has reaped much benefit from the great abilities which you have been able to place at its disposal; and in mentioning this, I have been especially glad to record that, notwithstanding the many calls upon your time, you have never permitted your other avocations to interfere with your Post Office work, which has been faithfully and indeed energetically performed.' (There was a touch of irony in this word 'energetically,' but still it did not displease me.)

'In accepting your resignation, which he does with much regret, the Duke of Montrose* desires me to convey to you his own sense of the value of your services, and to state how alive he is to the loss which will be sustained by the department in which you have long been an ornament, and where your place will with difficulty be replaced.

(Signed) J. TILLEY.'

Readers will no doubt think that this is official flummery; and so in fact it is. I do not at all imagine that I was an ornament to the Post Office, and have no doubt that the secretaries and assistant-secretaries very often would have been glad to be rid of me; but the letter may be

taken as evidence that I did not allow my literary enterprises to interfere with my official work. A man who takes public money without
earning it is to me so odious that I can find no pardon for him in my
heart. I have known many such, and some who have craved the power
to do so. Nothing would annoy me more than to think that I should
even be supposed to have been among the number.

And so my connection was dissolved with the department to which
I had applied the thirty-three best years of my life;—I must not say
devoted, for devotion implies an entire surrender, and I certainly had
found time for other occupations. It is however absolutely true that
during all those years I had thought very much more about the Post
Office than I had of my literary work, and had given to it a more
unflagging attention. Up to this time I had never been angry, never
felt myself injured or unappreciated in that my literary efforts were
slighted. But I had suffered very much bitterness on that score in
reference to the Post Office; and I had suffered not only on my own
personal behalf, but also and more bitterly when I could not procure*
to be done the things which I thought ought to be done for the benefit
of others. That the public in little villages should be enabled to buy
postage stamps; that they should have their letters delivered free and
at an early hour; that pillar letter-boxes* should be put up for them
(of which accommodation in the streets and ways of England I was
the originator, having, however, got the authority for the erection of
the first at St Heliers in Jersey); that the letter-carriers and sorters
should not be overworked; that they should be adequately paid, and
have some hours to themselves, especially on Sundays; above all, that
they should be made to earn their wages; and latterly that they should
not be crushed by what I thought to be the damnable system of so-
called merit;—these were the matters by which I was stirred to what
the secretary was pleased to call energetic performance of my duties.
How I loved, when I was contradicted,—as I was very often and no
doubt very properly,—to do instantly as I was bid, and then to prove
that what I was doing was fatuous, dishonest, expensive, and impracticable! And then there were feuds,—such delicious feuds! I was
always an anti-Hillite, acknowledging, indeed, the great thing which
Sir Rowland Hill had done for the country, but believing him to be
entirely unfit to manage men or to arrange labour. It was a pleasure
to me to differ from him on all occasions;—and looking back now,
I think that in all such differences I was right.

Having so steeped myself, as it were, in postal waters, I could not go out from them without a regret. I wonder whether I did anything to improve the style of writing in official reports! I strove to do so gallantly, never being contented with the language of my own reports unless it seemed to have been so written as to be pleasant to be read. I took extreme delight in writing them, not allowing myself to re-copy them, never having them re-copied by others, but sending them up with their original blots and erasures,—if blots and erasures there were. It is hardly manly, I think, that a man should search after a fine neatness at the expense of so much waste labour; or that he should not be able to exact from himself the necessity of writing words in the form in which they should be read. If a copy be required, let it be taken afterwards,—by hand or by machine, as may be. But the writer of a letter, if he wish his words to prevail with the reader, should send them out as written by himself, by his own hand, with his own marks, his own punctuation, correct or incorrect, with the evidence upon them that they have come out from his own mind.

And so the cord was cut, and I was a free man to run about the world where I would.

A little before the date of my resignation, Mr James Virtue,* the printer and publisher, had asked me to edit a new magazine for him, and had offered me a salary of £1000 a year for the work, over and above what might be due to me for my own contributions. I had known something of magazines, and did not believe that they were generally very lucrative. They were, I thought, useful to some publishers as bringing grist to the mill; but as Mr Virtue's business was chiefly that of a printer, in which he was very successful, this consideration could hardly have had much weight with him. I very strongly advised him to abandon the project, pointing out to him that a large expenditure would be necessary to carry on the magazine in accordance with my views,—that I could not be concerned in it on any other understanding, and that the chances of an adequate return to him of his money were very small. He came down to Waltham, listened to my arguments with great patience, and then told me that if I would not do the work he would find some other editor.

Upon this I consented to undertake the duty. My terms as to salary were those which he had himself proposed. The special stipulations which I demanded were: firstly, that I should put whatever I pleased into the magazine, or keep whatever I pleased out of it, without interference; secondly, that I should from month to month give in to him a list of payments to be made to contributors, and that he should pay them, allowing me to fix the amounts; and thirdly, that the arrangement should remain in force at any rate for two years. To all this he made no objection; and during the time that he and I were thus bound together, he not only complied with these stipulations, but also with every suggestion respecting the magazine that I made to him. If the use of large capital, combined with wide liberality and absolute confidence on the part of the proprietor, and perpetual good humour, would have produced success, our magazine certainly would have succeeded.

In all such enterprises the name is the first great difficulty. There is the name which has a meaning and the name which has none,—of which two the name that has none is certainly the better, as it never belies itself. *The Liberal* may cease to be liberal, or *The Fortnightly*, alas! to come out once a fortnight. But *The Cornhill* and *The Argosy* are under any set of circumstances as well adapted to these names as under any other. Then there is the proprietary name, or possibly the editorial name, which is only amiss because the publication may change hands. *Blackwood's* has indeed always remained *Blackwood's*, and *Fraser's*, though it has been bought and sold, still does not sound amiss. Mr Virtue, fearing the too attractive qualities of his own name, wished the magazine to be called *Anthony Trollope's*. But to this I objected eagerly. There were then about the town—still are about the town—two or three literary gentlemen, by whom to have had myself editored would have driven me an exile from my country. After much discussion, we settled on *St Paul's* as the name for our bantling,— not as being in any way new, but as enabling it to fall easily into the ranks with many others. If we were to make ourselves in any way peculiar, it was not by our name that we were desirous of doing so.

I do not think that we did make ourselves in any way peculiar,—and yet there was a great struggle made. On the part of the proprietor, I may say that money was spent very freely. On my own part, I may declare that I omitted nothing which I thought might tend to success. I read all manuscripts sent to me, and endeavoured to judge impartially. I succeeded in obtaining the services of an excellent literary corps. During the three years and a half of my editorship I was assisted by Mr Goschen, Captain Brackenbury, Edward Dicey, Percy Fitzgerald, A. H. Layard, Allingham, Leslie Stephen,

Mrs Lynn Linton, my brother, T. A. Trollope, and his wife, Charles Lever, E. Arnold, Austin Dobson, R. A. Proctor, Lady Pollock, G. H. Lewes, C. Mackay, Hardman (of the *Times*), George Macdonald, W. R. Greg, Mrs Oliphant, Sir Charles Trevelyan, Leoni Levi, Dutton Cook,*—and others, whose names would make the list too long. It might have been thought that with such aid the *St Paul's* would have succeeded. I do not think that the failure—for it did fail—arose from bad editing. Perhaps too much editing might have been the fault. I was too anxious to be good, and did not enough think of what might be lucrative.

It did fail, for it never paid its way. It reached, if I remember right, a circulation of nearly 10,000—perhaps on one or two occasions may have gone beyond that. But the enterprise had been set on foot on a system too expensive to be made lucrative by anything short of a very large circulation. Literary merit will hardly set a magazine afloat, though when afloat it will sustain it. Time is wanted,—or the hubbub, and flurry, and excitement created by ubiquitous sesquipe-dalian advertisement. Merit and time together may be effective, but they must be backed by economy and patience.

I think, upon the whole, that publishers themselves have been the best editors of magazines, when they have been able to give time and intelligence to the work. Nothing certainly has ever been done better than *Blackwood's*. The *Cornhill*, too, after Thackeray had left it and before Leslie Stephen had taken it, seemed to be in quite efficient hands,—those hands being the hands of proprietor and publisher. The proprietor, at any rate, knows what he wants and what he can afford, and is not so frequently tempted to fall into that worst of literary quicksands, the publishing of matter not for the sake of the readers, but for that of the writer. I did not so sin very often, but often enough to feel that I was a coward. 'My dear friend, my dear friend, this is trash!' It is so hard to speak thus,—but so necessary for an editor! We all remember the thorn in his pillow* of which Thackeray complained. Occasionally I know that I did give way on behalf of some literary aspirant whose work did not represent itself to me as being good; and as often as I did so, I broke my trust to those who employed me. Now, I think that such editors as Thackeray and myself—if I may for the moment be allowed to couple men so unequal—will always be liable to commit such faults, but that the natures of publishers and proprietors will be less soft.

Nor do I know why the pages of a magazine should be considered to be open to any aspirant who thinks that he can write an article, or why the manager of a magazine should be doomed to read all that may be sent to him. The object of the proprietor is to produce a periodical that shall satisfy the public, which he may probably best do by securing the services of writers of acknowledged ability.

CHAPTER 16

Beverley

VERY early in life, very soon after I had become a clerk in St Martin's le Grand, when I was utterly impecunious and beginning to fall grievously into debt, I was asked by an uncle of mine,* who was himself a clerk in the War Office, what destination I should like best for my future life. He probably meant to inquire whether I wished to live married or single, whether to remain in the Post Office or to leave it, whether I should prefer the town or the country. I replied that I should like to be a Member of Parliament. My uncle, who was given to sarcasm, rejoined that, as far as he knew, few clerks in the Post Office did become Members of Parliament. I think it was the remembrance of this jeer which stirred me up to look for a seat as soon as I had made myself capable of holding one by leaving the public service. My uncle was dead, but if I could get a seat, the knowledge that I had done so might travel to that bourne* from whence he was not likely to return, and he might there feel that he had done me wrong.

Independently of this, I have always thought that to sit in the British Parliament should be the highest object of ambition to every educated Englishman. I do not by this mean to suggest that every educated Englishman should set before himself a seat in Parliament as a probable or even a possible career; but that the man in Parliament has reached a higher position than the man out,—that to serve one's country without pay is the grandest work that a man can do,—that of all studies the study of politics is the one in which a man may make himself most useful to his fellow-creatures,— and that of all lives, public political lives are capable of the highest efforts. So thinking,— though I was aware that fifty-three was too late an age at which to commence a new career,— I resolved with much hesitation that I would make the attempt.

Writing now at an age beyond sixty, I can say that my political feelings and convictions have never undergone any change. They are now what they became when I first began to have political feelings and convictions. Nor do I find in myself any tendency to modify them as

I have found generally in men as they grow old. I consider myself to be an advanced, but still a Conservative-Liberal,* which I regard not only as a possible but as a rational and consistent phase of political existence. I can, I believe, in a very few words, make known my political theory; and as I am anxious that any who know aught of me should know that, I will endeavour to do so.

It must, I think, be painful to all men to feel inferiority. It should, I think, be a matter of some pain to all men to feel superiority, unless when it has been won by their own efforts. We do not understand the operations of Almighty wisdom, and are therefore unable to tell the causes of the terrible inequalities that we see,—why some, why so many, should have so little to make life enjoyable, so much to make it painful, while a few others, not through their own merit, have had gifts poured out to them from a full hand. We acknowledge the hand of God and His wisdom, but still we are struck with awe and horror at the misery of many of our brethren. We who have been born to the superior condition,—for in this matter I consider myself to be standing on a platform with dukes and princes, and all others to whom plenty and education and liberty have been given,—cannot, I think, look upon the inane, unintellectual, and toil-bound* life of those who cannot even feed themselves sufficiently by their sweat, without some feeling of injustice, some feeling of pain.

This consciousness of wrong has induced in many enthusiastic but unbalanced minds a desire to set all things right by a proclaimed equality. In their efforts such men have shown how powerless they are in opposing the ordinances of the Creator. For the mind of the thinker and the student is driven to admit, though it be awestruck by apparent injustice, that this inequality is the work of God. Make all men equal today, and God has so created them that they shall be all unequal tomorrow. The so-called Conservative, the conscientious philanthropic Conservative, seeing this, and being surely convinced that such inequalities are of divine origin, tells himself that it is his duty to preserve them. He thinks that the preservation of the welfare of the world depends on the maintenance of those distances between the prince and the peasant by which he finds himself to be surrounded;—and perhaps, I may add, that the duty is not unpleasant, as he feels himself to be one of the princes.

But this man, though he sees something, and sees that very clearly, sees only a little. The divine inequality is apparent to him, but not the equally divine diminution of that inequality. That such diminution is taking place on all sides is apparent enough; but it is apparent to him as an evil, the consummation of which it is his duty to retard. He cannot prevent it; and therefore the society to which he belongs is, in his eyes, retrograding. He will even, at times, assist it; and will do so conscientiously, feeling that, under the gentle pressure supplied by him, and with the drags and holdfasts which he may add, the movement would be slower than it would become if subjected to his proclaimed and absolute opponents. Such, I think, are Conservatives;—and I speak of men who, with the fear of God before their eyes and the love of their neighbours warm in their hearts, endeavour to do their duty to the best of their ability.

Using the term which is now common, and which will be best understood, I will endeavour to explain how the equally conscientious Liberal is opposed to the Conservative. He is equally aware that these distances are of divine origin, equally averse to any sudden disruption of society in quest of some Utopian blessedness;—but he is alive to the fact that these distances are day by day becoming less, and he regards this continual diminution as a series of steps towards that human millennium of which he dreams. He is even willing to help the many to ascend the ladder a little, though he knows, as they come up towards him, he must go down to meet them. What is really in his mind is,—I will not say equality, for the word is offensive, and presents to the imaginations of men ideas of communism, of ruin, and insane democracy,—but a tendency towards equality. In following that, however, he knows that he must be hemmed in by safeguards, lest he be tempted to travel too quickly; and therefore he is glad to be accompanied on his way by the repressive action of a Conservative opponent. Holding such views, I think I am guilty of no absurdity in calling myself an advanced Conservative-Liberal. A man who entertains in his mind any political doctrine, except as a means of improving the condition of his fellows, I regard as a political intriguer, a charlatan, and a conjurer,—as one who thinks that, by a certain amount of wary wire-pulling, he may raise himself in the estimation of the world.

I am aware that this theory of politics will seem to many to be stilted, overstrained, and, as the Americans would say, high-faluten. Many will declare that the majority even of those who call themselves politicians,—perhaps even of those who take an active part in politics,—are stirred by no such feelings as these, and acknowledge no such motives. Men become Tories or Whigs, Liberals or Conservatives, partly by education,—following their fathers,—partly by chance, partly as openings come, partly in accordance with the bent of their minds, but still without any far-fetched reasonings as to distances and the diminution of distances. No doubt it is so;—and in the battle of politics, as it goes, men are led further and further away from first causes, till at last a measure is opposed by one simply because it is advocated by another, and members of Parliament swarm into lobbies, following the dictation of their leaders, and not their own individual judgments. But the principle is at work throughout. To many, though hardly acknowledged, it is still apparent. On almost all it has its effect; though there are the intriguers, the clever conjurers, to whom politics is simply such a game as is billiards or rackets, only played with greater results. To the minds that create and lead and sway political opinion, some such theory is, I think, ever present.

The truth of all this I had long since taken home to myself. I had now been thinking of it for thirty years, and had never doubted. But I had always been aware of a certain visionary weakness about myself in regard to politics. A man, to be useful in Parliament, must be able to confine himself and conform himself, to be satisfied with doing a little bit of a little thing at a time. He must patiently get up everything connected with the duty on mushrooms, and then be satisfied with himself when at last he has induced a Chancellor of the Exchequer to say that he will consider the impost at the first opportunity. He must be content to be beaten six times in order that, on a seventh, his work may be found to be of assistance to some one else. He must remember that he is one out of 650, and be content with 1-650th part of the attention of the nation. If he have grand ideas, he must keep them to himself, unless by chance he can work his way up to the top of the tree. In short, he must be a practical man. Now I knew that in politics I could never become a practical man. I should never be satisfied with a soft word from the Chancellor of the Exchequer, but would always be flinging my over-taxed ketchup in his face.

Nor did it seem to me to be possible that I should ever become a good speaker. I had no special gifts that way, and had not studied the art early enough in life to overcome natural difficulties. I had found that, with infinite labour, I could learn a few sentences by heart, and deliver them, monotonously indeed, but clearly. Or, again, if there were something special to be said, I could say it in a commonplace fashion,—but always as though I were in a hurry, and with the fear before me of being thought to be prolix. But I had no power of combining, as a public speaker should always do, that which I had studied with that which occurred to me at the moment. It must be all lesson,—which I found to be best; or else all impromptu,—which was very bad indeed, unless I had something special on my mind. I was thus aware that I could do no good by going into Parliament,—that the time for it, if there could have been a time, had gone by. But still I had an almost insane desire to sit there, and be able to assure myself that my uncle's scorn had not been deserved.

In 1867 it had been suggested to me that, in the event of a dissolution, I should stand for one division of the county of Essex; and I had promised that I would do so, though the promise at that time was as rash a one as a man could make. I was instigated to this by the late Charles Buxton,* a man whom I greatly loved, and who was very anxious that the county for which his brother had sat, and with which the family were connected, should be relieved from what he regarded as the thraldom of Toryism. But there was no dissolution then. Mr Disraeli passed his Reform Bill, by the help of the Liberal member for Newark,* and the summoning of a new Parliament was postponed till the next year. By this new Reform Bill Essex was portioned out into three instead of two electoral divisions, one of which—that adjacent to London—would, it was thought, be altogether Liberal. After the promise which I had given, the performance of which would have cost me a large sum of money absolutely in vain, it was felt by some that I should be selected as one of the candidates for the new division,—and as such I was proposed by Mr Charles Buxton. But another gentleman, who would have been bound by previous pledges to support me, was put forward by what I believe to have been the dissenting interest,* and I had to give way. At the election this gentleman, with another Liberal, who had often stood for the county, were returned without a contest. Alas! alas! They were both unseated at the next election, when the great Conservative reaction* took place.

In the spring of 1868 I was sent to the United States on a postal mission, of which I will speak presently. While I was absent the dissolution took place. On my return I was somewhat too late to look out for a seat, but I had friends who knew the weakness of my ambition; and it was not likely, therefore, that I should escape the peril of being put forward for some impossible borough as to which the Liberal party would not choose that it should go to the Conservatives without a struggle. At last, after one or two others, Beverley* was proposed to me, and to Beverley I went.

I must, however, exculpate the gentleman who acted as my agent,* from undue persuasion exercised towards me. He was a man who thoroughly understood Parliament, having sat there himself,—and he sits there now at this moment. He understood Yorkshire,—or at least the East Riding of Yorkshire, in which Beverley is situated,— certainly better than any one alive. He understood all the mysteries of canvassing, and he knew well the traditions, the condition, and the prospect of the Liberal party. I will not give his name, but they who knew Yorkshire in 1868 will not be at a loss to find it. 'So,' said he, 'you are going to stand for Beverley?' I replied gravely that I was thinking of doing so. 'You don't expect to get in?' he said. Again I was grave. I would not, I said, be sanguine, but nevertheless I was disposed to hope for the best. 'Oh no!' continued he, with good-humoured raillery, 'you won't get in. I don't suppose you really expect it. But there is a fine career open to you. You will spend £1000, and lose the election. Then you will petition, and spend another £1000. You will throw out the elected members. There will be a commission, and the borough will be disfranchised. For a beginner such as you are, that will be a great success.' And yet, in the teeth of this, from a man who knew all about it, I persisted in going to Beverley!

The borough, which returned two members, had long been represented by Sir Henry Edwards, of whom, I think, I am justified in saying that he had contracted a close intimacy with it for the sake of the seat. There had been many contests, many petitions, many void elections, many members, but, through it all, Sir Henry had kept his seat, if not with permanence, yet with a fixity of tenure next door to permanence. I fancy that with a little management between the parties the borough might at this time have returned a member of each colour quietly;—but there were spirits there who did not love political quietude, and it was at last decided that there should be two Liberal and two Conservative candidates. Sir Henry was joined by a young man of fortune* in quest of a seat, and I was grouped with Mr Maxwell,* the eldest son of Lord Herries, a Scotch Roman Catholic peer who lives in the neighbourhood.

When the time came I went down to canvass, and spent, I think, the most wretched fortnight of my manhood. In the first place, I was subject to a bitter tyranny from grinding vulgar tyrants. They were doing what they could, or said that they were doing so, to secure me a seat in Parliament, and I was to be in their hands for at any rate the period of my candidature. On one day both of us, Mr Maxwell and I, wanted to go out hunting. We proposed to ourselves but the one holiday during this period of intense labour; but I was assured, as was he also, by a publican who was working for us, that if we committed such a crime he and all Beverley would desert us. From morning to evening every day I was taken round the lanes and by-ways of that uninteresting town, canvassing every voter, exposed to the rain, up to my knees in slush, and utterly unable to assume that air of triumphant joy with which a jolly, successful candidate should be invested. At night, every night I had to speak somewhere,—which was bad; and to listen to the speaking of others,— which was much worse. When, on one Sunday, I proposed to go to the Minster Church,* I was told that was quite useless, as the Church party were all certain to support Sir Henry! 'Indeed,' said the publican, my tyrant, 'he goes there in a kind of official profession, and you had better not allow yourself to be seen in the same place.' So I stayed away and omitted my prayers. No Church of England church in Beverley would on such an occasion have welcomed a Liberal candidate. I felt myself to be a kind of pariah in the borough, to whom was opposed all that was pretty, and all that was nice, and all that was—ostensibly—good.

But perhaps my strongest sense of discomfort arose from the conviction that my political ideas were all leather and prunella* to the men whose votes I was soliciting. They cared nothing for my doctrines, and could not be made to understand that I should have any. I had been brought to Beverley either to beat Sir Henry Edwards,—which, however, no one probably thought to be feasible,—or to cause him the greatest possible amount of trouble, inconvenience, and expense. There were, indeed, two points on which a portion of my wished-for supporters seemed to have opinions, and on both these two points I was driven by my opinions to oppose them. Some were anxious for the Ballot,*—which had not then become law,—and some desired the Permissive Bill.* I hated, and do hate, both these measures, thinking it to be unworthy of a great people to free itself from the evil results of vicious conduct by unmanly restraints. Undue influence on voters is a great evil from which this country had already done much to emancipate itself by extended electoral divisions and by an increase of independent feeling. These, I thought, and not secret voting, were the weapons by which electoral intimidation should be overcome. And as for drink, I believe in no Parliamentary restraint; but I do believe in the gradual effect of moral teaching and education. But a Liberal, to do any good at Beverley, should have been able to swallow such gnats* as those. I would swallow nothing, and was altogether the wrong man.

I knew, from the commencement of my candidature, how it would be. Of course that well-trained gentleman who condescended to act as my agent, had understood the case, and I ought to have taken his thoroughly kind advice. He had seen it all, and had told himself that it was wrong that one so innocent in such ways as I, so utterly unable to fight such a battle, should be carried down into Yorkshire merely to spend money and to be annoyed. He could not have said more than he did say, and I suffered for my obstinacy. Of course I was not elected. Sir Henry Edwards and his comrade became members for Beverley, and I was at the bottom of the poll. I paid £400 for my expenses, and then returned to London.

My friendly agent in his raillery had of course exaggerated the cost. He had, when I arrived at Beverley, asked me for a cheque for £400, and told me that that sum would suffice. It did suffice. How it came to pass that exactly that sum should be required I never knew, but such was the case. Then there came a petition,—not from me, but from the town. The inquiry was made, the two gentlemen were unseated, the borough was disfranchised,* Sir Henry Edwards was put on his trial for some kind of Parliamentary offence and was acquitted. In this way Beverley's privilege as a borough and my Parliamentary ambition were brought to an end at the same time.

When I knew the result I did not altogether regret it. It may be that Beverley might have been brought to political confusion and Sir Henry Edwards relegated to private life without the expenditure of my hard-earned money, and without that fortnight of misery; but connecting the things together, as it was natural that I should do, I did flatter myself that I had done some good. It had seemed to me that nothing could be worse, nothing more unpatriotic, nothing more absolutely opposed to the system of representative government, than the time-honoured practices of the borough of Beverley. It had come to pass that political cleanliness was odious to the citizens. There was something grand in the scorn with which a leading Liberal there turned up his nose at me when I told him that there should be no bribery, no treating, not even a pot of beer on our* side. It was a matter for study to see how at Beverley politics were appreciated because they might subserve electoral purposes, and how little it was understood that electoral purposes, which are in themselves a nuisance, should be endured in order that they may subserve politics. And then the time, the money, the mental energy, which had been expended in making the borough a secure seat for a gentleman who had realised the idea that it would become him to be a member of Parliament! This use of the borough seemed to be realised and approved in the borough generally. The inhabitants had taught themselves to think that it was for such purposes that boroughs were intended! To have assisted in putting an end to this, even in one town, was to a certain extent a satisfaction.

CHAPTER 17

*The American Postal Treaty—the Question of Copyright
with America—Four More Novels*

IN the spring of 1868,—before the affair of Beverley, which, as
being the first direct result of my resignation of office, has been
brought in a little out of its turn,—I was requested to go over to
the United States and make a postal treaty at Washington. This, as
I had left the service, I regarded as a compliment, and of course
I went. It was my third visit to America, and I have made two since.
As far as the Post Office work was concerned, it was very far from
being agreeable. I found myself located at Washington, a place I do
not love, and was harassed by delays, annoyed by incompetence, and
opposed by what I felt to be personal and not national views. I had
to deal with two men,*—with one who was a working officer of the
American Post Office, than whom I have never met a more zealous,
or, as far as I could judge, a more honest public servant. He had his
views and I had mine, each of us having at heart the welfare of the
service in regard to his own country,—each of us also having certain
orders which we were bound to obey. But the other gentleman, who
was in rank the superior,—whose executive position was dependent
on his official status, as is the case with our own Ministers,—did not
recommend himself to me equally. He would make appointments
with me and then not keep them, which at last offended me so grievously, that I declared at the Washington Post Office that if this treatment were continued, I would write home to say that any further
action on my part was impossible. I think I should have done so
had it not occurred to me that I might in this way serve his purpose
rather than my own, or the purposes of those who had sent me. The
treaty, however, was at last made,—the purport of which was, that
everything possible should be done, at a heavy expenditure on the
part of England, to expedite the mails from England to America,
and that nothing should be done by America to expedite the mails
from thence to us. The expedition I believe to be now equal both
ways; but it could not be maintained as it is without the payment of

a heavy subsidy from Great Britain, whereas no subsidy is paid by the States.[1]

I had also a commission from the Foreign Office, for which I had asked, to make an effort on behalf of an international copyright between the United States and Great Britain,—the want of which is the one great impediment to pecuniary success which still stands in the way of successful English authors. I cannot say that I have never had a shilling of American money on behalf of reprints of my work; but I have been conscious of no such payment. Having found many years ago—in 1861, when I made a struggle on the subject, being then in the States, the details of which are sufficiently amusing[2]— that I could not myself succeed in dealing with American booksellers, I have sold all foreign right to the English publishers; and though I do not know that I have raised my price against them on that score, I may in this way have had some indirect advantage from the American market. But I do know that what the publishers have received here is very trifling. I doubt whether Messrs Chapman & Hall, my present publishers, get for early sheets sent to the States as much as 5 per cent on the price they pay me for my manuscript. But the American readers are more numerous than the English, and taking them all through, are probably more wealthy. If I can get £1000 for a book here (exclusive of their market), I ought to be able to get as much there. If a man supply 600 customers with shoes in place of 300, there is no question as to such result. Why not, then, if I can supply 60,000 readers instead of 30,000?

I fancied that I knew that the opposition to an international copyright was by no means an American feeling, but was confined to the bosoms of a few interested Americans. All that I did and heard in

[1] This was a state of things which may probably have appeared to American politicians to be exactly that which they should try to obtain. The whole arrangement has again been altered since the time of which I have spoken.

[2] In answer to a question from myself, a certain American publisher*—he who usually reprinted my works—promised me that *if any other American publisher republished my work on America before he had done so,* he would not bring out a competing edition, though there would be no law to hinder him. I then entered into an agreement with another American publisher, stipulating to supply him with early sheets; and he stipulating to supply me a certain royalty on his sales, and to supply me with accounts half-yearly. I sent the sheets with energetic punctuality, and the work was brought out with equal energy and precision—by my old American publishers. The gentleman who made the promise had not broken his word. No other American edition had come out before his. I never got any account, and, of course, never received a dollar.

reference to the subject on this further visit,—and having a certain authority from the British Secretary of State with me I could hear and do something,— altogether confirmed me in this view. I have no doubt that if I could poll American readers, or American senators,—or even American representatives, if the polling could be unbiassed,— or American booksellers,[1] that an assent to an international copyright would be the result. The state of things as it is is crushing to American authors, as the publishers will not pay them on a liberal scale, knowing that they can supply their customers with modern English literature without paying for it. The English amount of production so much exceeds the American, that the rate at which the former can be published rules the market. It is equally injurious to American booksellers,— except to two or three of the greatest houses. No small man can now acquire the exclusive right of printing and selling an English book. If such a one attempt it, the work is printed instantly by one of the leviathans,—who alone are the gainers. The argument of course is, that the American readers are the gainers,— that as they can get for nothing the use of certain property, they would be cutting their own throats were they to pass a law debarring themselves from the power of such appropriation. In this argument all idea of honesty is thrown to the winds. It is not that they do not approve of a system of copyright,—as many great men have disapproved,—for their own law of copyright is as stringent as is ours. A bold assertion is made that they like to appropriate the goods of other people; and that, as in this case, they can do so with impunity, they will continue to do so. But the argument, as far as I have been able to judge, comes not from the people, but from the bookselling leviathans, and from those politicians whom the leviathans are able to attach to their interests. The ordinary American purchaser is not much affected by slight variations in price. He is at any rate too high-hearted to be affected by the prospect of such variation. It is the man who wants to make money, not he who fears that he may be called upon to spend it, who controls such matters as this in the United States. It is the large speculator who becomes powerful in the lobbies of the House, and understands how wise it may be to incur a great expenditure either in the creation of a great business, or in protecting that which he has created

---

[1] I might also say American publishers, if I might count them by the number of heads, and not by the amount of work done by the firms.

from competition. Nothing was done in 1868,—and nothing has been done since (up to 1876). A Royal Commission on the law of copyright is now about to sit in this country, of which I have consented to be a member; and the question must then be handled, though nothing done by a Royal Commission here can affect American legislators. But I do believe that if the measure be consistently and judiciously urged, the enemies to it in the States will gradually be overcome. Some years since we had some *quasi* private meetings, under the presidency of Lord Stanhope, in Mr John Murray's dining-room, on the subject of international copyright. At one of these I discussed this matter of American international copyright with Charles Dickens, who strongly declared his conviction that nothing would induce an American to give up the power he possesses of pirating British literature. But he was a man who, seeing clearly what was before him, would not realise the possibility of shifting views. Because in this matter the American decision had been, according to his thinking, dishonest, therefore no other than dishonest decision was to be expected from Americans. Against that idea I protested, and now protest. American dishonesty is rampant; but it is rampant only among a few. It is the great misfortune of the community that those few have been able to dominate so large a portion of the population among which all men can vote, but so few can understand for what they are voting.

Since this was written the Commission on the law of copyright* has sat and made its report. With the great body of it I agree, and could serve no reader by alluding here at length to matters which are discussed there. But in regard to this question of international copyright with the United States, I think that we were incorrect in the expression of an opinion that fair justice,—or justice approaching to fairness,—is now done by American publishers to English authors by payments made by them for early sheets. I have just found that £20 was paid to my publisher in England for the use of the early sheets of a novel for which I received £1600 in England. When asked why he accepted so little, he assured me that the firm with whom he dealt would not give more. 'Why not go to another firm?' I asked. No other firm would give a dollar, because other firms would fear* to run counter to that great firm which had assumed to itself the right of publishing my books. I soon after received a copy of my own novel in the American form, and found that it was published for 7½d. That a great sale was expected can be argued from the fact that without a

great sale the paper and printing necessary for the republication of
a three-volume novel could not be supplied. Many thousand copies
must have been sold. But from these the author received not one shilling. I need hardly point out that the sum of £20 would not do more
than compensate the publisher for his trouble in making the bargain.
The publisher here no doubt might have refused to supply the early
sheets, but he had no means of exacting a higher price than that
offered. I mention the circumstance here because it has been boasted,
on behalf of the American publishers, that though there is no international copyright, they deal so liberally with English authors as to
make it unnecessary that the English author should be so protected.
With the fact of the £20 just brought to my knowledge, and with the
copy of my book published at 7½d. now in my hands, I feel that an
international copyright is very necessary for my protection.

They among Englishmen who best love and most admire the
United States, have felt themselves tempted to use the strongest language in denouncing the sins of Americans. Who can but love their
personal generosity, their active and far-seeking philanthropy, their
love of education, their hatred of ignorance, the general convictions
in the minds of all of them that a man should be enabled to walk
upright, fearing no one and conscious that he is responsible for his
own actions? In what country have grander efforts been made by
private munificence to relieve the sufferings of humanity?* Where
can the English traveller find any more anxious to assist him than
the normal American, when once the American shall have found
the Englishman to be neither sullen nor fastidious? Who, lastly, is
so much an object of heart-felt admiration of the American man
and the American woman as the well-mannered and well-educated
Englishwoman or Englishman? These are the ideas which I say spring
uppermost in the minds of the unprejudiced English traveller as
he makes acquaintance with these near relatives. Then he becomes
cognisant of their official doings, of their politics, of their municipal
scandals, of their great ring-robberies,* of their lobbyings and briber-
ies, and the infinite baseness of their public life. There at the top of
everything he finds the very men who are the least fit to occupy high
places. American public dishonesty is so glaring that the very friends
he has made in the country are not slow to acknowledge it,—speaking
of public life as a thing apart from their own existence, as a state of
dirt in which it would be an insult to suppose that they are concerned!

In the midst of it all the stranger, who sees so much that he hates and so much that he loves, hardly knows how to express himself.

'It is not enough that you are personally clean,' he says, with what energy and courage he can command,—'not enough though the clean outnumber the foul as greatly as those gifted with eyesight outnumber the blind, if you that can see allow the blind to lead you. It is not by the private lives of the millions that the outside world will judge you, but by the public career of those units whose venality is allowed to debase the name of your country. There never was plainer proof given than is given here, that it is the duty of every honest citizen to look after the honour of his State.'

Personally, I have to own that I have met Americans,—men, but more frequently women,—who have in all respects come up to my ideas of what men and women should be: energetic, having opinions of their own, quick in speech, with some dash of sarcasm at their command, always intelligent, sweet to look at (I speak of the women), fond of pleasure, and each with a personality of his or her own which makes no effort necessary on my own part in remembering the difference between Mrs Walker and Mrs Green, or between Mr Smith and Mr Johnson. They have faults. They are self-conscious, and are too prone to prove by ill-concealed struggles that they are as good as you,—whereas you perhaps have been long acknowledging to yourself that they are much better. And there is sometimes a pretence at personal dignity among those who think themselves to have risen high in the world which is deliciously ludicrous. I remember two old gentlemen,—the owners of names which stand deservedly high in public estimation,—whose deportment at a public funeral turned the occasion into one for irresistible comedy. They are suspicious at first, and fearful of themselves. They lack that simplicity of manners which with us has become a habit from our childhood. But they are never fools, and I think that they are seldom ill-natured.

There is an American woman,* of whom not to speak in a work purporting to be a memoir of my own life would be to omit all allusion to one of the chief pleasures which has graced my later years. In the last fifteen years she has been, out of my family, my most chosen friend. She is a ray of light to me, from which I can always strike a spark by thinking of her. I do not know that I should please her or do any good by naming her. But not to allude to her in these pages would amount almost to a falsehood. I could not write truly of myself without saying that such a friend had been vouchsafed to me. I trust she may live to read the words I have now written, and to wipe away a tear as she thinks of my feeling while I write them.

I was absent on this occasion something over three months, and on my return I went back with energy to my work at the *St Paul's Magazine*. The first novel in it from my own pen was called *Phineas Finn*, in which I commenced a series of semi-political tales.* As I was debarred from expressing my opinions in the House of Commons, I took this method of declaring myself. And as I could not take my seat on those benches where I might possibly have been shone upon by the Speaker's eye, I had humbly to crave his permission for a seat in the gallery, so that I might thus become conversant with the ways and doings of the House in which some of my scenes were to be placed. The Speaker was very gracious, and gave me a running order for, I think, a couple of months. It was enough, at any rate, to enable me often to be very tired,—and, as I have been assured by members, to talk of the proceedings almost as well as though Fortune had enabled me to fall asleep within the House itself.

In writing *Phineas Finn*, and also some other novels which followed it, I was conscious that I could not make a tale pleasing chiefly, or perhaps in any part, by politics. If I write politics for my own sake, I must put in love and intrigue, social incidents, with perhaps a dash of sport, for the benefit of my readers. In this way I think I made my political hero interesting. It was certainly a blunder to take him from Ireland—into which I was led by the circumstance that I created the scheme of the book during a visit to Ireland.* There was nothing to be gained by the peculiarity, and there was an added difficulty in obtaining sympathy and affection for a politician belonging to a nationality whose politics are not respected in England. But in spite of this Phineas succeeded. It was not a brilliant success,—because men and women not conversant with political matters could not care much for a hero who spent so much of his time either in the House of Commons or in a public office. But the men who would have lived with Phineas Finn read the book, and the women who would have lived with Lady Laura Standish* read it also. As this was what I had intended, I was contented. It is all fairly good except the ending,—as to which till I got to it I made no provision. As I fully intended to bring my hero again into the world, I was wrong to marry him to a simple pretty Irish girl, who could only be felt as an encumbrance on such return.

When he did return I had no alternative but to kill the simple pretty Irish girl, which was an unpleasant and awkward necessity.

In writing *Phineas Finn* I had constantly before me the necessity of progression in character,—of marking the changes in men and women, which would naturally be produced by the lapse of years. In most novels the writer can have no such duty, as the period occupied is not long enough to allow of the change of which I speak. In *Ivanhoe*, all the incidents of which are included in less than a month, the characters should be, as they are, consistent throughout. Novelists who have undertaken to write the life of a hero or heroine have generally considered their work completed at the interesting period of marriage, and have contented themselves with the advance in taste and manners which are common to all boys and girls as they become men and women. Fielding, no doubt, did more than this in *Tom Jones*, which is one of the greatest novels in the English language, for there he has shown how a noble and sanguine nature may fall away under temptation and be again strengthened and made to stand upright. But I do not think that novelists have often set before themselves the state of progressive change,—nor should I have done it, had I not found myself so frequently allured back to my old friends. So much of my inner life was passed in their company, that I was continually asking myself how this woman would act when this or that event had passed over her head, or how that man would carry himself when his youth had become manhood, or his manhood declined to old age. It was in regard to the old Duke of Omnium, of his nephew and heir, and of his heir's wife, Lady Glencora, that I was anxious to carry out this idea; but others added themselves to my mind as I went on, and I got round me a circle of persons as to whom I knew not only their present characters, but how those characters were to be affected by years and circumstances. The happy motherly life of Violet Effingham, which was due to the girl's honest but long-restrained love; the tragic misery of Lady Laura, which was equally due to the sale she made of herself in her wretched marriage; and the long suffering but final success of the hero, of which he had deserved the first by his vanity, and the last by his constant honesty, had been foreshadowed to me from the first. As to the incidents of the story, the circumstances by which these personages were to be effected, I knew nothing. They were created for the most part as they were described. I never could arrange a set of events before me. But the evil and the good of my puppets,* and how the evil would always lead to evil, and the good produce good,—that was clear to me as the stars on a summer night.

Lady Laura Standish is the best character in *Phineas Finn* and its sequel *Phineas Redux*,—of which I will speak here together. They are, in fact, but one novel, though they were brought out at a considerable interval of time and in different form. The first was commenced in the *St Paul's Magazine** in 1867, and the other was brought out in the *Graphic** in 1873. In this there was much bad arrangement, as I had no right to expect that novel-readers would remember the characters of a story after an interval of six years, or that any little interest which might have been taken in the career of my hero could then have been renewed. I do not know that such interest was renewed. But I found that the sequel enjoyed the same popularity as the former part, and among the same class of readers. Phineas, and Lady Laura, and Lady Chiltern—as Violet had become—and the old duke,—whom I killed gracefully, and the new duke, and the young duchess, either kept their old friends or made new friends for themselves. *Phineas Finn*, I certainly think, was successful from first to last. I am aware, however, that there was nothing in it to touch the heart like the abasement of Lady Mason when confessing her guilt to her old lover, or any approach in delicacy of delineation to the character of Mr Crawley.

Phineas Finn, the first part of the story, was completed in May 1867. In June and July I wrote *Linda Tressel* for *Blackwood's Magazine*, of which I have already spoken. In September and October I wrote a short novel, called *The Golden Lion of Granpère*, which was intended also for *Blackwood*,—with a view of being published anonymously; but Mr Blackwood did not find the arrangement to be profitable, and the story remained on my hands, unread and unthought of, for a few years. It appeared subsequently in *Good Words*. It was written on the model of *Nina Balatka* and *Linda Tressel*, but is very inferior to either of them. In November of the same year, 1867, I began a very long novel, which I called *He Knew He Was Right*, and which was brought out by Mr Virtue, the proprietor of the *St Paul's Magazine*, in sixpenny numbers, every week. I do not know that in any literary effort I ever fell more completely short of my own intention than in this story. It was my purpose to create sympathy for the unfortunate man who, while endeavouring to do his duty to all around him, should be led constantly astray by his unwillingness to submit his own judgment to the opinion of others. The man is made to be unfortunate enough, and the evil which he does is apparent. So far I did not fail, but the sympathy has not been created yet. I look upon the story as being nearly altogether bad. It is in part redeemed by certain scenes in the house and vicinity of an old maid in Exeter.* But a novel which in its main parts is bad cannot, in truth, be redeemed by the vitality of subordinate characters.

This work was finished while I was at Washington in the spring of 1868, and on the day after I finished it, I commenced *The Vicar of Bullhampton*, a novel which I wrote for Messrs Bradbury & Evans. This I completed in November 1868, and at once began *Sir Harry Hotspur of Humblethwaite*, a story which I was still writing at the close of the year. I look upon these two years, 1867 and 1868, of which I have given a somewhat confused account in this and the two preceding chapters, as the busiest in my life. I had indeed left the Post Office, but though I had left it I had been employed by it during a considerable portion of the time. I had established the *St Paul's Magazine*, in reference to which I had read an enormous amount of manuscript, and for which, independently of my novels, I had written articles almost monthly. I had stood for Beverley and had made many speeches. I had also written five novels, and had hunted three times a week during each of the winters. And how happy I was with it all! I had suffered at Beverley, but I had suffered as a part of the work which I was desirous of doing, and I had gained my experience. I had suffered at Washington with that wretched American Postmaster, and with the mosquitoes, not having been able to escape from that capital till July; but all that had added to the activity of my life. I had often groaned over those manuscripts; but I had read them, considering it—perhaps foolishly—to be a part of my duty as editor. And though in the quick production of my novels I had always ringing in my ears that terrible condemnation and scorn produced by the great man in Paternoster Row,* I was nevertheless proud of having done so much. I always had a pen in my hand. Whether crossing the seas, or fighting with American officials, or tramping about the streets of Beverley, I could do a little, and generally more than a little. I had long since convinced myself that in such work as mine the great secret consisted in acknowledging myself to be bound to rules of labour similar to those which an artisan or a mechanic is forced to obey. A shoemaker when he has finished one pair of shoes does not sit down and contemplate his work in idle satisfaction. 'There is my pair of shoes finished at last! What a pair of shoes it is!' The shoemaker who so indulged himself would be without wages half his time. It is the same with a professional writer of books. An author may of course want time to study a new subject. He will at any rate assure himself that there is some such good reason why he should pause. He does pause, and will be idle for a month or two while he tells himself how beautiful is that last pair of shoes which he has finished! Having thought much of all this, and having made up my mind that I could be really happy only when I was at work, I had now quite accustomed myself to begin a second pair as soon as the first was out of my hands.

CHAPTER 18

⸺ ∞∞∞ ⸺

'The Vicar of Bullhampton'—*'Sir Harry Hotspur'*— *'An Editor's Tales'*—*'Cæsar'*

IN 1869 I was called on to decide, in council with my two boys and their mother, what should be their destination in life. In June of that year the elder, who was then twenty-three, was called to the Bar; and as he had gone through the regular courses of lecturing tuition and study, it might be supposed that his course was already decided. But, just as he was called, there seemed to be an opening for him in another direction; and this, joined to the terrible uncertainty of the Bar, the terror of which was not in his case lessened by any peculiar forensic aptitudes, induced us to sacrifice dignity in quest of success. Mr Frederic Chapman, who was then* the sole representative of the publishing house known as Messrs Chapman & Hall, wanted a partner, and my son Henry went into the firm. He remained there three years and a half; but he did not like it, nor do I think he made a very good publisher. At any rate he left the business with perhaps more pecuniary success than might have been expected from the short period of his labours, and has since taken himself to literature as a profession. Whether he will work at it so hard as his father, and write as many books, may be doubted.

My second son, Frederic, had very early in life gone out to Australia, having resolved on a colonial career when he found that boys who did not grow so fast as he did got above him at school. This departure was a great pang to his mother and me; but it was permitted on the understanding that he was to come back when he was twenty-one, and then decide whether he would remain in England or return to the Colonies. In the winter of 1868 he did come to England, and had a season's hunting in the old country; but there was no doubt in his own mind as to his settling in Australia. His purpose was fixed, and in the spring of 1869 he made his second journey out. As I have since that date made two journeys to see him,—of one of which at any rate I shall have to speak, as I wrote a long book on the Australasian Colonies,—I will have an opportunity of saying a word or two further on of him and his doings.

The Vicar of Bullhampton was written in 1868 for publication in *Once a Week*,* a periodical then belonging to Messrs Bradbury & Evans. It was not to come out till 1869, and I, as was my wont, had made my terms long previously to the proposed date. I had made my terms and written my story and sent it to the publisher long before it was wanted; and so far my mind was at rest. The date fixed was the first of July, which date had been named in accordance with the exigencies of the editor of the periodical. An author who writes for these publications is bound to suit himself to these exigencies, and can generally do so without personal loss or inconvenience, if he will only take time by the forelock. With all the pages that I have written for magazines I have never been a day late, nor have I ever caused inconvenience by sending less or more matter than I had stipulated to supply. But I have sometimes found myself compelled to suffer by the irregularity of others. I have endeavoured to console myself by reflecting that such must ever be the fate of virtue. The industrious must feed the idle. The honest and simple will always be the prey of the cunning and fraudulent. The punctual, who keep none waiting for them, are doomed to wait perpetually for the unpunctual. But these earthly sufferers know that they are making their way heavenwards,—and their oppressors their way elsewards. If the former reflection does not suffice for consolation, the deficiency is made up by the second. I was terribly aggrieved on the matter of the publication of my new Vicar, and had to think very much of the ultimate rewards of punctuality and its opposite. About the end of March 1869 I got a dolorous letter from the editor. All the *Once a Week* people were in a terrible trouble. They had bought the right of translating one of Victor Hugo's* modern novels, *L'Homme Qui Rit*; they had fixed a date, relying on positive pledges from the French publishers; and now the great French author had postponed his work from week to week and from month to month, and it had so come to pass that the Frenchman's grinning hero would have to appear exactly at the same time as my clergyman. Was it not quite apparent to me, the editor asked, that *Once a Week* could not hold the two? Would I allow my clergyman to make his appearance in the *Gentleman's Magazine** instead?

My disgust at this proposition was, I think, chiefly due to Victor Hugo's latter novels, which I regard as pretentious and untrue to nature. To this perhaps was added some feeling of indignation that

I should be asked to give way to a Frenchman. The Frenchman had broken his engagement. He had failed to have his work finished by the stipulated time. From week to week and from month to month he had put off the fulfilment of his duty. And because of these laches* on his part,—on the part of this sententious French Radical,—I was to be thrown over! Virtue sometimes finds it difficult to console herself even with the double comfort. I would not come out in the *Gentleman's Magazine*, and as the Grinning Man could not be got out of the way, my novel was published in separate numbers.

The same thing has occurred to me more than once since. 'You no doubt are regular,' a publisher has said to me, 'but Mr —— is irregular. He has thrown me out, and I cannot be ready for you till three months after the time named.' In these emergencies I have given perhaps half what was wanted, and have refused to give the other half. I have endeavoured to fight my own battle fairly, and at the same time not to make myself unnecessarily obstinate. But the circumstances have impressed on my mind the great need there is that men engaged in literature should feel themselves to be bound to their industry as men know that they are bound in other callings. There does exist, I fear, a feeling that authors, because they are authors, are relieved from the necessity of paying attention to everyday rules. A writer, if he be making £800 a year, does not think himself bound to live modestly on £600, and put by the remainder for his wife and children. He does not understand that he should sit down at his desk at a certain hour. He imagines that publishers and booksellers should keep all their engagements with him to the letter;— but that he, as a brain-worker, and conscious of the subtle nature of the brain, should be able to exempt himself from bonds when it suits him. He has his own theory about inspiration which will not always come,—especially will not come if wine-cups overnight have been too deep. All this has ever been odious to me, as being unmanly. A man may be frail in health, and therefore unable to do as he has contracted in whatever grade of life. He who has been blessed with physical strength to work day by day, year by year—as has been my case—should pardon deficiencies caused by sickness or infirmity. I may in this respect have been a little hard on others,—and, if so, I here record my repentance. But I think that no allowance should be given to claims for exemption from punctuality, made if not absolutely on the score still with the conviction of intellectual superiority.

The *Vicar of Bullhampton* was written chiefly with the object of exciting not only pity but sympathy for a fallen woman, and of raising a feeling of forgiveness for such in the minds of other women. I could not venture to make this female the heroine of my story. To have made her a heroine at all would have been directly opposed to my purpose. It was necessary therefore that she should be a second-rate personage in the tale;—but it was with reference to her life that the tale was written, and the hero and the heroine with their belongings are all subordinate. To this novel I affixed a preface,—in doing which I was acting in defiance of my old-established principle. I do not know that any one read it; but as I wish to have it read, I will insert it here again:—

'I have introduced in the *Vicar of Bullhampton* the character of a girl whom I will call,—for want of a truer word that shall not in its truth be offensive,—a castaway. I have endeavoured to endow her with qualities that may create sympathy, and I have brought her back at last from degradation, at least to decency. I have not married her to a wealthy lover, and I have endeavoured to explain that though there was possible to her a way out of perdition, still things could not be with her as they would have been had she not fallen.

'There arises, of course, the question whether a novelist, who professes to write for the amusement of the young of both sexes, should allow himself to bring upon his stage a character such as that of Carry Brattle. It is not long since,—it is well within the memory of the author,—that the very existence of such a condition of life as was hers, was supposed to be unknown to our sisters and daughters, and was, in truth, unknown to many of them. Whether that ignorance was good may be questioned; but that it exists no longer is beyond question. Then arises the further question,—how far the conditions of such unfortunates should be made a matter of concern to the sweet young hearts of those whose delicacy and cleanliness of thought is a matter of pride to so many of us. Cannot women, who are good, pity the sufferings of the vicious, and do something perhaps to mitigate and shorten them without contamination from the vice? It will be admitted probably by most men who have thought upon the subject that no fault among us is punished so heavily as that fault, often so light in itself but so terrible in its consequences to the less faulty of the two offenders, by which a woman falls. All her own sex is against her, and all those of the other sex in whose veins runs the blood which she is thought to have contaminated, and who, of nature, would befriend her, were her trouble any other than it is.

'She is what she is, and she remains in her abject, pitiless, unutterable misery, because this sentence of the world has placed her beyond the helping hand of Love and Friendship. It may be said, no doubt, that the severity of this judgment acts as a protection to female virtue,—deterring, as all known punishments do deter, from vice. But this punishment, which is horrible beyond the conception of those who have not regarded it closely, is not known beforehand. Instead of the punishment, there is seen a false glitter of gaudy life,— a glitter which is damnably false,—and which, alas! has been more often portrayed in glowing colours, for the injury of young girls, than have those horrors which ought to deter, with the dark shadowings which belong to them.

'To write in fiction of one so fallen as the noblest of her sex, as one to be rewarded because of her weakness, as one whose life is happy, bright, and glorious, is certainly to allure to vice and misery, But it may perhaps be possible that if the matter be handled with truth to life, some girl, who would have been thoughtless, may be made thoughtful, or some parent's heart may be softened.'

Those were my ideas when I conceived the story, and with that feeling I described the characters of Carry Brattle and of her family. I have not introduced her lover on the scene, nor have I presented her to the reader in the temporary enjoyment of any of those fallacious luxuries, the longing for which is sometimes more seductive to evil than love itself. She is introduced as a poor abased creature, who hardly knows how false were her dreams, with very little of the Magdalene about her—because though there may be Magdalenes they are not often found—but with an intense horror of the sufferings of her position. Such being her condition, will they who naturally are her friends protect her? The vicar who has taken her by the hand endeavours to excite them to charity; but father, and brother, and sister are alike hard-hearted. It had been my purpose at first that the hand of every Brattle should be against her; but my own heart was too soft to enable me to make the mother cruel,—or the unmarried sister who had been the early companion of the forlorn one.

As regards all the Brattles, the story is, I think, well told. The characters are true, and the scenes at the mill are in keeping with human nature. For the rest of the book I have little to say. It is not very bad, and it certainly is not very good. As I have myself forgotten what the heroine does and says—except that she tumbles into a ditch—I cannot expect that any one else should remember her. But I have forgotten nothing that was done or said by any of the Brattles.

The question brought in argument is one of fearful importance. As to the view to be taken first, there can, I think, be no doubt. In regard to a sin common to the two sexes, almost all the punishment and all the disgrace is heaped upon the one who in nine cases out of ten has been the least sinful. And the punishment inflicted is of such a nature that it hardly allows room for repentance. How is the woman to return to decency to whom no decent door is opened? Then comes the answer: It is to the severity of the punishment alone that we can trust to keep women from falling. Such is the argument used in favour of the existing practice, and such the excuse given for their severity by women who will relax nothing of their harshness. But in truth the severity of the punishment is not known beforehand; it is not in the least understood by women in general, except by those who suffer it. The gaudy dirt, the squalid plenty, the contumely of familiarity, the absence of all good words and all good things, the banishment from honest labour, the being compassed round with lies, the flaunting glare of fictitious revelry, the weary pavement, the horrid slavery to some horrid tyrant,—and then the quick depreciation of that one ware of beauty, the substituted paint, garments bright without but foul within like painted sepulchres,* hunger, thirst, and strong drink, life without a hope, without the certainty even of a morrow's breakfast, utterly friendless, disease, starvation, and a quivering fear of that coming hell which still can hardly be worse than all that is suffered here! This is the life to which we doom our erring daughters, when because of their error we close our door upon them! But for our erring sons we find pardon easily enough.

Of course there are houses of refuge, from which it has been thought expedient to banish everything pleasant, as though the only repentance to which we can afford to give a place must necessarily be one of sackcloth and ashes. It is hardly thus that we can hope to recall those to decency who, if they are to be recalled at all, must be induced to obey the summons before they have reached the last stage of that misery which I have attempted to describe. To me the mistake which we too often make seems to be this,—that the girl who has gone astray is put out of sight, out of mind if possible, at any rate out of speech, as though she had never existed, and that this ferocity comes not only from hatred of the sin, but in part also from a dread of the taint which the sin brings with it. Very low as is the degradation to which a girl is brought when she falls through love or vanity, or perhaps from a longing for luxurious ease, still much lower is that to which she must descend perforce when, through the hardness of the world around her, she converts that sin into a trade. Mothers and sisters, when the misfortune comes upon them of a fallen female from among their number, should remember this, and not fear contamination so strongly as did Carry Brattle's married sister and sister-in-law.

In 1870 I brought out three books,—or rather of the latter of the three I must say that it was brought out by others, for I had nothing to do with it except to write it. These were *Sir Harry Hotspur of Humblethwaite*, *An Editor's Tales*, and a little volume on Julius Cæsar. *Sir Harry Hotspur* was written on the same plan as *Nina Balatka* and *Linda Tressel*, and had for its object the telling of some pathetic incident in life rather than the portraiture of a number of human beings. *Nina* and *Linda Tressel* and *The Golden Lion* had been placed in foreign countries, and this was an English story. In other respects it is of the same nature, and was not, I think, by any means a failure. There is much of pathos in the love of the girl, and of paternal dignity and affection in the father.

It was published first in *Macmillan's Magazine*,* by the intelligent proprietor of which I have since been told that it did not make either his fortune or that of his magazine. I am sorry that it should have been so; but I fear that the same thing may be said of a good many of my novels. When it had passed through the magazine, the subsequent use of it was sold to other publishers by Mr Macmillan, and then I learned that it was to be brought out by them as a novel in two volumes. Now it had been sold by me as a novel in one volume, and hence there arose a correspondence.

I found it very hard to make the purchasers understand that I had reasonable ground for objection to the process. What was it to me? How could it injure me if they stretched my pages by means of lead and margin into double the number I had intended. I have heard the same argument on other occasions. When I have pointed out that in this way the public would have to suffer, seeing that they would have to pay Mudie* for the use of two volumes in reading that which ought to have been given to them in one, I have been assured that the public are pleased with literary short measure, that it is the object of novel-readers to get through novels as fast as they can, and that the shorter each volume is the better! Even this, however, did not overcome me, and I stood to my guns. *Sir Harry* was published in one volume, containing something over the normal 300 pages, with an average of 220 words to a page,—which I had settled with my conscience to be the proper length of a novel volume. I may here mention that on one occasion, and on one occasion only, a publisher got the better of me in a matter of volumes. He had a two-volume novel of mine running through a certain magazine, and had it printed complete in three volumes before I knew where I was,—before I had seen a sheet of the letterpress. I stormed for a while, but I had not the heart to make him break up the type.*

The *Editor's Tales* was a volume republished from the *St Paul's Magazine*, and professed to give an editor's experience of his dealings with contributors. I do not think that there is a single incident in the book which could bring back to any one concerned the memory of a past event. And yet there is not an incident in it the outline of which was not presented to my mind by the remembrance of some fact:—how an ingenious gentleman got into conversation with me, I not knowing that he knew me to be an editor, and pressed his little article on my notice; how I was addressed by a lady with a becoming pseudonym and with much equally becoming audacity; how I was appealed to by the dearest of little women whom here I have called Mary Gresley; how in my own early days there was a struggle over an abortive periodical* which was intended to be the best thing ever done; how terrible was the tragedy of a poor drunkard, who with infinite learning at his command made one sad final effort to reclaim himself, and perished while he was making it; and lastly how a poor weak editor was driven nearly to madness by threatened litigation from a rejected contributor. Of these stories *The Spotted Dog*, with the struggles of the drunkard scholar, is the best. I know now, however, that when the things were good they came out too quick one upon another to gain much attention;—and so also, luckily, when they were bad.

The *Cæsar* was a thing of itself. My friend John Blackwood* had set on foot a series of small volumes called *Ancient Classics for English Readers*, and had placed the editing of them, and the compiling of many of them, in the hands of William Lucas Collins,* a clergyman who, from my connection with the series, became a most intimate friend. The *Iliad* and the *Odyssey* had already come out when I was at Edinburgh with John Blackwood, and, on my expressing my very strong admiration for those two little volumes,—which I here recommend to all young ladies as the most charming tales they can read,— he asked me whether I would not undertake one myself. *Herodotus* was in the press, but, if I could get it ready, mine should be next. Whereupon I offered to say what might be said to the readers of English on *The Commentaries of Julius Cæsar*.

I at once went to work, and in three months from that day the little book had been written. I began by reading through the Commentaries twice, which I did without any assistance either by translation or English notes. Latin was not so familiar to me then as it has since become,—for from that date I have almost daily spent an hour with some Latin author, and on many days many hours. After the reading what my author had left behind him, I fell into the reading of what others had written about him, in Latin, in English, and even in French,—for I went through much of that most futile book by the late Emperor of the French.* I do not know that for a short period I ever worked harder. The amount I had to write was nothing. Three weeks would have done it easily. But I was most anxious, in this soaring out of my own peculiar line, not to disgrace myself. I do not think that I did disgrace myself. Perhaps I was anxious for something more. If so, I was disappointed.

The book I think to be a good little book. It is readable by all, old and young, and it gives, I believe accurately, both an account of Cæsar's Commentaries,—which of course was the primary intention,— and the chief circumstances of the great Roman's life. A well-educated girl who had read it and remembered it would perhaps know as much about Cæsar and his writings as she need know. Beyond the consolation of thinking as I do about it, I got very little gratification from the work. Nobody praised it. One very old and very learned friend* to whom I sent it thanked me for my 'comic Cæsar,' but said no more. I do not suppose that he intended to run a dagger into me. Of any suffering from such wounds, I think, while living, I never showed a sign; but still I have suffered occasionally. There was, however, probably present to my friend's mind, and to that of others, a feeling that a man who had spent his life in writing English novels could not be fit to write about Cæsar. It was as when an amateur gets a picture hung on the walls of the Academy.* What business had I there? *Ne sutor ultra crepidam.** In the press it was most faintly damned by most faint praise. Nevertheless, having read the book again within the last month or two, I make bold to say that it is a good book. The series, I believe, has done very well. I am sure that it ought to do well in years to come, for, putting aside Cæsar, the work has been done with infinite scholarship, and very generally with a light hand. With the leave of my sententious and sonorous friend, who had not endured, that subjects which had been grave to him should be treated irreverently, I will say that such a work, unless it be light, cannot answer the purpose for which it is intended. It was not exactly a school-book that was wanted, but something that would carry the purposes of the schoolroom even into the leisure hours of adult pupils. Nothing was ever better suited for such a purpose than the *Iliad* and the *Odyssey*, as done by Mr Collins. The *Virgil*, also done by him, is very good; and so is the *Aristophanes* by the same hand.

CHAPTER 19

—◦◦◦—

'Ralph the Heir'—*'The Eustace Diamonds'* — *'Lady Anna'*—*'Australia'*

IN the spring of 1871 we,—I and my wife,—had decided that we would go to Australia to visit our shepherd son.* Of course before doing so I made a contract with a publisher for a book about the Colonies. For such a work as this I had always been aware that I could not fairly demand more than half the price that would be given for the same amount of fiction; and as such books have an indomitable tendency to stretch themselves, so that more is given than what is sold, and as the cost of travelling is heavy, the writing of them is not remunerative. This tendency to stretch comes not, I think, generally from the ambition of the writer, but from his inability to comprise the different parts in their allotted spaces. If you have to deal with a country, a colony, a city, a trade, or a political opinion, it is so much easier to deal with it in twenty than in twelve pages! I also made an engagement with the editor of a London daily paper* to supply him with a series of articles,—which were duly written, duly published, and duly paid for. But with all this, travelling with the object of writing is not a good trade. If the travelling author can pay his bills, he must be a good manager on the road.

Before starting there came upon us the terrible necessity of coming to some resolution about our house at Waltham. It had been first hired, and then bought, primarily because it suited my Post Office avocations. To this reason had been added other attractions,—in the shape of hunting, gardening, and suburban hospitalities. Altogether the house had been a success, and the scene of much happiness. But there arose questions as to expense. Would not a house in London be cheaper? There could be no doubt that my income would decrease, and was decreasing. I had thrown the Post Office, as it were, away, and the writing of novels could not go on for ever. Some of my friends told me already that at fifty-five I ought to give up the fabrication of love-stories. The hunting, I thought, must soon go, and I would not therefore allow that to keep me in the country. And then, why should

I live at Waltham Cross now, seeing that I had fixed on that place in reference to the Post Office? It was therefore determined that we would flit, and as we were to be away for eighteen months, we determined also to sell our furniture. So there was a packing up, with many tears, and consultations as to what should be saved out of the things we loved.

As must take place on such an occasion, there was some heart-felt grief. But the thing was done, and orders were given for the letting or sale of the house. I may as well say here that it never was let, and that it remained unoccupied for two years before it was sold. I lost by the transaction about £800. As I continually hear that other men make money by buying and selling houses, I presume I am not well adapted for transactions of that sort. I have never made money by selling anything except a manuscript. In matters of horseflesh I am so inefficient that I have generally given away horses that I have not wanted.

When we started from Liverpool, in May 1871, *Ralph the Heir* was running through the *St Paul's*. This was the novel of which Charles Reade afterwards took the plot and made on it a play. I have always thought it to be one of the worst novels I have written, and almost to have justified that dictum that a novelist after fifty should not write love-stories. It was in part a political novel; and that part which appertains to politics, and which recounts the electioneering experiences of the candidates at Percycross, is well enough. Percycross and Beverley were, of course, one and the same place. Neefit, the breeches-maker, and his daughter, are also good in their way,—and Moggs, the daughter's lover, who was not only lover, but also one of the candidates at Percycross as well. But the main thread of the story,—that which tells of the doings of the young gentlemen and young ladies,—the heroes and the heroines,—is not good. Ralph the heir has not much life about him; while Ralph who is not the heir, but is intended to be the real hero, has none. The same may be said of the young ladies,—of whom one, she who was meant to be the chief, has passed utterly out of my mind, without leaving a trace of remembrance behind.*

I also left in the hands of the editor of *The Fortnightly*, ready for production on the 1st of July following, a story called *The Eustace Diamonds*. In that I think that my friend's dictum was disproved. There is not much love in it; but what there is, is good. The character of Lucy Morris is pretty; and her love is as genuine and as well told as that of Lucy Robarts or Lily Dale.

But *The Eustace Diamonds* achieved the success which it certainly did attain, not as a love-story, but as a record of a cunning little woman of pseudo-fashion, to whom, in her cunning, there came a series of adventures, unpleasant enough in themselves, but pleasant to the reader. As I wrote the book, the idea constantly presented itself to me that Lizzie Eustace was but a second Becky Sharp; but in planning the character I had not thought of this, and I believe that Lizzie would have been just as she is though Becky Sharp had never been described. The plot of the diamond necklace is, I think, well arranged, though it produced itself without any forethought. I had no idea of setting thieves after the bauble till I had got my heroine to bed in the inn at Carlisle; nor of the disappointment of the thieves, till Lizzie had been wakened in the morning with the news that her door had been broken open. All these things, and many more, Wilkie Collins would have arranged before with infinite labour, preparing things present so that they should fit in with things to come. I have gone on the very much easier plan of making everything as it comes fit in with what has gone before. At any rate, the book was a success, and did much to repair the injury which I felt had come to my reputation in the novel-market by the works of the last few years. I doubt whether I had written anything so successful as *The Eustace Diamonds* since *The Small House at Allington*. I had written what was much better,—as, for instance, *Phineas Finn* and *Nina Balatka*; but that is by no means the same thing.

I also left behind, in a strong box, the manuscript of *Phineas Redux*, a novel of which I have already spoken, and which I subsequently sold to the proprietors of the *Graphic* newspaper. The editor of that paper greatly disliked the title, assuring me that the public would take Redux for the gentleman's surname,—and was dissatisfied with me when I replied that I had no objection to them doing so. The introduction of a Latin word, or of a word from any other language, into the title of an English novel is undoubtedly in bad taste; but after turning the matter much over in my own mind, I could find no other suitable name.

I also left behind me, in the same strong box, another novel, called *An Eye for an Eye*, which then had been some time written, and of which, as it has not even yet been published, I will not further speak.* It will probably be published some day, though, looking forward, I can see no room for it, at any rate, for the next two years.

If therefore the Great Britain, in which we sailed for Melbourne, had gone to the bottom, I had so provided that there would be new novels ready to come out under my name for some years to come.* This consideration, however, did not keep me idle while I was at sea. When making long journeys, I have always succeeded in getting a desk put up in my cabin, and this was done ready for me in the Great Britain, so that I could go to work the day after we left Liverpool. This I did; and before I reached Melbourne I had finished a story called *Lady Anna*. Every word of this was written at sea, during the two months required for our voyage, and was done day by day—with the intermission of one day's illness—for eight weeks, at the rate of 66 pages of manuscript in each week, every page of manuscript containing 250 words.* Every word was counted. I have seen work come back to an author from the press with terrible deficiencies as to the amount supplied. Thirty-two pages have perhaps been wanted for a number, and the printers with all their art could not stretch the matter to more than twenty-eight or -nine! The work of filling up must be very dreadful. I have sometimes been ridiculed for the methodical details of my business. But by these contrivances I have been preserved from many troubles; and I have saved others with whom I have worked—editors, publishers, and printers—from much trouble also.

A month or two after my return home, *Lady Anna* appeared in *The Fortnightly*, following *The Eustace Diamonds*. In it a young girl, who is really a lady of high rank and great wealth, though in her youth she enjoyed none of the privileges of wealth or rank, marries a tailor who had been good to her, and whom she had loved when she was poor and neglected. A fine young noble lover is provided for her, and all the charms of sweet living with nice people are thrown in her way, in order that she may be made to give up the tailor. And the charms are very powerful with her. But the feeling that she is bound by her troth to the man who had always been true to her overcomes everything,— and she marries the tailor. It was my wish of course to justify her in doing so, and to carry my readers along with me in my sympathy with her. But everybody found fault with me for marrying her to the tailor. What would they have said if I had allowed her to jilt the tailor and marry the good-looking young lord? How much louder, then, would have been the censure! The book was read, and I was satisfied. If I had not told my story well, there would have been no feeling in favour of the young lord. The horror which was expressed to me at the evil thing I had done, in giving the girl to the tailor, was the strongest testimony I could receive of the merits of the story.

I went to Australia chiefly in order that I might see my son among his sheep. I did see him among his sheep, and remained with him for four or five very happy weeks. He was not making money, nor has he made money since. I grieve to say that several thousands of pounds which I had squeezed out of the pockets of perhaps too liberal publishers have been lost on the venture. But I rejoice to say that this has been in no way due to any fault of his. I never knew a man work with more persistent honesty at his trade than he has done.

I had, however, the further intentions of writing a book about the entire group of Australasian Colonies; and in order that I might be enabled to do that with sufficient information, I visited them all. Making my head-quarters at Melbourne, I went to Queensland, New South Wales, Tasmania, then to the very little known territory of Western Australia, and then, last of all, to New Zealand. I was absent in all eighteen months, and think that I did succeed in learning much of the political, social, and material condition of these countries. I wrote my book as I was travelling, and brought it back with me to England all but completed in December 1872.

It was a better book than that which I had written eleven years before on the American States, but not so good as that on the West Indies in 1859. As regards the information given, there was much more to be said about Australia than the West Indies. Very much more is said,—and very much more may be learned from the latter than from the former book. I am sure that any one who will take the trouble to read the book on Australia, will learn much from it. But the West Indian Volume was readable. I am not sure that either of the other works are, in the proper sense of that word. When I go back to them I find that the pages drag with me;—and if so with me, how must it be with others who have none of that love which a father feels even for his ill-favoured offspring. Of all the needs a book has the chief need is that it be readable.

Feeling that these volumes on Australia were dull and long, I was surprised to find that they had an extensive sale. There were, I think, 2000 copies circulated of the first expensive edition; and then the book was divided into four little volumes, which were published separately, and which again had a considerable circulation. That some facts were stated inaccurately, I do not doubt; that many opinions were crude, I am quite sure; that I had failed to understand much which I attempted to explain, is possible. But with all these faults the book was a thoroughly honest book, and was the result of unflagging labour for a period of fifteen months. I spared myself no trouble in inquiry, no trouble in seeing, and no trouble in listening. I thoroughly imbued my mind with the subject, and wrote with the simple intention of giving trustworthy information on the state of the Colonies. Though there be inaccuracies,—those inaccuracies to which work quickly done must always be subject,—I think I did give much valuable information.

I came home across America from San Francisco to New York, visiting Utah and Brigham Young* on the way. I did not achieve great intimacy with the great polygamist of the Salt Lake City. I called upon him, sending to him my card, apologising for doing so without an introduction, and excusing myself by saying that I did not like to pass through the territory without seeing a man of whom I had heard so much. He received me in his doorway, not asking me to enter, and inquired whether I were not a miner. When I told him that I was not a miner, he asked me whether I earned my bread. I told him I did. 'I guess you're a miner,' said he. I again assured him that I was not. 'Then how do you earn your bread?' I told him that I did so by writing books. 'I'm sure you're a miner,' said he. Then he turned upon his heel, went back into the house, and closed the door. I was properly punished, as I was vain enough to conceive that he would have heard my name.

I got home in December 1872, and in spite of any resolution made to the contrary, my mind was full of hunting as I came back. No real resolutions had in truth been made, for out of a stud of four horses I kept three, two of which were absolutely idle through the two summers and winter of my absence. Immediately on my arrival I bought another, and settled myself down to hunting from London three days a week. At first I went back to Essex, my old country, but finding that to be inconvenient, I took my horses to Leighton Buzzard,* and became one of that numerous herd of sportsmen who rode with the 'Baron' and Mr Selby Lowndes. In those days Baron Meyer was alive, and the riding with his hounds was very good. I did not care so much for Mr Lowndes. During the winters of 1873, 1874, and 1875, I had my horses back in Essex, and went on with my hunting, always trying to resolve that I would give it up. But still I bought fresh horses, and, as I did not give it up, I hunted more than ever. Three times a week the cab has been at my door in London very punctually, and not unfrequently before seven in the morning. In order to secure this attendance, the man has always been invited to have his breakfast in the hall. I have gone to the Great Eastern Railway,*—ah! so often with the fear that frost would make all my exertions useless, and so often too with that result! And then, from one station or another station, have travelled on wheels at least a dozen miles. After the day's sport, the same toil has been necessary to bring me home to dinner at eight. This has been work for a young man and a rich man, but I have done it as an old man and comparatively a poor man. Now at last, in April 1876, I do think that my resolution has been taken. I am giving away my old horses, and anybody is welcome to my saddles and horse-furniture.

> 'Singula de nobis anni prædantur euntes;
> Eripuere jocos, venerem, convivia, ludum;
> Tendunt extorquere poëmata.'*

> 'Our years keep taking toll as they move on;
> My feasts, my frolics, are already gone,
> And now, it seems, my verses must go too.'

This is Conington's translation, but it seems to me to be a little flat.

> 'Years as they roll cut all our pleasures short;
> Our pleasant mirth, our loves, our wine, our sport.
> And then they stretch their power, and crush at last
> Even the power of singing of the past.'

I think that I may say with truth that I rode hard to the very* end.

> 'Vixi puellis nuper idoneus,
> Et militavi non sine gloria;
> Nunc arma defunctumque bello
> Barbiton hic paries habebit.'*

> 'I've lived about the covert side,
> I've ridden straight, and ridden fast;
> Now breeches, boots, and scarlet pride
> Are but mementoes of the past.'

CHAPTER 20

*'The Way We Live Now' and 'The Prime Minister'—
Conclusion*

IN what I have said at the end of the last chapter about my hunting, I have been carried a little in advance of the date at which I had arrived. We returned from Australia in the winter of 1872, and early in 1873 I took a house in Montagu Square,*—in which I hope to live and hope to die. Our first work in settling there was to place upon new shelves the books which I had collected round myself at Waltham. And this work, which was in itself great, entailed also the labour of a new catalogue.*As all who use libraries know, a catalogue is nothing unless it show the spot on which every book is to be found,—information which every volume also ought to give as to itself. Only those who have done it know how great is the labour of moving and arranging a few thousand volumes. At the present moment I own about 5000 volumes, and they are dearer to me even than the horses which are going, or than the wine in the cellar, which is very apt to go, and upon which I also pride myself.

When this was done, and the new furniture had got into its place, and my little book-room was settled sufficiently for work, I began a novel, to the writing of which I was instigated by what I conceived to be the commercial profligacy of the age. Whether the world does or does not become more wicked as years go on, is a question which probably has disturbed the minds of thinkers since the world began to think. That men have become less cruel, less violent, less self-ish, less brutal, there can be no doubt;—but have they become less honest? If so, can a world, retrograding from day to day in honesty, be considered to be in a state of progress. We know the opinion on this subject of our philosopher Mr Carlyle. If he be right, we are all going straight away to darkness and the dogs. But then we do not put very much faith in Mr Carlyle,—nor in Mr Ruskin* and his other followers. The loudness and extravagance of their lamentations, the wailing and gnashing of teeth* which comes from them, over a world which is supposed to have gone altogether shoddy-wards, are so contrary to the convictions of men who cannot but see how comfort has been increased, how health has been improved, and education extended,—that the general effect of their teaching is the opposite of what they have intended. It is regarded simply as Carlylism to say that the English-speaking world is growing worse from day to day. And it is Carlylism to opine that the general grand result of increased intelligence is a tendency to deterioration.

Nevertheless a certain class of dishonesty, dishonesty magnificent in its proportions, and climbing into high places, has become at the same time so rampant and so splendid that there seems to be reason for fearing that men and women will be taught to feel that dishonesty, if it can become splendid, will cease to be abominable. If dishonesty can live in a gorgeous palace with pictures on all its walls, and gems in all its cupboards, with marble and ivory in all its corners, and can give Apician dinners,* and get into Parliament, and deal in millions, then dishonesty is not disgraceful, and the man dishonest after such a fashion is not a low scoundrel. Instigated, I say, by some such reflections as these, I sat down in my new house to write *The Way We Live Now.* And as I had ventured to take the whip of the satirist into my hand, I went beyond the iniquities of the great speculator who robs everybody, and made an onslaught also on other vices,—on the intrigues of girls who want to get married, on the luxury of young men who prefer to remain single, and on the puffing propensities of authors who desire to cheat the public into buying their volumes.

The book has the fault which is to be attributed to almost all satires, whether in prose or verse. The accusations are exaggerated. The vices are coloured, so as to make effect rather than to represent truth. Who, when the lash of objurgation is in his hands, can so moderate his arm as never to strike harder than justice would require? The spirit which produces the satire is honest enough, but the very desire which moves the satirist to do his work energetically makes him dishonest. In other respects *The Way We Live Now* was, as a satire, powerful and good. The character of Melmotte is well maintained. The Bear-garden is amusing,—and not untrue. The Longestaffe girls and their friend, Lady Monogram, are amusing,—but exaggerated. Dolly Longestaffe is, I think, very good. And Lady Carbury's literary efforts are, I am sorry to say, such as are too frequently made. But here again the young lady with her two lovers is weak and vapid. I almost doubt whether it be not impossible to have two absolutely distinct parts in a novel, and to imbue them both with interest. If they be distinct, the one will seem to be no more than padding to the other. And so it was in *The Way We Live Now*. The interest of the story lies among the wicked and foolish people,—with Melmotte and his daughter, with Dolly and his family, with the American woman, Mrs Hurtle, and with John Crumb and the girl of his heart. But Roger Carbury, Paul Montague, and Henrietta Carbury are uninteresting. Upon the whole, I by no means look upon the book as one of my failures; nor was it taken as a failure by the public or the press.

While I was writing *The Way We Live Now*, I was called upon by the proprietors of the *Graphic* for a Christmas story. I feel, with regard to literature, somewhat as I suppose an upholsterer and undertaker feels when he is called upon to supply a funeral. He has to supply it, however distasteful it may be. It is his business, and he will starve if he neglect it. So have I felt that, when anything in the shape of a novel was required, I was bound to produce it. Nothing can be more distasteful to me than to have to give a relish of Christmas to what I write. I feel the humbug implied by the nature of the order. A Christmas story, in the proper sense, should be the ebullition of some mind anxious to instil others with a desire for Christmas religious thought, or Christmas festivities,—or, better still, with Christmas charity. Such was the case with Dickens when he wrote his two first Christmas stories. But since that the things written annually—all of which have been fixed to Christmas like children's toys to a Christmas tree—have had no real savour of Christmas about them. I had done two or three before. Alas! at this very moment I have one to write, which I have promised to supply within three weeks of this time,—the picture-makers always require a long interval,—as to which I have in vain been cudgelling my brain for the last month. I can't send away the order to another shop, but I do not know how I shall ever get the coffin made.

For the *Graphic*, in 1873, I wrote a little story about Australia. Christmas at the antipodes is of course midsummer, and I was not loth to describe the troubles to which my own son had been subjected, by the mingled accidents of heat and bad neighbours, on his station in the bush. So I wrote *Harry Heathcote of Gangoil*, and was well through my labour on that occasion. I only wish I may have no worse success in that which now hangs over my head.

When *Harry Heathcote* was over, I returned with a full heart to Lady Glencora and her husband. I had never yet drawn the completed picture of such a statesman as my imagination had conceived. The personages with whose names my pages had been familiar, and perhaps even the minds of some of my readers—the Brocks, De Terriers, Monks, Greshams, and Daubeneys*—had been more or less portraits, not of living men, but of living political characters. The strong-minded, thick-skinned, useful, ordinary member, either of the Government or of the Opposition, had been very easy to describe, and had required no imagination to conceive. The character reproduces itself from generation to generation; and as it does so, becomes shorn in a wonderful way of those little touches of humanity which would be destructive of its purposes. Now and again there comes a burst of human nature, as in the quarrel between Burke and Fox;* but, as a rule, the men submit themselves to be shaped and fashioned, and to be formed into tools, which are used either for building up or pulling down, and can generally bear to be changed from this box into the other, without, at any rate, the appearance of much personal suffering. Four-and-twenty gentlemen will amalgamate themselves into one whole, and work for one purpose, having each of them to set aside his own idiosyncrasy, and to endure the close personal contact of men who must often be personally disagreeable, having been thoroughly taught that in no other way can they serve either their country or their own ambition. These are the men who are publicly useful, and whom the necessities of the age supply,—as to whom I have never ceased to wonder that stones of such strong calibre should be so quickly worn down to the shape and smoothness of rounded pebbles.

Such have been to me the Brocks and the Mildmays, about whom I have written with great pleasure, having had my mind much exercised in watching them. But I had also conceived the character of a statesman of a different nature—of a man who should be in something perhaps superior, but in very much inferior, to these men—of one who could not become a pebble, having too strong an identity of his own. To rid one's self of fine scruples—to fall into the traditions of a party—to feel the need of subservience, not only in acting but also even in thinking—to be able to be a bit, and at first only a very little bit,—these are the necessities of the growing statesman. The time may come, the glorious time when some great self action shall be possible, and shall be even demanded, as when Peel gave up the Corn Laws; but the rising man, as he puts on his harness, should not allow himself to dream of this. To become a good, round, smooth, hard, useful pebble is his duty, and to achieve this he must harden his skin and swallow his scruples. But every now and again we see the attempt made by men who cannot get their skins to be hard—who after a little while generally fall out of the ranks. The statesman of whom I was thinking—of whom I had long thought—was one who did not fall out of the ranks, even though his skin would not become hard. He should have rank, and intellect, and parliamentary habits, by which to bind him to the service of his country; and he should also have unblemished, unextinguishable, inexhaustible love of country. That virtue I attribute to our statesmen generally. They who are without it are, I think, mean indeed. This man should have it as the ruling principle of his life; and it should so rule him that all other things should be made to give way to it. But he should be scrupulous, and, being scrupulous, weak. When called to the highest place in the council of his Sovereign, he should feel with true modesty his own insufficiency; but not the less should the greed of power grow upon him when he had once allowed himself to taste and enjoy it. Such was the character I endeavoured to depict in describing the triumph, the troubles, and the failure of my Prime Minister. And I think that I have succeeded. What the public may think, or what the press may say, I do not yet know, the work having as yet run but half its course.[1]

That the man's character should be understood as I understand it—or that of his wife's, the delineation of which has also been a matter of much happy care to me—I have no right to expect, seeing that the operation of describing has not been confined to one novel, which might perhaps be read through by the majority of those who commenced it. It has been carried on through three or four, each of which will be forgotten even by the most zealous reader almost as soon as read. In *The Prime Minister*, my Prime Minister will not allow his wife to take office among, or even over, those ladies who are attached by office to the Queen's court. 'I should not choose,' he says to her, 'that my wife should have any duties unconnected with our joint family and home.' Who will remember in reading those words that, in

---

[1] Writing this note in 1878, after a lapse of nearly three years, I am obliged to say that, as regards the public, *The Prime Minister* was a failure. It was worse spoken of by the press than any novel I had written. I was specially hurt by a criticism on it in the *Spectator*. The critic who wrote the article* I know to be a good critic, inclined to be more than fair to me; but in this case I could not agree with him, so much do I love the man whose character I had endeavoured to portray.

a former story, published some years before, he tells his wife, when she has twitted him with his willingness to clean the Premier's shoes, that he would even allow her to clean them if it were for the good of the country? And yet it is by such details as these that I have, for many years past, been manufacturing within my own mind the characters of the man and his wife.

I think that Plantagenet Palliser, Duke of Omnium, is a perfect gentleman. If he be not, then am I unable to describe a gentleman. She is by no means a perfect lady; but if she be not all over a woman, then am I not able to describe a woman. I do not think it probable that my name will remain among those who in the next century will be known as the writers of English prose fiction;—but if it does, that permanence of success will probably rest on the character of Plantagenet Palliser, Lady Glencora, and the Rev. Mr Crawley.

I have now come to the end of that long series of books written by myself, with which the public is already acquainted. Of those which I may hereafter be able to add to them I cannot speak; though I have an idea that I shall even yet once more have recourse to my political hero as the mainstay of another story.* When *The Prime Minister* was finished, I at once began another novel, which is now completed in three volumes, and which is called *Is He Popenjoy?* There are two Popenjoys in the book, one succeeding to the title held by the other; but as they are both babies, and do not in the course of the story progress beyond babyhood, the future readers, should the tale ever be published, will not be much interested in them. Nevertheless the story, as a story, is not, I think, amiss. Since that I have written still another three-volume novel, to which, very much in opposition to my publisher, I have given the name of *The American Senator.*[1] It is to appear in *Temple Bar,** and is to commence its appearance on the first of next month. Such being its circumstances, I do not know that I can say anything else about it here.

And so I end the record of my literary performances,—which I think are more in amount than the works of any other living English author. If any English authors not living have written more—as may probably have been the case—I do not know who they are. I find

---

[1] *The American Senator* and *Popenjoy* have appeared, each with fair success. Neither of them has encountered that reproach which, in regard to *The Prime Minister,* seemed to tell me that my work as a novelist should be brought to a close. And yet I feel assured that they are very inferior to *The Prime Minister.*

that, taking the books which have appeared under our names, I have published much more than twice as much as Carlyle. I have also published considerably more than Voltaire,* even including his letters. We are told that Varro,* at the age of eighty, had written 480 volumes, and that he went on writing for eight years longer. I wish I knew what was the length of Varro's volumes; I comfort myself by reflecting that the amount of manuscript described as a book in Varro's time was not much. Varro, too, is dead, and Voltaire; whereas I am still living, and may add to the pile.

The following is a list of the books I have written, with the dates of publication and the sums I have received for them. The dates given are the years in which the works were published as a whole, most of them having appeared before in some serial form.

Names of Works	Date of Publication	Total Sums Received		
The Macdermots of Ballycloran	1847	£48	6	9
The Kellys and the O'Kellys	1848	123	19	5
La Vendée	1850	20	0	0
The Warden	1855	727	11	3
Barchester Towers	1857			
The Three Clerks	1858	250	0	0
Doctor Thorne	1858	400	0	0
The West Indies and the Spanish Main	1859	250	0	0
The Bertrams	1859	400	0	0
Castle Richmond	1860	600	0	0
Framley Parsonage	1861	1000	0	0
Tales of All Countries—1st Series	1861	1830	0	0
,, ,, 2d ,,	1863			
,, ,, 3d ,,	1870			
Orley Farm	1862	3135	0	0
North America	1862	1250	0	0
Rachel Ray	1863	1645	0	0
The Small House at Allington	1864	3000	0	0
Can You Forgive Her?	1864	3525	0	0
Miss Mackenzie	1865	1300	0	0
The Belton Estate	1866	1757	0	0
The Claverings	1867	2800	0	0
The Last Chronicle of Barset	1867	3000	0	0
Nina Balatka	1867	450	0	0
Linda Tressel	1868	450	0	0
Phineas Finn	1869	3200	0	0
He Knew He Was Right	1869	3200	0	0
Carry forward		£34,361	17	5

Name of Works	Date of Publication	Total Sums Received		
Brought forward		£34,361	17	5
Brown, Jones, and Robinson	1870	600	0	0
The Vicar of Bullhampton	1870	2500	0	0
An Editor's Tales	1870	378	0	0
Cæsar (Ancient Classics)	1870[1]	0	0	0
Sir Harry Hotspur of Humblethwaite	1871	750	0	0
Ralph the Heir	1871	2500	0	0
The Golden Lion of Granpère	1872	550	0	0
The Eustace Diamonds	1873	2500	0	0
Australia and New Zealand	1873	1300	0	0
Phineas Redux	1874	2500	0	0
Harry Heathcote of Gangoil	1874	450	0	0
Lady Anna	1874	1200	0	0
The Way We Live Now	1875	3000	0	0
The Prime Minister	1876	2500	0	0
The American Senator	1877	1800	0	0
Is He Popenjoy?	1878	1600	0	0
South Africa	1878	850	0	0
John Caldigate	1879	1800	0	0
Sundries		7800	0	0
		£68,939	17	5

It will not, I am sure, be thought that, in making my boast as to quantity, I have endeavoured to lay claim to any literary excellence. That, in the writing of books, quantity without quality is a vice and a misfortune, has been too manifestly settled to leave a doubt on such a matter. But I do lay claim to whatever merit should be accorded to me for persevering diligence in my profession. And I make the claim, not with a view to my own glory, but for the benefit of those who may read these pages when young and who may intend* to follow the same career. *Nulla dies sine lineâ.** Let that be their motto. And let their work be to them as is his common work to the common labourer. No gigantic efforts will then be necessary. He need tie no wet towels round his brow, nor sit for thirty hours at his desk without moving,— as men have sat, or said that they have sat. More than nine-tenths of my literary work has been done in the last twenty years, and during twelve of those years I followed also* another profession. I have never been a slave to this work, giving due time, if not more than due time,

---

[1] This was given by me as a present to my friend John Blackwood.

to the amusements I have loved. But I have been constant,—and constancy in labour will conquer all difficulties. *Gutta cavat lapidem non vi, sed saepe cadendo.**

It may interest some if I state that during the last twenty years I have made by literature something near £70,000. As I have said before in these pages, I look upon the result as comfortable, but not splendid.

It will not, I trust, be supposed by any reader that I have intended in this so-called autobiography to give a record of my inner life. No man ever did so truly,—and no man ever will. Rousseau probably attempted it, but who doubts but that Rousseau has confessed* in much the thoughts and convictions rather than the facts of his life? If the rustle of a woman's petticoat has ever stirred my blood; if a cup of wine has been a joy to me; if I have thought tobacco at midnight in pleasant company to be one of the elements of an earthly paradise; if now and again I have somewhat recklessly fluttered a £5 note over a card-table;—of what matter is that to any reader? I have betrayed no woman. Wine has brought me to no sorrow. It has been the companionship of smoking* that I have loved, rather than the habit. I have never desired to win money, and I have lost none. To enjoy the excitement of pleasure, but to be free from its vices and ill effects,—to have the sweet, and leave the bitter untasted,—that has been my study. The preachers tell us that this is impossible. It seems to me that hitherto I have succeeded fairly well. I will not say that I have never scorched a finger,—but I carry no ugly wounds.

For what remains to me of life I trust for my happiness still chiefly to my work—hoping that when the power of work be over with me, God may be pleased to take me from a world in which, according to my view, there can be no joy; secondly, to the love of those who love me; and then to my books. That I can read and be happy while I am reading, is a great blessing. Could I remember, as some men do, what I read, I should have been able to call myself an educated man. But that power I have never possessed. Something is always left,—something dim and inaccurate,—but still something sufficient to preserve the taste for more. I am inclined to think that it is so with most readers.

Of late years, putting aside the Latin classics, I have found my greatest pleasure in our old English dramatists,*—not from any excessive love of their work, which often irritates me by its want of truth to nature, even while it shames me by its language,—but from curiosity in searching their plots and examining their character. If I live a few years longer, I shall, I think, leave in my copies of these dramatists, down to the close of James I, written criticisms on every play. No one who has not looked closely into it knows how many there are.

Now I stretch out my hand,* and from the further shore I bid adieu to all who have cared to read any among the many words that I have written.

THE END.

OTHER WRITINGS

Trollope on Jane Austen

SINCE the writing of Pepys's Diary, Miss Austen has perhaps gone the nearest towards giving us a true insight into the houses of the people of her day. With Mr and Mrs Bennet and Lady Catherine de Burgh we are quite at home. With the Mansfields and the Crofts* we have our sympathies and antipathies as we have with the surrounding families in our own village or our own circle. The return of Sir Thomas is as when our own father came upon us in our juvenile delinquencies; and we can hardly help believing that we ourselves received Mr Collins' letters each with one of Rowland Hill's penny stamps in the corner of the envelope.

(From *The New Zealander*, written 1855–6, Chapter 10, 'Society')

EMMA is undoubtedly very tedious;—thereby shewing rather the patience of readers in the authors day than any incapacity on her part to avoid the fault. The dialogues are too long and some of them are unnecessary.

But the story shews wonderful knowledge of female character, and is severe on the little foibles of women with a severity which no man would dare to use. Emma, the heroine, is treated almost mercilessly. In every passage of the book she is in fault for some folly, some vanity, some ignorance,—or indeed for some meanness. Her conduct to her friend Harriet,—her assumed experience and real ignorance of human nature—are terribly true; but nowadays we dare not make our heroines so little. Her weaknesses are all plain to us, but of her strengths we are only told; and even at the last we hardly know why Mr Knightley loves her.

The humour shewn in some of the female characters in Emma is very good. Mrs Elton with her loud Bath-begotten vulgarity is excellent; and Miss Bates, longwinded, self-denying, ignorant, and eulogistic has become proverbial. But the men are all weak. There is nothing in Emma like Mr Bennet and Mr Collins the immortal heroes of Pride and Prejudice. Mr Woodhouse, the malade imaginaire,* is absurd and the Knightleys and Westons are simply sticks. It is as a portrait of female life among ladies in an English village 50 years ago that Emma is to be known and remembered.

We have here, given to us unconsciously, a picture of the clerical life of 1815 which we cannot avoid comparing with the clerical life of 1865. After a modest dinner party, when the gentlemen join the ladies, the parson of the parish, a young man, is noticed as having taken too much wine. And no one else has done so. But allusion is made to this, not because he is a clergyman, nor is he at all a debauched or fast-living clergyman. It simply suits the story that he should be a little flushed & free of speech. The same clergyman, when married, declines to dance because he objects to the partner proposed to him; and special mention is made of card parties at this clergyman's house. How must the mouths of young parsons water in these days as they read these details, if they are ever allowed to read such books as Emma.

I cannot but notice Miss Austens timidity in dealing with the most touching scenes which come in her way, and in avoiding the narration of those details which a bolder artist would most eagerly have seized. In the final scene between Emma and her lover,—when the conversation has become almost pathetic,—she breaks away from the spoken dialogue, and simply tells us of her hero's success. This is a cowardice which robs the reader of much of the charm which he has promised himself—Augt. 17, 1864.

(Trollope's annotation to his copy of *Emma*, made in 1864, transcribed by Bradford A. Booth and first published in *Nineteenth-Century Fiction*, 4 (December 1949), 245–7; the copy of *Emma* was then in the possession of Miss Muriel Rose Trollope)

'On English Prose Fiction as a Rational Amusement'

No man, I fancy, can work long at any trade without being brought to consider whether that which he is doing daily tends to evil or to good. All of you probably have asked yourself that question, and have answered it after some fashion. A man must, I think, have but a sorry existence upon whose bosom is forced a conviction that he gets his bread by doing evil and not good in the world. My own trade is that of a writer of novels. I may probably have the honour of address-ing many here who are readers of novels. I stand before you now to vindicate my own profession and your amusement. I have often asked myself this question; and I have done so with the full conviction that there are many good men, even in these days, who regard the writer of novels as a doer of evil, and the reader of novels as one who wastes that time which has been given to us all to be so used that we may become fit for eternity. My friends, this is for me a serious question; and it is no unimportant matter for those of you if you are readers of novels. More important still is it, as regards your consideration, if you have sons and daughters as to whom you have yet to decide whether works of English Prose Fiction shall or shall not be put into their hands with your sanction.

The large dimensions of this question are, I think, proved by the extent to which novels are circulated among us, and by the spread of education,—which, though we regard it as a blessing, may have its evil side, if it enable the thoughtless to occupy themselves with that which will teach them evil. It cannot be doubted that the reading of novels has of late increased in a greater degree than has the reading of other works. I could give you figures in support of this statement; but I do not think any figures could support it so strongly as those palpable circumstances of our ordinary literature with which I cannot but presume you to be acquainted. In every household we see the monthly and weekly periodicals of the day which never appear with-out a novel,—and in regard to which proprietors, publishers, editors, and contributors, all know that without a novel they would have no chance of success . . . It must be admitted that novels are diligently read among us. Nevertheless, hard words are said of novels; words that are hard to the novel-reader,—and very hard indeed to the novel-writer, if he have a conscience. Mr Carlyle,—for whom of all living men I feel perhaps the highest veneration,—has dealt upon him whom he calls the distressed novel-wright* the hardest blow of all, and, as I think, the most unjust and the most thoughtless. A bishop gets up now and then to lecture against novels;*—as I am now getting up to lecture in their defence. Some grave and thoughtful writer will at intervals attack us, himself believing, and therefore very properly trying to prove, that the propagation of novels is a propagation of evil. Sometimes we have novels attacked in sermons. And it must probably have occurred to most of you, as it has often to me, to hear discussions in private life,—to hear them and to take part in them,—on this great subject,—whether the reading of novels be good for young people.

Now I wish first to assure you, on my own behalf, that simple success is not sufficient to justify to me my own profession. I am not entitled to speak on behalf of others; but I may express my conviction that that which I say for myself may be said of nearly all those whose works you probably know as belonging to the literature of English Prose Fiction in the present day. I could tell you of one novelist, whose name you would hear with acclaim, that on the opening day of a certain year he penned a prayer that he might be hindered by God's grace from writing a word that year that might be injurious to any young person. Do you not think that Walter Scott was animated by such intention; that Thackeray desired to be so guided;—that such was the inward resolve and conscientious struggle of Miss Austen and of Maria Edgeworth? It is not my intention to mention to you this evening the name of any living novelist; but I think that you could continue the list yourself with writers of fiction who are still among us. Simple success in a profession,—by which I mean the making of money or the gaining of a reputation,—cannot be sufficient for any man or woman with a conscience. Labour that is useless,—unproductive,—will break the heart even of a convict. Do you believe it possible then that an enlightened man,—one, at least, so far enlightened as to be able to produce for you pictures of life that shall delight you,—can do so from year to year, contentedly, without a self-inquiry whether he be producing any good by his work,—without at least satisfying himself that he does not produce evil? I shall endeavour to show you the ground on which a novelist may consider himself to enjoy that satisfaction; and in doing so I shall endeavour also to prove to you that you may be satisfied when you see your sons and daughters reading novels,—providing always that some judgement has been used in their selection.

This task I shall attempt to perform by describing to you very shortly the manner in which English novels have become what they are; and by explaining how it is that the taste of the community forms the writer, while the power of the writer,—such as it may be,—reacts upon the public taste. I shall mention to you the names of a few English novelists who lived in times now somewhat removed from us, and of some who went from us, so to say, but the other day. This, however, I must beg of your charity; that in speaking to you of Prose Fiction, which has been the work of my own life, I may not be supposed to speak in my own praise. I do desire to vindicate in your judgement my own profession, and to make you believe that your children may be benefited by the reading of novels; but I do not desire to vindicate my own work.

I think it is admitted by all who have given attention to the subject, that Sir Walter Scott inaugurated altogether a new era in Prose Fiction. This he did so completely that readers who are not at all disposed to be critics, nevertheless feel that there are two distinct epochs of English novel production,—the period before Sir Walter Scott, and that which he commenced and made and consecrated. This arose partly, no doubt, from the fact that immediately before his time the desire of the public for Prose Fiction had grown quicker than the wholesome supply, and that therefore the novel-reading world had been deluged with trash. There had come forth a flood of stories,—which was said in those days to go quickly to the trunkmakers, for it was supposed that the trunkmakers used up the waste paper of the time. These stories were usually known as the production of the Minerva Press.* The Minerva Press was a publishing establishment from which the love stories of the day emanated, and very weak and wonderfully vapid they were;—not often immoral according to our usual ideas of immorality; never I think indecent; but powerless to teach to man or woman any lessons which could be of real service. The only story which I can recommend to my hearers as connected with the Minerva Press is a satire on its productions called the 'Heroine,' written by Mr Barrett* avowedly as a quiz on Mrs Radcliffe's school, but in truth a burlesque, and a very excellent burlesque, on the tales which came from that once flourishing establishment, the Minerva Press. Then Walter Scott blazed forth, annihilating the Minerva Press, and making for himself his own aera. The result was the fact that the production of the first half-dozen of the Waverley Novels instituted a new epoch in English Prose Fiction.

Of the British novelists who wrote before Scott I must say something to you, though I do not think it likely that you often read their works. There are not many of these earlier novels which you who are fathers and mothers will wish to see,—at any rate in the hands of your daughters. But this indisposition on your own part to read, or to select for reading for others, old English novels does not arise from the bad lessons which are taught therein, but from the fact that the writers wrote them to suit the taste of times whose tastes are not our tastes. Many of these novels, though they were produced in years by no means remote, do not amuse now because we do not see the manners which they describe. The novelist is bound to adapt himself to his age; and is almost forced to be ephemeral. In his own age he can have great effect for good or evil; but we know as yet of no prose novelist who has influenced after-ages, except in so far as one age is the product of all ages that have gone before it. Cervantes is said to have laughed Spain's chivalry away; but no Spaniard now dresses himself in this or that garb because of the lessons which he has learned from 'Don Quixote.' This is as true of historical novels as of those which are devoted to social life. For the historical novel, though it deals with the names, and perhaps with the facts, of a bygone period, describes only the vices and virtues of the day. I fear that the novelist can expect no centuries of popularity. But the poet adapts himself to all ages by the use of language, thoughts, and scenes which are not ephemeral.

Not thinking that you will care to go back to black-letter lore, I may say that the earliest English novels we know are 'The Euphues,' by Lylie, and 'The Arcadia,' by Sir Philip Sidney. Both of them were written about 1580,—nearly three centuries ago,—though the latter was not printed for many years after that date. It is not probable that you will wish to read either of them; but they cannot hurt you if you do read them. One wonders now at the patience of those who, in the days of Queen Elizabeth, took delight in these stories. The language of 'Euphues' is so affected as to be to our ears unbearable. We know it best in the caricature of Sir Piercie Shafton,* the Euphuist. That of the 'Arcadia' has undoubtedly much beauty. It is very perfect and often charming in its language, though also very quaint in its form of expression. The sentiments are noble and virtuous. But the plot is hopelessly complex and long. And the story is so told that it is almost impossible for the modern reader to distinguish one character from another. Musidorus and Pyrocles, Philoclea and Pamela, lose their identities in endless ambiguity. These writers took their stories, through the French, from the Greek Romancists; and their plots, or portions of their plots, were borrowed by some of our greatest dramatists.

This may be remarked of them and of their work;—that they endeavoured to represent their heroes and their heroines as possessing those virtues which were then esteemed. Their women were modest, frugal, given much to poetry, and content to be wooed by their swains in very long sentences, and for very long periods. The men were brave, and, if intended to be represented as good, were constant in their loves. They rode about the country in an unintelligible state of perplexed battling, and seem upon the whole to have had a bad time of it. But, no doubt, these pictures did, as far as they were circulated, tend to reproduce those aspirations which gave them birth. The authors I have mentioned had various imitators, with whose names I will not attempt to burden your memories; but we can see in examining their works how they gradually adapted themselves to the times in which they lived.

Then we come to the latter novelists of Charles II;—for the school of which I have spoken, modified by degrees and by no means improved, did furnish whatever prose fictions were used in England up to the Restoration, and for some time after it. At this period there arose as novelists Mrs Manley, Mrs Afra Behn, and some others, who bear a very bad name indeed. We all know what were the plays of that time and of some succeeding years,—how poor in incident, how abominable in morals, how disgusting in language, and how false in humanity! I need only say of the novels, that though they are bad, they are not nearly so bad as the plays, and that their greatest fault lies in their terrible dullness.

The English novel earliest in date that you have all probably read is 'Robinson Crusoe.' It was published in 1719, just a century and a half ago. It is not my purpose to speak in detail of a story so common in our hands. What 'Robinson Crusoe' is you all know. It is singular that the man who wrote it, Defoe, should have been able to produce for us a work so faultless, as regards offences which were still common in his times, whereas his other novels, of which there are three or four, are by no means fitted for general reading. 'Robinson Crusoe' is as yet only a hundred and fifty years old, and we will make no predictions as to an immortality of fame on its behalf. Many such prophecies have been made and belied in the history of literature. But we may declare that the book has caught a hold of the reading public of all countries which nothing yet has shaken, and that it has made a stronger claim to immortality than any other work of English prose Fiction.

Passing by names with which I need not trouble you, we now reach Richardson and Fielding, who came forward as novelists very nearly at the same date. This was about 1740, little more than a century and a half after the production of the 'Arcadia.' In the meantime how great had been the change in English taste! Both Richardson and Fielding wrote of the private life of the day, and their stories are altogether removed from the romances of the Paladins. Indeed, who could be less like a Paladin than Tom Jones, or more removed from the forlorn lady of a castle than Miss Harriet Biron?* The period of which we are speaking is distant from our own by hardly more than a century;—is distant by not a century from that epoch of Scott's which we identify with our own. And yet, again, how great is the distance in the manners represented, and in the language and style of the artists! Richardson and Fielding were the first English novelists who wrote with a distinct intention to deal with the circumstances of the life amidst which they lived. They are still read by men who choose to make themselves acquainted with the English literature of the last century; and there are no doubt some who relish the long-drawn pathos of Richardson, and the wonderful constructive skill of Fielding. It is customary in literary conversation to presume that men are acquainted with their works. But we no longer find them lying about the houses of our friends. They stand on the shelves of our libraries, and people think that they have read them. They describe coarse things in coarse language, and are not in accordance with the tastes or with the sympathies of the age.

I have named these two novelists together, as though they were of the same class; but in truth no two writers could be more essentially different in their treatment of life. Richardson was, as it were, a saint among novelists,—and Fielding a sinner. Richardson laid himself out to support high-toned feminine virtue. The praise of strict matrons and of severe elders was the very breath of his nostrils. He placed himself on a pedestal of morality, and dictated to Propriety at large what should and what should not be considered becoming for young women. And he lived up to his preaching, preferring good old ladies to naughty young men, and a dish of tea to a glass of punch. Fielding was in every respect the reverse of his rival,—whom he loved to flout. One of Fielding's novels was written, or at least commenced, as a parody on Richardson.* Fielding palliated the vices which Richardson denounced, and made his heroes heroic in doing those things, for the doing of which Richardson's personages were made to be Satanic. Nevertheless the two are I think to be classed together. They each wrote of the actual life around them, and were the first among English novelists to teach practically to their readers what virtues they should follow, and what vices they should shun. In Fielding, when he tells us in his 'Amelia' how Mr Booth fell away from virtue, and how in 'Tom Jones' his hero was led into wickedness, though he describes the improprieties of the gentleman with a minuteness which is not now gratifying, is nevertheless preaching morality after his fashion. This is the way men fall, says Fielding; and this is the way in which women stand. Therefore let the men worship the women, and, if it may be possible, imitate them a little. But Richardson's men are fiends,— such as men I think never were. There may have been a man as bad as Lovelace,* but one doubts even the single instance. And Richardson the saint, in describing to us the injuries which female virtue may be made to suffer, is quite as circumstantial as the sinner Fielding. So thoroughly is this the case that Tom Jones is less repulsive to me than Clarissa; though Tom Jones is of all heroes the least heroic, and Clarissa of all heroines the most ill-used and the most divine.

Such of you as have read the works of these two authors will hardly wish those who come after you to pursue the study. Nor will they do so. 'Tom Jones' and 'Clarissa' will gradually be banished from our ordinary home bookshelves, as 'Euphues' and the 'Arcadia' have been banished before them. Nevertheless we must remember that in their time these writers did their work, and that they made a great step towards a wholesome condition of Prose Fiction. The Prose Fiction of Queen Elizabeth, the first that our literature knew, had been heroic and grand after a fashion, but it had not been real. The men and women described are hardly more to us than the gods and goddesses of the Greek mythology. Then came the style of the Stuart period in which Rochester was a poet, Wycherley a dramatist, and Afra Behn a novelist. From that it was much to rise to the manliness and conscience of Richardson and

Fielding. In each case the author expressed his age, and, in expressing, taught it; and in each case it must be remembered that the growing education of the country demanded from the writers of the day some accommodation to its wants. The 'Arcadia' of Sir Philip Sidney was written for the delight of a sister;—with no view probably to publication. A reading public did not then exist. Men and women could see and listen and appreciate poetry on the stage; but they did not read. In the days of the Stuarts education was progressing, but taste had retrograded. Mrs Manley and Mrs Behn intended, no doubt, to teach moral lessons, but they were poor creatures who could teach nothing. Fielding and Richardson were real teachers, who dealt powerfully with life as they found it.

Then Smollett came, a man of infinite humour. But it cannot be boasted on his behalf, that he did much to improve the literature of Prose Fiction. He was coarser even than Fielding, and seems to have written with less of a fixed purpose.

The name of Goldsmith is familiar to you all, and we must not pass by the 'Vicar of Wakefield'. It is a marvel of simplicity and of honest story-telling, creating in the reader's mind that momentary conviction of its reality which the novelist should ever strive to produce. But the 'Vicar' has its faults. To say that it lacks purity would be unjust. But, though it be pure in its morals, it is occasionally coarse in its delineations.

But even yet the public taste in prose fiction was wavering, and returned for a while to a class of narrative as unreal and fictitious as were the old French romances of the Paladins. We have the 'Castle of Otranto' from Horace Walpole, which we may sufficiently condemn by saying that up to the present day no one knows whether it was intended as a burlesque or as a serious work. And we have those fearful stories, the 'Romance of the Forest,' the 'Italian,' and the 'Mysteries of Udolpho.'*

I doubt whether in these practical and unpoetic days there is left, even among the young, enough of the true spirit of romance to comprehend even what was once the effect of these wonderful compositions. I remember, myself, to have been unable to leave my chair during the whole night when I was reading that awful book, the 'Mysteries of Udolpho,' alone, amidst the gloom of a dark, flock-papered dining-room. It was not that I could not put down the book,—as good-natured critics sometimes say of the novels of the day,—but that I did not dare to stir from my chair, to turn my head, or to glance at the dark curtain behind which some horrible living ruffian, or more horrible departed hero, was at that moment so probably half hidden,—half ready to come forth and freeze the marrow of my bones! So the unsnuffed candles burned themselves out; and I remained sleepless,—and, at last, sleeping,—in my chair. There is no such faith among the young of this age. I found that to my boys the 'Mysteries of Udolpho' were an old woman's tale, very dull and very long. And very dull and very long it is. The reading of it now I find to be a task almost impossible to perform. The fault is, that it lacks that which we all demand. It is unreal, and unlife-like. It is not true.

And now, before we come to the great epoch of modern English Prose Fiction, I must mention the names of two ladies who wrote novels which were true to life, full of excellent teaching, and free from an idea or a word that can pollute. I speak of Maria Edgeworth and of Miss Austen. Scott has told us that he was instigated to write his own novels by the extended and well-merited fame of Miss Edgeworth. 'Without being so presumptuous,' he tells us, 'as to hope to emulate the rich humour, pathetic tenderness, and admirable tact of my accomplished friend, I felt that something might be attempted for my own country of the same kind with that which Miss Edgeworth so fortunately achieved for Ireland.' I will not pause to make an easy comparison, but will say simply that Scott expressed the general opinion of the works of that lady. She had hit the taste of the public, which now demanded that Prose Fiction should be life-like and clear. It was becoming weary of the fantastic romance of Mrs Radcliffe, as it had long since been weary of the more fantastic romance of Sir Philip Sidney. And it had so far refined itself as to feel the coarseness of Fielding and Smollett to be distasteful. I shall not enter here upon a criticism of Miss Edgeworth's works, which in my judgement lack a certain strength which those of Miss Austen possess; but I may assert that no mother need hesitate to place the tales of Maria Edgeworth in the hands of her daughter.

Miss Austen was surely a great novelist. I do not know how far I may presume that you are acquainted with her works, but I recommend such of you as may not be so, to lose no time in mending that fault. What she did, she did perfectly. Her work, as far as it goes, is faultless. She wrote of the times in which she lived, of the class of people with which she associated, and in the language which was usual to her as an educated lady. Of romance,—what we generally mean when we speak of romance,—she had no tinge. Heroes and heroines with wonderful adventures there are none in her novels. Of great criminals and hidden crimes she tells us nothing. But she places us in a circle of gentlemen and ladies, and charms us while she tells us with an unconscious accuracy how men should act to women, and women to men. It is not that her people are all good;—and, certainly, they are not all wise. The faults of some are the anvils on which the virtues of others are hammered until they are bright as steel. In the comedy of folly I know no novelist who has beaten her. The letters of Mr Collins, a clergyman in 'Pride and Prejudice' would move laughter in a low-church archbishop. Throughout all her works, and they are not many, a sweet lesson of homely household womanly virtue is ever being taught.

From the short list with which I have ventured to trouble you, I have purposely omitted three works of great reputation for reasons which I will give you. The first in date is Bunyan's 'Pilgrim's Progress,'—as to which, were I to claim it simply as a work of English Prose Fiction, I think you would blame me. It has another character which forbids me to treat it as such. The second is Swift's 'Gulliver's Travels,' which so many of us have read in our youth as though they were wonderful stories told simply for recreation. The book contains the bitterest satire and, as I think, the foulest calumnies on the age in which it was written that disgrace our language. Satire may be virtuous,—may also be useful. To be the first it should spring from a hatred of vice, and not from disappointed hopes. To be the latter it should at least be true. The history of Gulliver is the emanation of a wounded ambition, in which the author has revelled in foul-mouthed vengeance against the institutions of his country. The third is Godwin's 'Caleb Williams,' which I should not have mentioned had it not been made the subject of eulogies which I cannot myself understand. Macintosh* said of this work, that it was 'the finest novel produced by man,—at least, since the "Vicar of Wakefield."' Other critics have spoken of it in similar language. It was written to depict the agony of one who suffered innocently from the despotic power of the English aristocracy, and is intended as a denunciation of the injustice of the time. But the sufferer was anything but innocent, and his sufferings were not compatible with the practice of law or the usages of life in those days. To my idea the book is false. It is certainly unreal, harsh, gloomy, and devoid of light. The writer was a fierce democrat, attacking every existing institution. He died a sinecurist* and pensioner on the public purse.

We have now come to the epoch of Sir Walter Scott, and I hope I need not state that in the few details with which I have troubled you I have not intended to give any catalogue, much less any complete criticism of English novels down to the time we have reached. It has been my object simply to explain how the writing of novels sprung up among us, and to show you that the supply has followed the demand. This, I think, will always be the case in literature as in commerce. We cannot, certainly, have at our will a Shakespeare, let the demand be ever so great,—or even a Scott. But the poetic temperament of an age will produce poetry. And the realistic tendencies of a people will cause them to be furnished with works of art which are life-like. Again, the propensity of public taste to what I will call cleanliness of morals will protect it from the pollution of dirt. You may, I think, be sure of this, that, in regard to all literature, the effort of reformers must be to teach the people to want good books rather than to teach authors to write them. The writers, let them be who they may, will write the books which the people demand.

And now, before I attempt to say what was done for us by Scott, and by a few who followed him,—for I shall be restrained to the naming of one or two by an unwillingness to mention those who are still living among us;—before I do this, I will say a few words on that important subject;—whether the reading of novels is, or is not, good for young people. I do so at this period in my discourse because I wish to insist on my opinion that from henceforth the literature of Prose Fiction in England became wholesome and salutary. And I will begin by suggesting that if novel-reading be bad for young people, it is bad also for the old. I am disposed to think that the distinction which so many of us make in this matter is similar in its nature to that which we have instituted between the one-o'clock and the seven-o'clock dinner. We who are the elders have the richer puddings and the more piquant sauces,—not because they agree with us better than with our children, but because we are able to get them. When I hear of ladies beginning to read French novels after they are married, I always think of the privilege which grown-up people have in spoiling their digestive organs. And I will refer to the distinction between the sexes as well as to that between young and old. If novels, or any classes of novels, be bad for young women, then they are also bad for young men. I do not understand why it should be allowed, as by implication it is, that a man's thoughts may be impure. Of this I am sure, that he who condemns the reading of novels for his daughter, should condemn it for his son; and that he who condemns it for his children, should condemn it for himself. Can any man say of himself that he has arrived at a time of life in which he can learn no evil? If so, it must be because in the learning of evil he can go no lower. We are all learning from the cradle to the grave, from our first to our last action of thought, learning good or evil; and the lessons of our mature years are at least as important to us as those of our youth. I think, too, that honest manliness is as necessary to us as feminine grace, and that vicious teaching mars the one as it effaces the other.

Does the reading of novels tend to mar the one or to efface the other? If so, for the love of heaven, let us have no more novel-reading. Let us, at any rate, make up our minds about it. Here is the fact. We have become a novel-reading people. Novels are in the hand of us all; from the Prime Minister down to the last-appointed scullery maid. We have them in our library, our drawing-rooms, our bedrooms, our kitchens,—and in our nurseries. Our memories are laden with the stories which we read, with the plots which are unravelled for us, and with the characters which are drawn for us. Poetry also we read and history, biography and the social and political news of the day. But all our other reading put together hardly amounts to what we read in novels. Let any father of a family, with a houseful of people and of books, say whether it is not so. If it be so, let us know what it is that we receive from this daily literary occupation. That we must receive much either of good or evil is beyond questioning.

The book which we call a novel contains, we may say always, a love story. Indeed, taking the general character of novels as our guide, we may say that the love stories are their mainstay and the staff of their existence. They not only contain love stories, but they are written for the sake of the love stories. They have other attractions, and deal with every phase of life; but the other attractions hang round and depend on the love story as the planets depend upon the sun. There are novel worlds, no doubt, in which the planets are brighter than the sun; in which the love-making is less interesting than the life by which it is surrounded; but these are erratic worlds, novels out of the course of nature, and to be spoken of as exceptional. The love story is the thing. In what way did this special John make himself pleasant to that particular Jane;—how did Jane receive John's attentions, and what became of it at last? This is the nucleus of all this mass of ephemeral literature which is so voluminous;—and in which the wanderings of the planets round the centre sun are so various that it is hardly too much to say that in every action of our life we are more or less guided by what is so imparted to us.

If I were to make my way into the house of any one of you as a chance visitor, and begin to teach your sons and daughters how to make love and how to receive love-making, you would think me to be a very dangerous and impertinent fellow. Your son would tell me that he understands it a great deal better than an old fogie such as I am. Your daughter would think the same thing, but would probably walk out of the room without saying it. But when I, or some greater professor, come on the same errand with Mr Mudie's ticket* on my back, you admit me, and accept my teaching. The teaching of the professor, no doubt, is taken and used. Would the love-making of our world be done better without the teaching of such professors? That it should be done is an essential necessity of our existence. That it should be done well is, perhaps, of all matters in our own private life, the most important to us. It is in itself,—in the doing of it, the brightest spot in our existence. Upon it,—the manner in which it is done, the causes by which it is actuated, depends the happiness of our future life. No social question has been so important to us as that of the great bond of matrimony. And why? Because every most wholesome joy and most precious duty of our existence depends upon our inner family relations. For what, after all, are made those outer struggles of existence, but that these may be satisfactory to us and those belonging to us? Now, of what nature is the teaching of the professor I have named? Is the man-pupil taught that it is well to be false to the woman, to triumph over her, and then to be indifferent; to lie to her, and then to despise her; or is he taught to be true and honest, and to be desirous of that which he seeks to win for noble and manly purposes? And is she taught to be bold-faced, mean in spirit, fond of pleasure, and exacting; or to be modest, devoted, and unselfish? I think you must have chosen your novels unfortunately if you have found in them the bad and not the good lessons. That the novelist deals with the false and forward, as well as with the good and gracious, with lust as well as love, with the basest of characters as well as with the best, is of course true. How else shall he do his work as professor? Does not all our sacred teaching do the same? Are we not specially warned against murder, theft, adultery, and covetousness in the Scriptures? In treating of vice does the British novelist whom you know make vice alluring, or does he make it hideous? Which course does he recommend to you,—honour or dishonour? That happy ending with the normal marriage and the two children,—is it the lot of the good girl, who has restrained all her longings by the operations of her conscience, or of the bold, bad, scheming woman who has been unwomanly and rapacious? Which attracts you, Amelia,—Thackeray's Amelia, who is not clever but good; or Becky Sharp, who is all intellect and all vileness?

But there are many planets surrounding the suns in these novel-worlds. Much is intended to be inculcated quite independent of the love lessons. All the habits and ways of our domestic and public lives are portrayed to us in novels. We have political novels, social-science novels, law-life novels, civil-service novels, commercial novels, fashionable-life novels,—and I am told that novels even of clerical life have been written. In all of them there is probably some backbone of a love story; but, over and beyond that, lessons of life are being taught from the first page to the last. Looking back upon the novels which you know, can you say that the teaching is other than good, straightforward, and in the right direction? The novels may be bad novels, and yet the lessons taught may be in the right direction. My experience tells me that this community, the British reading public, is upon the whole utterly averse to the teaching of bad lessons, and will not have it. They will accept bad work, but they reject an immoral or injurious theory of life. Mr James's* heroes may not always be life-like, but they are always made so to act as to leave on the reader's mind an idea that vice is injurious and virtue attractive. Would the hands at any mill be rendered worse as men and women by the reading of 'Mary Barton'?* There are of course exceptions. There are modern novels, as well as old novels, in which the teaching is bad. Very injurious they may be,—and have been. But you do not reject your daily food because there are butchers who sell unwholesome meat. There is adulterated tea in the market, but you get your tea good if you take the trouble to look for it. Take the same trouble about your novels, and I am sure you may save yourselves from evil teaching in that direction.

But there are two other objections made to the reading of novels;—made by some who scrupulously exclude such books from their houses, and by others who admit them, but admit them with hesitation. The first of these is very strong, and up to a certain point, is unanswerable. Time is devoted to an amusement which should be given to work. The novel-reading girl will have her novel in her hand all day, and the novel-reading young man will hide it even under his Blackstone.* And these objectors will go further than this, and will say that not only may such an evil afflict this or that irrational and over-greedy consumer of novels, but that the tendency of the amusement is to create idleness, desultory thinking, and a pernicious vagueness and unreality of character. There is, doubtless, much truth in the allegation. All our amusements have a tendency to impose upon us, and to obtain for themselves an undue importance,—as though they were the chief instead of secondary objects of our lives. I may exemplify this by referring to the athletic sports of the day, which, with many young men, have assumed all the characteristics of a serious life's occupation. The stroke-oar of a boat is as intent on what he does in his boat, and on the manner in which he is seen to do it, as is a Prime Minister or a Poet Laureate. It is the same with hunting, shooting, dancing, and what not. You may hunt and dance too much, and undoubtedly you may read too many novels. Let those who have the control of the hours of others see to this;—and let those who have the control of their own hours see to it also. As to that pernicious way of looking at the affairs of life which is attributed to novel-reading,—that Lydia Languish determination, for instance, not to be married without the aid of a rope ladder,—I do not think that such result comes from the novels of our period. To be too romantic is not the fault of our time. It may, perhaps, rather be the fault of our novelists that there is not sufficient of romance left among them. The manner of looking at life engendered by the novels of the day is realistic, practical, and, though upon the whole serviceable, upon the whole also unpoetical rather than romantic.

Amusement of some kind,—what our forefathers, understanding the matter very well, used to call distraction,—all the world admits to be necessary. The harder we work the more needful it is that we should at intervals take our minds away from the matters that most engross us and disport ourselves at our ease. But the mind will not sleep or be at rest. What the mind requires is change,—not tranquillity. In all the changes that are sought and found some lesson is still being learned. The girl is learning to be a woman, and the boy is learning to be a man in every waking hour; and in every waking hour the man and woman are learning,—a further lesson still. I am not here to tell you that these great lessons can be best learned from novels. But I do say that much must be learned in the lighter hours, and that the lessons which are learned from novels may be, and generally are, lessons of good and not of evil.

The further objection to novels of which I have spoken is, to my mind, so palpably groundless that I should not allude to it were it not that it has frequently been raised against me by those who disapprove of novel-reading. They say that novels are false;—meaning that they are untrue in the broadest sense, because they are fictions. The hero and heroine, who are said by the novelist so to act or so to speak, never acted or spoke at all; and the whole thing is untrue. Of course it is all fiction; but fiction may be as true as fact. These objectors seem to me to misunderstand Truth and Untruth;—which consist in the desire of the speaker or actor to reveal or to deceive. If I write for you a story, giving you a picture of life as true as I can make it, my story, though a fiction, is not false. It may be as true a book as ever was written. A novel may indeed be false,—hideously false. I could name to you novels that are very false. A novelist is false who, in dealing with this or that phase of life, bolsters up a theory of his own with pictures which are in themselves untrue. There is at this moment a great question forward as to the tenure of Land in Ireland.* I may have my ideas upon it, and may desire to promulgate them in a novel. But if for the sake of promulgating my theory, I draw a picture of Irish landlords which is not a true picture,—which I have no ground for believing to be true,—in which I make them out to be cruel, idle, God-abandoned reprobates, because I have a theory of my own to support in my novel, then my book is a false book, and I am a liar. In this way a novel may be false, and much of this falseness, sometimes in large and often in very small proportions, is to be found in novels; but to say that a novel is false because it deals with an imagined and not with a real world of people, seems to me to be an absurdity.

Now, having made my apology for my trade, and having endeavoured to show that the lessons which the novelist undoubtedly does teach, need not necessarily be evil, I will revert to Walter Scott, the great master of modern fiction, and to the lessons which he taught. It may be said of him,—as of the two ladies whom I mentioned to you as his immediate precursors,—that in his teaching there is no mixture of immorality. He has taught us many lessons, and we have probably failed to analyse his teaching so as to know exactly what we have got from him; but we are all probably aware that we have not been fostered in vice, in meanness, or in greed, by any word written by him. He has probably taught us all to be more or less Cavalier in our Scotch politics, and we have been unconscious of the teaching. He has imbued us with a love of lakes and mountains, and we, individually, have been unconscious of that teaching. With many of us he has had an effect upon our tendencies in religion, teaching us to revere establishments and perhaps endowments. In his time he made a great many conservatives who never knew why they were so. And he taught the world of those days, without the world being in the least aware of the lesson, a certain somewhat cold grace of courtship in which there was more of poetry than of nature,—which lesson, however, under other subsequent teaching, the world has now altogether unlearned. From Scott's view in these matters you may differ, and to his lessons you may demur. You may dislike the Cavaliers, disregard lakes and mountains, may object to Church Establishments, and hate endowments. You may despise conservatism, and think that romantic grace is absurd in the affairs of every-day life. But still you cannot but admit that the teaching was good of its kind. It tended to elevate the mind, and left the reader better than it found him.

These works made with great quickness a revolution in the English mind in reference to Prose Fiction. Gradually under their influence was removed the embargo which had hitherto been laid upon novels in many English domestic circles, and which Miss Edgeworth and Miss Austen had not been strong enough to dislodge. Mothers allowed their daughters to read them, and a new world of romance was opened to that wholesome portion of the community which consists of parents who are anxious for their children, and of children who obey their parents. Is there anyone here present who thinks that any injury was thus done to morals? And yet Scott told tales which freeze the blood,—as of Lucy Ashton; of fallen womanhood,—as of Effie Deans; of broad farce,—as with Baillie Nicol Jarvie; of faerie-land,— as of the White Maid of Avenel;—of villainy,—as of Varney; and also of somewhat too forward feminine behaviour, as I have always thought was the case with Miss Julia Mannering.* But no woman became forward, and no man a villain under his teaching. Nor has he helped to produce domestic tragedies. No wife has left husband or child, stirred to mischief and vagabond propensities,—to what we, in the cant of the day, call Bohemianism,—through his influence. He has instructed no Lydia to be desirous of rope ladders. I grant you that if Lydias desirous of rope ladders are to be the result of novels, the less we have of novels the better. But I assert that propriety of life and that domestic security which is so ineffably precious to us all, have been advanced and not impeded by the reading of Scott's novels.

My object is rather to carry you with me in this opinion than to give you any minute criticism on the separate heads of Sir Walter Scott;—but I shall hardly carry out the purpose of my discourse without saying a word or two as to the special qualities of his works. As a novelist he was very great, but not great, I think, at all points. In creation of incidents he was unrivalled. 'Ivanhoe,' for the glory of exciting movement, has probably never been surpassed. In certain touches of pathos he has been almost divine. Who does not remember the rebuke of Evan Maccombich* to those in the court who laughed at his self-devoting proposal? 'But if they laugh because they think I would not keep my word, I can tell them they ken neither the heart of a Hielandman nor the honour of a gentleman.' Or the thrilling prophecy with which Meg Merrilies* rebuked the old laird who had turned against her and her people after years of neighbourly kindness? 'Ride your ways, laird of Ellangowan; ride your ways, Geoffrey Bertram. This day ye have quenched seven smoking hearths; see if the fire in your parlour burn the blither for that! Ye have riven the thack off seven cottar houses; look if your ain roof-tree stand the faster! Ye may stable your stirks in the shealings of Derncleugh; see that the hare does not couch on the hearthstane of Ellengowan!' I know no words in the English language better chosen for their intended purpose than those. And let me recall to you the tragedy between Balfour of Burley and Bothwell,* and repeat to you the final words of the scene. ' "Base peasant churl," says Bothwell dying, "thou has spilt the blood of a line of kings."—"Die, wretch; die!" said Balfour. "Die, bloodthirsty dog; die as thou has lived! Die like the beasts that perish! Hoping nothing, believing nothing!"—"And fearing nothing!" said Bothwell.' I do not know whether I carry you with me; but there is, to my feeling, a strength of expression in Scott to which I know nothing equal in Prose Fiction. He was, too, very great in the creation of characters. Oldbuck, for instance, Meg Merrilies, Wamba, and Dugald Dalgetty,* are all marvels in their way.

In the delineation of ordinary human beings he was not, I think, equally happy. When he undertook the task of describing the every-day doings of life, he was somewhat stiff, and apt to be unlife-like. As I said before, there was something chilling in the grace of his lovers. If either in high life or in low life he had to do with things out of the common course, he could excite our pathos or our mirth; but with things in their common course he did not succeed so well. Counsellor Pleydell at high jinks is excellent; but Counsellor Pleydell in Colonel Mannering's drawing-room is not so good. Old Davie Deans, who in his life is beyond the common, charms us; but Reuben Butler is uninteresting. It is so with Lord Evandale, Edith Bellenden, and Henry Morton; with Rose Bradwardine, and I fear I must say also with the hero, Waverley.* Scott was a giant when describing the life outside the world,—the life which he himself created; but in drawing the life which we ourselves know, he was not so natural. His dialogues are marvellously fine, when, as in the passages which I have quoted, they refer to scenes the life of which we have never seen. But they hardly strike us as natural, or as containing such words as could have been spoken in scenes such as those to which we are accustomed. Most of us here,—I mean of the male sex,—have had love scenes of our own; but we did not conduct them as do Scott's heroes; and had we done so, we should hardly have succeeded,—even as well as we have done.

I insist on this for the sake of explaining the way in which the nature of novels has been altered since Scott's time. I have said that his aera divides our Prose Fiction into two epochs. But he himself belongs to both. He partook of that unreal romance which was the very base on which Prose Fiction was first founded. There is still the touch of the Paladin and the Princess about his men and women; but he wove them into stories of such vital interest, and threw such movement and passion and mirth into the telling of these stories, that he created a new system of Fiction. If he was not always life-like himself, he produced a love for such likeness which has imposed an obligation on all English novelists coming after him. In parting with his name I must again repeat my belief that from the reading of his novels nothing but good has come to the people for whom he wrote.

Of the novelists who have succeeded Scott I shall name to you but three. Luckily for us all, many of those who are most distinguished are still among us. But Thackeray has gone, and so too have two other great writers of Prose Fiction,—Mrs Gaskell and Charlotte Bronte. Of Thackeray, whom I knew and loved, I would wish to guard myself against speaking with an enthusiasm which, much as I feel it to be his due, may perhaps come from my love rather than from my judgement. According to my ideas he has described humanity—the real flesh and blood with the heart and mind working within them,—the human beings whom we see and know,—our very selves,—with an accuracy that has been within the reach of no other writer of English Prose Fiction. And his power went beyond accuracy. There is a fineness of touch in it, a grace of finish, a capacity for seeing and reproducing the minute workings of the heart, which warrant me in saying that he possessed an intellect combining both male and female qualities. Scott's intellect was wholly masculine. I do not imply by that that Scott's women are not feminine. No woman more feminine than Jeannie Deans ever walked through the pages of a novel. But she is a woman seen from a man's point of view,—as are all his women and all his men. But Thackeray sees his characters, both men and women, with a man's eye and with a woman's. He dissects with a knife and also with a needle. It is said of him that in his work he was a cynic. Those who say it mean to imply that he has put forth characters of men and women less noble, less genuine, less faultless than are generally found in novels. His heroes and heroines are much less heroic than those of Scott, and he has rarely described for us a man or a woman perfect at all points. Scott did so frequently. Ivanhoe was a model, though Saint Anthony* was never so tempted. Had Thackeray written the story, instead of the burlesque* upon the story, Ivanhoe would certainly have declared a passion for the Jewess,—even though his mind had been as firm as ever in regard to Rowena. Ravenswood never descends to any of the foibles of humanity. Edie Ochiltree as a beggar is without spot or flaw,—perfectly heroic. Jeanie Deans never lapses even for a moment into consciousness of self. Of his higher-class heroines it would be impossible to imagine that they would ever flirt, ever run in debt for bonnets and gilt boots, or pay sly visits to the pastry-cook. Of Flora MacIvor,* does anybody conceive that she required meat and drink to keep her alive? Thackeray's heroines do require meat, and his heroes a good deal of drink to wash the meat down. But then,—such is the way with men and women in the world! I do not remember a single heroine of Thackeray's who does not now and then fall off from the heroic. But I must say, speaking from my own experience, that the effulgence of woman's divinity is made fitter for the weak eyes of men by some few spots and clouds.

In the palmy days of Italian art,—or rather, when those palmy days were coming to an end,—there came up a school of painters in which it was the aim of the artist to endow the female face with beauties and graces which he found rather in his imagination than in the models which nature gave him. Whether or not he lost more than he gained we will not now inquire; but he certainly effected this,—that from that day to our own the portrait of a woman which shall give us that woman's face with its own colouring, its own expression, and its own natural inequalities of surface, is to us displeasing. An artist even now does not dare to paint such a portrait of a young woman. We have instructed our eyes to believe that the true portrait would be a caricature. The same fault of a fictitious grace arose in the Art of Literature. But Thackeray with his minute feminine glances into life, seeing the workings of the human heart with that magnifying-glass with which nature had supplied him, could not paint his portraits in the Raphaelistic manner. He saw what there was of good and evil in men and women, and he had to put it all down. He felt with intensity the duty of so writing that he should teach no evil;—and I make bold to say that he has taught none; but he could not describe the world around as other than he saw it. That he fell into the common fault of thinking all things to be evil, when his kind was dwelling on the special evils which he then saw, is quite true. It is the policeman's fault who looks on all men as thieves; the reformer's fault who regards all settled customs as abuses; the fault of all self-appointed censors, to whose eyes everything is bad. From this cause Thackeray's 'Snob Papers'* are faulty because, while scourging the snobs he saw, his mind for awhile became imbued with a conviction that all men were snobs. But this fault does not disfigure Thackeray's chief works; because in them it is his purpose to write in fiction what Life is and should be, and not to reform special abuses. I will take 'Esmond' as being in my judgement the most complete novel which he left in our hands, and ask you to study the characters of the two ladies, mother and daughter, which are there drawn. Regard the depth of the self-devoting love of Lady Castlewood,—a love which was at first the sweet affection of a woman for the youth whom it had been her duty to foster;—a love which grew upon her till in her purity she repented of it as a sin, though it hardly ever grew to be a fault;—a love which she buried in her own bosom, because the youth in his manhood had learned to love her own daughter! How gallantly she strove to make that daughter accept the man, whom she had found fit to be trusted as a lord and master! Lady Castlewood is a woman all over,—generous, self-devoting, full of jealousy, angry without cause, unjust, irrational, full of faith, full of piety, and true as steel! Do you remember the scene between her and Esmond when they first meet after his return from the wars? They had seen each other in the church, and she had been thinking of him as she listens to the anthem. And thus when they meet she tells him her thoughts:—'And today in the anthem when they sang it;—"When the Lord turned the captivity of Zion we were like them that dream;" I thought, yes, like them that dream, like them that dream. And then it went,—"They that sow in tears shall reap in joy, and he that goeth forth and weepeth shall doubtless come home with rejoicing, bringing his sheaves with him." I looked up from my book and saw you. I knew that you would come, my dear, and I saw the gold sunshine round your head. Do you know what day it is?' she continued,—'it is your birthday! But last year we did not drink it. No, no; my lord was cold, and my Harry was like to die, and my brain was in a fever; and we had no wine. But now,—now you are come again, bringing your sheaves with you.' I cannot quote to you the passage in which she reveals to her daughter's betrothed, the Duke of Hamilton, the story of Esmond's birth. It is too long for us now, though it occupies but a page or two. I have read it a score of times, but never without a tear. I think that nothing finer can be found in the whole range of English Prose Fiction; and I think that no woman has ever been drawn more life-like, with more of the mingled grace and purity, weakness and self-devotion of woman, than Lady Castlewood.

Then there is her daughter, Beatrix, a young girl who has seen and lived among the vices of the Court while her mother is still so innocent,—who is beautiful, witty, proud, scornful, hard, worldly,—and conscious through it all of her own mean condition in that she is hard and worldly; a terrible picture, drawn and finished with minute touches, which show the working of every evil thought and passion in the poor creature's bosom,—ambition that has killed the power of love, the craving for rank and wealth that has stifled all feminine softness – and yet with all these the consciousness that a woman to be worthy of the name should be tender and loving. Thackeray's Beatrix is more terrible to me than his Becky Sharp. But the story of her faults can make no other woman faulty. No girl will wish to be a Beatrix. The gems and jewels which she prized she herself knew to be worthless and paltry; and the tale is so told that the very child who reads it is made to feel that these things are but vanity and vexation of spirit.

Thackeray displays the same minute powers in most of his novels. 'Barry Lyndon,'—an unpleasant book to read,—is a marvel in this way. The hero, who is thoroughly a scoundrel, tells his own story with absolute belief in himself,—and yet never palliates a fault or blinks a vice! The result on the reader's mind is a detestation of the scoundrel and the scoundrel's selfishness. Of Colonel Newcome, I must say he is as fine a gentleman as Don Quixote, and as good a Christian. Laura,—Mrs Pendennis as she becomes,—is so thorough a woman that we can hardly understand that a man should have drawn the character,—so finely cut are those little traits which show that with all her virtues she is still human. In the old romances, and in some that are not old, the heroine is a marble goddess,—faultless as a goddess, but made of marble. Thackeray's heroines are not only flesh and blood; but they are so put before us that we can see the beating of every pulse. Seeing so much, of course we see the faults;—but I know no work of his which makes the faults alluring.

I have alluded to one novel written by Mrs Gaskell, and would tell you of others if time admitted. They are quite worthy of being mentioned as works of art that have done good by their teaching while they have charmed by their grace and truth. Let any mother of a family take the last which she wrote,—which she died while writing,—'Wives and Daughters,' and ask herself whether it contains any lesson that can do harm. I say of these books, and of hundreds like them, that harm may doubtless come from time devoted to them which should be given to graver pursuits; but that as recreation,—if recreation be required at all,—they are not only harmless but salutary. They teach the lessons which a mother would desire that her child should learn.

One word I must say of Charlotte Bronte,—Currer Bell as she called herself while she was writing;—because she also possessed that power of minutely seeing and describing the inner work of the heart which belonged so remarkably to Thackeray. The character of Rochester, and the intercourse between him and Jane Eyre which ultimately led to their marriage,—as is customary in novels,—is a wonderful piece of fine workmanship. Miss Bronte wrote while she was yet young, and wrote under various disadvantages. Circumstances had hidden from her much of the outside world, and she was feeble in health, and prone, as are all who are isolated, to be too conscious of her own self. This consciousness she displays in her writing to a fault; but her power and honesty of purpose, and intention to do good as far as it lay within her power to accomplish it, are not to be doubted. And there was a delicacy and fineness of touch in her hand, so rare, that I should be wrong were I not to name her among the novelists who have graced our language and are now no more.

You will understand that in bringing under your notice the few names that I have mentioned, I have not intended to give you any catalogue of English novelists. You may feel, perhaps, that I have spoken of those I have named with too much eulogy; but you will, I hope, remember that it has not been my intention to tell you of the weak, the indifferent, or the vicious. That we have many weak novels, some, also, that are vicious, you probably do not need to be told, and I shall not deny. I simply assert, on behalf of English novel-writers and novel-readers, that there is good conscientious work provided by the former, and that the latter may so choose their novels,—or have them chosen for them,—that no injury shall come from the lessons which they convey.

There is one other point to which I crave your attention, and then I will have done. There has arisen of late years a popular idea as to the division of novels into two classes, which is, I think, a mistaken idea. We hear of the sensational school of novels; and of the real-istic, or life-like school. Now, according to my view of the matter, a novel is bound to be both sensational and realistic. And I think that if a novel fail in either particular it is, so far, a failure in Art. No doubt a string of tragic incidents bound together without truth in details, and told as affecting personages without character,—wooden blocks who cannot make themselves known to the readers as men and women,—does not instruct or amuse. Horrors heaped upon horrors, which are horrors only in themselves, and not as touching any recognised and known person, cease even to horrify. And such tragic elements of a story may be increased without end and with-out difficulty. I may tell you of a woman murdered,—murdered in the same street with you, in the next house,—that she was a wife, murdered by her husband,—a bride not yet a week a wife. I may add to it for ever. I may say that the murderer roasted her alive,—that he had her served to table, that he himself sat at the banquet! There is no end to it. I may say that a former wife was treated with equal barbarity, and I may assert that as the murderer was led to execution he declared his only sorrow, his sole regret to be,—that he could not live to treat a third after the same fashion. There is nothing so easy as the creation and piling up of tragic incidents after this sort. And if such creation be the beginning and the end of the novelist's work,—and novels have been written seeming to want other attractions,—nothing can be more dull, more deadly, or more useless. But not on that account are we averse to tragedy in prose Fiction. As in poetry, so in prose, he who can deal adequately with tragic elements is a greater artist and reaches a higher aim than the writer whose efforts never carry him above the mild walks of every-day life. The passages which I quoted to you from Scott were all tragic; the 'Bride of Lammermoor' is a tragedy throughout, in spite of its comic elements; the life of Lady Castlewood, of which I have spoken to you, is all a tragedy. Rochester's wretched thraldom to his mad wife in 'Jane Eyre' is a tragedy. But these stories charm us not simply because they are tragic, but because we feel that men and women with flesh and blood, creatures with whom we can sympathise, are struggling amidst their woes. It all lies in that. No novel is anything, for purposes either of tragedy or of comedy, unless the reader can sympathise with the characters whose names he finds upon the page. Let an author so tell his tale as to touch your heart and draw your tears, and he has so far done his work well. Truth let there be;—truth of description, truth of character, human truth as to men and women. If there be such truth I do not know that a novel can be too sensational.

There is, indeed, a certain sensational interest,—to feel which we are all prone, though we ought not to feel it,—which is very evil in its tendencies. The taste is bad in the reader; but the sin of pandering to it is unpardonable in the writer. I speak of the interest which is aroused by dealing with the characters of those who are yet alive,—or who have lived so recently as to make their foibles, or perhaps their faults, a matter of interest to the public, and of most painful concern to those belonging to them. You know that were I to bring into my pages the name of some great man, and attempt to unravel the secrets of his private life, accusing him of this vice and of that folly, very many would rush to read it. It is an author's object to obtain readers, and I should be so far successful. The book would,—sell, and people would talk. But I as an author would have sinned grievously. Against that sensationalism I enter my protest. But in regard to the so-called ordinarily sensational novel, I beg to repeat my opinion that, as long as a novel be true to life, it cannot too strongly convey that feeling which we mean when we speak of sensation. To convey that is the very essence of the poet's art,—and also of the novelist's.

Ladies and Gentlemen, I have now finished my task, and I thank you for the patience with which you have heard my apology for the profession which I follow.

From *Thackeray*

As one reads, one is sometimes struck by a conviction that this or the other writer has thoroughly liked the work on which he is engaged. There is a gusto about his passages, a liveliness in the language, a spring in the motion of the words, an eagerness of description, a lilt, if I may so call it, in the progress of the narrative, which makes the reader feel that the author has himself greatly enjoyed what he has written. He has evidently gone on with his work without any sense of weariness, or doubt; and the words have come readily to him. So it has been with *Barry Lyndon*. 'My mind was filled full with those blackguards,' Thackeray once said to a friend. It is easy enough to see that it was so . . . his mind was running over with the idea that a rascal might be so far gone in rascality as to be in love with his own trade. (Chapter 2)

The object of a novel should be to instruct in morals while it amuses. I cannot think but that every novelist who has thought much of his art will have realised as much as that for himself. Whether this may best be done by the transcendental or by the commonplace is the question which it more behoves the reader than the author to answer, because the author may be fairly sure that he who can do the one will not, probably cannot, do the other. If a lad be only five feet high he does not try to enlist in the Guards. Thackeray complains that many ladies have 'remonstrated and subscribers left him,' because of his realistic tendency. Nevertheless he has gone on with his work, and, in *Pendennis*, has painted a young man as natural as Tom Jones . . . It has to be admitted that Pendennis is not a fine fellow. He is not as weak, as selfish, as untrustworthy as that George Osborne whom Amelia married in *Vanity Fair*; but nevertheless, he is weak, and selfish, and untrustworthy. He is not such a one as a father would wish to see his son, or a mother to welcome as a lover for her daughter. But then, fathers are so often doomed to find their sons not all that they wish, and mothers to see their girls falling in love with young men who are not Paladins. In our individual lives we are contented to endure an admixture of evil, which we should resent if imputed to us in the general. We presume ourselves to be truth-speaking, noble in our sentiments, generous in our actions, modest and unselfish, chivalrous and devoted. But we forgive and pass over in silence a few delinquencies among ourselves . . . Thackeray is always protesting . . . that no good is done by blinking the truth. He knows that we have our little home experiences. Let us have the facts out, and mend what is bad if we can. This novel of *Pendennis* is one of his loudest protests to this effect. (Chapter 4)

When we were young we used to be told, in our house at home, that 'elbow-grease' was the one essential necessary to getting a tough piece of work well done. If a mahogany table was to be made to shine, it was elbow-grease that the operation needed. Forethought is the elbow-grease which a novelist, or poet, or dramatist,—requires. It is not only his plot that has to be turned and re-turned in his mind, not his plot chiefly, but he has to make himself sure of his situations, of his characters, of his effects, so that when the time comes for hitting the nail he may know where to hit it on the head,—so that he may himself understand the passion, the calmness, the virtues, the vices, the rewards and punishments which he means to explain to others,—so that his proportions shall be correct, and he be saved from the absurdity of devoting two-thirds of his book to the beginning, or two-thirds to the completion of his task. It is from want of this special labour, more frequently than from intellectual deficiency, that the tellers of stories fail so often to hit their nails on the head. To think of a story is much harder work than to write it. The author can sit down with the pen in his hand for a given time, and produce a certain number of words. That is comparatively easy, and if he have a conscience in regard to his task, work will be done regularly. But to think it over as you lie in bed, or walk about, or sit cosily over your fire, to turn it all in your thoughts, and make the things fit,—that requires elbow-grease of the mind. The arrangement of the words is as though you were walking simply along a road. The arrangement of your story is as though you were carrying a sack of flour while you walked. Fielding had carried his sack of flour before he wrote *Tom Jones*, and Scott his before he produced *Ivanhoe*. So had Thackeray done,—a very heavy sack of flour,—in creating *Esmond*. In *Vanity Fair*, in *Pendennis*, and in *The Newcomes*, there was more of that mere wandering in which no heavy burden was borne. The richness of the author's mind, the

beauty of his language, his imagination and perception of character
are all there. For that which was lovely he has shown his love, and
for the hateful his hatred; but, nevertheless, they are comparatively
idle books. His only work, as far as I can judge them, in which there
is no touch of idleness, is *Esmond*. *Barry Lyndon* is consecutive, and
has the well-sustained purpose of exhibiting a finished rascal; but
Barry Lyndon is not quite the same from beginning to end. All his
full-fledged novels, except *Esmond*, contain rather strings of incidents
and memoirs of individuals, than a completed story. But *Esmond* is
a whole from beginning to end, with its tale well told, its purpose
developed, its moral brought home,—and its nail hit well on the head
and driven in. (Chapter 5)

Realism in style has not all the ease which seems to belong to it. It
is the object of the author who affects it so to communicate with his
reader that all his words shall seem to be natural to the occasion . . .
In one respect both the sublime and the ludicrous are easier than the
realistic. They are not required to be true. A man with an imagination and culture may feign either of them without knowing the ways
of men. To be realistic you must know accurately that which you
describe. How often do we find in novels that the author makes an
attempt at realism and falls into a bathos of absurdity, because he cannot use appropriate language? 'No human being ever spoke like that,'
we say to ourselves,—while we should not question the naturalness of
the production, either in the grand or the ridiculous.

    And yet in very truth the realistic must not be true,—but just so far
removed from truth as to suit the erroneous idea of truth which the
reader may be supposed to entertain. For were a novelist to narrate
a conversation between two persons of fair but not high education,
and to use the ill-arranged words and fragments of speech which are
really common in such conversations, he would seem to have sunk to
the ludicrous, and to be attributing to the interlocutors a mode of language much beneath them. Though in fact true, it would seem to be
far from natural. But on the other hand, were he to put words gram-
matically correct into the mouths of his personages, and to round
off and to complete the spoken sentences, the ordinary reader would
instantly feel such a style to be stilted and unreal. This reader would
not analyse it, but would in some dim but sufficiently critical manner be aware that his author was not providing him with a naturally

spoken dialogue. To produce the desired effect the narrator must go between the two. He must mount somewhat above the ordinary conversational powers of such persons as are to be represented,—lest he disgust. But he must by no means soar into correct phraseology,—lest he offend. The realistic,—by which we mean that which shall seem to be real,—lies between the two, and in reaching it the writer has not only to keep his proper distance on both sides, but has to maintain varying distances in accordance with the position, mode of life, and education of the speakers. (Chapter 9)

From 'The Genius of Nathaniel Hawthorne'

THERE never surely was a powerful, active, continually effective mind less round, more lop-sided than that of NATHANIEL HAWTHORNE. If there were aught of dispraise in this, it would not be said by me,—by an Englishman of an American whom I knew, by an English man of letters of a brother on the other side of the water, much less by me, an English novelist, of an American novelist . . . from Hawthorne we could not have obtained that weird, mysterious, thrilling charm with which he has awed and delighted us had he not allowed his mind to revel in one direction, so as to lose its fair proportions.

I have been specially driven to think of this by the strong divergence between Hawthorne and myself. It has always been my object to draw my little pictures as like to life as possible, so that my readers should feel that they were dealing with people whom they might probably have known, but so to do it that the every-day good to be found among them should allure, and the every-day evil repel; and this I have attempted, believing that such ordinary good and ordinary evil would be more powerful in repelling or alluring than great and glowing incidents which, though they might interest, would not come home to the minds of readers. Hawthorne, on the other hand, has dealt with persons and incidents which were often but barely within the bounds of possibility,—which were sometimes altogether without those bounds,—and has determined that his readers should be carried out of their own little mundane ways, and brought into a world of imagination in which their intelligence might be raised, if only for a time, to something higher than the common needs of common life . . . How was it that his mind wandered away always into those fancies, not jocund as are usually those of the tellers of fairy tales, not high-flown as are the pictures generally drawn by the poets, with no fearful adventures though so sad, often by no means beautiful, without an attempt even at the picturesque, melancholy beyond compare, as though the writer had drawn all his experiences from untoward accidents? That some remnant of Puritan asceticism should be found in the writings of a novelist from Concord, in Massachusetts, would seem natural to an English reader . . . But had that been the

Hawthorne flavour, readers both in England and in the States would have accepted it, without surprise.

It is, however, altogether different, though ascetic enough. The predominating quality of Puritan life was hard, good sense,—a good sense which could value the realities of life while it rejected the frivolities . . . Hawthorne is severe, but his severity is never of a nature to form laws for life. His is a mixture of romance and austerity, quite as far removed from the realities of Puritanism as it is from the sentimentalism of poetry. He creates a melancholy which amounts almost to remorse in the minds of his readers. There falls upon them a conviction of some unutterable woe which is not altogether dispelled until other books and other incidents have had their effects. The woe is of course fictitious, and therefore endurable,—and therefore alluring. And woe itself has its charm. It is a fact that the really miserable will pity the comfortable insignificance of those who are not unhappy, and that they are apt even to boast of their own sufferings . . . You are beyond measure depressed by the weird tale that is told to you, but you become conscious of a certain grandness of nature in being susceptible of such suffering. When you hear what Hawthorne has done to others, you long to search his volumes. When he has operated upon you, you would not for worlds have foregone it. You have been ennobled by that familiarity with sorrow. You have been, as it were, sent through the fire and purged of so much of your dross. For a time, at least, you have been free from the mundane touch of that beef and ale with which novelists of a meaner school will certainly bring you in contact. No one will feel himself ennobled at once by having read one of my novels. But Hawthorne, when you have studied him, will be very precious to you. He will have plunged you into melancholy, he will have overshadowed you with black forebodings, he will almost have crushed you with imaginary sorrows; but he will have enabled you to feel yourself an inch taller during the process. Something of the sublimity of the transcendent, something of the mystery of the unfathomable, something of the brightness of the celestial, will have attached itself to you, and you will all but think that you too might live to be sublime, and revel in mingled light and mystery.

The creations of American literature generally are no doubt more given to the speculative,—less given to the realistic,—than are those of English literature. On our side of the water we deal more with beef and ale, and less with dreams. Even with the broad humour of Bret

Harte, even with the broader humour of Artemus Ward and Mark Twain, there is generally present an undercurrent of melancholy, in which pathos and satire are intermingled. There was a touch of it even with the simple-going Cooper and the kindly Washington Irving. Melancholy and pathos, without the humour, are the springs on which all Longfellow's lines are set moving. But in no American writer is to be found the same predominance of weird imagination as in Hawthorne. There was something of it in M. G. Lewis—our Monk Lewis as he came to be called, from the name of a tale which he wrote; but with him, as with many others, we feel that they have been weird because they have desired to be so. They have struggled to achieve the tone with which their works are pervaded. With Hawthorne we are made to think that he could not have been anything else if he would. It is as though he could certainly have been nothing else in his own inner life. We know that such was not actually the case. Though a man singularly reticent,—what we generally call shy,—he could, when things went well with him, be argumentative, social, and cheery . . . And yet his imagination was such that the creations of his brain could not have been other than such as I have described . . . In the true enjoyment of Hawthorne's work there is required a peculiar mood of mind. The reader should take a delight in looking round corners, and in seeing how places and things may be approached by other than the direct and obvious route. No writer impresses himself more strongly on the reader who will submit to him; but the reader must consent to put himself altogether under his author's guidance, and to travel by queer passages, the direction of which he will not perceive till, perhaps, he has got quite to the end of them.

From 'A Walk in a Wood'

THE most difficult thing that a man has to do is to think. There are many that can never bring themselves really to think at all, but do whatever thinking is done by them in a chance fashion, with no effort . . . My purpose here is to describe how this operation, always so difficult, often so repugnant to us, becomes easier out among the woods, with the birds and the air and the leaves and branches around us, than in the seclusion of any closet.

But I have nothing to show for it beyond my own experience, and no performances of thought to boast of beyond the construction of combinations in fiction, countless and unimportant as the sand on the sea-shore. For in these operations of thinking it is not often the entire plot of a novel,—the plot of a novel as a whole,—that exercises the mind. That is a huge difficulty; one so arduous as to have been generally found by me altogether beyond my power of accomplishment. Efforts are made no doubt,—always out in the open air, and within the precincts of a wood if a wood be within reach; but to construct a plot so as to know, before the story is begun, how it is to end, has always been to me a labour of Hercules beyond my reach. I have to confess that my incidents are fabricated to fit my story as it goes on, and not my story to fit my incidents. I wrote a novel once in which a lady forged a will; but I had not myself decided that she had forged it till the chapter before that in which she confesses her guilt. In another a lady is made to steal her own diamonds,—a grand tour-de-force, as I thought,—but the brilliant idea only struck me when I was writing the page in which the theft is described . . . I say this to show that the process of thinking to which I am alluding has not generally been applied to any great effort of construction. It has expended itself on the minute ramifications of tale-telling;—how this young lady should be made to behave herself with that young gentleman;—how this mother or that father would be affected by the ill conduct or the good of a son or a daughter;—how these words or those other would be most appropriate and true to nature if used on some special occasion. Such plottings as these, with a fabricator of fiction, are infinite in number as they are infinitesimal in importance,—and are therefore, as I have said, like the sand of the sea-shore. But not one of them can be done fitly without thinking. My little effort will miss its wished-for result, unless I be true to nature; and to be true to nature I must think what nature would produce. Where shall I go to find my thoughts with the greatest ease and most perfect freedom?

Bad noises, bad air, bad smells, bad light, an inconvenient attitude, ugly surroundings, little misfortunes that are soon to come, hunger and thirst, overeating and overdrinking, want of sleep or too much of it, a tight boot, a starched collar, are all inimical to thinking. I do not name bodily ailments. The feeling of heroism which is created by the magnanimity of overcoming great evils will sometimes make thinking easy. It is not the sorrows but the annoyances of life which impede. Were I told that the bank had broken in which my little all was kept for me I could sit down and write my love story with almost a sublimated vision of love; but to discover that I had given half a sovereign instead of sixpence to a cabman would render a great effort necessary before I could find the fitting words for a lover. These little lacerations of the spirit, not the deep wounds, make the difficulty. Of all the nuisances named noises are the worst. I know a hero who can write his leading article for a newspaper in a club smoking-room while all the chaff of all the Joneses and all the Smiths is sounding in his ears;—but he is a hero because he can do it. To think with a barrel organ within hearing is heroic. For myself I own that a brass band altogether incapacitates me . . .

Whither shall a man take himself to avoid these evils, so that he may do his thinking in peace,—in silence if it may be possible? And yet it is not silence that is altogether necessary. The wood-cutter's axe never stopped a man's thought, nor the wind through the branches, nor the flowing of water, nor the singing of birds, nor the distant tingling of a chapel bell. Even the roaring of the sea and the loud splashing of the waves among the rocks do not impede the mind. No sounds coming from water have the effect of harassing. But yet the seashore has its disadvantages. The sun overhead is hot or the wind is strong,—or the very heaviness of the sand creates labour and distraction. A high road is ugly, dusty, and too near akin to the business of the world . . . if your mind flies beyond this;—if it attempts to deal with humour, pathos, irony, or scorn, you should take it away from the well-constructed walks of life. I have always found it impossible to utilise railroads for delicate thinking . . . On horseback something may be done. You may construct your villain or your buffoon as you are going across country. All the noise of an assize court or the low rattle of a gambling table may thus be arranged. Standing by the covert side I myself have made a dozen little plots, and were I to go back to the tales I could describe each point at the covert side at which the incident or the character was moulded and brought into shape. But this, too, is only good for rough work. Solitude is necessary for the task we have in hand; and the bobbing up and down of the horse's head is antagonistic to solitude.

I have found that I can best command my thoughts on foot, and can do so with the most perfect mastery when wandering through a wood. To be alone is of course essential. Companionship requires conversation,—for which indeed the spot is most fit; but conversation is not now the object in view. I have found it best even to reject the society of a dog, who, if he be a dog of manners, will make some attempt at talking . . . Even when quite alone, when all the surroundings seem to be fitted for thought, the thinker will still find a difficulty in thinking. It is not that the mind is inactive, but that it will run exactly whither it is not bidden to go. With subtle ingenuity it will find for itself little easy tasks instead of settling itself down on that which it is its duty to do at once. With me, I own, it is so weak as to fly back to things already done,—which require no more thinking, which are perhaps unworthy of a place even in the memory,—and to revel in the ease of contemplating that which has been accomplished rather than to struggle for further performance. My eyes which should become moist with the troubles of the embryo heroine, shed tears as they call to mind the early sorrows of Mr ——, who was married and made happy many years ago. Then,—when it comes to this,—a great effort becomes necessary, or that day will for him have no results. It is so easy to lose an hour in maundering over the past, and to waste the good things which have been provided in remembering instead of creating!

But a word about the nature of the wood! It is not always easy to find a wood, and sometimes when you have got it, it is but a muddy, plashy, rough-hewn congregation of ill-grown trees,—a thicket rather than a wood,—in which even contemplation is difficult and thinking is out of the question . . . A crowded undergrowth of hazel, thorn, birch, and alder, with merely a track through it, will by no means serve the occasion. The trees around you should be big and noble. There should be grass at your feet. There should be space for the felled or fallen princes of the forest . . . And it should be a wood,—perhaps a forest,—rather than a skirting of timber. You should feel that, if not lost, you are lose-able. To have trees around you is not enough unless you have many. You must have a feeling as of Adam in the garden. There must be a confirmed assurance in your mind that you have got out of the conventional into the natural,—which will not establish itself unless there be a consciousness of distance between you and the next ploughed field. If possible you should not know the East from the West, or, if so, only by the setting of the sun. You should recognise the direction in which you must return simply by the fall of water.

But where shall the wood be found? Such woodlands there are still in England, though, alas, they are becoming rarer every year . . . I will not say that a wood prepared, not as the home but the slaughter-ground of game, is altogether inefficient for our purpose. I have used such even when the sound of the guns has been near enough to warn me to turn my steps to the right or to the left. The scents are pleasant even in winter, the trees are there, and sometimes even yet the delightful feeling may be encountered that the track on which you are walking leads to some far off vague destination, in reaching which there may be much of delight because it will be new,—something also of peril because it will be distant. But the wood if possible should seem to be purposeless. It should have no evident consciousness of being there either for game or fagots . . . The mind should conceive that this wood never had been planted by hands, but had come there from the direct beneficence of the Creator,—as the first woods did come,—before man had been taught to recreate them systematically, and as some still remain to us, so much more lovely in their wildness than when reduced to rows and quincunces,* and made to accommodate themselves to laws of economy and order.

England, dear England,—and certainly with England Scotland also,—has advanced almost too far for this . . . In Devonshire there are still some sweet woodland nooks, shaws, and holts, and pleasant spinneys, through which clear water brooks run, and the birds sing sweetly, and the primroses bloom early, and the red earth pressing up here and there gives a glow of colour,—and the gamekeeper does not seem quite as yet to dominate everything. Here, perhaps, in all fair England the solitary thinker may have his fairest welcome.

But though England be dear, there are other countries not so small, not so crowded, in which every inch of space has not been made so available either for profit or for pleasure, in which the woodland rambler may have a better chance of solitude amidst the unarranged things of nature. They who have written and they who have read about Australia say little and hear little as to its charm of landscape, but here the primeval forests running for uninterrupted miles, with undulating land and broken timber, with ways open everywhere through the leafy wilderness, where loneliness is certain till it be interrupted by the kangaroo, and where the silence is only broken by the noises of quaint birds high above your head, offer all that is wanted by him whose business it is to build his castles carefully in the air. Here he may roam at will and be interrupted by no fence, feel no limits, be wounded by no art, and have no sense of aught around him but the forest, the air, and the ground . . .

But the woods of Australia, New Zealand, California, or South Africa are too far afield for the thinker for whom I am writing. If he is to take himself out of England it must be somewhere among the forests of Europe . . . in Switzerland there are pure forests still, standing or appearing to stand as nature caused them to grow, and here the poet or the novelist may wander and find all as he would have it. Or, better still, let him seek the dark shadows of the Black Forest, and there wander, fancy free,—if that indeed can be freedom which demands a bondage of its own.

Were I to choose the world all round I should take certain districts in the Duchy of Baden as the hunting ground for my thoughts. The reader will probably know of the Black Forest* that it is not continual wood. Nor, indeed, are the masses of timber, generally growing on the mountain sides, or high among the broad valleys, or on the upland plateaux, very large. They are interspersed by pleasant meadows and occasional cornfields, so that the wanderer does not wander on among them, as he does, perhaps hopelessly, in Australia. But as the pastures are interspersed through the forest, so is the forest through the pastures; and when you shall have come to the limit of this wood, it is only to be lured on into the confines of the next. You go upwards among the ashes and beeches, and oaks, till you reach the towering pines . . . It is when they are round me that, if ever, I can use my mind aright and bring it to the work which is required of it. There is a scent from them which reaches my brain and soothes it . . . If I can find myself here of an afternoon when there shall be another two hours for me, safe before the sun shall set, with my stick in my hand, and

my story half-conceived in my mind, with some blotch of a character
or two, just daubed out roughly on the canvas, then if ever I can go to
work, and decide how he, and she, and they shall do their work.

They will not come at once, those thoughts which are so anxiously
expected,—and in the process of coming they are apt to be troublesome, full of tricks, and almost traitorous. They must be imprisoned,
or bound with thongs, when they come, as was Proteus when Ulysses
caught him amidst his sea-calves,—as was done with some of the fairies
of old, who would, indeed, do their beneficent work, but only under
compulsion. It may be that your spirit should on occasion be as obedient
as Ariel, but that will not be often. He will run backwards,—as it were
downhill,—because it is so easy, instead of upward and onward . . . So
it is with the tricksy Ariel,—that Ariel which every man owns, though
so many of us fail to use him for much purpose, which but few of us
have subjected to such discipline as Prospero had used before he had
brought his servant to do his bidding at the slightest word.

It is right that a servant should do his master's bidding; and, with
judicious discipline, he will do it. The great thinkers, no doubt, are
they who have made their servant perfect in obedience, and quick
at a moment's notice for all work. To them no adjuncts of circumstances are necessary. Solitude, silence, and beauty of surroundings
are unnecessary. Such a one can bid his mind go to work, and the
task shall be done, whether in town or country, whether amid green
fields, or congregated books, or crowded assemblies. Such a master
no doubt was Prospero. Such were Homer and Cicero, and Dante.
Such were Bacon and Shakespeare. They had so tamed, and trained,
and taught their Ariels that each, at a moment's notice, would put
a girdle round the earth. With us, though the attendant Spirit will
come at last and do something at our bidding, it is but driving an
unwilling pig to market.

But at last I feel that I have him . . . When I have got him I have
to be careful that he shall not escape me till that job of work be done.
Gradually as I walk, or stop, as I seat myself on a bank, or lean against
a tree, perhaps as I hurry on waving my stick above my head till
with my quick motion the sweat-drops come out upon my brow, the
scene forms itself for me. I see, or fancy that I see, what will be fitting,
what will be true, how far virtue may be made to go without walking upon stilts, what wickedness may do without breaking the link
which binds it to humanity, how low ignorance may grovel, how high

knowledge may soar, what the writer may teach without repelling by severity, how he may amuse without descending to buffoonery; and then the limits of pathos are searched, and words are weighed which shall suit, but do no more than suit, the greatness or smallness of the occasion . . . for that which we do there are appropriate terms and boundaries which may be reached but not surpassed. All this has to be thought of and decided upon in reference to those little plotlings of which I have spoken, each of which has to be made the receptacle of pathos or of humour, of honour or of truth, as far as the thinker may be able to furnish them. He has to see, above all things, that in his attempts he shall not sin against nature, that in striving to touch the feelings he shall not excite ridicule, that in seeking for humour he does not miss his point, that in quest of honour and truth he does not become bombastic and strait-laced . . . he who tells tales in prose can hardly hope to be effective as a teacher unless he binds himself by the circumstances of the world which he finds around him. Honour and truth there should be, and pathos and humour, but he should so constrain them that they shall not seem to mount into nature beyond the ordinary habitations of men and women.

Such rules as to construction have probably been long known to him. It is not for them he is seeking as he is roaming listlessly or walking rapidly through the trees. They have come to him from much observation, from the writings of others, from that which we call study—in which imagination has but little immediate concern. It is the fitting of the rules to the characters which he has created, the filling in with living touches and true colours those daubs and blotches on his canvas which have been easily scribbled with a rough hand, that the true work consists. It is here that he requires that his fancy should be undisturbed; that the trees should overshadow him, that the birds should comfort him, that the green and yellow mosses should be in unison with him,—that the very air should be good to him. The rules are there fixed,—fixed as far as his judgement can fix them, and are no longer a difficulty to him. The first coarse outlines of his story he has found to be a matter almost indifferent to him. It is with these little plotlings that he has to contend. It is for them that he must catch his Ariel, and bind him fast;—but yet so bind him that not a thread shall touch the easy action of his wings. Every little scene must be arranged so that,—if it may be possible,—the proper words may be spoken and the fitting effect produced.

Alas, with all these struggles, when the wood has been found, when all external things are propitious, when the very heavens have lent their aid, it is so often that it is impossible! . . . How often is one prompted to fling oneself down in despair, and, weeping between the branches, to declare that it is not that the thoughts will wander, it is not that the mind is treacherous . . . Nevertheless, before all be given up, let a walk in a wood be tried.

APPENDIX
PASSAGES OMITTED FROM *AN AUTOBIOGRAPHY*

THE manuscript of *An Autobiography* contains some passages cancelled by Anthony Trollope, and others that were omitted by his son
Henry Trollope when he prepared the work for publication in 1883
(see Note on the Text, pp. 21–5). The longer passages are reproduced
here, keyed to the text by chapter and page number. An asterisk in the
text and an explanatory note indicate where they fall.

Chapter 5, p. 62

[. . . no peculiar intimacy with any clergyman.] In the treatment of
subjects the ephemeral writers of the day were apt to study—or in
slang phraseology to get up,—the subject matter of which they are
writing, than to take up a subject which they have studied. So it was
with me. [My archdeacon, . . .]

Cancelled in the manuscript by Anthony Trollope.

Chapter 8, p. 98

[Whether abroad as special correspondent, or at home amidst the
flurry of his newspaper work, he was a charming companion] but
hardly a staff to be trusted in a literary enterprise. He once promised
to write for me an article on the American telegraph wires. Much
after the time named the first half came;—long after the whole should
have been in print came the last quarter with an intimation that the
missing bit should reach me by the next post. The missing bit never
reached me, and the unconnected fragments were joined together at
the last moment by the printers' type. I did not hear that any one ever
found out the difference. It was useless on such occasions either to
argue with him or accuse him. [His ready wit always gave him the last
word.] He has fallen away latterly among Princes,* and his old friends
do not see much of him.

[Of Thackeray I will speak again . . .]

*Omitted by Henry Trollope after discussion with J. M. Langford, head of
Blackwood's London office.*

Chapter 8, p. 98

[. . . with those banquets.]

I do not know whether I did not put an end to these dinners by an indiscretion of my own. It was I think at the first of them that Thackeray, sitting opposite to his host, asked whether Dr Johnson was getting his dinner behind the screen.* The old story is too well known to require any further telling here. Our munificent publisher being engaged with his neighbour did not hear the question, and Thackeray, naturally anxious for his little joke, repeated it. Whereupon Mr Smith, who was still very eager with the friend at his elbow, replied across the table that he did not think there was anybody of the name of Johnson in the room. There was not much fun in it, but, what there was, consisted in Thackeray's vain attempts to have his allusion recognized. On the next morning I unfortunately told the story to a friend;—but I told it also in the presence of a man to whom nothing could be told quite safely.* He was, though I did not know it then, a literary gutter-scraper,—one who picked up odds and ends of scandal from chance sources, and turning them with a spice of malice into false records, made his money of them among such newspapers as would pay him. This story, altogether be-devilled and twisted from the truth,—crammed with bitterness, both against Thackeray & Smith, loaded with poison,—was sent to an American newspaper. That alone would not have mattered much because American newspapers are not much read in this country. But the Saturday,—which everybody reads, or at least everybody then read,—got hold by chance of the American paper, and, more suo, tore everybody concerned to pieces. Why were such dinners given? Why were such stories told? Was it creditable to anybody that the conversation of a private table in London should be made gossip to satisfy the evil cravings of New York readers? This article afflicted Thackeray much. It annoyed Mr Smith greatly. I taxed the gutter-scraper with his offence, and he owned his sin, praying to be forgiven. I confessed my fault to the others;—for it was a fault to have told anything in the presence of such a man. I was pardoned, but there were no more Cornhill dinners.

[Of *Framley Parsonage* I need only . . .]

Cancelled in the manuscript by Anthony Trollope.

Chapter 9, p. 109

Additional passage at the end of the chapter.

[. . . among my juniors.] And now came the question of abandoning it. At this moment I have not decided whether this season should be the last,—it is now February 1876,—or whether another year should be added. But, as I have gone along the fields alone, I have made my own epitaph—

> 'I have lived about the covert side
> I have ridden straight, and have ridden fast.
> Now breeches, boots and scarlet pride
> Are but mementoes of the past.'

Perhaps after all I shall not hang them on their pegs till another year shall have passed.

Cancelled in the manuscript by Anthony Trollope; the material, in slightly different form, was transferred to the end of Chapter 19. In the margin, Trollope scored through the Latin original of the 'epitaph', cited as 'Horace 3d book 26 ode'.

Chapter 10, p. 118

[. . . good.] Of course I informed him that I felt no anger. [There was . . .]

Omitted by Henry Trollope.

Chapter 11, p. 129

[. . . would probably have continued the experiment];—no doubt would have done so had I continued it without any price. [Another ten years . . .]

Omitted by Henry Trollope at the request of John Blackwood.

Chapter 12, p. 137

[. . . as to the work done by novelists.] As I write this there is still living among us one, venerable in age and venerable in position, whom I have ever revered as a thinker and valued as an author; whom I esteem as a man, and from whom I have myself learned very much. I was astounded when I first came across the following words from him. It is thus that Mr Carlyle* has written of the novel-writers of his day.

'How knowest thou', may the distressed novel-wright exclaim, 'that I, here where I sit, am the foolishest of existing mortals; that this my long ear of a fictitious biography shall not find one and the other into whose still longer ears it may be the means under providence of instilling somewhat?' We answer, 'No one knows; none can certainly know. Therefore write on, worthy brother, even as thou canst, even as it is given thee.'

I was at first confounded and as it were convicted of being a windbag. I and my friends—those whom I so greatly loved and esteemed, whose works were to me the objects of such close criticism and scrutiny,—were all windbags. But when, by degrees, I dared to examine and sift this saying of Carlyle in which he has so strangely confused that metaphor of the ass's ears I found it to be silly and arrogant. Our dear old prose Homer nods* sometimes, and had nodded here. But words such as those from such a man do not pass by one like the wind. [But when, by degrees, I dared to examine and sift . . .]

Cancelled in the manuscript by Anthony Trollope.

Chapter 13, p. 159

[. . . as belonging to Swift and not to himself.] On another occasion, during my absence in Australia, he took the plot of a novel of mine,* and, adapting it very cleverly to the stage, brought it out, with a notice on the title, that it was by 'Anthony Trollope and Charles Reade.' This he did without any concert with me, and without any former partnership, or even allusion to such partnership;—I may say without any word having ever passed between us in reference to joint workmanship. I felt myself bound to repudiate the play by writing to the newspapers. Had Mr Reade asked me for the plot for the purpose for which he used it, I should have felt myself honoured by the request. Had it been in my line to write a play in conjunction with another writer, I know no one with whom I would more willingly [have] embarked in such a task than with Mr Reade. But this unauthorized use of my name on a playbill angered me. I could not, however, make him understand that he had done wrong, and could only escape from the absurdity of a personal quarrel with a man I esteemed by suggesting to him that nothing more should be said about it by either of us.

[The novels of a man possessed of so singular a mind . . .]

Omitted by Henry Trollope after discussion with J. M. Langford.

Chapter 14, p. 166

[. . . but can never make an author successful.]

> 'Ponatur calculus, adsint
> Cum tabulâ pueri; numeras sestertia quinque
> Omnibus in rebus; numerentur deinde labores.'*

[I think it may be laid down as a golden rule . . .]

Omitted by Henry Trollope.

Chapter 15, p. 173

[. . . suitable, I am quite sure.] Of the copyright of 'The Last Chronicle' I did not sell the whole as I had done of all my works since 'Barchester Towers'. This came to pass in accordance with a proposition made by the publishers, and not by myself. The half which I hold has however never brought me sixpence. Why this should be, seeing that Messrs Longman pay me annually some small sum for 'Barchester Towers' I do not quite understand. I think it is because the publisher does not care to create a sale. It is the feeling of disappointment coming from such uncertainty as this which has induced me to part with so many of my copyrights. I cannot but think that the sale of 'The Last Chronicle' during the last eight years ought to have produced some profit.

[I have sometimes wished to see . . .]

Cancelled in the manuscript by Anthony Trollope.

Chapter 15, p. 173

[*Framley Parsonage*,] 'The Small House at Allington'* [and *The Last Chronicle of Barset*. But . . .]

Cancelled in the manuscript by Anthony Trollope.

Chapter 17, p. 194

[. . . sufferings of humanity?] Where is there a wider hospitality? [Where can the English traveller . . .]

Omitted by Henry Trollope.

Chapter 19, p. 212

[. . . without leaving a trace of remembrance behind.] I doubt whether I have produced any other character of whom I cannot call to mind the name.

[I also . . .]

Cancelled in the manuscript by Anthony Trollope.

Chapter 19, p. 213

[. . . I will not further speak.] I have not read it since it was finished and, as it has not been impressed on my memory by its passage
through the press, hardly know whether it is good or bad. [It will
probably be published . . .]

Cancelled in the manuscript by Anthony Trollope.

Chapter 19, p. 214

[. . . for some years to come.] I do not know how many posthumous
books the public would receive from an author's pen, one after the
other, when the author had been long buried. That one novel should
be accepted, as was the case with 'Kenelm Chillingly'* I can understand; but I fear that the numbers appearing month after month, and
year after year, with persistent regularity—when the man who wrote
them was all but forgotten,—would weary the British public. From
the shade of Dickens they would have been accepted, but not, I fear,
from mine. [This consideration, however, . . .]

Omitted by Henry Trollope.

Chapter 19, p. 214

[. . . containing 250 words.] I may say here that for twenty years
I have had every word I have written counted,* so that I might not
get into the habit of putting less into a page of manuscript than a page
was supposed to contain. [Every word was counted . . .]

Cancelled in the manuscript by Anthony Trollope.

EXPLANATORY NOTES

These notes are built on foundations laid by previous annotators, especially P. D. Edwards (World's Classics, 1980) and David Skilton (Penguin Classics, 1996). The present editor gratefully acknowledges his debt to their work and to Richard Mullen, with James Munson, for their *Penguin Companion to Trollope* (1996), to R. C. Terry for his *Oxford Reader's Companion to Trollope* (1999), to *The Letters of Anthony Trollope*, ed. N. John Hall with the assistance of Nina Burgis, 2 vols. (1983), and to the biographies written by Helen Heineman (of Frances Trollope, 1979), R. H. Super (1988), Richard Mullen (1990), N. John Hall (1991), and Victoria Glendinning (1992). References to Shakespeare are to the text of *The Complete Works*, ed. Stanley Wells and Gary Taylor (Oxford: Clarendon Press, 1988). Anthony Trollope's father and brother were both called Thomas: here 'Thomas' is the father and 'Tom' the brother. In textual notes, *MS* indicates a reading adopted from Anthony Trollope's manuscript and *1883* the first-edition reading which it replaces.

AN AUTOBIOGRAPHY

9 *tell everything of himself*: Trollope is distinguishing his book from Jean-Jacques Rousseau's *Confessions* (1781–8), which claimed to 'display a portrait in every way true to nature' of 'myself'. Trollope returns, more explicitly, to the comparison with Rousseau in his final chapter (see p. 226).

set down naught in malice: Shakespeare, *Othello*, Act 5, Scene 2, ll. 350–2: 'When you shall these unlucky deeds relate, | Speak of me as I am. Nothing extenuate, | Nor set down aught in malice.'

Keppel Street: a street of substantial terraced houses in the Bloomsbury area of London, built *c*.1800 and originally running from Gower Street to Russell Square. The houses were mostly demolished in 1932 for the building of London University's Senate House, and the site of No. 16, where Trollope was born, is now under its car park.

Lord Northwick: John Rushout, FSA, 2nd Baron Northwick (1770–1859), whose estate is commemorated in the name of the underground station Northwick Park. Although Northwick sold his house there in 1823, he retained his agricultural holdings in Middlesex. The Trollopes dealt chiefly with his agent, Quilton, but sometimes wrote to him directly; he, in turn, was a reader of Frances Trollope's novels (Mullen, 1990, 75).

Wykamist . . . New College: Winchester College is a school founded in 1382 by the Bishop of Winchester, William of Wykeham (its pupils therefore being known as 'Wykehamists'), in conjunction with New College, Oxford, for which it was a feeder school; 't' other school' is a piece of

Winchester College slang (or 'notion') for the establishment previously attended: usually a prep school rather than a rival like Harrow (see next note). Thomas Trollope became a scholar at Winchester in 1785, moving to New College, Oxford, in 1794.

9 *Harrow*: Harrow School was founded in 1572 at Harrow on the Hill in Middlesex. Originally set up to provide a free education for boys from the parish, by the nineteenth century a majority of its pupils were 'foreigners' (fee-payers from elsewhere), with local boys paying a reduced fee.

10 *Chancery barrister*: the Court of Chancery was, until 1873, the equity court of the English legal system, providing remedies where the strict application of the common law produced unfair outcomes. Trollope's father was admitted to the Middle Temple in 1799, was called to the bar in 1804, and practised as a Chancery barrister from 1806 (with chambers in Lincoln's Inn). He published *A Treatise of the Mortgage of Ships, as Affected by the Registry Acts* (London: Joseph Butterworth, 1823), which argues that the Registry Act of 1794 should not be interpreted in a way that 'deprives the Court of Chancery of its power of decreeing a redemption' (p. vi).

Julians: the Trollopes moved in 1815 to Ilotts Farm, a property of 157 acres on the southern slope of Harrow Hill, which Thomas Trollope had leased from Lord Northwick in October 1813; a new lease, for twenty-one years, would be signed in 1819. In 1817 he made a proposal to his landlord to build a more elegant house on the land. Northwick agreed and reduced the rent to cover the costs of the mortgage which Trollope used to fund the building. The new house was completed in 1818 and called Julians. A year later, however, losses on the farm obliged the Trollope family to sub-let Julians (to J. W. Cunningham, Vicar of Harrow; see note to p. 98) and move back to Ilotts Farmhouse, which they improved and renamed Julian Hill. This would be the model for 'Orley Farm' in Anthony Trollope's novel of that name. In 1827 Thomas Trollope added a second, cheaper farm in Harrow Weald to his rented estate and Julian Hill was sub-let while Anthony boarded at Winchester and his mother went to America. From 1830 to 1832 Anthony and his father lived together at the 'tumble-down' farmhouse in Harrow Weald. When his mother got back she insisted that they should return to Julian Hill, where they lived until they were obliged to flee to Belgium, to escape their creditors, in 1834. Julian Hill, later known as 'Orley Farm School', was demolished between 1900 and 1905. Julians survives but is now, confusingly, called Julian Hill.

old uncle: Adolphus Meetkerke (1753–1841), brother of Thomas Trollope's mother, was a descendant of the Flemish ambassador to Elizabeth I, and owner of an estate in Hertfordshire. His first wife died, childless, in 1817. He remarried and in 1819, at the age of 66, had a son and heir, also called Adolphus.

John Millais: John Everett Millais (1829–96; created baronet 1885), painter, founder-member of the Pre-Raphaelite Brotherhood, and Royal Academician. Trollope met him in 1860 and they became close friends.

Millais would provide illustrations for *Framley Parsonage*, *Orley Farm*, *The Small House at Allington*, *Phineas Finn*, and *Kept in the Dark*.

11 *Dr Butler*: the Revd George Butler (1774–1853), mathematician and Fellow of Sidney Sussex College, Cambridge, was appointed headmaster of Harrow School in 1805, in preference to the internal candidate, Mark Drury (see note below). He had persistent problems with discipline and resigned in 1829. After a period as a country clergyman, he became Dean of Peterborough in 1842.

private school at Sunbury: Sunbury is a small town on the banks of the Thames in Surrey (then Middlesex), south-west of London. A 'public school' was a charitable foundation which offered at least some free or subsidized places. A private school was an institution run for profit by its proprietor.

Arthur Drury . . . Henry Drury: Joseph Drury, headmaster of Harrow 1785–1805, founded a dynasty of Drurys at the school. His brother, the Revd Mark Drury, was second master but was obliged to flee his creditors and move to the Continent in 1826. Mark Drury's son William opened a school in Brussels, where Anthony Trollope would work as a classical usher in 1834; his son Arthur ran the private school in Sunbury which Trollope attended in 1825–7. Joseph's son, the Revd Henry Drury (1778–1841), was an assistant master at Harrow for over forty years, where he was tutor (at different times) to both Byron and Trollope. Joseph's daughter Louisa married John Herman Merivale (1779–1844, see note to p. 40) and it was probably through the Merivales that the Trollopes knew 'masters at Harrow'.

the curled darlings of the school: Shakespeare, *Othello*, Act 1, Scene 2, l. 69: 'The wealthy curlèd darlings of our nation'.

12 *lily-livered curs*: Shakespeare, *Macbeth*, Act 5, Scene 3, ll. 15–16: 'Go prick thy face and over-red thy fear, | Thou lily-livered boy.'

13 *Cincinnati*: Frances Trollope, with three of her children, Henry, Cecilia, and Emily, left England in November 1827 to join the idealistic community run by Frances Wright (see note to p. 22) at Nashoba, Tennessee. Disillusioned, they travelled up the Mississippi to Cincinnati, Ohio, arriving on 10 February 1828. Thomas and Tom Trollope joined Frances there in September 1828, leaving Anthony alone in England, and returned six months later after agreeing to the plan to open a 'Bazaar' (part cultural centre, part shopping mall). This was a financial disaster; Henry returned to England in 1830, Frances and her daughters in 1831.

Draco: Athenian legislator who codified the laws of Athens in 621 BC, with results which involved the death penalty for most offences. Tom Trollope, in his own autobiography, *What I Remember* (3 vols., 1887–9), rejected the claim that he had beaten his brother 'daily' and 'with a big stick', insisting that the practice of 'scourging' at Winchester was a harmless ritual: 'the pain was really not worth speaking of . . . a mere form and farce' (i. 115–16).

14 *Pariah*: (Tamil) 'social outcast', 'untouchable'.

secured: *MS*; 'served' *1883*.

15 *twelve miles*: three miles four times a day: Trollope came home from school for dinner (that is, lunch).

sizar . . . *Bible-clerk*: a sizar was a Cambridge student who worked as a domestic servant in exchange for tuition; a Bible-clerk was the Oxford equivalent, with duties which included reading the lessons at services in the college chapel.

home-boarder: *MS*; 'house-boarder' *1883*.

16 *fight*: with James Lewis, son of a prosperous London book-binder.

Encyclopædia Ecclesiastica: the first (and only) volume of *An Encyclopædia Ecclesiastica; or, A Complete History of the Church* by Thomas Anthony Trollope, covering 'Abaddon' to 'Funeral Rites', was published by John Murray in 1834. Written in a liberal, Broad Church spirit, it offers lucid summaries of historical, liturgical, and doctrinal topics.

17 *Lexicon and Gradus*: a lexicon is a dictionary, usually of ancient Greek. 'Gradus' is an abbreviation of *Gradus ad Parnassum* ('a step to Parnassus'), a handbook of versification, used by schoolboys when writing Latin verse exercises (see note to p. 147).

Cooper's novel . . . *Hookham's library*: the American novelist James Fenimore Cooper (1789–1851) published *The Prairie*, the third of his 'Leatherstocking Tales', in 1827. Thomas Hookham ran one of the sub-scription libraries from which nineteenth-century readers borrowed novels; the 1829 Addenda to the *Catalogue of Hookham's Circulating Library* include 'Prairie, by the Author of the Spy, 3 vol.'.

Dr Longley: the Revd Charles Longley (1794–1868) succeeded George Butler as headmaster of Harrow in 1829. A handsome, charming man, and a High Churchman of the old school, he had been an Oxford tutor, Hampshire rector and rural dean; he afterwards became Bishop of Ripon 1836, Bishop of Durham 1856, Archbishop of York 1860, and Archbishop of Canterbury 1862. Bishop Yeld in *The Way We Live Now* (1875), called 'Yelgnol' in Trollope's working diary for the novel, appears to be a portrait of him.

18 *a book written about the United States*: Frances Trollope, *The Domestic Manners of the Americans* (London: Whittaker, 1832).

Colonel Grant: Major-General James Grant, CB (1778–1852), and his wife, Penelope (1795–1861), were the Trollopes' neighbours at Julian Hill. Grant had served with distinction in India, and in the Peninsula and France from 1811 to 1815. The Grants' daughters Mary (b. 1819) and Kate (b. 1821) would be bridesmaids at the marriage of Trollope's sister Cecilia to John Tilley (see note to p. 41) in 1839; Anna (b. 1820) would marry Trollope's friend Peregrine Birch in 1843. Trollope would write to

Mary in 1861 to say of her mother that, 'Of all the friends that I have ever had out of my own family she has been the dearest' (*Letters*, i. 140); for Mary's husband see note to p. 126.

Elysium: Elysium, or the Elysian Fields, was the paradise of ancient Greek religion, where the souls of the virtuous enjoyed a life like that of the gods.

19 *ferule*: flat ruler with a pierced end, used for punishing boys.

how little I knew of Latin or Greek: Trollope knew rather more of both languages than he here suggests. In 1840 he found that he could read Horace and Cicero in Latin without difficulty (the mistakes in his Latin quotations from Horace and Virgil in *An Autobiography* suggest that he was quoting from memory); his 1833 marginalia to Longinus consisted of quotations in Greek from the *Iliad*.

never got a prize: not for Classics, though he may have won prizes for English essays.

20 *the Rev. William Milton*: the Revd William Milton (1741–1824), educated at Winchester and St John's College, Oxford, and Fellow of New College, was vicar of Heckfield, Hampshire, from 1773, though resident there only from 1801. In Chapter 11 of *Ralph the Heir* (1870–1) Trollope will praise the countryside around Heckfield ('there is no prettier district').

no novel of Richardson's or Miss Burney's: Samuel Richardson (1689–1761) published the epistolary novels *Pamela, or Virtue Rewarded* (1740–1), *Clarissa* (1747–8), and *Sir Charles Grandison* (1753–4), which Thomas Trollope read aloud to his family in 1832–3. Frances (Fanny) Burney (1752–1840) published *Evelina* (1778), *Cecilia* (1782), and *Camilla* (1796).

on circuit: a circuit is the journey made by lawyers to hold assize courts in provincial towns.

21 *Chollerton*: Cecilia Tilley's *Chollerton; A Tale of Our Own Times, by a Lady* (London: John Ollivier, 1846) is often described as 'High Church' but is actually a Trollopian defence of 'High and Dry' Anglicanism, since the hero chooses to marry the sensibly middle-of-the-road Charlotte Fosdyke rather than the beautiful but austerely Puseyite Anna Marsden.

the persecution of Lord Byron: George Gordon, Lord Byron (1788–1824), was driven abroad by debt and rumours about incest with his half-sister in 1816, attacked by the government for his satirical poem *The Vision of Judgement* in 1822, and refused burial at Harrow in 1824; the Rector of Harrow's earlier refusal to install a memorial tablet to Byron's illegitimate daughter, Allegra (1817–22), prompted Frances Trollope's satirical poem 'Salmagundi Aliena'.

the then unknown Scott . . . Miss Edgeworth: the Waverley novels of Sir Walter Scott (1771–1832) were published anonymously, the author's identity emerging only in 1827. The greatest 'triumph' of the Irish novelist Maria Edgeworth (1768–1849) came in 1803, when she was feted in London after the publication of *Castle Rackrent* (1800) and *Belinda* (1801).

21 *money troubles*: *MS*; 'many troubles' *1883*.

    Mathias: Thomas Mathias (1754–1835), court official and scholar, editor of Thomas Gray, translator, and author of verse in the manner of Gray, including (anonymously) *The Pursuits of Literature: A Satirical Poem* (1794–7), an attack on contemporary authors, especially Radicals. He moved to Italy in 1817, so Trollope's memories of him must be very early ones.

    Henry Milman: Henry Hart Milman (1791–1868), clergyman, historian, Sanskrit scholar, and poet, whose parents lived near the Trollopes, at Pinner Grove. His verse tragedy *Fazio* (published 1815) was a hit at Covent Garden in 1818, the year in which he also published his epic poem *Samor* and became Rector of St Mary's, Reading. He maintained his unflagging literary output by writing for an hour before breakfast every day.

    Miss Landon: Letitia Elizabeth Landon (1802–38), novelist and poet (as 'L. E. L'). Her father was a London army agent, who, like Trollope's father but a little earlier (1809–15), tried unsuccessfully to run a farm in Barnet. Her verse appeared in the *Literary Gazette* from 1820 and by the end of the decade she was a famous and commercially successful poet. Briefly engaged to John Forster (see note to p. 56), she married the colonial governor George Maclean in 1838, went out with him to West Africa, and was found dead two months later.

22 *Miss Wright*: Frances Wright (1795–1852), born in Scotland, the daughter of a wealthy political Radical, published her *Views of Society and Manners in America* in 1821. Frances Trollope met her in Paris in 1823. She returned to America in 1824 and visited Robert Owen's utopian community at New Harmony, Indiana. The following year she founded her own idealistic settlement at Nashoba, near Memphis, Tennessee, which Frances Trollope briefly visited in 1827. After the failure of the Nashoba experiment in 1830, Wright resumed her career as a writer and lecturer on feminist, abolitionist, and egalitarian topics. She married a French doctor, Guillaume Sylvan Phiquepal-d'Arusmont, in 1838.

    first two novels . . . a book on . . . Germany: *The Refugee in America: A Novel* (1832); *The Abbess: A Romance* (1833); *Belgium and Western Germany in 1833* (1834).

24 *Bruges*: the Château d'Hondt in the hamlet of St Baess, where the Trollope family settled, was an ugly suburban villa. Charles Lever (see note to p. 97) said that Bruges was one of the cheapest places to live in the whole of Europe. Trollope sets his play *The Noble Jilt* there (see note to p. 58) and gives a picture of émigré life in Belgium in *Mr Scarborough's Family* (1882–3).

25 *classical usher*: an assistant schoolmaster teaching Latin and Greek.

26 *Sir Francis Freeling*: Francis Freeling (1764–1836; created baronet 1828) rose from the ranks in the Bristol Post Office to become Secretary to the Post Office (that is, chief administrator) in 1798. He was also a Fellow of the Society of Antiquaries and a notable book collector.

three: *MS*; 'these' *1883*.

about this period of her career . . . written: Frances Trollope wrote *Tremordyn Cliff* (1835) from September 1833 to January 1835, and *Jonathan Jefferson Whitlaw* (1836) from December 1835 to March 1836.

27 *Hadley*: properly Monken Hadley, a village then in Middlesex, subsequently in Hertfordshire, now part of the London Borough of Barnet, where Frances Trollope lived from January 1836 until the summer of 1838; Trollope's sister Emily died there and is buried in the churchyard. His novel *The Bertrams* (1859) is partly set there.

29 *St Martin's-le-Grand*: a London street just north of St Paul's Cathedral, called after a medieval religious house. In the nineteenth century it was almost entirely taken over by the Post Office, which moved from Lombard Street in 1829. The building was enlarged in 1845 and demolished in 1912.

Henry Freeling: George Henry Freeling (1789–1841; 2nd baronet from 1836), eldest of the five sons of Sir Francis Freeling (see note to p. 26), student at New College, Oxford, and Assistant Secretary to the Post Office 1810–36.

rule of three . . . conic sections. the rule of three (or 'golden rule') is a convenient technique for cross-multiplication and -division; conic sections are the complex geometry of the intersections of cones and planes (the hyperbola, the parabola, and the ellipse).

Gibbon: Edward Gibbon (1737–94), whose *History of the Decline and Fall of the Roman Empire* was published 1776–88.

30 *a very great change indeed*: competitive examination would replace patronage as the mode of entry to the Civil Service after 1855, though the change would not be complete until 1870.

32 *The music of the Miltonic line*: John Milton (1608–74) used the English iambic pentameter, previously found chiefly in drama, for epic and elegiac verse: his *Lycidas* (1638) was Trollope's favourite poem. Although Frances Trollope's family name was Milton, there was no relationship.

Ivanhoe . . . Esmond: Sir Walter Scott's *Ivanhoe* (1819); William Makepeace Thackeray's *The History of Henry Esmond, Esquire* (1852).

33 *Antinous*: a beautiful young man who became the favourite of the Emperor Hadrian.

34 *Colonel Maberly*: William Leader Maberly (1798–1885), army officer, MP (1819–34), and civil servant, succeeded Sir Francis Freeling as Secretary to the Post Office in 1836. His tenure was troubled by the campaign launched in 1837 by Rowland Hill (see note to p. 86) for postal reform. Hill was made Secretary to the Post-Master General in 1846 and replaced Maberly in 1854. Maberly's Irish wife, Catherine, was a prolific writer of silver-fork and historical novels in the 1840s and '50s; Maberly was a model for Sir Boreas Bodkin in Trollope's *Marion Fay* (1881–2).

34 *écarté*: a two-player card game, similar to whist but played with a pack of only thirty-two cards. Originally French, it became popular in England in the 1820s.

35 *symposiums*: drinking parties, sometimes with philosophical discussion (from Greek).

36 *Mecklenburgh Square*: a three-sided 'square' between the Foundling Hospital and Gray's Inn Road in London. In Chapter 18 of *The Three Clerks* Charley Tudor travels 'towards Mecklenburg Square' to visit the money-lender Jabesh M'Ruen, and goes north 'across Theobald's Road' to find his house.

37 *Queen of . . . Saxony*: if this was indeed the Queen of Saxony, she was Princess Maria Anna of Bavaria (1805–77), who married the crown prince in 1833; he became King Frederick Augustus II in 1836.

two intervals: in the spring of 1838 Anthony seems to have been living with his mother at Hadley and commuting to work. That summer Frances Trollope took a house at 20 York Street, Marylebone, where Cecilia, Tom, and Anthony lived with her until Cecilia's wedding in February 1839. In December 1839 she took Anthony on a trip to Paris and when, after his return to London, he fell ill, she stayed with him in lodgings in Wyndham Street from June to September 1840. No mention is made of this serious illness in *An Autobiography*, though it may have been a significant prelude to the change in Trollope's life in 1841.

38 *Sheriffs' officers . . . a prisoner*: until 1869 people unable to pay debts could be held in debtors' prisons, such as the King's Bench Prison and the Marshalsea (closed in 1842); sheriffs' officers were the officials who arrested them.

ever: MS; 'even' *1883*.

39 *Horace*: Quintus Horatius Flaccus (65–8 BC), Roman poet.

Johnson . . . Lycidas: Samuel Johnson (1709–84) published his *Lives of the English Poets* in 1779–81, in which he attacked the artificiality of *Lycidas* and called it 'easy, vulgar, and therefore disgusting'. Romantic taste had since turned against this judgement.

Northumberland Street by the Marylebone Workhouse: from 1835 to 1837 Trollope lodged at 22 Northumberland Street, now Luxborough Street, Marylebone; the workhouse, built in 1775 and later known as Luxborough Lodge, was demolished in 1965. Joseph Emilius lodges in this 'somewhat obscure neighbourhood' in *Phineas Redux* (Chapter 47) and, in Chapter 56, Madame Max Goesler walks up 'that very uninviting street' and knocks 'at a door just opposite to the deadest part of the dead wall of the Marylebone Workhouse'. In Chapter 49 of *Orley Farm*, however, reflecting on the pleasures of youth, Trollope speaks of 'happy days . . . in dirty lodgings . . . somewhere near the Marylebone workhouse'.

40 *after breakfast I had to pay day by day*: MS; 'often breakfast to pay day by day' *1883*.

an uncle: Henry Milton (1784–1850), civil servant in the War Office and writer. Educated at Winchester College and New College, Oxford, he published *Letters on the Fine Arts Written from Paris during the Year 1815* (1816) and two novels, *Rivalry* (1840) and *Lady Cecilia Farrencourt* (1846).

John Merivale . . . Herman Merivale . . . Charles Merivale: sons of John Herman Merivale (1779–1844), translator, writer, and lawyer, who was called to the bar in the same year as Thomas Trollope and also had chambers in Old Square, Lincoln's Inn. John Lewis Merivale (1815–86) became a long-serving registrar in the Court of Chancery. Herman Merivale (1806–74) was a star pupil at Harrow, who went on to be a successful barrister and permanent under-secretary at the Colonial and India Offices. Charles Merivale (1808–93), also a star pupil at Harrow, became a Fellow of St John's College, Cambridge, an authority on Roman history and, from 1869, Dean of Ely. Trollope reviewed the first five volumes of his *History of the Romans under the Empire* (1850–64) in the *Dublin University Magazine* in May 1851 and July 1856 (see note to p. 68).

W—— A——: Walter Herbert Awdry (1812–69), educated at Winchester and Oxford, where he was at Magdalen Hall with Tom Trollope. He became a schoolteacher, and from 1861 to 1869 was a curate in Shropshire and the Isle of Man.

the rustle of a lady's dress: *MS*; 'a lady's dress' *1883*.

first loomed: *MS*; 'loomed' *1883*.

41 *John Tilley*: Sir John Tilley (1813–98; knighted 1880). He joined the Post Office as a clerk in 1829, and became successively a Surveyor in northern England in 1838 and Assistant Secretary in 1848; he was successor to Sir Rowland Hill as Secretary to the Post Office from 1864 to 1880. He married Trollope's sister Cecilia in 1839.

Peregrine Birch . . . daughters of Colonel Grant: Peregrine Birch (1817–98) married Anna Grant in 1843.

42 *£400*: His net income was actually £313 in his first year in Ireland, and £326 in his second (travel account books, Morris L. Parrish Collection of Victorian Novelists, Princeton University Library, cited in *Letters*, i. 11).

43 *cursed the hour in which I was born*: 'Let the day perish wherein I was born', Job 3:3.

'Sin aliquem . . . vitam': 'But if, Fortune, you threaten some dreadful disaster, let me now, oh now, end my cruel life', Virgil, *Aeneid*, Book 8, ll. 578–9. Trollope misquotes l. 579, which should read 'nunc, nunc o liceat'.

44 *a dear old cousin*: John Young, a cousin of Trollope's father on the Meetkerke side of the family.

Connaught: Connaught (or Connacht) is a province in the west of Ireland, which includes the counties of Galway, Leitrim, Mayo, Roscommon, and Sligo.

44 *Banagher*: town in County Offaly (then King's County), used by the Surveyor of the Central Postal District because of its transport links on the River Shannon. Trollope lived there from September 1841 until late 1844 in the Shannon Hotel. The Surveyor to whom he reported, James Drought, would be forced to resign for 'misconduct' in 1855. The traditional saying 'That beats Banagher! (And Banagher beats the devil)' derives either from its status as a notorious pocket borough or from a reputation for sharp dealing at its famous horse fair.

45 *Secretary of the Irish Post Office*: Augustus Godby.

Tales of All Countries: 'Father Giles of Ballymoy', which originally appeared in *The Argosy* (May 1866), was actually published in *Lotta Schmidt and Other Stories* (1867), not *Tales of All Countries* (1st series 1861; 2nd series 1863). 'The O'Conors of Castle Conor, County Mayo' appeared in *Harper's Magazine* (May 1860), before being reprinted in the 1st series.

46 *Charles Buxton*: Charles Buxton (1822–71), partner in the Truman, Hanbury & Buxton Brewery, and, from 1857, Liberal MP. In the 1850s he established a model farm in County Kerry. He argued for clemency after the Indian Mutiny, for the referral of the Trent question to arbitration (see note to p. 105), and for Church reform. He published *The Ideas of the Day on Policy* (1866), which Trollope reviewed (*Fortnightly Review*, January 1866), and was a keen fox hunter. The 'run on another man's horse' is used in Chapter 38 of *The Eustace Diamonds*.

47 *County Cavan*: in the Northern District of the Irish Post Office, not the Central District to which Trollope was officially attached from 1841 to 1844.

encounter: MS; 'remember' *1883*.

48 *Rose Heseltine*: Rose Heseltine (1820–1917), born in Rotherham, Yorkshire, was the daughter of a bank manager, Edward Heseltine (1782–1855), who after his retirement in 1853 was discovered to have defrauded the bank of a sum of more than £4,000 and fled to France. Her mother had died in November 1841, and in July and August 1842 she was on holiday in Kingstown (Dún Laoghaire, a port and seaside resort south of Dublin) with her father and younger sister. Trollope went to Kingstown, on Post Office business, in July 1842, where he may have had an introduction to the Heseltines from Joseph Bland, a Post Office clerk whose brother or cousin was a clerk in the Rotherham bank. After two weeks of work in Kingstown, Trollope returned by taking his fortnight's annual leave there in August, by the end of which time he and Rose were engaged. They married in June 1844, had two sons in 1846 and 1847, and later adopted two orphaned nieces. Rose won a bronze medal for embroidery at the Great Exhibition. She was the only person allowed to read and comment on Trollope's novels before they went to the publisher, read manuscripts for him when he was editor of *St Paul's Magazine*, and sometimes acted as his amanuensis.

49 *'is born to blush unseen . . . desert air'*: Thomas Gray, 'Elegy Written in a Country Churchyard' (1751), l. 55.

Drumsna: a village in County Leitrim on the River Shannon. Trollope stayed there for a month from 5 September 1843, chiefly on Post Office business, though John Merivale joined him for a holiday, during which they walked to the hamlet of Headford and discovered the ruined house (still extant). Trollope gives a slightly different account of the matter at the beginning of *The Macdermots of Ballycloran*, where the narrator is by himself when he finds the ruin.

the potato disease . . . Encumbered Estates Bill: the Irish Famine or 'Great Hunger' (1845–50) was caused by a potato blight (*Phytophthora infestans*), which arrived in Europe from America in 1844. Its effects were widespread but particularly severe in Ireland, where almost a quarter of the population depended on potatoes for survival. Trollope was working for the Post Office in the worst-affected areas at the time and defended the government's response in a series of letters to *The Examiner* in 1849–50 (see note to p. 56). Despite these measures, the population of Ireland fell from eight to six million people, half of the loss resulting from emigration and half from starvation or disease. The Encumbered Estates Acts of 1848 and 1849 sought to bring new capital into Irish agriculture by facilitating the sale of estates whose owners were unable to redeem their mortgages.

50 *Clonmel*: the county town of South Tipperary, where Trollope and his wife lived from June 1845 in furnished rooms. The Surveyor of the Southern District was the efficient James Kendrick, with whom Trollope chose to move to Mallow, County Cork, in 1848 when Clonmel was split off into the new South Midland District. After an abortive uprising at Ballingary in July 1848 (see note to p. 51), the Young Ireland leaders were tried at Clonmel.

51 *the treachery of the Union . . . Mr Butt*: after the Irish Rebellion of 1798, an Act of Union between Ireland and Great Britain was passed by the Irish Parliament in 1801, in part because of a promise of Catholic Emancipation; George III subsequently blocked that measure which would not be introduced until 1829. Daniel O'Connell (1775–1847), MP for County Clare from 1830, campaigned for repeal of the Act of Union, holding 'monster meetings' throughout Ireland in the 1840s. William Smith O'Brien (1803–64) led an abortive revolution against British rule in 1848 which ended in a skirmish in a cabbage patch at Ballingary. The republican Fenian Brotherhood was founded in 1858 by James Stephens (1825–1901) and waged a campaign of violent protest in America, Britain, and Ireland. Isaac Butt (1813–79), MP for Youghal, who as a young lawyer had cross-examined Trollope during the trial of a Post Office employee accused of theft in 1849, founded the Home Government Association of Ireland in 1870; renamed the Home Rule League in 1873, it won fifty-nine seats in the Commons in 1874.

51 *My brother had commenced*: Tom Trollope had by 1845 published *A Summer in Brittany* (1840) and *A Summer in Western France* (1841).

52 *Mr Newby*: Thomas Cautley Newby (1797–1882) founded Newby & Co. (1843–74) in Mortimer Street, London, moving to Welbeck Street in 1849. An imitator of Henry Colburn (see note to p. 52) as a producer of novels for circulating libraries, he published the first novels of Emily and Anne Brontë, as well as Anthony Trollope, but was known for his sharp practice.

any notice taken of it: There were, in fact, at least seven reviews of *The Macdermots of Ballycloran* in May and June 1847, including notices in *The Spectator* and *The Athenaeum*, and a good deal of the comment was favourable.

Mr Colburn: Henry Colburn (1784/5–1855) founded Colburn and Co. (1808–53). Best known for silver-fork fiction, he withdrew from London publishing in 1833 but re-established himself in Great Marlborough Street in 1836. There he became a leading publisher of three-volume novels for circulating libraries. His gift for publicity earned him the nickname 'The Prince of Puffers'.

53 *Facilis descensus Averni*: 'The descent to Hell is easy', Virgil, *Aeneid*, Book 6, l. 126 (actually 'Averno'). Lake Avernus was believed to be the gate to the underworld.

review in The Times: Trollope quotes the review of 7 September 1848 very partially: it also said: 'There is a native humour and a bold reality in the delineation of the characters, which honourably distinguish it from a host of abstract insipidities.'

55 *this morsel of criticism*: not so: there were at least two reviews of *La Vendée*, one in *The Athenaeum* (6 July 1850), the other in *The Examiner* on the same day as the appearance there of the last of Trollope's letters about 'The Real State of Ireland' (15 June 1850).

56 *the pestilence . . . Sir Robert Peel . . . Lord John Russell*: a cholera epidemic in 1849 caused many deaths in Ireland; the Tory Prime Minister Sir Robert Peel split his party in 1846 by repealing the protectionist Corn Laws to remove an impediment to the import of grain during the Famine; Lord John Russell, his Whig successor, though initially opposed to interventions which would hamper the free market in food, introduced relief measures, including public-works schemes and soup kitchens, in 1847.

S. G. O.: the Revd Sydney Godolphin Osborne (1808–89; Lord Sydney Godolphin Osborne from 1859), Dorset clergyman well known for his letters and 'lay sermons' in *The Times* from 1844 to 1884, written in a Tory paternalist and anti-Tractarian spirit, and published over the initials 'S. G. O'.

Mr John Forster: John Forster (1812–76), writer, editor, and literary adviser, close friend and biographer of Dickens, was editor of *The Examiner*

1847–55. Trollope's six letters to *The Examiner* on 'Irish Distress' and 'The Real State of Ireland' appeared 25 August 1849–15 June 1850; they were republished as *The Irish Famine*, ed. Lance O. Tingay (London: Silverbridge, 1987).

57 *Bentley and Gifford*: Richard Bentley (1662–1742), classical scholar and critic, and William Gifford (1756–1826), critic and editor of the *Quarterly Review*, both notorious for the severity of their judgements. Forster's review of *The Warden* (*The Examiner*, 6 January 1855) called it 'a clever novel' but found 'the caricatures and burlesques of living writers' to be 'in very bad taste . . . and not calculated to raise Mr Trollope in the estimation of the public'.

Dickens had given that reading: Forster lived, until 1856, at 58 Lincoln's Inn Fields, where Dickens gave a famous reading of *The Chimes* on 2 December 1844, of which Daniel Maclise made a drawing, reproduced in the second volume of Forster's *Life of Charles Dickens* (1872–4).

58 *The Noble Jilt*: a five-act play written in 1850–1, immediately after the completion of *La Vendée*, and similarly set in the period of the French Revolution, though in Bruges rather than Brittany. Written in the quasi Shakespearian manner of the pre 1843 'legitimate drama', its two plots would be re-used for the novel *Can You Forgive Her?* (1864–5). Trollope describes a performance of it at the Haymarket Theatre in Chapter 52 of *The Eustace Diamonds* (1871–3); in reality it has never been performed and was first published only in 1923.

George Bartley: George Bartley (1782–1858), comic actor and stage manager of Covent Garden Theatre, who played leading roles on the London stage from 1802 to 1852; he was best known for his Falstaff.

59 *Mr John Murray*: John Murray (1808–92), the third generation of his family to run the publishing house, founded the Murray Handbooks in 1836, a pioneering series of guidebooks, which would become the Blue Guides in 1915. He also published Herman Melville's first two novels as (supposedly) literal travel narratives, Darwin's *Voyage of the Beagle* (2nd edn. 1845), and David Livingstone's *Missionary Travels* (1857).

60 *an Irish groom*: Barney, Trollope's long-serving groom, is referred to as 'Bernard Smith, groom, 63, born Ireland' in the 1861 census at Waltham Cross (*Letters*, i. 215). James Pope Hennessy, after research at Banagher, gave the surname as MacIntyre (*Anthony Trollope* (London: Cape, 1971), 75); Trollope's granddaughter Muriel says he was remembered in the family as Barney Fitzpatrick ('What I Was Told', *Trollopian*, 2 (March 1948), 230). Originally hired at Banagher in 1841, he had retired there by 1882 (*Letters*, ii. 941).

61 *damnable habit*: MS; 'habit' *1883*.

62 *cathedral city . . . clergyman*: not strictly true: Trollope lived in Winchester as a schoolboy in 1827–30, and had stayed with his mother's cousin Fanny Bent in the cathedral close at Exeter; later in this chapter Trollope

will remark that in the early 1850s he 'lived' in the cathedral cities of 'Exeter . . . Bristol . . . and . . . Worcester'. Both his grandfathers were Anglican clergymen (though one of them had died in 1806), as were two of his uncles by marriage; he also 'knew well' the Revd R. W. Thackeray, Rector of Hadley (*Thackeray*, 1879, Chapter 1). For a passage in the MS omitted in *1883* see Appendix, p. 274.

64 *some daily Jupiter*: the *Jupiter* is the name of the daily national newspaper in the Barsetshire series, which closely resembles *The Times*.

29th of July 1853 . . . Worcestershire: incorrectly given as '1852' and 'Herefordshire' in *MS*; corrected *1883*.

just at this time: Trollope's appointment as acting Surveyor of the Northern District began on 6 September 1853; he was given the substantive post of Surveyor on 9 October 1854. In Belfast the Trollopes are said to have lived first in Custom House Square, then at Whiteabbey.

65 *two sons*: Henry Merivale Trollope (1846–1926) and Frederic Trollope (1847–1910), both born in Clonmel. Henry would be a partner in the publishers Chapman & Hall 1869–73; he later became a minor man of letters and editor of his father's *Autobiography*. Frederic was a sheep farmer in Australia 1865–76, then a civil servant in the Australian Land Department.

Mallow: a market town in County Cork, where Trollope lived from the autumn of 1848 until August 1851 in a house in the High Street. *Castle Richmond* (1860) is set around Mallow.

Donnybrook: a suburb of Dublin, south of the city and close to the sea. The Trollopes took a semi-detached Georgian house at 5 Seaview Terrace, where they lived from June 1855 to November 1859.

end of 1853 . . . autumn of 1854: incorrectly given as '1852' and '1853' in both *MS* and *1883*.

William Longman: William Longman (1813–77) ran the publishing house jointly with his brother Thomas (1804–79) as the fourth generation of the family to manage the firm. Their predecessors had published Wordsworth, Coleridge, Southey, and the *Edinburgh Review*; William and Thomas published Macaulay, Matthew Arnold, John Stuart Mill, J. A. Froude, and Disraeli.

notices: there were reviews of *The Warden* in *The Examiner* ('a clever novel'), *The Spectator* ('great cleverness'), *The Athenaeum* ('clever, spirited, sketchy'), *The Leader* ('a new and excellent subject . . . treated very cleverly'), and the *Eclectic Review* ('spirited and clever'), though they all regretted Trollope's refusal to take sides about ecclesiastical charities.

66 *stone-breaking*: breaking stones into rubble for road-mending was seen as the lowest form of work because welfare recipients were sometimes required to do it.

an article: the review (in *The Times*, 13 August 1857) was by E. S. Dallas (see note to p. 98).

67 *a little book*: Trollope's *The Commentaries of Caesar* (Edinburgh and London: Blackwood, 1870), a paraphrase of Julius Caesar's *Commentarii de bello Gallico* and *Commentarii de bello civili*, describing campaigns between 58 and 48 BC (see note to p. 209).

Bismarck: Otto von Bismarck (1815–98), the so-called 'Iron Chancellor' who united the states of Germany into a single country under Prussian leadership. After his defeat of Austria (1866) and France (1871), Germany became the greatest power in continental Europe.

68 *other articles*: apart from his two reviews (May 1851 and July 1856) of Charles Merivale's *History of the Romans* (see note to p. 40), only one other article by Trollope is known to have appeared in the *Dublin University Magazine*: 'The Civil Service' (October 1855).

Carlyle: Thomas Carlyle (1795–1881), writer and critic. Trollope parodied Carlyle as 'Dr Pessimist Anticant' in *The Warden* (1855) but spoke of him as the person 'for whom of all living men I feel perhaps the highest veneration' in his lecture 'On English Prose Fiction as a Rational Amusement' (1870; see 'Other Writings', p. 233). G. H. Lewes introduced them in 1861; Trollope's attitude is best suggested by his remark to Lewes in 1864: 'what a mixture of wisdom and folly flows from him!' (*Letters*, i. 258).

a most laborious and voluminous criticism: a transcript of the reader's report (by Joseph Cauvin (d. 1875), author and translator) is printed in Sadleir's *Commentary*, 169–70, and *Letters*, i. 45–6.

71 *the 'last infirmity of noble mind'*: 'Fame is the spur that the clear spirit doth raise | (That last infirmity of Noble mind) | To scorn delights, and live laborious days', Milton, *Lycidas*, ll. 70–2.

72 *the august columns of Paternoster Row*: Thomas Longman founded his publishing house in 1724 by taking over two shops known as the Black Swan and the Ship in Paternoster Row, near St Paul's Cathedral. The firm remained in these large and increasingly grand premises until they were destroyed by bombing in December 1940.

Hurst & Blackett: publishing company (1852–1926) that took over the business of Henry Colburn (see note to p. 52) and continued his policy of producing three-volume novels for circulating libraries.

73 *Mr Bentley*: Richard Bentley (1794–1871) began publishing in 1829 in partnership with Henry Colburn, but worked independently from 1832, becoming the leading producer of three-volume fiction for circulating libraries. His son George Bentley (1828–95) assumed the leading role in the firm in the late 1860s and became the editor of *Temple Bar*, which serialized Trollope's *The American Senator* in 1874–5.

Chaffanbrass: a brilliantly effective courtroom barrister, known for his browbeating of witnesses, who defends Alaric Tudor in *The Three Clerks*, Lady Mason in *Orley Farm*, and Phineas Finn in *Phineas Redux*.

73 *Sir Charles Trevelyan . . . Lady Trevelyan . . . Sir Stafford Northcote*: Charles Trevelyan (1807–86; KCB 1848), civil servant in India, then at the Treasury (1840–59), was latterly in India again before returning to England in 1865; the Lady Trevelyan here referred to is his first wife Hannah Macaulay (d. 1873), sister of the historian. Sir Stafford Northcote (1818–87) was Gladstone's private secretary in 1843, then a civil servant, Tory MP from 1855, President of the Board of Trade 1866, and Chancellor of the Exchequer 1874–80. Trevelyan and Northcote jointly produced the report *The Organisation of the Permanent Civil Service* in November 1853 which led to the introduction of entrance exams for the Civil Service.

74 *the Medical Venus*: the Medici Venus, or Venus de' Medici, is a Hellenistic marble sculpture, in the Uffizi Gallery, Florence. Hailed as 'a miracle of art' by John Evelyn in 1677, it became an indispensable part of the aristocratic Grand Tour of Europe.

75 *the Austrian authorities*: northern Italy was part of the Austrian Empire from 1814 to 1859, an arrangement made at the end of the Napoleonic Wars to block any future French invasion of Italy; this 'visit' was in the summer of 1855.

zwanzigers: an Austrian silver coin worth about one tenth of a pound.

76 *the Pasha*: Muhammad Sa'id Pasha (1822–63) ruled Egypt from 1854, technically as a province of the Ottoman Empire, in practice independently. Railway building in Egypt had begun in 1854; the need for more rapid communication between Britain and India had been made urgent by the Indian Mutiny, or Uprising, between March 1857 and July 1858.

came to me the next morning: Trollope appears to have 'improved' this anecdote: Bentley reduced his offer by letter, not visit, on 25 January 1858 (*Letters*, i .62). Trollope may that day have rushed to Chapman and Hall in his lunch hour but did not sign the agreement with them until the 29th. He took the boat train for Paris on 30 January.

Chapman & Hall: Edward Chapman (1804–80) and William Hall (1800–47) began as booksellers and publishers in the Strand in 1830, moving to 193 Piccadilly in 1850. They published Dickens's early fiction, also Thackeray, Carlyle, and the Brownings. *Doctor Thorne*, in 1858, was the first of thirty-two books that Trollope published with the firm. Frederic Chapman (1823–95) became manager in 1864, when Trollope was involved with him in the launch of the *Fortnightly Review*. In 1869 Trollope bought a third share of the business to create a partnership for his son Henry. Henry left after four years and Trollope became a director in 1880 when the firm was reorganized as a limited company.

Charles Merewether: Charles George Merewether (1823–84), barrister, MP for Northampton 1874–80. Modern commentators have suggested that the legal opinion he supplied (as 'Mr Thomas Dove') for Chapter 25 of *The Eustace Diamonds* (1871–2) was right on heirlooms but wrong on paraphernalia and *inter vivos* gifts.

77 *Hounslow Heath*: now the site of Heathrow Airport, Hounslow Heath was a large area of wild countryside, notorious for the highwaymen and robbers who preyed on coaches travelling between London and the west of England.

78 *Labor omnia vincit improbus*: 'Persistent work conquers everything' (Virgil, *Georgics*, Book 1, ll. 145–6, where the verb is actually in the past tense, 'vicit': 'has conquered').

always prepared a diary: Trollope began to do this while writing *Barchester Towers* in 1856; many of the diaries are now in the Bodleian Library.

79 *Hercules . . . tortoise*: Hercules, or Heracles, was a Greek mythic hero, with exceptional strength and courage. The story of the tortoise and the hare is one of Aesop's fables.

80 *Mens sana in corpore sano*: 'A sound mind in a sound body' (Juvenal, *Satires*, 10, l. 356).

cobbler's wax: a sticky wax, used to coat the thread used by cobblers, and proverbially used to make workers stick to their task.

81 *Nubar Bey*: Nubar Nubarian (1825–99), Egyptian official, at this date (in effect) Minister of Transport; he later became Nubar Pasha and, with French and British backing, the first Prime Minister of Egypt 1878–9.

82 *'John Bull on the Guadalquivir'*: a short story based on an incident during Trollope's brief holiday in Spain, on his way back from Egypt in April 1858; first published in *Cassell's Illustrated Family Paper* (November 1860), it was collected in *Tales of All Countries*, 1st series (1861).

The Bertrams has had quite an opposite fortune. Although *The Bertrams* is thought of as an unpopular novel, it was reprinted and translated surprisingly often: there was a fourth edition by 1861; German, Dutch, Danish, and French translations appeared 1859–66; and it was being serialized in the *Manchester Weekly Times* (30 January 1876–9 June 1877) while Trollope was writing *An Autobiography*.

Tom Jones . . . Meg Merrilies: *Tom Jones* (1749) and *Ivanhoe* (1819) are novels by Henry Fielding and Sir Walter Scott respectively. Amelia is the heroine of Fielding's later novel *Amelia* (1751); John Balfour of Burley is a character in Scott's *Old Mortality* (1816), and Meg Merrilies in his *Guy Mannering* (1815).

83 *cleanse the Augean stables*: one of the labours of Hercules was to clean, in a single day, the stables of Augeas, King of Elis, where thousands of oxen had not been mucked out for thirty years.

84 *the best book*: *The West Indies and the Spanish Main* (Chapman and Hall, 1859).

85 *currente calamo*: (Latin) 'with running pen'.

three articles: *The Times* published a two-part review of *The West Indies and the Spanish Main* (6 and 18 January 1860; usually attributed to E. S.

Dallas, though possibly by Mowbray Morris, the paper's manager and son of a West Indian planter), but it was not this notice which enabled him to demand £600 for *Castle Richmond*: the agreement for that novel had been signed in August 1859. Trollope is probably confusing this notice with a review of his fiction by Dallas (*The Times*, 23 May 1859), which called him 'the Apollo of the circulating library'.

86 *squeezed out*: MS; 'squeezed into' *1883*.

Mr Rowland Hill: Rowland Hill (1795–1879; knighted 1860), a teacher in his family's progressive schools in Edgbaston and Tottenham, published a pamphlet on Post Office reform in 1837 and campaigned for the introduction of the penny post in 1840. In 1846 he was made Secretary to the Postmaster-General, thus functioning as an internal rival to the Secretary to the Post Office, Colonel Maberly, whom he replaced in 1854. Though praised by some as a reformer, insiders such as Trollope and Tilley disliked him; Lord Palmerston saw him as the 'spoilt child of the Post Office'. His brother Frederic Hill (1803–96) was also a teacher before becoming an Inspector of Prisons. In 1851 he joined his brother as Assistant Secretary to the Postmaster-General, remaining in that post until 1875.

87 *a lecture on The Civil Service*: delivered on 4 January 1861, reported in the newspapers the next day, and published as 'The Civil Service as a Profession' in the *Cornhill Magazine* in February 1861. The Postmaster-General was Lord Stanley of Alderley (1802–69).

no one in the Post Office could even vote: this prohibition had been introduced in 1782; it would be abolished by the Revenue Officers' Disabilities Removal Act, 1868 (see note to p. 221).

88 *among the great*: MS; 'the greatest' *1883*.

penates: (Latin) 'household gods', figuratively 'domestic possessions'; images of the *lares et penates* (deified ancestors and gods of the storeroom) were kept in a shrine in ancient Roman houses.

Cornhill Magazine: the *Cornhill Magazine* (1860–1975) was founded by George Smith (1824–1901) of Smith, Elder & Co. (whose premises were at 65 Cornhill, London). It was an illustrated monthly magazine, costing only 1s., and the first issue sold 110,000 copies; it remained the leading outlet for high-quality, serialized fiction. Thackeray ceased to be editor in 1862. Trollope published *Framley Parsonage*, *The Struggles of Brown, Jones and Robinson*, *The Small House at Allington*, *The Claverings*, and three articles in the journal.

Thackeray: William Makepeace Thackeray (1811–63), novelist, journalist, humorous writer, and artist. Although Trollope did not meet Thackeray until 1860, he had admired his work since the 1830s, and would publish both an affectionate obituary (*Cornhill Magazine*, January 1864) and a life-and-works monograph, *Thackeray*, 1879 (see 'Other Writings', pp. 259–62).

89 *Paterfamilias*: (Latin) 'father of the family'.

second volume: the most common format for Victorian novels was publication in three volumes (the 'three-decker'); *The Three Clerks* was published in three volumes by Bentley in November 1857.

90 *no part . . . was completed*: not, in fact, an issue which had previously arisen, since *Framley Parsonage* was Trollope's first novel to appear as a serial (January 1860–April 1861). Dickens's *Edwin Drood* (1870) and Gaskell's *Wives and Daughters* (1864–6) were both appearing as serials at the time of their authors' deaths, though Gaskell's novel was substantially complete. Thackeray had written only eight chapters of *Denis Duval* at the time of his sudden death in December 1863, but none of them had yet been published; the fragment would be posthumously serialized in the *Cornhill* in March–June 1864, and Trollope, as he says in his obituary of Thackeray (*Cornhill Magazine*, 9 (February 1864), 134–7), was himself involved in the decision to print it.

'*Servetur ad imum . . . processerit*': 'As it unfolded from the beginning, so let it remain until the end' (Horace, *Ars Poetica*, ll. 126–7).

Achilles: a version of Horace, *Ars Poetica*, ll. 120–1, suggesting that Achilles must be consistently 'impiger, iracundus, inexorabilis, acer': 'indefatigable, angry, inexorable, fierce'.

Davus: Horace's *Ars Poetica*, l. 237, insists that 'Davus' ('Dave', a common name for comic slaves in Latin drama) must also be consistently characterized.

91 '*tanti*': (Italian) 'ample', 'plenty', 'lots of'. In Chapter 73 of *The American Senator* (1877) Reginald Morton recommends 'the great doctrine of "tanti"'.

never broken it since: in fact both *Can You Forgive Her?* (completed 28 April 1864; published in parts January 1864–August 1865) and *The Belton Estate* (completed 4 September 1865; serialized in the *Fortnightly Review*, 15 May 1865–1 January 1866) began to appear before they were completed.

In the meantime: that is, between seeing George Smith in London on 3 or 4 November and leaving London on the evening of the 4th. 'Conception' was followed by 'writing' (see Introduction, p. xiii) once he had taken his seat in the boat train to Dublin.

92 *tuft-hunting*: the sycophantic seeking of aristocratic or distinguished acquaintances.

93 *Nathaniel Hawthorne*: American novelist and short-story writer (1804–64). The comments which Trollope quotes were made in a letter of 11 February 1860 from Hawthorne to James T. Fields of the Boston publishers Ticknor and Fields, who published an extract in the *Atlantic Monthly* in February 1871 (though Fields may have told Trollope about it when he dined at Waltham House in May 1860). Trollope met Hawthorne in Boston in September 1861.

94 *Flora Macdonald*: Flora MacDonald, a Scottish Jacobite (1722–90) who helped Bonnie Prince Charlie to escape after his defeat at the Battle of Culloden in 1746, though Trollope is more likely to have meant Flora MacIvor, the heroine of Scott's novel *Waverley* (1814).

95 *George Smith*: George Smith (1824–1901), publisher and businessman, who took over Smith, Elder & Co. (1816–1917) from his father and made it an important imprint for prose fiction from the late 1840s onwards. He published five of Trollope's novels, shared his political views, and became a friend.

Charles Taylor: Sir Charles Taylor (1817–76), sportsman, bon vivant, and man about town, who had an estate near Battle in Sussex. A group portrait by Henry O'Neil, *Sir Charles Taylor and Others* (1869; Garrick Club), shows Taylor, Trollope, and forty-one other members watching a game of billiards.

Robert Bell: Robert Bell (1800–67), Anglo-Irish journalist, novelist, playwright, and editor. He was editor of *The Atlas*, the *Monthly Chronicle*, and *Home News*, wrote three plays, published two novels (one of which, *The Ladder of Gold*, 1850, has been seen as an influence on Trollope's *The Way We Live Now*), and is best remembered for his 29-volume *Annotated Edition of the English Poets* (1854–7).

G. H. Lewes: George Henry Lewes (1817–78), writer on philosophy and science, dramatist, novelist, editor, and, from 1854, partner of Mary Ann Evans (George Eliot). Trollope persuaded Lewes to edit the *Fortnightly Review*, got him to write for *St Paul's Magazine* (on 'The Dangers and Delights of Tobacco', November 1868; Trollope supplied Lewes with his Cuban cigars), and helped his son get a job in the Post Office.

Russell of the Times: *MS*; omitted from this list by Henry Trollope in *1883*. William Howard Russell (1820–1907; knighted 1895), Anglo-Irish journalist, made famous by his coverage of the Crimean War for *The Times*.

Monckton Milnes: Richard Monckton Milnes (1809–85; created Baron Houghton 1863), poet, biographer, and politician. His *Life and Letters of Keats* was published in 1848; his poem 'Unspoken Dialogue' (describing a situation like that in Trollope's *Castle Richmond*, where a mother and daughter are in love with the same man) appeared in the *Cornhill Magazine* in 1860.

96 *Garrick Club*: London club founded in 1831 and particularly associated with actors and writers; Trollope was elected on 5 April 1862.

97 *Canning*: George Canning (1770–1827), Tory politician, Foreign Secretary 1822–7, and Prime Minister 1827. Robert Bell's *Life of the Rt. Hon. George Canning* was published in 1846.

the Literary Fund Committees: the Literary Fund ('Royal' from 1842) was founded in 1790 to relieve authors in financial distress. Trollope joined the committee in May 1861 and worked hard to find speakers for the annual fund-raising dinner.

to hear the chimes go at midnight . . . to have ginger hot in his mouth: a combination of two Shakespearian lines: Falstaff in *2 Henry IV*, Act 3, Scene 2, ll. 197–8: 'We have heard the chimes at midnight, Master Shallow'; and Sir Toby Belch and Feste to Malvolio in *Twelfth Night*, Act 2, Scene 3, ll. 103–6: 'Dost thou think because thou art virtuous there shall be no more cakes and ale?' | *Feste* 'Yes, by Saint Anne, and ginger shall be hot i' th' mouth, too.'

George Eliot: Mary Ann (or Marian) Evans (1819–80), novelist, translator, and literary journalist, adopted the pseudonym George Eliot (which Trollope misspells in several different ways in the *MS* of *An Autobiography*) when she began to write fiction in 1857. Trollope met her in 1860, through her partner G. H. Lewes (see note to p. 95); he often dined with them (without Rose), and Lewes with the Trollopes (without Marian). Despite this observance of the prevailing social rules about unmarried couples, Trollope and Evans genuinely liked and admired each other: she said that she would not have planned her masterpiece, *Middlemarch*, 'on so extensive a scale' without the example of Trollope's work (T. H. S. Escott, *Anthony Trollope*, 1913, 185). *1883* corrects 'In one modern writer he does believe thoroughly' (*MS*) to 'did believe' because Lewes had died in 1878.

Charles Lever: Charles James Lever (1806–72), Anglo-Irish novelist. Trollope first met him at Coole Park, Sir William Gregory's house in Galway, in the 1840s. From 1845 he lived chiefly in Italy but published in the *Cornhill Magazine* and *Blackwood's Edinburgh Magazine*, was a member of the Garrick Club, and dined with Trollope on his last visit to London in April 1871.

98 *companion*: for a passage in the *MS* omitted in *1883* see Appendix, p. 274.

word: for a passage in the *MS* omitted in *1883* see Appendix, p. 274.

Albert Smith: Albert Richard Smith (1816–60), comic writer, traveller, and popular lecturer. He wrote songs, plays, and burlesques, and published several novels, but was best known for his entertaining lectures, especially those about his ascent of Mont Blanc in 1851.

Jacob Omnium: Matthew James Higgins (1810–68), journalist and controversialist, who had a private income and Peelite views. He published under several (transparent) pseudonyms, most famously as 'Jacob Omnium', and wrote for the *Morning Chronicle*, *The Times*, and, after 1863, the *Pall Mall Gazette*.

Dallas: Eneas Sweetland Dallas (1828–79), journalist and critic, was a staff writer on *The Times* from 1855, writing (anonymous) obituaries, political articles, and book reviews. He wrote the review (*The Times*, 23 May 1859) which established Trollope's reputation as 'the Apollo of the circulating library' (see note to p. 85).

George Augustus Sala: George Augustus Henry Sala (1828–96), journalist, initially for Dickens's *Household Words*; he was a foreign correspondent and writer of leaders and features for the *Daily Telegraph* from 1857.

Fitz-James Stephen: James Fitzjames Stephen (1829–94; knighted 1877), lawyer, author, and journalist (chiefly for the *Saturday Review*), would be

appointed a High Court judge in 1879. In 1855 he married Mary Cun-
ningham (1829–1912), daughter of John William Cunningham, Vicar of
Harrow, tenant of Julians (see note to p. 10), and the figure caricatured in
Frances Trollope's *The Vicar of Wrexhill* (1837).

banquets: for a passage in the *MS* omitted in *1883* see Appendix, p. 275.

a map of the dear county: Trollope's map of Barsetshire was published ('re-
drawn from the sketch map made by the novelist himself') in Sadleir's
Trollope: A Commentary (1927).

99 *Rusticum*: (Latin) 'rural or rustic place', 'country village'.

100 *Waltham Cross*: a village in Hertfordshire, now part of the outer suburbs
of London. Trollope first rented then bought Waltham House, an early
eighteenth-century brick building; Anne Thackeray (see note to p. 160)
described it in her journal, in the winter of 1865, as 'a sweet old prim chill
house'. Later a rose farm, then a convent, it was demolished in 1936.

1861: actually 5 April 1862.

King Street: the Garrick Club moved from King Street to its current
premises in Garrick Street in 1864.

101 *the young tyrant of my household*: Florence Bland (1855–1908), daughter
of Rose Trollope's sister Isabella, who came to live with the Trollopes
when she was orphaned in 1863. From 1878 she would serve as Trollope's
amanuensis.

'my custom always in the afternoon': Shakespeare, *The Tempest*, Act 3,
Scene 2, ll. 82–3 (Caliban speaking of Prospero): ''tis a custom with him |
I'th' afternoon to sleep'.

Rip Van Winkle: 'Rip Van Winkle' is a short story by the American author
Washington Irving (1783–1859), published in *The Sketch Book of Geof-
frey Crayon* (1819–20); the hero meets some ghostly figures in the Catskill
Mountains, shares the liquor they are drinking, and falls asleep for twenty
years. The phrase 'swear off' is not actually used in the story, though Rip
Van Winkle regrets drinking from the flagon when he first wakes up.

one's: *MS*; 'men's' *1883*.

chiefly: *MS*; 'simply' *1883*.

pandemonium: (Greek) 'place of all the devils'—that is, hell. Originally
a Miltonic usage though Trollope may be remembering Byron's 'A Sketch'
(*Domestic Pieces*, 1816): 'To make a Pandemonium where she dwells, |
And reign the Hecate of domestic hells?'

after: *MS*; 'for' *1883*.

102 *Arts Club . . . Civil Service Club . . . Athenaeum*: the Arts Club was founded
in 1863, originally in Hanover Square, by a group which included Trollope,
Dickens, and Frederick Leighton. Although there were several attempts
in the nineteenth century to found Civil Service clubs, the current club

dates only from 1953. The Athenaeum, in Pall Mall, was founded in 1824 for 'individuals known for scientific, literary, or artistic accomplishments'; Trollope became a member on 12 April 1864.

Lord Stanhope: Philip Henry Stanhope, FRS, 5th Earl Stanhope (1805–75), Tory politician, historian, and President of the Royal Literary Fund from 1863.

the Cosmopolitan: the Cosmopolitan Club (1852–1902), with premises in an artist's studio in Mayfair, and open after dinner on just two nights a week, was a meeting place for literary men, journalists, publishers, artists, civil servants, and politicians; Trollope became a member in April 1861. It is depicted as the Universe in Chapter 34 of *Phineas Redux*.

Tom Hughes . . . Tom Taylor: THOMAS HUGHES (1822–96), novelist, lawyer, and Liberal MP, best remembered for *Tom Brown's Schooldays* (1857). WILLIAM STIRLING (1818–78; Stirling Maxwell, 9th baronet, from 1865), art historian, collector, and Tory MP. HENRY REEVE (1813–95), leader writer and foreign correspondent for *The Times* 1840–55, and editor of the *Edinburgh Review* 1855–95. ARTHUR RUSSELL (1825–92; Lord Arthur Russell from 1872), private secretary to his uncle Prime Minister Lord John Russell 1849–54, and Liberal MP for Tavistock 1857–85. TOM TAYLOR (1817–80), playwright, journalist, editor of *Punch* 1874–80, and civil servant (Board of Health, 1850–72), who rose at five each morning to write for three hours before walking to his Whitehall office.

Lord Ripon . . . Knatchbull Hugessen: LORD RIPON: GEORGE FREDERICK SAMUEL ROBINSON (1827–1909; Viscount Goderich 1853–59; Earl de Grey 1859–71; created Marquess of Ripon 1871), Christian Socialist Radical MP 1852–9, cabinet minister 1861–6 and 1868–73, and Viceroy of India 1880–5. LORD STANLEY, Edward Stanley (1826–93; Lord Stanley 1851–69; 15th Earl of Derby from 1869), Tory MP and cabinet minister, with progressive views, great wealth, a timid manner and (from 1870) a formidable political hostess as his wife (Lady Mary Catherine Sackville-West, 1824–1900, widow of James Gascoyne-Cecil, 2nd Marquess of Salisbury). WILLIAM EDWARD FORSTER (1818–86), Bradford manufacturer and Liberal MP (see note to p. 186), married to Matthew Arnold's sister, and chiefly responsible for the 1870 Elementary Education Act. LORD ENFIELD, George Byng (1836–98; Viscount Enfield 1860–86; 3rd Earl of Strafford from 1886), Liberal MP for Tavistock 1852–7 and Middlesex 1857–74, and junior cabinet minister in the 1860s and '70s. LORD KIMBERLEY, John Wodehouse (1826–1902; Lord Wodehouse 1826–66; 1st Earl of Kimberley from 1866), Liberal MP and cabinet minister. GEORGE BENTINCK (1821–91), lawyer, cricketer, and Tory MP. WILLIAM VERNON HARCOURT (1827–1904; knighted 1873), lawyer, journalist (for the *Saturday Review* and *The Times*), Liberal MP for Oxford 1868–80, cabinet minister, and leader of the opposition 1896–8; he was a capable but uncharismatic politician, sometimes mocked for his descent from the Plantagenets. WILLIAM BROMLEY DAVENPORT

(1821–84; Davenport-Bromley from 1822 and thus in *MS*, Bromley Davenport from 1867 and thus in *1883*), Tory MP for North Warwickshire 1864–84. EDWARD HUGESSEN KNATCHBULL-HUGESSEN (1829–93; created Baron Brabourne 1880), Liberal MP for Sandwich 1857–80, and junior cabinet minister; he was the first editor of the letters of Jane Austen (his mother's aunt).

102 *the Turf*: the Turf Club was founded in 1868 (originally as the Arlington) in Piccadilly, subsequently moving to Carlton House Terrace. A club for aristocrats and race-horse owners, it was a useful source of material for the horse-racing episodes in *The Duke's Children*.

sub silentio: (Latin) 'in silence', 'unnoticed'. Serialized in the *Cornhill Magazine* 1861–2, *The Struggles of Brown, Jones, and Robinson* was pirated by Harpers in New York in 1862 but not published in London as a book until 1870; it was reviewed in the *British Quarterly Review* (January 1871) and the *Westminster Review* (July 1871), and mentioned in the *Saturday Review*'s notice of *Miss Mackenzie* (March 1865).

103 *when I have published my work anonymously*: *Nina Balatka* (July 1866–January 1867) and *Linda Tressel* (October 1867–May 1868) were serialized in *Blackwood's Edinburgh Magazine*, where all work appeared anonymously; unusually Trollope insisted that they should remain anonymous when republished in book form (1867 and 1868). Although R. H. Hutton identified the author in his *Spectator* review (23 March 1867), both sold poorly and Blackwood reissued them in 1879 with Trollope's name on the title page. Trollope wished to do the same thing with *The Golden Lion of Granpère* (1872) but Blackwood refused.

the War of Secession: usually now referred to as the American Civil War (1861–5) but technically an attempt by eleven Southern states to secede from the federal union established by the constitution of 1787.

104 *Postmaster-General*: Lord Stanley of Alderley.

August: Trollope was in America from September 1861 to March 1862. The first Battle of Bull Run had taken place in July, before his arrival, so he was present during the indecisive, smaller-scale fighting of the first winter of the war.

105 *Messrs Slidell and Mason*: John Slidell and James Mason were emissaries sent by the Confederacy to seek support from European governments. Travelling from Havana on the British Royal Mail ship the *Trent* (on which Trollope had himself travelled in 1858–9), they were seized by the USS *San Jacinto* on 8 November 1861. Although Northern public opinion was pleased, the government feared it might lead to war with Britain. Trollope's presence, as an Englishman, at William Seward's dinner party on 26 December, the day on which Lincoln's cabinet had considered the British ultimatum, was remarkable. His account of the roles played by Seward, Secretary of State, and Charles Sumner, Chairman of the Senate Foreign Relations Committee, is, however, only partly correct. Although

Sumner's wish for arbitration might have prolonged the crisis, he had always favoured a conciliatory response. Seward, by contrast, had earlier taken a hard line. Now he cut matters short by recommending the immediate release of the two men. He informed the British ambassador on 27 December; the news was made public on 29 December, and Slidell and Mason resumed their journey in January 1862.

106 *proud . . . proud*: MS; 'fond . . . fond' *1883*.

109 *juniors*: for a passage in *MS* omitted from *1883* see Appendix, p. 276.

110 *Fortnightly Review*: a highbrow Liberal periodical (1865–1954), published from the offices of Chapman and Hall but owned until 1871 by an independent group with Trollope as its chairman; it became a monthly after November 1866. The first issues contained Trollope's *The Belton Estate* and Walter Bagehot's *The English Constitution*; Trollope also serialized *The Eustace Diamonds* and *Lady Anna* here, and contributed more than twenty articles and reviews between 1865 and 1879.

113 *Gibbon . . . Macaulay*: Edward Gibbon (1737–94), whose *History of the Decline and Fall of the Roman Empire* was published 1776–88. Thomas Babington Macaulay (1800–59), politician, poet, and historian, published his best-selling *History of England* from 1849 to 1855.

single spies . . . battalions: Shakespeare, *Hamlet*, Act 4, Scene 5, ll. 74–5: 'When sorrows come they come not single spies, | But in battalions.'

female prig. MS; 'French prig' *1883*, a prig is an excessively punctilious or morally correct person.

114 *Mr Cobden . . . Mr Disraeli*: Richard Cobden (1804–65), Radical politician of the Manchester School; Benjamin Disraeli (1804–81; created Earl of Beaconsfield 1876), politician and novelist; he was effectively leader of the Tory party from the early 1850s but did not become Prime Minister until 1868.

115 *primogeniture*: the legal right of the firstborn son to inherit the whole of the family estate, customary in British titles of nobility.

very: added in *1883*.

to do her duty: the Anglican Catechism includes an undertaking 'to do my duty in that state of life, unto which it shall please God to call me'.

a distinguished dignitary of our Church: not identified, though Trollope's reply to him, on 31 October 1865, survives (*Letters*, i. 316).

117 *even*: MS; 'ever' *1883*.

He had been unfortunate: Thackeray came from a wealthy background but had lost his inheritance by 1833. He married Isabella Shawe (1816–93) in 1836; she became insane after the birth of their third child in 1840 and spent the rest of her life in care.

118 *Lady Castlewood*: a character in Thackeray's novel *Henry Esmond* (1852).

118 *Good Words*: a monthly magazine founded in 1860 and aimed at an Evangelical readership; by 1864 it was selling more than 100,000 copies a month and had become the single most popular outlet for serialized fiction. Trollope fails to mention that Macleod had good grounds for objecting to the hostile portrait, in *Rachel Ray*, of the Evangelical clergyman Mr Prong (*Letters*, i. 222–5).

make good: for a passage in *MS* omitted from *1883* see Appendix, p. 276.

119 *with the responsibility of his name attached*: see Trollope's article 'On Anonymous Literature', *Fortnightly Review* (1 July 1865).

the well-known French publication: *La Revue des Deux Mondes* was published fortnightly in Paris from August 1829, though it too eventually became a monthly. Trollope thanked George Smith, on 22 September 1860, for a copy of the *Revue* (15 September 1860) containing a perceptive discussion of his work by E. D. Forgues, but remarked that, 'for dull, hard reading, with nothing in it, recommend me to the deux mondes' (*Letters*, i. 121).

121 *John Morley*: John Morley (1838–1923; created Viscount Morley of Blackburn 1908), editor, biographer, and politician. He edited the *Fortnightly Review* 1867–82 and the *Pall Mall Gazette* 1880–3, became a Liberal MP in 1883, and would later be a cabinet minister.

Mr Freeman: Edward Augustus (E. A.) Freeman (1823–92), prolific historian and controversialist (especially in the *Saturday Review*), whose five-volume *History of the Norman Conquest* was published from 1867 to 1879. His 'The Morality of Field Sports' appeared in the *Fortnightly Review* on 1 October 1869, Trollope's reply on 1 December. They met in Rome in 1880 and became friends.

two on Cicero: 'Cicero as a Politician' and 'Cicero as a Man of Letters' (*Fortnightly Review*, April and September, 1877).

124 *I did not follow the habit*: Bishop Proudie is briefly mentioned in Chapter 2, and Clavering appears to be within his diocese, but there is no other link to previous novels.

125 *a further novel of mine*: *The Last Chronicle of Barset*, published in weekly parts from December 1866 to July 1867.

Pall Mall Gazette: a daily evening newspaper (1865–1923), founded by George Smith and Frederick Greenwood, which took its title from a fictitious journal in Thackeray's *Pendennis* (1850). Trollope was a regular feature writer and reviewer from 1865 to 1868 and again in 1880. Collections of his articles were republished as *Hunting Sketches* (1865), *Travelling Sketches* (1866), *Clergymen of the Church of England* (1866), and *London Tradesmen* (1927).

Hannay . . . Lord Strangford . . . Greenwood . . . Greg: James Hannay (1827–73), Scottish journalist and novelist, who edited the *Edinburgh Evening Courant* in 1861–4 but was in London from 1864 until 1868, when he became British consul in Barcelona. Percy Smythe (1825–69;

8th Viscount Strangford from 1857), linguist, author, and Middle East expert. Frederick Greenwood (1830–1909), novelist and editor (*Queen* 1861–3, *Cornhill Magazine* 1864–8, *Pall Mall Gazette* 1865–80), who had himself suggested the idea of an evening newspaper to George Smith and published an angry article ('Gossip about a Newspaper', *St James's Gazette*, 16 October 1883) about Trollope's claim that the *Pall Mall* was the result of Smith's 'unassisted energy'. W. R. Greg (1809–81), industrialist, civil servant (1856–77, Customs, then Stationery Office), writer, and social commentator.

the revelations of a visitor: 'A Night in a Casual Ward, by an Amateur Casual', a piece of sensational reportage written by Frederick Greenwood and his brother James (1832–1929), based on the latter's experiences, was published in the *Pall Mall Gazette* on 12, 13, and 15 January 1866.

126 *a great dean*: Henry Alford (1810–71), poet, critic, and clergyman, Dean of Canterbury from 1857. His article 'Mr Anthony Trollope and the English Clergy' was published in the *Contemporary Review* (June 1866). The suggestion that the dean 'may revisit the glimpses of the metropolitan moon' had been made in Trollope's article 'The Normal Dean of the Present Day' (*Pall Mall Gazette*, 2 December 1865) as part of an argument that deans were redundant.

A gentleman: William Dougal Christie (1816–74), British Minister to Brazil from 1859 to 1863, who had married Trollope's childhood friend Mary Grant (see note to p. 18) in 1841. His behaviour in Brazil led to a severing of diplomatic relations and a critical debate in the House of Commons. He sought to justify his conduct in a pamphlet, which Trollope discussed in 'Notes on the Brazilian Question', *Pall Mall Gazette* (11 February 1865).

127 *Exeter Hall*: a building in the Strand (constructed 1829–31, demolished 1907), used for the meetings of philanthropic and religious organizations, including the Bible Society, the Ragged School Union, and the Temperance Society, and for sermons by Charles Spurgeon, the charismatic Baptist preacher. Trollope's 'A Zulu in Search of a Religion' appeared in the *Pall Mall Gazette* on 10 May 1865.

128 *Mr Hutton*: Richard Holt Hutton (1826–97), Unitarian theologian, mathematician, and literary editor of *The Spectator* from 1861 to 1897; his review of *Nina Balatka* appeared in *The Spectator* on 23 March 1867.

129 *Prague . . . Nuremberg*: Trollope visited Prague and Nuremberg on a family holiday in the autumn of 1865.

experiment: for a passage in *MS* omitted from *1883* see Appendix, p. 276.

130 *Fortnum & Mason*: a fashionable London grocery store, opened on its present site in Piccadilly in 1707.

walk: MS; 'work' *1883*.

131 *Milton . . . mute and inglorious*: Thomas Gray, 'Elegy Written in a Country Churchyard' (1751), l. 59: 'Some mute inglorious Milton here may rest'.

131 *article on the early verses of Lord Byron*: Henry Brougham's criticism of Byron's volume *Hours of Idleness* as 'so much stagnant water' (*Edinburgh Review*, January 1808) is said to have provoked Byron into writing his satirical poem, *English Bards and Scotch Reviewers* (1809).

The Biliad: Terence McMahon Hughes (1812–49) privately published his satirical poem about reviewers, *The Biliad, or, How to Criticize; A Satire, with The Dirge of Repeal, and Other Jeux d'Esprit*, in 1846; the other poems in the collection were chiefly concerned with Irish politics, which may at the time have recommended the volume to Trollope. Richard Payne Knight's *An Analytical Enquiry into the Principles of Taste* had first appeared in 1805; Pindar was a Greek lyric poet of the 5th century BC.

attorney-general: a politician who is the government's senior legal adviser and the Crown's representative in the law courts; in the nineteenth century he was allowed to combine this public role with a lucrative private practice at the bar.

132 *Charles Reade*: Charles Reade (1814–84), dramatist and novelist. For his later quarrel with Trollope see note to p. 277.

133 *crown*: a coin worth 5s. (25 pence).

135 *a history of English prose fiction*: Trollope may have 'proposed' this project in the mid–1850s but the surviving material apparently dates from 1866: Sadleir prints 'the few pages of introduction that were actually written' as an appendix to his *Trollope: A Commentary* (1927) and describes the 'list of novels . . . to be read' attached to the manuscript (277).

May meetings: at Exeter Hall in the Strand (see note to p. 127).

Arcadia . . . Robinson Crusoe: Sir Philip Sidney's *The Arcadia* is a prose romance written in the 1580s; Trollope would have known the hybrid text available between 1593 and 1907, when the 'Old' and 'New' versions of *The Arcadia* were distinguished. Scott's *Ivanhoe* was published 1819, Daniel Defoe's *The Life and Strange and Surprising Adventures of Robinson Crusoe* in 1719.

when Dickens and Bulwer died: in 1870 and 1873 respectively. Bulwer refers to Edward Bulwer Lytton, 1st Baron Lytton, writer and politician.

Aphra Behn: Aphra Behn (1640?–89), Playwright, poet, and novelist, whose *Oroonoko* (1688) has been seen as the first philosophical novel in English.

137 *novelists*: for a passage in *MS* omitted from *1883* see Appendix, p. 276.

Lydia . . . under the sofa: in Sheridan's play *The Rivals* (1775), Lydia Languish tells her maid to hide the novels she has been reading: 'Fling *Peregrine Pickle* [by Tobias Smollett, 1751] under the toilet . . . thrust *Lord Aimworth* [Anon., *The History of Lord Aimsworth*, 1773] under the sofa . . . and leave *Fordyce's Sermons* open upon the table' (Act 1, Scene 2).

139 *Cagliostros*: Count Cagliostro was the alias of Joseph Balsamo (1743–95), magician and confidence trickster, who was implicated in the notorious

'Affair of the Diamond Necklace' in 1785, which helped to discredit the Bourbon monarchy before the French Revolution.

Jack Sheppards . . . Macheaths: the highwaymen heroes of Harrison Ainsworth's novel *Jack Sheppard* (1839) and John Gay's play *The Beggar's Opera* (1728).

140 *Lydia Bennet . . . Earl Leicester . . . Beatrix*: Lydia Bennet is seduced by Wickham in Jane Austen's *Pride and Prejudice* (1813); Leicester conceals his marriage to Amy Robsart in Scott's *Kenilworth* (1821) and is complicit in her murder; Beatrix has an affair with James Stuart, the Old Pretender, in Thackeray's *The History of Henry Esmond* (1852).

141 *Sir Anthony . . . Mrs Malaprop*: characters in Sheridan's play *The Rivals* (1775).

Laura Bell: exemplary character in Thackeray's *Pendennis* (1850).

'*Naturam expellas furcâ, tamen usque recurret*': 'You may drive nature out with a pitchfork but it will still return' (Horace, *Epistles*, Book 1, no. 10, l. 24).

142 *sensational novels*: sensation fiction was a school of novel writing in the 1860s, which relied on complex plots, rather than complex characterization, and featured bigamy, violent crime, guilty secrets, and insanity. Its leading practitioners were Wilkie Collins, Mrs Henry Wood, and Mary Braddon.

Rebecca . . . Burley . . . the mad lady . . . Lady Castlewood . . . Lady Mason: incidents in Scott's *Ivanhoe* (1819) and *Old Mortality* (1816), Charlotte Brontë's *Jane Eyre* (1847), Thackeray's *Henry Esmond* (1852), and Trollope's *Orley Farm* (1862) respectively.

143 *Bride of Lammermoor*: a novel by Sir Walter Scott, published in 1819.

145 '*Solve senescentem mature . . . ridendus*': 'Be sensible and let the old horse loose, so that it does not break down and look ridiculous' (Horace, *Epistles*, Book 1, no. 1, ll. 8–9).

know them well unless: 'know them unless' *1883*.

146 *Gil Blas' canon*: *Gil Blas* (4 vols., 1715–35) is a picaresque novel by Alain-René Le Sage (1668–1747); in the second volume the hero encounters a canon who, despite his age and the good advice of his doctor, persists in over-eating and drinking.

147 *Macaulay says . . . 'How little . . . thinks of it.'*: The remark is from a diary entry by Macaulay for 12 January 1850, quoted in G. O. Trevelyan's *Life and Letters of Macaulay* (1876).

the prosody of a Sapphic stanza: Trollope is thinking of the refinement of the Greek Sapphic stanza, developed for Latin verse by Horace: a four-line stanza, with three lines of five trochaic and dactylic feet (the lesser Sapphic), and a short line of two feet (the Adonic). Trollope's inversion puts a trochee where a dactyl should be.

148 *'Mercuri, nam te docilis magistro . . . Callida nervis'*: 'I call upon you Mercury—for you were the master by whom docile Amphion was taught to make stones move by his singing—and you, tortoise shell, skilled in making seven strings resonate' (Horace, *Odes*, Book 3, no. 11, ll. 1–4). The shell of a tortoise was used as the sounding-box of a lyre.

  The Curious Impertinent . . . the Man of the Hill: celebrated 'episodes', or inserted stories not linked to the plot, in Cervantes' *Don Quixote* (1605–15) and Fielding's *Tom Jones* (1749) respectively.

150 *Caleb Williams . . . Adam Blair*: William Godwin's novel *Caleb Williams* (1794); John Gibson Lockhart's novel *Some Passages in the Life of Mr Adam Blair* (1822).

152 *Colonel Newcome*: a character in Thackeray's novel *The Newcomes* (1853–5).

  Becky Sharp . . . Lady Castlewood . . . Esmond . . . Warrington, Pendennis . . . the Major . . . Colonel Newcome . . . Barry Lyndon: characters in Thackeray's novels *Vanity Fair* (1847–8), *Henry Esmond* (1852), *Pendennis* (1848–50), *The Newcomes* (1853–5), and *The Luck of Barry Lyndon* (1844). Trollope frequently misspells the names 'Newcome' and 'Becky Sharp'.

153 *The Virginians . . . Philip*: Thackeray's novels *The Virginians* (1857–9) and *The Adventures of Philip on His Way through the World* (1861–2).

  Felix Holt, Middlemarch, or Daniel Deronda: these novels (published in 1866, 1872, and 1876 respectively) are examples of George Eliot's later, more intellectually demanding manner.

154 *Seth Bede, Adam Bede, Maggie and Tom Tulliver, . . . Silas Marner, . . . Tito, . . . Mrs Poyser*: Seth and Adam Bede and Mrs Poyser are characters in George Eliot's *Adam Bede* (1859), Maggie and Tom Tulliver in *The Mill on the Floss* (1860), Silas Marner in *Silas Marner* (1861), and Tito Melema in *Romola* (1862–3).

  Mrs Gamp, Micawber, and Pecksniff: Mrs Gamp and Pecksniff are characters in Dickens's *Martin Chuzzlewit* (1843–4), Mr Micawber in *David Copperfield* (1849–50).

  biography by John Forster: Forster's *Life of Charles Dickens* was published in three volumes in 1872–4. Trollope's letter to George Eliot and G. H. Lewes of 27 February 1872 explains his dislike of it: 'Forster's first volume is distasteful to me . . . Dickens was no hero; he was a powerful, clever, humorous, and, in many respects, wise man;—very ignorant, and thick-skinned . . . Forster tells of him things which should disgrace him . . . but Forster himself is too coarse-grained, (though also a very powerful man) to know what is and what is not disgraceful; what is or is not heroic' (*Letters*, ii. 557–8).

155 *Smike . . . Nicholas . . . Kate*: characters in Dickens's *Nicholas Nickleby* (1838–9).

  Boucicault: Dion Boucicault (1820–90), Irish actor and playwright, famous

for comedies such as *London Assurance* (1841), the immensely successful melodrama *The Corsican Brothers* (1852), and, later, a series of 'strong
dramas' with Irish settings: *The Colleen Bawn* (1860), *Arrah-na-Pogue*
(1864), and *The Shaughraun* (1874).

Boffins and Veneerings: characters in Dickens's *Our Mutual Friend* (1864–5).

156 *Pelham . . . Ernest Maltravers . . . My Novel . . . The Caxtons*: novels
by Edward Bulwer Lytton, published in 1828, 1837, 1853, and 1850
respectively.

157 *Corney Delaney*: actually Corny Delany, a character in Charles Lever's
novel *Jack Hinton the Guardsman* (1842).

felt with: MS; 'felt' *1883*.

158 *Jane Eyre . . . Villette . . . Shirley*: novels by Charlotte Brontë, published
in 1847, 1853, and 1849 respectively. *Harry Lorrequer* (1839) was one of
Charles Lever's most popular novels.

The Eighth Commandment . . . a plot taken from a play: Charles Reade
adapted the plot of Auguste Macquet's play *Le Château de Grantier*
(1852) for his novel *White Lies* (1857); Macquet (1813–88) was used to
such arrangements, as he had supplied (for a fee) material for many of
the novels of Alexandre Dumas. Reade published *The Eighth Commandment* (1860) at his own expense in order to defend the rights of authors
and declare his dislike of plagiarism ('Thou shalt not steal'), despite his
tendency to commit it.

159 *a dialogue which he took from Swift*: Charles Reade's version of the topical
issue of the Tichborne claimant, *The Wandering Heir*, published as prose
fiction in the 1872 Christmas number of *The Graphic* and performed
as a play from November 1873, included, without acknowledgement,
a passage from Jonathan Swift's poem, 'The Journal of a Modern Lady'
(1729). Accused of plagiarism by Mortimer Collins, Reade printed his
reply as an appendix when the story was published as a book in 1873.

himself: for a passage in *MS* omitted from *1883* see Appendix, p. 277.

The Cloister and the Hearth: a historical novel by Charles Reade (1861;
serialized as *A Good Fight*, 1859) about the life of Erasmus's father.
Reade's campaigning (or muck-raking) novels about 'paupers', 'lunatics',
and 'the wickedness of certain classes' are *It Is Never Too Late to Mend*
(1856), *Hard Cash* (1863), and *Put Yourself in His Place* (1869–70).

160 *Annie Thackeray and Rhoda Broughton*: Anne Thackeray Ritchie (1837–
1919; Ritchie from 1877, Lady Ritchie from 1907), Thackeray's daughter and herself a novelist, whose books include *The Story of Elizabeth*
(1863), *The Village on the Cliff* (1867), and *Old Kensington* (1873). Rhoda
Broughton (1840–1920), novelist, whose tomboy heroines, witty dialogue,
and mildly improper plots made her a best-seller with books like *Cometh
Up as a Flower* (1867), *Not Wisely but Too Well* (1867), and *Nancy* (1873,
the novel quoted in the next paragraph).

161 *Mr Disraeli*: Benjamin Disraeli (see note to p. 114) combined his career as a politician with another as a novelist, publishing silver-fork fiction in the 1820s and '30s (*Vivian Grey*, 1826–7), Condition-of-England novels in the 1840s (*Coningsby*, *Sybil*, and *Tancred*, 1844–7), and two late novels written after his first spell as Prime Minister: *Lothair* (1870) and *Endymion* (1880). Lady Corisande is a character in *Lothair*; Venetia and Henrietta are the eponymous heroines of *Venetia* (1837) and *Henrietta Temple* (1837).

buhl: furniture inlaid with ornamental patterns of brass or tortoiseshell, hence something showy or extravagant.

164 *Barsetshire Gazette . . . Dillsborough Herald . . . Evening Pulpit*: fictitious newspapers, the first of which might have appeared in the Barsetshire series (a *West Barsetshire Gazette* is mentioned in the short story 'Mrs Brumby', 1870), and the second in *The American Senator*; the third does appear, edited by Ferdinand Alf, in *The Way We Live Now*.

Facilis descensus Averni: see note to p. 291.

165 *a critic of the day*: E. S. Dallas (see note to p. 66), who was given the manuscript of Dickens's *Our Mutual Friend* (1864–5); Dallas reviewed the novel in *The Times* (29 November 1865).

a straining at gnats: 'Ye blind guides, which strain at a gnat, and swallow a camel' (Matthew 23:24).

166 *successful*: for a passage omitted in the MS in *1883* see Appendix, p. 277.

dew . . . from heaven: Shakespeare, *The Merchant of Venice*, Act 4, Scene 1, ll. 179–80: 'The quality of mercy is not strained. | It droppeth as the gentle rain from heaven'.

167 *Mentor*: in the *Odyssey*, a friend of Odysseus who acts as teacher and adviser to his son Telemachus.

tanquam ex cathedrâ: (Latin) 'as though from the throne': that is, spoken with the authority of a bishop in his cathedral.

168 *on the tapis*: (French) 'on the tablecloth': that is, available for discussion.

169 *the Roothing country*: the Roothings, or Rodings, are a group of villages in Essex, all of which have the word 'Roding' as part of their name.

the Shoreditch Station: Shoreditch Station (later Bishopsgate Station) was opened in 1844 by the Eastern Counties Railway, which ran a service over a stretch of Northern & Eastern Railway Company line via Waltham Cross to Hertford. Small and inconvenient, it was superseded by Liverpool Street Station in 1874 and became a goods depot.

5.30 a.m.: there are differing accounts of the hour at which Barney was required to wake Trollope, and good reason to suppose that it did not happen every day. Anne Thackeray Ritchie says in her journal in 1865 that she heard him being called at four o'clock. In *Thackeray* (1879), Trollope states that a novel-writing civil servant will need to 'have risen at five, and have sat at his private desk for three hours before he began his official routine at the public one'. In Chapter 15 of *An Autobiography*, however, it emerges that, during the Waltham Cross years, Trollope often spent several nights a week at his club in London, and did his writing in the club library later in the day; see notes to p. 21 and p. 102.

171 *three such*: *An Eye for an Eye* (written 1870 but not published until 1878–9), *Is He Popinjoy?* (written 1874–5, published 1877–8), and *The American Senator* (written 1875, published 1876).

dean . . . deanery: actually it is Septimus Harding, the precentor (not the dean), who is dying at the deanery in *The Last Chronicle of Barset*.

rectory: *MS*; 'victory' *1883*.

172 *It was thus that it came about*: there is reason to doubt the literal truth of this famous anecdote. Trollope was writing *The Last Chronicle of Barset* between 21 January and 15 September 1866. Archdeacon Grantly had last appeared in *Framley Parsonage* (serialized 1860–1) and the 'old duke' of Omnium in *The Small House at Allington* (serialized 1862–4), so the 'two clergymen' would have been reading very out-of-date magazines. Augustus Hare records another version of the story in which Trollope is heard to say that 'Mrs Proudie shall die in the very next book I write' (Hare, *The Story of My Life*, vol. 5 (London: George Allen, 1900), 300). This was probably a response to hostile reviews of his re-use of characters and situations, such as those in the *Saturday Review*'s notices of *Can You Forgive Her?* (19 August 1865) and *The Belton Estate* (3 February 1866). While planning *The Last Chronicle*, Trollope might have overheard fellow members of the Athenaeum discussing these. The *Saturday Review* would welcome the departure of Mrs Proudie in an article on 'Ambitious Wives' on 6 July 1867. Trollope would deplore 'the elephantine tread of *The Saturday*' in his *Thackeray* (1879).

173 *Did He Steal It?*: *Did He Steal It? A Comedy in Three Acts* was a dramatization of *The Last Chronicle of Barset*, made by Trollope in 1869. It was not performed, but Trollope had some copies privately printed by James Virtue. There is a modern edition of Trollope's two plays: *'The Noble Jilt' and 'Did He Steal It?'*, with an introduction by Robert H. Taylor (New York: Arno Press, 1981).

sure: for a passage in *MS* omitted from *1883* see Appendix, p. 278.

a combined republication: achieved as *The Chronicles of Barsetshire*, 8 vols. (London: Chapman and Hall, 1878–9): a uniform series of six novels, despite the fact that Trollope deleted 'The Small House at Allington' from the *MS* here and the title remained absent from the list in *1883*.

174 *Mr Scudamore*: Frank Ives Scudamore (1823–84) joined the Post Office in 1840 and was promoted to Assistant Secretary in 1864, despite never having served as a departmental Surveyor. The key proponent of the Post Office Savings Bank, established in 1861, he launched the sale of life insurance through the Post Office in 1864, and recommended and ran the nationalization of the telegraph system in 1869. In 1873 it was revealed that he

had spent £800,000, without official approval, on expanding the telegraph service. The Postmaster-General, William Monsell, and Chancellor of the Exchequer, Robert Lowe, were obliged to resign; Scudamore resigned in 1875 and went to work for the Turkish postal system. Trollope comments wryly on this scandal in Chapter 50 of *The Way We Live Now* (1874–5).

175 *the Duke of Montrose*: James Graham, 4th Duke of Montrose (1799–1874), Postmaster-General in the Conservative government of 1866–8.

176 *procure*: MS; 'promise' *1883*.

pillar letter-boxes: Trollope's report on the Channel Islands postal service in 1851 recommended the adoption in Jersey of 'a plan [that] has obtained in France of fitting up letter boxes in posts fixed at the road side'. The first such boxes were opened in Jersey and Guernsey in November 1852; by the mid-1850s they were appearing throughout Britain.

177 *Mr James Virtue*: James Virtue (1829–92) took over his father's business as printer and publisher of illustrated books in 1855. In 1866, owed money for the printing of Alexander Strahan & Co.'s periodicals, he considered taking over *The Argosy* in lieu of the debt. Thinking better of this, but attracted by the idea of owning a journal, he instead founded, in 1867, the monthly *St Paul's Magazine* (1867–74), with Trollope as editor (1867–70) and a title which, like the *Cornhill Magazine* and *Temple Bar*, referred to a London landmark. Trollope serialized *Phineas Finn* (1867–9) and *Ralph the Heir* (1870–1) in *St Paul's*, novels which reflected his wish to use the magazine as a platform for his political interests. It was unprofitable and Virtue transferred it to Strahan in 1869.

179 *Mr Goschen . . . Dutton Cook*: GEORGE JOACHIM GOSCHEN (1831–1907; created Viscount Goschen 1900), merchant banker, political economist, Liberal MP (for the City of London 1863–80), and youthful cabinet minister (he gained his first post in 1865); he was the author of articles in *St Paul's* in October and November 1867, voicing anxiety that the new voters enfranchised by the Reform Act would not appreciate the merits of laissez-faire economics. HENRY BRACKENBURY (1837–1914; Lieutenant-General 1888; KCB 1894), soldier and writer on military theory and army reform. EDWARD DICEY (1832–1911), author and journalist (he was special correspondent for the *Daily Telegraph* 1862–9, and editor of *The Observer* 1870–89), who was Trollope's assistant editor at *St Paul's*. PERCY HETHERINGTON FITZGERALD (1834–1925), prolific novelist, biographer, and theatre critic (writing on 'The Decay of the Stage' for *St Paul's*, November 1867), who, in his *Recreations of a Literary Man, or Does Writing Pay?* (1882), calculated his earnings from fiction to be almost £3,000. AUSTEN HENRY LAYARD (1817–94; KCB 1878), archaeologist, art collector, Liberal MP (for Aylesbury 1852–7, and Southwark 1860–9), and diplomat, who published articles in *St Paul's* on the Eastern Question (1867–8). WILLIAM ALLINGHAM (1824–89), Irish civil servant and poet (poems by him appeared in December 1867 and April 1868). LESLIE STEPHEN (1832–1904; KCB 1902), author, literary critic,

and first editor of the *Dictionary of National Biography*. ELIZA LYNN
LINTON (1822–98), novelist, journalist, and essayist, who contributed
'Cumberland Photographs' to the magazine (December 1867); FRANCES
ELEANOR TROLLOPE (1834–1913), sister of Dickens's mistress, Ellen
Ternan, and second wife of Trollope's brother Tom, whose novel *The
Sacristan's Household* was serialized in 1868–9. EDWIN ARNOLD (1832–
1904; knighted 1888), poet, Orientalist, and journalist (editor of the *Daily
Telegraph* from 1873), who contributed a poem in March 1868. AUSTIN
DOBSON (1840–1921), civil servant, poet, and biographer, who reprinted
his poems from *St Paul's* in his first volume, *Vignettes in Rhyme* (1873),
and dedicated it to Trollope. RICHARD ANTHONY PROCTOR (1837–88),
astronomer and popular science writer. JULIET CREED, LADY POLLOCK
(1819–99), biographer and children's writer, who wrote for *St Paul's* on
'Fashion in Poetry' (March 1868) and 'Jane Austen' (March 1870), and
reviewed Victor Hugo's *L'Homme qui rit* (July 1869; see note to p. 202).
CHARLES MACKAY (1814–99), poet, journalist, and editor. FREDERICK
HARDMAN (1814–74), short-story writer and journalist, correspondent
for *The Times* in Spain, the Crimea, Austria, Italy, and France. GEORGE
MACDONALD (1824–1905), versatile novelist, now best remembered for
his romances and fantasies, whom Trollope asked to supply a Christmas
story, 'weird . . . and of a Christmas-ghostly flavour' (*Letters*, i. 442),
which was published as 'Uncle Cornelius: His Story' in January 1869.
MARGARET OLIPHANT (1828–97), prolific novelist, whose novel *The
Three Brothers* was serialized in *St Paul's* in 1869–70. LEONE LEVI
(1821–88), lawyer and statistician, Professor of Commercial Law at King's
College London. EDWARD DUTTON COOK (1829–83), dramatist, novelist, and drama critic (*Pall Mall Gazette* 1867–75), editor of the *Cornhill
Magazine* 1868–71.

thorn in his pillow: W. M. Thackeray, 'Thorns in the Cushion', Roundabout Paper, No. 5, *Cornhill Magazine*, 2 (July 1860).

181 *an uncle of mine*: Henry Milton (see note to p. 40).

travel to that bourne: Shakespeare, *Hamlet*, Act 3, Scene 1, ll. 80–2: 'the
dread of something after death, | The undiscovered country from whose
bourn | No traveller returns'.

182 *an advanced, but still a Conservative-Liberal*: Trollope was a Whig but the
term was dying out in the 1870s, hence this awkward formulation. For
other accounts of his views see Chapter 68 of *The Prime Minister* (1876)
and Chapter 49 of *Ralph the Heir* (1870–1).

toil-bound: *MS*; 'tost-bound' *1883*.

185 *Charles Buxton*: see note to p. 46. Buxton's elder brother Edward had been
MP for South Essex 1847–52.

the Liberal member for Newark: Grosvenor Hodgkinson (1818–81), Liberal
MP for Newark 1859–74. Previously an obscure backbencher, he became
famous on 17 May 1867 when he moved 'Hodgkinson's amendment' to

the Representation of the People Bill. In a thinly attended House, and without consulting his colleagues, Disraeli unexpectedly accepted it, with the result that more than 400,000 'compound householders' (whose rates were paid by their landlord) were added to the electoral register.

185 *dissenting interest*: MS; 'defeating interest' *1883*. The 'dissenting interest' were Protestant Nonconformists, who saw the Tories as the voice of the Anglican Church and the Liberals as their most effective means of resisting it. The candidate they supported was Andrew Johnson, Chairman of Essex County Council, who would be MP for South Essex 1868–74.

the great Conservative reaction: the Liberal majority of 106 in 1868 became a Conservative majority of 52 in 1874, and the Tories would stay in power until 1880—their first extended period of government since the 1840s.

186 *Beverley*: Beverley is a market town in the East Riding of Yorkshire; it had been a parliamentary borough since 1563. Although Trollope invented a 'Bishop of Beverley' in *The Warden* (1855), the town actually lies within the diocese of York. There were 2,100 electors, of whom half were newly enfranchised in 1868.

my agent: the Liberal agent in the constituency was W. S. Hind, a local solicitor. But Hind was never an MP and the advice reported here seems to have been from someone who was an 'agent' in a more informal sense, probably Trollope's friend and fellow member of the Cosmopolitan Club (see note to p. 102) William Edward (W. E.) Forster (1818–86), Liberal MP for Bradford.

Sir Henry Edwards . . . a young man of fortune: Henry Edwards (1812–86; created baronet 1866), Chairman of the Beverley Iron and Waggon Company, Tory MP for Halifax 1847–52, and Beverley 1857–69. The 'young man' was Captain Edmund Hegan Kennard (1835–1912), Tory MP for Beverley 1868–9, and Lymington 1874–85.

Mr Maxwell: the Hon. Marmaduke Francis Constable-Maxwell (1837–1908; Baron Herries from 1884), Lord Lieutenant of the East Riding; he was the son of William Constable-Maxwell (1804–76) for whom the title of Lord Herries of Terregles had been restored in 1858. A Catholic family, they lived near Beverley at Everingham Park.

187 *the Minster Church*: a magnificent collegiate or monastic church which became Beverley's parish church after the Reformation; the tomb of Lady Eleanor Percy (*c.*1340) suggested the name 'Percycross' in Trollope's novel about the election, *Ralph the Heir* (1870–1).

leather and prunella: 'Worth makes the man, and want of it, the fellow: | The rest is all but leather and prunella' (Alexander Pope, *Essay on Man*, Epistle 4, ll. 204–5); prunella was a woollen fabric from which the clothes of clergymen were often made.

the Ballot: voting by secret ballot would be introduced by the Ballot Act of 1872.

the Permissive Bill: the Permissive Prohibitory Liquor Bill, first proposed by the Liberal MP Sir Wilfred Lawson in 1863 and repeatedly debated between 1869 and 1878, was a temperance measure which would have banned the sale of alcohol in any district where two-thirds of the ratepayers voted to prohibit it. Lawson finally achieved a parliamentary majority for a similar measure in 1880, though the Gladstone government chose not to enact it.

188 *swallow such gnats*: see note to p. 165.

the borough was disfranchised: Beverley was one of four constituencies disfranchised in 1870, the others being Bridgwater, Sligo, and Cashel; its voters were added to the electorate of the larger East Riding seat.

189 *our*: MS; 'one' *1883*.

190 *two men*: Alexander Randall (1819–72), Governor of Wisconsin 1858–61, and American Postmaster-General 1866–9, and his senior clerk, Joseph Fanwood.

191 *a certain American publisher*: Harper & Brothers (1817–1962, now part of HarperCollins), New York publisher. Between 1859 and 1882 they published nine novels by Trollope, as well as some of his non-fiction and short stories, and claimed to have paid him a total of £3,080; Trollope, however, spoke of 'that beast Harper' in a letter to Kate Field (23 August 1862; *Letters*, i. 192). For Trollope's public letter to James Russell Lowell about American copyright piracy and Harper's role in it (*The Athenaeum*, 6 September 1862), and for the subsequent exchange of views, see *Letters* i. 193–202.

193 *the Commission on the law of copyright*: Trollope was an active member of the Royal Commission on Copyright, 1876–7. An Anglo-American Copyright Act would finally be agreed in 1891.

other firms would fear: MS; 'no other firm would care' *1883*.

194 *humanity?*: for a passage in *MS* omitted from *1883* see Appendix, p. 278.

ring-robberies: price-fixing cartels, which would be outlawed by the Sherman Antitrust Act of 1890.

195 *an American woman*: MS; 'a woman' *1883*. The writer, actress, and feminist Kate Field (1838–96), whom Trollope first met in Florence in 1860, when she was 22 and he 45. They met again in America in 1861–2 and 1868; she visited England in the 1870s. He wrote more than twenty affectionate letters to her and on 8 July 1868, writing from Washington, dropped a hint that she might meet him at the seaside, sending 'a kiss that shall be semi-paternal—one third brotherly, and as regards the small remainder, as loving as you please' (*Letters*, i. 438). There is, however, no reason to suppose that the relationship was other than chaste: Kate also corresponded with Rose Trollope, and Anthony was one of several older literary men whom she cultivated; some modern commentators have identified her as lesbian (see Kate Flint, 'Queer Trollope', *Cambridge Companion*, 105). Henry Trollope probably removed the word 'American' to make it harder

to identify her; in practice, its absence made the relationship seem more significant than his father had intended by removing it from the context of an account of his attitude to Americans.

196 *a series of semi-political tales*: the six Palliser, or parliamentary, novels (1864–80).

a visit to Ireland: Trollope and his wife had a holiday at Glengariff, a seaside village on Bantry Bay, County Cork, in late September 1866.

Lady Laura Standish: a character in *Phineas Finn* and *Phineas Redux*.

197 *my puppets*: an uncharacteristic usage by Trollope, who elsewhere insists that his characterization does not have the artificial, puppet-like quality found in Dickens or in Thackeray's *Vanity Fair*.

198 *St Paul's Magazine*: see note to p. 177.

the Graphic: a weekly illustrated newspaper (1869–1932), founded as a rival to the *Illustrated London News* (1842–2003). Trollope published *Phineas Redux* (1873–4), *Marion Fay* (1881–2), and two Christmas stories, *Harry Heathcote of Gangoil* (1871) and 'Christmas at Thompson Hall' (1876), in its pages.

199 *an old maid in Exeter*: Jemima Stanbury, a character probably based on Fanny Bent, a cousin of Trollope's mother.

the great man in Paternoster Row: William Longman (see note to p. 65).

201 *Frederic Chapman, who was then*: followed in *MS* by the words 'and is now'; omitted in *1883* because, in 1880, when Chapman and Hall became a limited liability company, Chapman ceased to be the chief proprietor of a privately owned partnership.

202 *Once a Week*: the publishing firm of Bradbury and Evans founded *Once a Week* (1859–80) when Dickens closed down their *Household Words* (1850–9) and set up his independent *All the Year Round* (1859–95). It was a 6*d.* illustrated weekly, with serial fiction and a body of artists and writers shared with *Punch*.

Victor Hugo: Victor Hugo (1802–85), French poet, playwright, and novelist, famous for *Notre-Dame de Paris* (1831) and *Les Misérables* (1862). Trollope would print a hostile review by his friend Juliet Pollock of *L'Homme qui rit* (1869) in *St Paul's Magazine* (July 1869).

the Gentleman's Magazine: a monthly publication (1731–1922), which, in 1868, moved away from its previous mix of news, obituaries, and learned notes to become a middlebrow magazine running serial fiction. It failed to attract first-rank novelists and abandoned long fiction in the mid–1880s.

203 *laches*: negligence, delay in the performance of a legal duty (from Old French: *laschesse*).

206 *painted sepulchres*: 'Woe unto you, scribes and Pharisees, hypocrites! for ye are like unto whited sepulchres, which indeed appear beautiful outward,

but are within full of dead men's bones, and of all uncleanness' (Matthew 23:27).

207 *Macmillan's Magazine*: *Macmillan's Magazine* (1859–1907) was the first 1*s.* monthly, appearing only very shortly before the *Cornhill Magazine* (1860–1975). It published Trollope's *Sir Harry Hotspur of Humblethwaite* (1870) but rejected *Ayala's Angel* in 1879. The owner, Alexander Macmillan (1818–96), was a friend of Trollope's and entertained him the night before he suffered a stroke in 1882.

Mudie: Charles Mudie's circulating library (1842–1937) was until the 1880s the chief source of new novels for Victorian readers.

208 *break up the type*: the novel that had been set in type in three- rather than two-volume form was *The Belton Estate* (1866), previously serialized in the *Fortnightly Review* (1865–6).

my own early days . . . abortive periodical: 'The Panjandrum' (1870) is Trollope's autobiographical story about his attempt to found a literary magazine in the late 1830s (see Introduction, p. xvii).

John Blackwood: John Blackwood (1818–79) took over the family publishing house of Blackwood & Sons (1804–1980) in 1852. Either in serial form in *Blackwood's Edinburgh Magazine* (1817–1980) or as books (sometimes as both), the firm published six novels and two other books (*The Commentaries of Caesar* and *An Autobiography*) by Trollope between 1867 and 1884.

William Lucas Collins: the Revd William Lucas Collins (1817–87), clergyman and author. Educated at Rugby School (under Thomas Arnold), he became Diocesan Inspector of Education for Northamptonshire in the 1850s, Vicar of Kilsby from 1867, and Rector of Lowick after 1873. A regular contributor to *Blackwood's Edinburgh Magazine*, especially on educational topics (where he took a sceptical view of Arnold's achievement), he also wrote perceptive reviews of George Eliot's works. He edited the *Blackwood's* series Ancient Classics for English Readers, meeting Trollope in that capacity in 1870; they became good friends.

209 *that most futile book . . . Emperor of the French*: Charles Louis Napoléon Bonaparte (1808–73; Emperor Napoléon III of France 1852–70) published *L'Histoire de Jules César* (1865–6); his attempt to suggest parallels between his own policies and Caesar's became ridiculous after his defeat in the Franco-Prussian War (1870–1).

old and very learned friend: Charles Merivale (see note to p. 40). R. H. Super has suggested that Merivale actually wrote 'your Comm[entaries of] Caesar', and that Trollope misread the abbreviation. But Margaret Oliphant, who reviewed the book for *Blackwood's* (November 1871), told John Blackwood privately that it made her laugh (see Mullen, *Anthony Trollope*, 578).

210 *an amateur . . . walls of the Academy*: the Royal Academy's Summer Exhibition is an open competition to which amateur, as well as professional, artists can submit work.

210 *Ne sutor ultra crepidam*: 'The cobbler should not judge things beyond the sandal.' Pliny's *Natural History* (AD 77) describes how a shoemaker criticized a sandal in a painting by Apelles. When he went on to criticize the leg, the painter responded in a phrase 'that has passed into a proverb' (Book 35, Chapter 36, Section 85) in the form used here by Trollope.

211 *our shepherd son*: Frederic Trollope was a sheep farmer in Australia from 1865 to 1876.

a London daily paper: the *Daily Telegraph* printed ten letters, signed 'Antipodean', between 23 December 1871 and 28 December 1872.

212 *behind*: for a passage in *MS* omitted from *1883* see Appendix, p. 278.

213 *speak*: for a passage in *MS* omitted from *1883* see Appendix, p. 278.

214 *come*: for a passage in *MS* omitted from *1883* see Appendix, p. 279.

words: for a passage in *MS* omitted from *1883* see Appendix, p. 279.

216 *Brigham Young*: Brigham Young (1801–77) was the leader of the Mormon, or Latter-Day Saint, movement from 1847 to 1877. He led the Mormons to Utah in 1847 and founded Salt Lake City.

Leighton Buzzard: a market town in Bedfordshire. Trollope kept horses there in the spring of 1873, hunting with Baron Meyer de Rothschild's deer hounds and with the Whaddon Chase fox hounds in Buckinghamshire, whose Master was William Selby Lowndes (1807–86); see *Letters*, ii. 579.

217 *Great Eastern Railway*: 'Eastern Counties Railway' in *MS*; altered by Henry Trollope in *1883* to reflect the fact that the old Eastern Counties Railway had been absorbed into the Great Eastern Railway in 1862; see note to p. 169.

'Singula de nobis . . . poëmata': Horace, *Epistles*, Book 2, no. 2, ll. 55–7; the translation is from John Conington, *The Satires, Epistles, and Art of Poetry of Horace Translated into English Verse* (1874), 163.

the very: *MS*; 'my' *1883*.

'Vixi puellis . . . habebit': 'Until now I have lived to please young women, and have campaigned not without glory; now both my weapons and my lyre—its warfare is over—will be hung on this wall' (Horace, *Odes*, Book 3, no. 26, ll. 1–4); in l. 3, 'chordis' *MS*, corrected to 'bello' *1883*. Trollope makes a very free adaptation, or imitation, of the original.

218 *Montagu Square*: 39 Montagu Square, a terraced house in Marylebone, built in 1811 and only a few streets away from where Trollope had lodged in the 1830s. He bought the house in February 1873 and lived there from April 1873 to July 1880.

new catalogue: Trollope had two catalogues of his library privately printed, the first in 1867 when the books were at Waltham Cross, the second in 1874 after the move to Montagu Square; both are described by R. H. Grossman and A. Wright in *Nineteenth-Century Fiction*, 31 (1976), 48–64.

Mr Ruskin: John Ruskin (1819–1900), art critic and social theorist. Trollope reviewed his *Sesame and Lilies* and *The Crown of Wild Olive* in the *Fortnightly Review* (15 July 1865 and 15 June 1866).

wailing and gnashing of teeth: 'The Son of man shall send forth his angels, and they shall gather out of his kingdom all things that offend . . .; | And shall cast them into a furnace of fire: there shall be wailing and gnashing of teeth' (Matthew 13:42).

219 *Apician dinners*: Apicius was a celebrated gourmet in the reign of Tiberius (AD 14–37), though the Latin cookery book which bears his name is of later date.

221 *Brocks, De Terriers . . . Daubeneys*: there is some degree of resemblance between Lord Brock and Lord Palmerston, Lord De Terrier and Lord Derby, Mr Gresham and Gladstone, and Mr Daubeney and Disraeli. Joshua Monk has been linked to Richard Cobden, though he also partially resembles Sir George Cornewall Lewis (1806–63), and the name may be taken from the Liberal MP Charles James Monk, whose Revenue Officers' Disabilities Removal Act (1868) gave Post Office officials the right to vote.

Burke and Fox: the Whig politicians Edmund Burke (1729–97) and Charles James Fox (1749–1806) were friends and political allies, who fell out over the French Revolution, which Fox welcomed but Burke deplored. After an emotional confrontation in the Commons on 6 May 1791, with Fox in tears, Burke crossed the floor of the House to sit with the government, declaring that, 'I have done my duty though I have lost my friend.'

222 *The critic who wrote the article*: although Trollope thought the writer was R. H. Hutton (see note to p. 128), this review (*Spectator*, 22 July 1876) was actually by Meredith White Townsend (1831–1911), the paper's political editor.

223 *another story*: *The Duke's Children* (1879–80).

Temple Bar: a monthly magazine (1860–1906) and rival of the *Cornhill*, with an emphasis on serial fiction. Trollope was offered the editorship in 1861 but declined; it serialized *The American Senator* in 1876–7.

224 *Voltaire*: pen name of François-Marie Arouet (1694–1778), French philosopher and writer of 2,000 books and pamphlets; Trollope must be calculating by number of words, rather than titles.

Varro: Marcus Terentius Varro (116–27 BC), Roman scholar whose encyclopedic interests produced seventy-four works in 620 books, most of which survive only in fragments.

225 *when young and who may intend*: MS; 'and when young may intend' *1883*.

Nulla dies sine lineâ: 'No day without a line'. Pliny's *Natural History* (AD 77) describes the Greek painter Apelles' determination never to let a day be so fully occupied with other matters that he did not 'practise his art by drawing a line' (Book 35, Chapter 36, Section 84). This practice had become a proverb ('quod ab eo in proverbium venit') in the form used here by Trollope.

225 *followed also*: MS; 'followed' *1883*.

226 *Gutta cavat lapidem . . . cadendo*: 'the drop of rain maketh a hole in the stone, not by violence, but by oft falling', Hugh Latimer (1492–1555), *Seventh Sermon before Edward VI* (1549), extending Ovid's 'gutta cavat lapidem' ('the drop hollows the stone'; *Epistulae ex Ponto*, Book 4, no. 10, l. 5).

Rousseau . . . confessed: see note to p. 9.

smoking: Trollope was an enthusiastic smoker who imported his own cigars from Cuba; an entire wall of the study at Waltham House was devoted to cabinets for them.

our old English dramatists: Trollope had a large collection of Elizabethan and Jacobean drama, most of it now in the Folger Shakespeare Library, Washington DC; between 1866 and 1882 he read and annotated more than 270 such plays.

227 *I stretch out my hand*: 'tendebantque manus ripae ulterioris amore' (Virgil, *Aeneid*, Book 6, l. 314: 'And they stretched out their hands in yearning for the farther shore'), actually describing dead souls longing to be transported across the Styx to the underworld, though often, as here, used of the dead stretching out their hands to the living.

OTHER WRITINGS
TROLLOPE ON JANE AUSTEN

Trollope is the Victorian novelist who worked most directly in the tradition of Jane Austen. As early as 1848, *The Athenaeum*, in its review of *The Kellys and the O'Kellys*, could observe that 'Lord and Lady Cashel are a pair whom Miss Austen need not have disowned', and the *Saturday Review*'s notice of *The Small House at Allington*, in 1864, claimed that 'He can do . . . what Miss Austen did, only that he does it in the modern style'. In the essays written about Trollope immediately after his death, the link was almost automatic: *The Times*, for example, on 7 December 1882 remarked that 'his world is the heir of Miss Austen's'. Trollope was fully conscious of his debt to his great predecessor. In Chapter 3 of *An Autobiography* he says that by the age of nineteen, in 1834, 'I had already made up my mind that *Pride and Prejudice* was the best novel in the English language'. Although he goes on to say that he 'partially withdrew' this palm 'after a second reading of *Ivanhoe*', and 'did not completely bestow [it] elsewhere till *Esmond* was written', he appears to have returned to his original judgement by November 1869, when, as editor of *St Paul's Magazine*, he asked Richard Bentley for a review copy of J. E. Austen-Leigh's *A Memoir of Jane Austen* (1870) and referred to her as 'my chief favourite among novelists' (*Letters*, i. 486). The catalogues made of Trollope's library in 1867 and 1874 show that he owned the five-volume edition of Austen's work published by Bentley in 1833 (the only complete edition before

1882) in its 1856 reissue; he had clearly read the novels before then in other editions. He discusses her work on several occasions, admiringly but from the viewpoint of an experienced fellow novelist, and two examples are given here: a passage from *The New Zealander* (his quasi-Carlylean review of the state of the nation, written in 1855–6 but not published until 1972), and the manuscript note made in 1864 on the endpapers of his copy of *Emma*. A third can be found in his 1870 lecture 'On English Prose Fiction as a Rational Amusement' (see p. 233).

231 *De Burgh . . . Crofts*: Trollope is writing from memory; he misspells 'de Bourgh' and means Bertrams (of *Mansfield Park*), not 'Mansfields'. 'Crofts' is either an error for Crawfords (in *Mansfield Park*) or a reference to Admiral and Mrs Croft in *Persuasion*.

malade imaginaire: (French) 'imaginary invalid' or hypochondriac, as in Molière's play *Le Malade imaginaire* (1673).

'ON ENGLISH PROSE FICTION AS A RATIONAL AMUSEMENT'

Trollope wrote 'On English Prose Fiction' as a lecture for delivery in Edinburgh on 28 January 1870, though by the time it was read there he had already given it in Hull (24 January) and Glasgow (27 January); it was repeated on three subsequent occasions in Britain and several in Australia during Trollope's visit of 1871–2. The text was privately printed for Trollope by James Virtue (possibly in 1871 for use on the Australian trip) and first published, from the copy now in the Morris L. Parrish Collection of Victorian Novelists at Princeton University Library, in Morris L. Parrish (ed.), *Anthony Trollope: Four Lectures* (London: Constable, 1938). Trollope excluded discussion of living authors from his original lecture but added a section about Dickens in 1871 (printed in *Four Lectures*, 127–9; Dickens had died in June 1870) and re-used a good deal of the material in his article, 'Novel-Reading: The Works of Charles Dickens, the Works of W. Makepeace Thackeray' (*Nineteenth Century*, January 1879).

234 *novel-wright*: 'Of no given Book, not even of a Fashionable Novel, can you predicate with certainty that its vacuity is absolute . . . How knowest thou, may the distressed Novelwright exclaim, that I . . . am the Foolishest of existing mortals; that this my Long-ear of a Fictitious Biography shall not find one, and the other, into whose still longer ears it may be the means, under Providence, of instilling somewhat? We answer, None knows, none can certainly know: therefore, write on, worthy Brother . . .', Thomas Carlyle, 'Biography', *Fraser's Magazine*, 27 (April 1832), here quoted from *The Works of Thomas Carlyle*, Centenary Edition, 30 vols. (London: Chapman and Hall, 1899), xxviii. 48–9); see note to p. 68.

bishop . . . lecture against novels: William Thomson (1819–90), Archbishop of York 1862–90, attacked the taste for 'sensational stories' in a talk to the Huddersfield Church Institute, which *The Times* reported on 2 November 1864 and endorsed in a leading article the following day. Trollope wrote to George Smith on 4 November 1864 seeking space in the *Cornhill Magazine* for a reply (*Letters*, i. 285–6). On the same day, however, *The Times* published a leader seeking 'to state what may be said on the other side' and defending the recreational value of prose fiction as 'harmless distraction'.

235 *Minerva Press*: a publishing house established *c.*1790 in Leadenhall Street, London, by William Lane (1745–1814), and known for its Gothic and Sentimental fiction. Lane's partner and successor, Anthony Newman, dropped the Minerva Press imprint in the 1820s.

Mr Barrett: Eaton Stannard Barrett (1786–1820), Anglo-Irish poet and satirist, who published his comic novel *The Heroine, or Adventures of a Fair Romance Reader* in 1813.

236 *Sir Piercie Shafton*: a character in Scott's novel *The Monastery* (1820).

238 *Miss Harriet Biron*: Harriet Byron is the heroine of Samuel Richardson's novel *Sir Charles Grandison* (1754).

239 *parody on Richardson*: Henry Fielding's *An Apology for the Life of Mrs Shamela Andrews* (1741) is a parody of Richardson's *Pamela* (1740–1), as is his *Joseph Andrews* (1742), especially in its early chapters.

Lovelace: the principal male character in Richardson's *Clarissa* (1747–9).

240 *'Romance of the Forest' . . . 'Mysteries of Udolpho'*: Gothic novels published in 1791, 1797, and 1794 by Ann Radcliffe (1764–1823).

242 *Macintosh*: Sir James Mackintosh (1765–1832), Scots lawyer, historian, and Whig politician.

243 *a sinecurist*: despite his anarchist views, William Godwin accepted the nominal post of Office Keeper and Yeoman Usher of the Receipt of the Exchequer from the Whig government in 1833, moving into rooms in New Palace Yard. Although the job was abolished in October 1834 and the Houses of Parliament burned down six days later, the incoming Tory government continued to pay him the salary until his death in April 1836.

245 *Mr Mudie's ticket*: Charles Mudie's circulating library (1842–1937) was the chief outlet for novels in the mid-nineteenth century; the books had a prominent yellow label on their cover.

246 *Mr James*: G. P. R. James (1799–1860), popular and prolific writer of historical romances.

'Mary Barton': Elizabeth Gaskell's *Mary Barton: A Tale of Manchester Life* (1848).

247 *Blackstone*: the *Commentaries on the Laws of England* (1765–9) by Sir William Blackstone (1723–80) was the standard text which trainee lawyers had to master.

248 *Land in Ireland*: the Irish Land Act (or Landlord and Tenant, Ireland, Act) 1870, for the first time gave tenants a legal interest in their holdings, and thus challenged the traditional conception of property rights and freedom of contract. Twelve years later, in June 1882, after the Second Irish Land Act (1881), Trollope would write a novel to 'promulgate' his ideas about

the tenure of land in Ireland: *The Land-Leaguers* (unfinished at the time of his death; serialized in its incomplete form 1882–3); *The Spectator* called it 'a long pamphlet, under the guise of fiction' (15 December 1883).

249 *Lucy Ashton . . . Julia Mannering*: characters (in one case a supernatural being) in Scott's novels *The Bride of Lammermoor* (1819), *The Heart of Midlothian* (1818), *Rob Roy* (1817), *The Monastery* (1820), *Kenilworth* (1821), and *Guy Mannering* (1815) respectively.

250 *Evan Maccombich*: a character in Scott's novel *Waverley* (1814).

Meg Merrilies: a character in Scott's novel *Guy Mannering* (1815).

Balfour . . . Bothwell: characters in Scott's novel *Old Mortality* (1816).

251 *Oldbuck . . . Wamba . . . Dugald Dalgetty*: Jonathan Oldbuck is the principal character in Scott's *The Antiquary* (1816), Wamba is the jester in his *Ivanhoe* (1819), and Dugald Dalgetty appears in Scott's *The Legend of Montrose* (1819).

Counsellor Pleydell . . . Waverley: characters in Scott's novels *Guy Mannering* (1815), *The Heart of Midlothian* (1818), *Old Mortality* (1816), and *Waverley* (1814).

252 *Saint Anthony*: St Antony the Great (251–356) was a hermit who was tempted by devils in the form of beautiful naked women.

the burlesque: Thackeray's *Rebecca and Rowena* (1850) was a comic sequel to Scott's *Ivanhoe*, in which the hero, who in the original novel marries the Saxon Rowena rather than the beautiful Jewess Rebecca, changes his mind.

Ravenswood . . . Edie Ochiltree . . . Jeanie Deans . . . Flora MacIvor: Characters in Scott's *The Bride of Lammermoor* (1819), *The Antiquary* (1816), *The Heart of Midlothian* (1818), and *Waverley* (1814) respectively.

253 '*Snob Papers*': Thackeray's 'The Snobs of England by One of Themselves' appeared in *Punch* (1846–7) and were republished as *The Book of Snobs* (1848).

FROM *THACKERAY*

John Morley, the editor of Macmillan's series English Men of Letters, asked Trollope to write the volume on Thackeray in the winter of 1878. It was written between 27 January and 31 March 1879 (*Letters*, ii. 812–13), with some material repeated from the then unpublished manuscript of *An Autobiography*, and appeared in May 1879; Henry James's volume, in the same series, on Nathaniel Hawthorne appeared the same year. This was a 'life-and-works' series and because no biography of Thackeray had yet been published, Morley urged Trollope to provide as much biographical information as possible. Trollope sent a questionnaire (written by his wife, Rose) to Thackeray's daughter, and made enquiries of some mutual friends (*Letters*, ii. 812); on 20 February he wrote to William Howard Russell to say that, 'My biographical chapter will be finished today' (*Letters*, ii. 816). In the same tone of apologetic self-depreciation that he used when describing some of his best novels in *An Autobiography*, Trollope told John Blackwood on 6 February that he had, 'got the Thackeray in hand and a terrible job I find it. There is absolutely nothing to say,—except washed out criticism' (*Letters*, ii. 815). In fact, as J. Hillis Miller has argued, Trollope's criticism anticipates many of the key features of the modern view of Thackeray's achievement, while his theoretical account of the procedures of prose fiction, 'is a Victorian version of assumptions about "realism" which are as old as Aristotle in one historical direction, and still of great force today in the other' (*Nineteenth-Century Fiction*, 37 (December 1982), 353).

FROM 'THE GENIUS OF NATHANIEL HAWTHORNE'

Published in the *North American Review* (September 1879); on Hawthorne see note to p. 93. Trollope would publish another essay in this American journal, 'Henry Wadsworth Longfellow', in April 1881.

FROM 'A WALK IN A WOOD'

Published in *Good Words* (September 1879). This was the second of two essays written by Trollope for the 'Half Hours in the Fresh Air' series in *Good Words*. His first contribution, 'In the Hunting Field', appeared in February 1879. This second essay was finished by the end of May, at which point the editor decided that it would not, after all, be included in the 'Half Hours' series and Trollope, accordingly, suggested that the title might be changed to 'How we write our books' (*Letters*, ii. 829). No change was made and it appeared with its original title in September.

269 *quincunces*: a quincunx is a pattern made by placing each of five items at the centre and four corner points of a square.

270 *Switzerland . . . Black Forest*: the Black Forest, or Schwarzwald, is a wooded mountain range in Baden-Württemberg. In 1874, 1876, 1878, and 1879 Trollope spent several long holidays there, in the Hollenthal valley near Freiburg, and at Felsenegg, near Zug, in Switzerland. During these periods he was writing *The Prime Minister*, *Is He Popenjoy?*, *The Duke's Children*, *Ayala's Angel*, and *Marion Fay*.

APPENDIX

274 *fallen away latterly among Princes*: Skilton suggests a reference to Psalm 82:6–7, but it seems more likely that Trollope is continuing his Shakespeare allusion and echoing Falstaff's statement, after spending time in the company of Prince Hal, 'Bardolf, am I not fallen away vilely since this last action?' (*2 Henry IV*, Act 3, Scene 3, ll. 1–2). W. H. Russell became part of the Prince of Wales's circle from 1868 and accompanied him on tours of the Near East (1869) and India (1875–6), publishing books and articles about them.

275 *Dr Johnson . . . behind the screen*: Samuel Johnson (1709–84), poet, critic, essayist, and lexicographer. In 1744 Walter Harte dined with Edward Cave

and praised Johnson's recently published *Life of Savage*. Cave told Harte, when they next met, that he had made a man very happy. ' "How could that be?" says Harte; "none were present but you and I." Cave replied, "You might observe I sent a plate of victuals behind the screen. There skulked the Biographer, one Johnson, whose dress was so shabby that he durst not make his appearance" ' (note by Edward Malone, added to Boswell's *Life of Johnson*, 3rd edn., 4 vols., 1799, i. 136–7). Henry Wallis's painting *Dr Johnson at Cave's, the Publisher* (Royal Academy, 1854) had helped to make the incident famous.

a man to whom nothing could be told quite safely: Edmund Yates (1831–94), Post Office official (1847–72), novelist, dramatist, and gossip column- ist, initially for the *Illustrated Times* (1855–63), was editor of *Temple Bar* and *Tinsley's Magazine*, and from 1874 owner and editor of the profitable society magazine *The World*. Expelled from the Garrick Club in 1858 for a story about Thackeray in *Town Talk*, he sold his account of the *Corn- hill* dinner (describing George Smith as 'totally unread') to the *New York Times* ('Echoes from London Clubs', 26 May 1860; reported in the *Satur- day Review* as 'Newspaper Gossip', 23 June 1860). Thackeray responded with 'On Screens in Dining Rooms', Roundabout Paper, No. 6, *Cornhill Magazine*, 2 (August 1860).

276 *Mr Carlyle*: Thomas Carlyle's essay 'Biography', scorning novelists for writing merely imaginary biographies, was first published in *Fraser's Magazine*, 27 (April 1832), and reprinted in his *Critical and Miscellaneous Essays* (1839); see note to p. 68.

277 *Homer nods*: 'Quandoque bonus dormitat Homerus' (Horace, *Ars Poetica*, l. 359; 'Even good Homer sometimes slumbers', that is, makes a mistake).

the plot of a novel of mine: Reade used one of the plots of Trollope's *Ralph the Heir* (1870–1) for his play *Shilly-Shally* (Gaiety Theatre, 1 April 1872). A farce, with the popular comic actor John Toole as Neefit the breeches- maker, it had a successful one-month run. Trollope did not receive Reade's letter of explanation until 20 May, was outraged, sent letters of protest to the *Pall Mall Gazette* (16 July) and *Daily Telegraph* (6 August), and did not speak to Reade again (despite playing whist with him at the Garrick Club) until 1877.

'Ponatur calculus . . . labores': Juvenal, *Satires*, 9, ll. 40–2 (actually 'numera', not 'numeras' in l. 41): 'Get out the calculator, have the boys present with their records, count the five thousand sesterces paid, and then count up my labours.' In its original context a very improper piece of verse (about paying for pederastic sex), which is probably why Henry Trollope omitted it in *1883*.

278 *'The Small House at Allington'*: Trollope's deletion of this title here in *MS* was reflected in his original scheme for The Chronicles of Barsetshire as a series of only five novels; at some point in the May or June of 1878 Fred- erick Chapman intervened to insist on the inclusion of *The Small House at*

Allington and the rights were expensively acquired from Smith, Elder to make this possible.

279 *'Kenelm Chillingly'*: Bulwer Lytton's novel *Kenelm Chillingly* was published a few days after his death in January 1873; his novel *The Parisians* was being serialized (October 1872–January 1874) in *Blackwood's Edinburgh Magazine* at the time; a further novel, the unfinished *Pausanias the Spartan*, would be published in 1876.

have had every word I have written counted: Trollope's original formulation here suggests that this chore was undertaken by somebody else, most probably his wife.

The Oxford World's Classics Website

www.worldsclassics.co.uk

- Browse the full range of Oxford World's Classics online
- Sign up for our monthly e-alert to receive information on new titles
- Read extracts from the Introductions
- Listen to our editors and translators talk about the world's greatest literature with our Oxford World's Classics audio guides
- Join the conversation, follow us on Twitter at OWC_Oxford
- Teachers and lecturers can order inspection copies quickly and simply via our website

www.worldsclassics.co.uk

American Literature

British and Irish Literature

Children's Literature

Classics and Ancient Literature

Colonial Literature

Eastern Literature

European Literature

Gothic Literature

History

Medieval Literature

Oxford English Drama

Philosophy

Poetry

Politics

Religion

The Oxford Shakespeare

A complete list of Oxford World's Classics, including Authors in Context, Oxford English Drama, and the Oxford Shakespeare, is available in the UK from the Marketing Services Department, Oxford University Press, Great Clarendon Street, Oxford OX2 6DP, or visit the website at www.oup.com/uk/worldsclassics.

In the USA, visit www.oup.com/us/owc for a complete title list.

Oxford World's Classics are available from all good bookshops. In case of difficulty, customers in the UK should contact Oxford University Press Bookshop, 116 High Street, Oxford OX1 4BR.

ANTHONY TROLLOPE   **The American Senator**
An Autobiography
Barchester Towers
Can You Forgive Her?
Cousin Henry
Doctor Thorne
The Duke's Children
The Eustace Diamonds
Framley Parsonage
He Knew He Was Right
Lady Anna
The Last Chronicle of Barset
Orley Farm
Phineas Finn
Phineas Redux
The Prime Minister
Rachel Ray
The Small House at Allington
The Warden
The Way We Live Now

GUY DE MAUPASSANT	**A Day in the Country and Other Stories**
	A Life
	Bel-Ami
PROSPER MÉRIMÉE	**Carmen and Other Stories**
MOLIÈRE	**Don Juan and Other Plays**
	The Misanthrope, Tartuffe, and Other Plays
BLAISE PASCAL	**Pensées and Other Writings**
ABBÉ PRÉVOST	**Manon Lescaut**
JEAN RACINE	**Britannicus, Phaedra, and Athaliah**
ARTHUR RIMBAUD	**Collected Poems**
EDMOND ROSTAND	**Cyrano de Bergerac**
MARQUIS DE SADE	**The Crimes of Love**
	Justine
	The Misfortunes of Virtue and Other Early Tales
GEORGE SAND	**Indiana**
MME DE STAËL	**Corinne**
STENDHAL	**The Red and the Black**
	The Charterhouse of Parma
PAUL VERLAINE	**Selected Poems**
JULES VERNE	**Around the World in Eighty Days**
	Journey to the Centre of the Earth
	Twenty Thousand Leagues under the Seas
VOLTAIRE	**Candide and Other Stories**
	Letters concerning the English Nation
	A Pocket Philosophical Dictionary

A SELECTION OF OXFORD WORLD'S CLASSICS